LIVING HOPE TODAY

A Daily Devotional

Pastor Scott Kalevik

iUniverse, Inc.
Bloomington

Living Hope Today
A Daily Devotional

Copyright © 2011 Pastor Scott Kalevik

iUniverse books may be ordered through booksellers or by contacting:

iUniverse
1663 Liberty Drive
Bloomington, IN 47403
www.iuniverse.com
1-800-Authors (1-800-288-4677)

ISBN: 978-1-4620-0469-0 (pbk)
ISBN: 978-1-4620-0754-7 (ebk)

Printed in the United States of America

iUniverse rev. date: 4/7/2011

It is my prayer that you grow in Christ as you use this

Living Hope Today Devotional!

The people of Living Hope Community Church and I invite you to use this devotional as a daily tool to strengthen your walk with Christ. Living Hope Today supplies you with the following:

a)   A daily Scripture to meditate upon
b)   Comments by Pastor or other Authors
c)   A daily Bible reading program that will take you through the Old Testament once each year and the New Testament twice each year

I believe God has several goals for us in this devotional:

First, I know He wants to strengthen our daily walk with Christ. There is no substitute for time in prayer and in His word!

Second, I know Jesus wants our obedience to all He has commanded us. I trust the Lord will move our hearts to forsake our sin and to walk in step with His Holy Spirit as we serve Him.

Lastly, it is my prayer that you will be inspired by God's Spirit to participate in the daily reading schedule. The Lord draws near to those who draw near to Him.

Let's make today a day spent reading God's word and communing with Him in prayer knowing that as we abide in Him, He will produce His fruit in us. Glory be to God.

Pastor Scott

Acknowledgments

This devotional is written to honor and glorify our Lord and Savior, Jesus Christ. To Him is due all the praise and the glory!

I also want to thank the dear people of Living Hope Community Church. Your love, patience, and desire to follow Jesus will never leave my heart.

This devotional is a work of love that has been written and edited by several. My deepest appreciation and sincere gratitude go first to my lovely wife, Peggy Kalevik, and also to Beth Nelson, Kathy Bryant, Gwen Taylor, Jazmine Rosbia, Cissie Mullaney, Mike Scheimann, David Fundenberger, Herb Hubbard, and Mike Nelson. Thank you for the hundreds of hours spent making this project possible.

Our dear brother David Fundenberger succumbed to cancer in February 2011. His contribution to our lives and to this effort is immeasurable. In honor of his life and the love God expressed to us through David, I wish to dedicate this devotional to the memory of James David Fundenberger. David, I thank God that you are now at peace and I can't wait to see you again in heaven. Thank you for living your life following Jesus.

Pastor Scott

January 1

TRYING TO SEE
By Scott Kalevik

Luke 19:4 So he (Zacchaeus) ran ahead and climbed a sycamore-fig tree to see him, since Jesus was coming that way.

Why did Zacchaeus climb that tree? Zacchaeus was a rich guy. He made his money by collecting taxes for the Roman Empire. Rich guys don't typically humiliate themselves in public to see some carpenter walk down the road.

Why did Zacchaeus climb that tree? Zacchaeus was very unpopular among the people. Helping people suffer while you get rich off of their tax money leads to low ratings. Wouldn't it be better for him to lay low and not risk being spotted by the rock throwers while he hung out in a tree?

Why did Zacchaeus climb that tree? The answer is simple. Zacchaeus had reached a point in his life where finding peace was more important than any humiliation or suffering that might come his way. He knew he needed a change of heart. He was tired of feeling guilty, empty, and alone. So, he did whatever it took to see Jesus!

When Jesus walked under that tree, he stopped, looked up and told Zacchaeus to come down! Jesus knew his name! Instead of hating him, Jesus went over to his house! Zacchaeus changed his ways and gave his heart to Jesus right then and there. Jesus said salvation had come to Zacchaeus. It's interesting that while Zacchaeus thought he was seeking Jesus, Jesus says He came seeking to save the lost! Jesus was seeking him! Jesus seeks us!

Zacchaeus did three things: a. He tried to see Jesus; b. He believed that Jesus is the Christ; c. He changed his ways. Jesus knows your name too. If you draw near to Him, He'll draw near to you (James 4:8). Are you seeking Him? Have you surrendered to Him? Are you living in obedience to His word?

Point: Jesus seeks us as we seek Him. When He finds us, He invites us to change our behavior to honor Him.

Prayer: God, You're all I want in this life. Thank you for seeking me. Please help me honor you in my behavior today.

Practice: What behaviors need to change in my life to honor God?

Today's Reading:
Genesis 1-2; Matthew 1-2

January 2

WHO CAN YOU TRUST?
By Beth Nelson

Philippians 2:5 *"Your attitude should be the same as that of Christ Jesus: Who..took the very nature of a servant..humbled himself and became obedient to death on a cross!"*

My husband is not perfect. Oh, he's nearly perfect, but like me, he makes an occasional mistake. Abraham was not a perfect man, either. Sometimes he feared man more than he trusted God. In the course of Abraham and Sarah's journey to the Promised Land, he deeply wronged his wife not once, but twice. Because Sarah was strikingly beautiful, Abraham hatched a plan to protect his own skin when they traveled through Egypt. Sarah was to agree to lie and say that she was his sister, which means the Egyptians could take Sarah and leave him alone. After all, being a man, he was more important. Wrong! He found out that God valued Sarah just as much because God Himself came to her rescue. The truth was, Sarah could appeal to God to save her because she had the proper attitude toward her husband. Pharaoh did take Sarah for himself, just as Abraham had feared, but God spoke to Pharaoh personally and told him that she was Abraham's wife. Aghast at the thought, Pharaoh let them both go.

Our culture thinks of the word "submission" as an ugly word. It brings connotations of being a doormat, keeping someone in subservience, allowing someone to step on you. But submission is a profound concept, rooted in the trustworthiness of God, not man, and vital to the releasing of God's blessing and protection in our lives. The Apostle Peter sets Sarah up as a prime example for believers to follow: *"This is the way the holy women of the past put their hope in God...like Sarah, who obeyed Abraham and called him her master. You are her daughters if you do what is right and do not give way to fear."* (1Pet 3:5,6)

When we submit to those in authority over us, we, like Sarah, can appeal to a higher power. *"Obey your leaders and submit to their authority...they must give an account."* (Heb 13:17) The Apostle Paul even says to have this attitude of humility with one another, *"Submit to one another out of reverence for Christ."* (Eph 5:21) And it was the very attitude of Christ Himself, who of His own free will submitted to the Father and went to the cross for us all. If we ignore this teaching, we're missing out on a great blessing!

Today's Reading:
Genesis 3-5; Matthew 3

January 3

Why Hell?

By Scott Kalevik

Revelation 20:15 *If anyone's name was not found written in the book of life, he was thrown into the lake of fire.*

God clearly and repeatedly tells us that there will be a day of judgment. God also has made it clear that on the day of judgment, some will enter into paradise through faith in Jesus Christ, and others will be condemned. The Bible talks about "Hades" or "The Lake Of Fire" or "Hell" or "The Pit" as an actual physical place that God will send all who are not in Christ.

What should we do with this kind of information? Why has God told us all of this? There are two or three basic reasons God wants us to know about Hell:

First, God wants us to examine our own lives. Is your name written in the book of life or not? If you don't know or if you have to honestly answer, "No", God gives you a chance today to make your peace with Him. Ask Jesus to forgive you and invite Him to enter your heart. Turn away from sin. Trust your life to Him.

The second reason God tells us about Hell is to encourage us to warn others. Jn 3:36 *Whoever believes in the Son has eternal life, but whoever rejects the Son will not see life, for God's wrath remains on him."* Is there someone in your life today that doesn't understand? Do you love that person enough to warn them? Ask God to give you opportunity to share. Ask God to open their eyes to the truth.

The third reason God tells us about Hell is to remind us that He is a God of justice. It might seem like the wicked prosper in this life, but God is going to set things right. Although we don't delight in the idea that someone else receives punishment from God, God's justice stands true. If we suffer at the hands of people who hate God, we can love them enough to tell them about salvation and then rest in the fact that God's actions – even actions of judgment – are always right.

Point: There is a lake of fire.
Prayer: God, thank you for saving me and please lead me to warn others today.
Practice: Today is the day to tell someone about the saving grace of Jesus. Let the Spirit lead you and be bold.

Today's Reading:
Genesis 6-7; Matthew 4-5

January 4

PRIDE - A DOUBLE-EDGED SWORD
By Mike Scheimann

Proverbs 8:13 *To fear the Lord is to hate evil; I hate pride and arrogance, evil behavior and perverse speech.*

Like many human emotions, pride can be both good and evil. Love and hate are two examples. You can love others, and you can also love money. You can hate your brother, or hate sin. The same emotion with two very different end results. Pride is the same way. You can take pride in your children, your country, and our soldiers. You can be proud to be a Christian, a servant of God.

However, as we know all too well, pride can be a very evil emotion. Nebuchadnezzar was the most important king of the Neo-Babylonian Empire. He restored old religious monuments and improved canals. He is best known for his legendary Hanging Gardens of Babylon, one of the 7 wonders of the ancient world. But Daniel 5:20 tells us that when King Nebuchadnezzar's heart became arrogant and hardened with pride; God deposed him from his royal throne and stripped him of his glory.

Pride has brought kings to their knees, destroyed great kingdoms and armies, as well as caused God's punishment upon His people throughout the scriptures. Pride can cause you to have road rage, make fun of others, or to become totally self-reliant. The Bible tells us that pride goes before destruction, in pride the wicked man does not seek God, and in all his thoughts there is no room for God. (Prov 16:18; Psalms 10:4). Am I living a life of pride or is there room in my thoughts and heart for God?

Point: Seek humility, it is better to be proud of others, not yourself. Self-pride may cross the line and become destructive and may even be evil.

Prayer: Father Almighty, you have told us over and over in your word that you love a humble heart, and that pride in ourself only leads to sin and your wrath. Lord show us the areas in our lives where we have pride, and feel superior. Help us to remember that the first shall be last, and the last shall be first.

Practice: Ask God to show you any area in your life where you have pride and then pray and diligenlty work to turn that area over to God and release it to Him.

Today's Reading:
Genesis 8-10; Matthew 6

January 5

Surviving The Flood!
By Scott Kalevik

Genesis 6:17 *I am going to bring floodwaters on the earth to destroy all life under the heavens, every creature that has the breath of life in it. Everything on earth will perish.*

When God created man He said that it was good (Gen. 1:31). But the serpent tempted Adam and Eve and they sinned against God. Death entered the world. Cain murdered Abel. Sin ran rampant. God finally had enough. God decided to destroy the world by flood. Every living creature that had breath, besides Noah and his family, would be destroyed in the flood. Judgment came.

We like to talk about how God's mercy lasts forever. We are right to say it. For those who are in the Ark of salvation, judgment will not destroy. God's mercy will last forever for them. But make no mistake. God will not tolerate sin forever. Just like God's mercy ran out for the wicked people of Noah's day, God's mercy will run out for the wicked now too.

So how do we survive God's judgment? By being in Christ. Ro 8:1 *Therefore, there is now no condemnation for those who are in Christ Jesus.* Instead of an ark, God built a cross. Instead of us dying for our sins, God died for us. He clothes us who believe with the righteousness of Christ so that we will survive His awesome judgment against sin. Not through our merit, but through His work of salvation on the cross. Noah obeyed God, built the ark, and survived! God asks each of us to obey Him by receiving His son and living for Him.

Take heart! The end of evil is coming! The question each of us must answer before God's judgment comes is whether or not we are in His ark of salvation. God has told us to repent from sin and believe in the Lord Jesus Christ. He has told us to deny ourselves and take up our cross daily and follow Him. If we do what He has told us, we will be protected from the wrath of God coming on the Day of the Lord! Praise God!

Point: All are offered the chance to avoid God's judgment through Christ.
Prayer: Lord, thank you for the cross. Strengthen me to follow.
Practice: Today I will rejoice in the salvation of the Lord!

Today's Reading:
Genesis 11-12; Matthew 7-8

5

January 6

The "Perfect Ten"

By Mike Scheimann

Matthew 19:17 *"Why do you ask me about what is good?" Jesus replied. "There is only one who is good. If you want to enter life, obey the commandments."*

Many Christians know the story of how God gave Moses the Ten Commandments, over 4000 years ago. Unfortunately, most people think that they are ancient history, and not applicable to life today. Atheists want them out of our schools and courthouses, and many people say that half of them are irrelevant or out-dated. They say now that we are Christians, we don't need the Old Testament laws anymore.

However, Jesus Himself lived by the laws of the old Testament, and told us He is not changing a jot or tittle of God's commandments. We will still be judged by them when we die. We are still accountable when we break them.

Point: Even though Jesus has died for us and has saved us by grace, we are still commanded to live perfect and blameless lives, and are not given a free pass to do whatever we want.

Prayer: Jesus, our Redeemer, you gave your very life as a perfect sacrifice, that we may be forgiven. Let us not waste the blood that you shed, by continuing to willfully live in sin and disobedience.

Practice: Take some time to read the 10 Commandments in Ex 20 and ask yourself how many times you are sinning against God by breaking and disobeying His commands. Do you tell lies? Do you covet? Do you lust in your heart?

Today's Reading:
Genesis 13-15; Matthew 9

January 7

Believing In God When Things Go Wrong!

By Scott Kalevik

Job 23:9 When he is at work in the north, I do not see him; when he turns to the south, I catch no glimpse of him. 10 But he knows the way that I take; when he has tested me, I will come forth as gold.

If there was ever a guy who knew what a bad day was all about, it was Job. He lost his family, his wealth, his possessions, and his health. As if that wasn't enough, Job was subjected to the constant haranguing of his three 'friends' Eliphaz, Bildad, and Zophar. He sat penniless and homeless day after day in the dirt scraping his sores with broken pottery. His 'friends' kept telling him that these bad things must have happened to him because of his sin. Total misery seems like an understatement.

Job kept calling out to God. But he received no response. By the grace of God, Job never accused God of being unfair or unloving. He knew that it was God's right to give or to take away. Job worshiped God despite all of the trouble.

How do you think you would react to this kind of trouble? Who among us could bless God and worship Him while life as we know it was obliterated?

How did Job survive? First, Job believed he was in God's hands. Job assures himself that "God knows the way I take."

More than that, Job knows that God still has his best interest at heart. He tells himself that he will come out as pure gold when this test is over. WOW! Job is already looking past his circumstances to see the goodness of God! Job clearly sees that God is working out his refinement through all his suffering. He's going to be just like gold when this is over! What faith!

So, if things are going badly for you right now, please remember that if you're in Christ, God knows the way you take. After He's tested you, you will come forth as gold! God restored Job! He is faithful!

Point: Despite terrible hardship, Job believed God was good!
Prayer: God forgive me for doubting you when my life is hard. Help me stand!
Practice: Today I will deliberately focus my thinking on the FACT that God is watching me!

Today's Reading:
Genesis 16-17; Matthew 10-11

January 8

A Whole New You!

By Scott Kalevik

Isaiah 26:19 *But your dead will live; their bodies will rise. You who dwell in the dust, wake up and shout for joy. Your dew is like the dew of the morning; the earth will give birth to her dead.*

The idea of people being raised from the dead did not originate on the day Jesus conquered death that first Easter. Isaiah spoke about the earth giving birth to her dead some 700 years earlier (see above).

Daniel spoke about resurrection in Daniel 12:2 *Multitudes who sleep in the dust of the earth will awake: some to everlasting life, others to shame and everlasting contempt.*

Abraham believed that if God allowed him to follow through with sacrificing Isaac, He would raise Isaac from the dead (Gen. 22:1-12; Heb. 11:19). Ezekiel 37:12-14 is another OT text regarding the resurrection of the dead. Job describes his own resurrection in Job 19:26 *And after my skin has been destroyed, yet in my flesh I will see God; 27 I myself will see him with my own eyes—I, and not another. How my heart yearns within me!*

The New Testament declares Jesus' resurrection in all four gospels. Jesus describes the resurrection of all people: John 5:28 *"Do not be amazed at this, for a time is coming when all who are in their graves will hear his voice 29 and come out—those who have done good will rise to live, and those who have done evil will rise to be condemned.*

So please understand that those aches and pains and struggles you might be experiencing today, are only temporary. If you are in Christ, there's going to be a whole new you! God promised it centuries before Christ!

As we endure the hardships and struggles of this life, God encourages us to focus on the hope He gives us regarding the next life. Don't be discouraged. Don't despair. Through Christ a whole new you is on the way!

Point: The resurrection from the dead is written of in the Old Testament too!

Prayer: Lord, allow my meditation to be on the future hope you have for me!

Practice: Imagine meeting Jesus face to face. Does your heart yearn within you like Job or are you afraid? What does that tell you?

Today's Reading:
Genesis 18-20; Matthew 12

January 9

Let Me Alone

By Peggy Kalevik

Deuteronomy 9:13-14 *And the LORD said to me, "I have seen this people, and they are a stiff-necked people indeed! 14 Let me alone, so that I may destroy them and blot out their name from under heaven. And I will make you into a nation stronger and more numerous than they.*

What is your state of mind and heart when you ask your loved ones to leave you alone? Usually, we are hurt, confused, distraught or angry. Well, God created us in His image; we can sometimes exhibit some of His traits. God got angry and asked Moses to "leave him alone". What a terrifying thought! God is so angry with His people He wants to be left alone while He contemplates destroying them.

In verse 12 of this same chapter He calls them "Moses' people" not "my people". In Exodus He called them "my people" at least 30 times, now they have displeased Him so badly, they are "Moses' people". Note that while he understood God's anger, Moses pleaded for the Israelites anyway (Exodus 32:11-13). Moses goes to the people and destroys all traces of evil which the people created during his absence. Moses goes on to tell the people how they have been rebellious against the Lord ever since He has known them (verse 24).

As Moses pleads for the Israelites while laying prostrate before the Lord, we get a sense of why God was so upset with the people. After all He had done for them they still remained obstinate and rebellious. We are upset with our children if they react to our love and caring with stubborn disobedience. In this instance God is no different; yet He forgave them. Can we, like God, come back from "let me alone" to "let me forgive and love them" in spite of what they have done or are doing? In addition, we are never alone. God is always there listening to our every thought and holding our hand; He won't leave us alone.

Point: God won't leave us alone, but we can walk away

Prayer: God help me to find calm and peace in you. Let me use my time away from other people to strengthen myself in You.

Practice: I will not lose my reason in anger today

Today's Reading:
Genesis 21-22; Matthew 13-14

January 10

Turning The World On Its Ear!
By Scott Kalevik

Matthew 5:44 *But I tell you: Love your enemies and pray for those who persecute you,*

Jesus said things that are truly revolutionary. Even today the majority of people read His teachings and scratch their heads at how unorthodox He is. Who would ever seriously counsel people to love their enemies? Aren't we better served by seeking revenge against our enemies? We're supposed to pay our enemies back – not pray for them … aren't we?

Yet, despite our sensibilities, Jesus doesn't seem at all affected by our conventional, earthly wisdom. He continues to insist that His followers be people who LOVE their enemies. His followers are distinguished by their willingness to PRAY for people that persecute them!

Mohammed obviously didn't agree with Jesus' teaching about loving enemies. Radical Muslims vow to kill anyone who insults Allah. Remember the Danish cartoon writer that drew a cartoon poking fun at Islam? He's been running for his life ever since.

Nevertheless, Jesus asserts that one of the characteristics of a godly person is his or her willingness to love and pray for their enemies. It's hard to understand the power of God's truth here. All of our natural tendencies are bent towards revenge.

Perhaps we can understand it better if we see it in action. I recall the life of Dr. Martin Luther King, Jr. He refused to hate back. He never retaliated. He committed his life to nonviolent measures seeking justice for the oppressed. He stood up for the truth that God created all men equal. God used him to move a nation.

Do you love your enemies? Do you pray for people that have hurt you? Obeying Christ here proves that His character resides in us! His love still has the power to turn the world on its ear!

Point: Jesus teaches us to love and pray for our enemies.
Prayer: Lord, please forgive me for hating my enemies. Teach me how to love like you love.
Practice: Today, with a heart of love, I will pray for someone who has hurt me.

Today's Reading:
Genesis 23-25; Matthew 15

January 11

THE DEVIL GOES TO CHURCH!

By Scott Kalevik

2 Corinthians 11:13-15 *For such men are false apostles, deceitful workmen, masquerading as apostles of Christ. 14 And no wonder, for Satan himself masquerades as an angel of light. 15 It is not surprising, then, if his servants masquerade as servants of righteousness. Their end will be what their actions deserve.*

Take a minute and read today's passage again. The Bible clearly tells us that NOT everyone who proclaims Jesus belongs to Jesus! One of Satan's greatest deceptions is that he masquerades as an angel of light. And so do his servants! In other words, there are people who may look good and sound good and do good things, but in the end they are serving Satan and not Christ!!!

How can you tell? First, what are they saying about God? Are they preaching the Bible diligently and honestly? A preacher is a waiter not a chef. His job isn't to cook something up that he has made. The preacher's job is to deliver what God has already said. Oh, he may add a garnish or two, but the meal comes from God!

Second, what does the fruit of their life tell you? Obviously people can hide some sins in their lives, but sin usually always eventually comes to the surface. If you see lying, strife, and corruption of heart, proceed with caution; pray; perhaps confront.

If the devil goes to church, how can I protect myself? Know the word of God so well that you discern false doctrine and ungodly living. The Secret Service trains agents to recognize counterfeit money by studying real money. Once the agent can positively identify the real thing, the fakes are much more obvious. Do you know your Bible so well that false doctrine is obvious to you? Are you so familiar with walking with the Lord that you can discern truth and error?

Studying and reading our Bibles is more than just a 'nice' thing to do. God uses His instruction in our lives to equip us to recognize counterfeits.

Point: False teachers exist in the church.
Prayer: Lord, please give me discernment.
Practice: Set aside a time to regularly study God's word.

Today's Reading:
Genesis 26-27; Matthew 16-17

January 12

ARE YOU A TRUE DISCIPLE, OR A MEMBER OF THE CROWDS?
By Mike Scheimann

Luke 14:27 *And anyone who does not carry his cross
and follow me cannot be my disciple.*

We all love a good show. We all love to be entertained, often at other's expense. But when it comes to your walk with Christ, are you there to be a spectator, or are you actively involved? Many Christians think that if they go to church on Sundays, and give their tithes, that they have done their duty. However, God has called us to do MUCH MORE than that. He has called us to be disciples, to be active followers of Christ. Not on-lookers.

We all expect the Pastor and those in service at the church to do all the work, while we enjoy "the show", but God wants, actually demands, that we ALL participate in His ministry and His work. God has given us each a cross to bear, and a gift of ministry. We all endure hardships, and we all have something that we've learned that can edify the body of Christ.

Point: Next time you find yourself in church, just sitting back and enjoying the show, or at a Bible study, listening to what everyone else has learned from the study, remember that God asks each of us to serve! How are you serving Him?

Prayer: Lord, help me to be willing, just as you were 2000 years ago, to take up my cross and follow you. If that means getting out of my comfort zone, or giving up my free time, in order to help serve you and minister to others, give me the strength, Lord

Practice: Pray to God for guidance, and ask Him to show you what gifts He has given you. Then make this year the year that you get up the courage to stop being a spectator, and become a disciple.

Today's Reading:
Genesis 28-30; Matthew 18

January 13

Now Is The Time!
By Scott Kalevik

Isaiah 55:6 *Seek the LORD while he may be found; call on him while he is near.*

Communication between the people of this planet has never been easier in the history of mankind. I can email our friends in Liberia today and get all the answers I need within minutes. Cell phones span thousands of miles in seconds. Cables and communication satellites have made virtually every nook and cranny of the earth accessible to communication.

But all our technology has never come close to matching the communication system of the Lord. Since time began, the Lord has told us that we can speak with Him anytime we choose through prayer. No batteries necessary. No dropped calls. No static. We don't even have to pray out loud. All we need is the desire to honestly speak with Him. He'll hear and answer every time. And, you'll never get a bill for going over your allotment of minutes!

Isaiah 55:6 and many other passages encourage us to take advantage of the opportunity to speak with the Lord. Yet, if you read closely, you'll see a warning.

When we're told that we should seek the Lord while he may be found, the implication is that there is coming a day when He cannot be found. When we're asked to call on him while he is near, the implication is that there will be a day when God is not near.

The Lord warns us that if we refuse Him in this life, there will come a day when the opportunity to speak with Him is revoked. Hebrews 9:27 tells us that each of us is destined to die and after that to face judgment. In other words, God's offer to redeem us expires at our physical death. If we're found in Christ when we pass from this world, He promises us that we'll spend eternity with Him. But if we've never called on Him in this life, our opportunity to call on Him will not extend into the next. Call on the Lord now! He's waiting to hear from you.

Point: God invites us to call on Him and warns us that now is the time!
Prayer: Lord help me live in the urgency of your salvation.
Practice: Lord please help me tell someone about You today knowing that time is running out!

Today's Reading:
Genesis 31-32; Matthew 19-20

13

January 14

THE CRY OF A DESPERATE HEART!

By Scott Kalevik

1 Samuel 1:18 She said, "May your servant find favor in your eyes." Then she went her way and ate something, and her face was no longer downcast.

Have you ever lived at the brink of despair? Hannah is a dear saint in the Old Testament that can teach us a few things about despair. She was married to Elkanah but she could not have children. Elkanah had another wife named Peninnah and she bore lots of children.

Peninnah compounded Hannah's grief by constantly provoking Hannah with the fact that Peninnah had lots of children and Hannah had none. It's one thing to know you have a problem. It's another to have someone constantly rubbing it in!

What would you do if you were Hannah? Would you conceive of some plot to silence Peninnah's provocations? Would you appeal to Elkanah to make her shut up? Would you run away and feel sorry for yourself? Depression?

Hannah chose the most effective remedy for the situation. She prayed! Scripture tells us that in bitterness of soul she wept much and prayed to God. She laid her heart out before God and she made God a promise. She not only asked God for a child, but Hannah promised to give the child back to God if He blessed her with a son.

Hannah coped with her despair by prayer. When she had unloaded her burden to the Lord, she left it with Him! She got up. She ate. The countenance of her face lightened up! In other words, Hannah prayed believing that God heard her and that He would respond according to His will.

The Lord did respond. Hannah gave birth to Samuel. Remember Hannah today if you're feeling low. Cry out to God in earnest prayer. Tell Him about your deepest desires in life! You will not be disappointed!

Point: Hannah turned to the Lord with her greatest desire.

Prayer: Lord, please help me lay my desires at your feet with faith knowing that You will respond according to your will.

Practice: Today I will set aside a time to discuss my most pressing concerns with the Lord!

Today's Reading:
Genesis 33-35; Matthew 21

14

January 15

ONE WAY!

By Scott Kalevik

Isaiah 43:11 *I, even I, am the LORD, and apart from me there is no savior.*

I learned about choices the last time I went out for dinner. My waiter asked, "What would you like for dinner?" I said, "I'll have a steak." "How would you like that cooked?" "Medium." Then I was asked about my choices for soup, salad, dressing, vegetables, potato toppings, drink and dessert. By the time I was done ordering I wasn't just hungry, I was tired and hungry! So many choices to make!

We are bombarded with choices everyday. What cell phone company will we choose? What soap will we use? Who is going to cut our hair? How will we spend our time today? The list goes on and on.

Given all the choices we are asked to make, I guess it should come as no surprise to us that most people in our culture believe they should be able to choose how they get to heaven as well. This street theology says sincere belief is more important than believing truth. If I sincerely believe whatever I believe, I'll go to heaven. And so will you, if you sincerely believe whatever you believe. But in reality, truth always triumphs over sincerely believing error.

When it comes to salvation, God says there is no choice but Him! "Apart from me there is no savior." ONLY ONE CHOICE! And, therefore, every other choice other than the Lord is wrong! Every other choice leads to death. As you recall, Jesus said, *"I am the way, the truth, and the life. No one comes to the Father except through me."* (John 14:6)

Remember, even though we make a multitude of choices about our daily lives, there is no savior other than Jesus Christ. God has made it so. There is only one way.

Point: There is only one way to heaven.
Prayer: God help me stand up for this truth in a culture that disdains it.
Practice: Thank God for having mercy and seek Him about with whom to share this truth.

Today's Reading:
Genesis 36-37; Matthew 22-23

January 16

ARE YOU PLAYING YOUR PART?
By Scott Kalevik

1 Corinthians 12:7 *Now to each one the manifestation of the Spirit is given for the common good.*

My wife and I recently went to hear Andrea Bocelli sing! He sang wonderfully. But I noticed those 50 or so people behind him. The conductor directed the symphony orchestra's every move with precision and it sounded fabulous! All the instruments were dedicated to playing their parts perfectly so that Bocelli could shine!

Watching Bocelli sing while the symphony played behind him reminded me of what God says about us, the body of Christ. The Lord has given each of us gifts and talents to use in service to Him. Like orchestra members, all of us are called to play our parts for the glory of Jesus Christ. Each of us should use our gifts for the common good of the church. We should play in harmony. We should never be jealous of each other's gifts. Instead, we should encourage each other to use the gift(s) God gave us to build up the body of Christ.

Question: What instrument does God have you playing in His orchestra?

Many people view church as a place to go once a week. They attend church regularly, but rarely do they ever take God home with them. They feel that by attending church, they've fulfilled their obligation to God. Nothing could be further from God's truth!

The church is NOT a place to go. The church is every believer in the body of Christ. We can have all the buildings in the world, but if we don't have anyone who loves Jesus with all of his or her heart, soul, mind and strength, we don't have a church!

We are called to allow God to lead our lives; to deny ourselves and take up our crosses and follow Jesus. That means we use everything at our disposal to glorify God in our lives! What part are you playing?

Point: We each have a part to play in our service to God.
Prayer: Give me the strength to use the gifts you've given me for Your glory!
Practice: Get involved serving Christ using the gifts and talents He's given you.

Today's Reading:
Genesis 38-40; Matthew 24

January 17

KEEPING HOPE ALIVE; TRUST THE WORD.
By Peggy Kalevik

Micah 5:2 *"But you, Bethlehem Ephrathah, though you are small among the clans of Judah, out of you will come for me one who will be ruler over Israel, whose origins are from of old, from ancient times."*

In Micah 3:12 and 5:1, the prophet saw the impending exile of Jerusalem in 586 B.C... However in today's scripture, Micah 5:2, the prophet makes a shift. Micah predicts the coming of a King who will bring lasting security to Israel and his influence and power will extend to the ends of the earth.

The prophets of the Old Testament purpose was to proclaim God's word, to exalt God; and to encourage, warn, teach and rebuke God's people in an effort to keep them moving toward a fresh new beginning and a new relationship with God.

Like Micah, Isaiah (9:6-7) and Zechariah (13:7), both made predictions of Christ coming. It must have seemed impossible for one man to fulfill all the prophecies predicted of Him by the Old Testament prophets. Yet God had foretold Christ victory over Satan long before the prophets predicted or spoke of His coming (Genesis 3:15). God was preparing, even at the time of creation, Christ's life, death and resurrection, fulfilling the prophecies of His prophets. From the little village of Bethlehem came the redeemer of the world. God used this small insignificant place to change the world.

Let us look back over our lives and see how God has moved on our behalf. All these things should give us hope and greater faith in the word, the power and the person of God. The Bible says Jesus will return (Revelation 22:12). Hope is alive!

Point: We need not despair over the things of this world. There is nothing too hard for God! Trust Him and His word.

Prayer: Father, strengthen my faith, give me wisdom, as I read, study and pray lead me in living out Your word in my life.

Practice: Whenever I feel discouraged I will find strength in God's word and move forward in His will.

Today's Reading:
Genesis 41-42; Matthew 25-26

January 18

RULES FOR THE HARD HEART

By Peggy Kalevik

Matthew 5:38-39 *"You have heard that it was said, 'Eye for eye, and tooth for tooth.' 39 But I tell you, Do not resist an evil person. If someone strikes you on the right cheek, turn to him the other also.*

The first writing of this Old Testament Law ('Eye for eye, and tooth for tooth.') is found in Exodus 21:23-25. The so called law of retaliation (*lex talionis*), was a way of providing the Old Testament justice system with a formula for fair punishment, but it forbade revenge, and or vendetta's. While it may appear that Jesus in today's scripture could be contradicting the Old Testament, He is not; He is invoking the law of love. Recall that in Matthew 19:3-12, Jesus explains that God gave man divorce because mans heart was hard. Today's passage has the same reasoning; the law of retaliation was given because of the hardness of man's heart.

In verse 17 Jesus tells us: *"Do not think that I have come to abolish the Law or the Prophets; I have not come to abolish them but to fulfill them.* Certainly we have heard this spoken from many pulpits and from many Sunday school, and Bible study teachers, the prophecy of the Old Testament points to Jesus. There are those scholars that say Jesus in these verses presents himself as the goal of these Old Testament laws. I think that is what we believe, that the entire Bible points to Him. That being the case, it is clear that He does not want us to extract an "eye for an eye or a tooth for a tooth." He wants us to forgive, to show love and to live in peace with each other. Jesus wants us to have a generous spirit, not a heart that wants to exact revenge.

How thoughtful of God to allow for our hard hearts, He did not overlook anything. There is no need to look for revenge or repayment, God has covered it with the blood of His Son. *"Do not let your hearts be troubled. Trust in God; trust also in me.* (John 14:1)

Point: Jesus said we can't have a hard heart
Prayer: Lord, let my heart be soft and pliable in Your hand.
Practice: I will forgive the one who has offended me, and I will have a generous heart.

Today's Reading:
Genesis 43-45; Matthew 27

January 19

LEAVE IT BEHIND
By Beth Nelson

Genesis 12:1 The Lord said to Abram, "Leave your country, your people and your father's household and go to the land I will show you."

Most people don't like change, especially when it means leaving something behind. We're creatures of habit and the familiar is comforting to us.

Often God calls people to let go of the old in order to embrace something new that He has for them. Look at His call to Abram. He asked Abram to leave behind everything: his family, his people and his country, take his wife and travel to a faraway land. His goal? *"I will make you into a great nation and I will bless you."*

Could He have accomplished the same purpose if Abram had stayed home? Apparently not. When God is starting something new He requires our full, undivided attention. Moving away from the familiar, whether physically or emotionally, is not only symbolic of a new life, it's often necessary to focus on, listen to and rely upon, God. Could that be where the concept of being 'set apart' originated? To be set apart implies distance from something; moving away from the old to focus on the new that God has for us.

Abraham and Sarah sacrificed much in their obedience to God. They knew that they might never see their parents, families, or homeland, again. They were physically set apart. Because they were willing to not only hear God's voice, but to obey, God became their Father, their Protector, their Provider. He also fulfilled His promise to them. He made them into a great nation and through them, all of the earth was blessed.

Today's Reading:
Genesis 46-47; Matthew 28-Mark 1

January 20

GET READY FOR REAL GLOBAL WARMING!
By Scott Kalevik

Revelation 21:1 *Then I saw a new heaven and a new earth, for the first heaven and the first earth had passed away, and there was no longer any sea.*

What's wrong with the earth? Tsunamis, earthquakes, hurricanes and volcanoes rock various parts of the globe on an increasingly routine basis. The February meeting of the United Nations-backed Intergovernmental Panel on Climate Change reported that there is a 90 percent chance greenhouse gases are cooking the planet and that the trend will accelerate through this century. They estimate that temperatures will rise 3.2 to 7.1 degrees Fahrenheit by the year 2100. This rise in temperature may melt polar ice caps raising sea levels worldwide. The increased temperatures may also lead to climate changes causing widespread drought leading potentially to famine.

How should we as Christians respond to these cataclysmic reports? First, we recognize that Jesus prepared us for these events by telling us about them thousands of years ago: Mt 24:7 *Nation will rise against nation, and kingdom against kingdom. There will be famines and earthquakes in various places. 8 All these are the beginning of birth pains.* God is sovereign over all of these changes.

Second, we remember what God's plan is for this earth! 2Pe 3:7 *By the same word the present heavens and earth are reserved for fire, being kept for the day of judgment and destruction of ungodly men.* Worried about global warming? Wait until you see what Jesus does to this planet when His divine plan comes to pass!

Third, we rest in the fact that God has promised to create a new heaven and a new earth for those in Christ. Certainly we want to live responsibly when it comes to taking care of the planet. But instead of fretting about the future, let's spend today growing in Christ and sharing His love with others so that they too may escape the judgment of God when REAL global warming comes!

While we do all we can to care for our environment, we must remember: Our security is NOT in planet earth. Our security is in Christ!

Point: Security is in Christ, not in planet earth!

Prayer: Lord, help me responsibly care for this earth but help me remember that life with you is the main priority of my life.

Practice: Today I'll praise God for the security He gives to His own!

Today's Reading:
Genesis 48-50; Mark 2

January 21

God is our Hiding Place
By Mike Scheimann

Psalm 32:7 7 You are my hiding place; you will protect me from trouble and surround me with songs of deliverance. Selah

Ever since I was a young child, "You are my hiding place" has been one of my most cherished and beloved songs. Sometimes, when I'm feeling low, I'll program the CD player in my car to "repeat" mode, and listen to it over and over. The words of the song are so simple, yet so profound and comforting. "Whenever I am afraid, I will trust in You." What a statement! This verse in Psalm is truly a song of deliverance written by someone who knew what it meant to be very afraid. The writer also knew what it meant to be delivered by God's mighty hand when all hope seemed lost.

I have only been afraid for my life a very few times, but sometimes I do feel like I am surrounded by enemies. Do you ever get that feeling? Do you ever feel like you are being overwhelmed by your enemies and you just want to hide? Perhaps you or a loved one is fighting an illness, or legal battle, or financial crisis. Perhaps you feel like your family or friends are the enemy? Sometimes the people who have the opportunity or ability to hurt us the most, are the ones closest to us. Or maybe your battle is with some addiction or temptation? Whatever it is, God is able to overcome!

Point: Praise God! He is bigger than any enemy or battle that comes against us. He will hide us and protect us; He will go out and defeat the enemy with a mighty hand. The same God who delivered David is our God!

Prayer: Heavenly Father, you are such a mighty and awesome God! We are so blessed to have you in our lives. You truly do bless us with songs of deliverance whenever we are afraid. Thank you for who you are.

Practice: Are you feeling like you are under attack right now? Seek your refuge, your strength, and your deliverance in God's mighty embrace. Let Him erase the sorrow that holds you captive and fill your heart with a song.

Today's Reading:
Exodus 1-2; Mark 3-4

January 22

GOD IS OMNISCIENT
By Peggy Kalevik

Numbers 22:28 *Then the LORD opened the donkey's mouth, and she said to Balaam, "What have I done to you to make you beat me these three times?"*

In his time, Balaam was a sorcerer, prophet, and diviner of great reputation. It was said of him, whoever he blesses will be blessed and whoever he curses will be cursed. But Balaam underestimated the power of the true God. Balaam's reputation was built on his ability to examine the internal organs of animals and observe natural phenomena to determine the will of "the gods". He thought the God of Israel was the same as all the pagan gods.

Balaam is on his way to the camp of Balak, where he is expected to bring a curse on the Israelites so the Moabites will be able to defeat them in battle. The Moabites had seen and heard about the victories of the Israelites and they were terrified.

Balaam refused to go with the first messengers who Balak had sent; so he sent a second group. This time God gave Balaam permission to go but he could only say what God wanted him to say. However, God was angry with Balaam and sent an angel to block his path. Balaam was noted for his ability to handle animals so it was strange that he was having so much trouble with his donkey. Balaam's treatment of the donkey gives us a look into the heart of the pagan prophet. The donkey, after being beaten three times by Balaam, spoke up, and enlightened Balaam about the presence of the angel on the path.

God sent the angel because He knew Balaam was planning to say whatever he wanted to say when he met Balak. God knew Balaam's thoughts and his heart. Once Balaam reached the camp of the Moabites he made pagan sacrifices but, to Balak's chagrin, he could only bless the Israelites. The spirit of God came upon Balaam as he realized God's intent was to bless Israel. The Lord opened the mouth of a donkey to open the eyes of a pagan prophet.

Point: God knows everything!! Even our every thought. He is Omniscient!

Prayer: Lord let my thoughts glorify you, cleanse my heart and my mind.

Practice: Make a conscious effort to repent of thoughts which do not glorify God or edify His people. God knows all.

Today's Reading:
Exodus 3-5; Mark 5

January 23

The Center of God's Word
By Mike Scheimann

Psalm 118:8 *It is better to take refuge in the Lord than to trust in man.*

We've all read or heard that Psalm 119 is the longest chapter in the Bible, and Psalm 117 is the shortest. It is also said that, through God's divine providence, Psalm 118 happens to be the exact middle chapter of the Bible. And Psalm 118:8 is the middle verse in the Bible.

I don't think it's any coincidence this psalm gives thanks to God for His deliverance. Or, how we're told by the psalmist to put our trust in God, not in man. Isn't this what being a Christian essentially means? Either you trust in God, in His Word, His commands, and His teachings, and follow and obey Him; or you trust what man says, and live life any way you like.

God tells us to trust in Him and He will guide us, protect us, teach us, love us, and one day bring us home to live with Him for all eternity. Man says there is no "one" true god. We can worship whoever or whatever god we want, and if we're basically good people, we'll either all go to heaven, or perhaps come back as a racehorse instead of a rat.

Man tells us to trust in ourselves and in our own wisdom and might. Man relies on himself for protection and to make a better life for himself. If you take a look at the news around the world, or even around our own city, you will see how well that plan is working out for everyone. Who do you think is right? God or man?

Point: The Bible is the only true Word of God and has withstood the test of time.

Prayer: Heavenly Father, You have seen the folly of mankind in their effort to prove their greatness. Yet you continue to patiently love us and discipline us. We have seen and heard what men do in their own power and wisdom and the destruction it causes. Help us to seek you rather than worldly riches or prominence.

Practice: God gave us His Holy Word as a testimony of His wisdom. Everything in His word has its purpose, and nothing is coincidence. Read it and trust in what it says, for it is the spoken word of God. Take refuge in it.

Today's Reading:
Exodus 6-7; Mark 6-7

January 24

Touching the Word

By Peggy Kalevik

John 20:27 *Then he said to Thomas, "Put your finger here; see my hands. Reach out your hand and put it into my side. Stop doubting and believe."*

When Jesus visited the apostles after His resurrection, Thomas was not with them. When he heard of Jesus' appearance among them, he doubted. So, one week later Jesus appeared to them again while Thomas was present. After a greeting to all present, Jesus said to Thomas, *"Put your finger here; see my hands. Reach out your hand and put it into my side. Stop doubting and believe."* An interesting thing happens here which doesn't often get attention. Thomas is given the opportunity to touch the "Word".

In chapter 1 of John's Gospel, he writes: *"In the beginning was the Word, and the Word was with God, and the Word was God."* He was with God in the beginning. Generally the "word" used here refers to the spoken word, however in this instance John is expressing how the Word is the source of all that is visible and antedates the entire material world. John is saying the Word is creative in power because God spoke creation into existence through His Word. He's also indicating that Jesus has universal significance and He speaks with the ultimate authority.

Thomas in his humanness, his weak faith as it were, is blessed by the opportunity to see, hear and touch the Word of God. Wow! When we have bad days, how often do we long for Jesus to appear at our side in a way that we could see him face to face; to help us through a really rough situation. But Jesus also says to Thomas, *"Because you have seen me, you have believed; blessed are those who have not seen and yet have believed."* While we have not seen nor physically touched Him, our faith should be strengthened by what we know and see of Him around us everyday. We can touch Him as He is revealed to us in His Word. We can see Him in His creation.

Point: The word is near you; it is in your mouth and in your heart, you can touch the Word

Prayer: Lord place Your Word in my heart and on my tongue that I may be able to feel your touch.

Practice: Study and memorize the Word for deeper understanding so you are able to hold onto the Word.

Today's Reading:
Exodus 8-10; Mark 8

January 25

AND WE ARE BLESSED!

By Peggy Kalevik

Ephesians 1:3 *"Praise be to the God and Father of our Lord Jesus Christ, who has blessed us in the heavenly realms with every spiritual blessing in Christ."*

As Christians we have a unique and special relationship with God the Father through Christ's death and resurrection. We are "blessed" by God through this saving action of Christ Jesus.

In the Old Testament we are shown how a blessing is given by the patriarch to his son(s) and in the case of Esau and Jacob, through Esau's ambivalence and Jacob's trickery it was a source of great contention. The blessing given in Ephesians 1:3 is eternal and the blessing given to one does not negate the blessing given to another. Your blessing from God does not change or take away mine; I am blessed as well.

The Old Testament blessing was characterized by the "giving of good"; it was usually material and specific. The New Testament blessing is spiritual, but definite. Our blessings are spiritual because they are communicated to us through the Holy Spirit. They are definite because they have been secured in the heavenly realms in Christ Jesus.

The Holy Spirit transfers to us all God achieved in Christ; and Christ, who is seated at the right hand of God, is victorious over the spiritual forces of darkness and evil. So we can say, Praise be to the God and Father of our Lord Jesus Christ, because he has loved us with the greatest love of all and we are blessed!

Point: This unique relationship is our greatest blessing; rejoice!
Prayer: We praise You Father, because it is from You that we are blessed.
Practice: Make an effort to consciously praise God each day for this great blessing.

Today's Reading:
Exodus 11-12; Mark 9-10

January 26

FRESH COMPASSIONS, EVERYDAY!

By Kathy Bryant

Lamentations 3:22-23 *22 Because of the LORD's great love we are not consumed, for his compassions never fail. 23 They are new every morning; great is your faithfulness.*

By the time we reach adulthood most of us have experienced some type of trouble or suffering (physical, financial, or relational) and we felt alone. In hindsight, we came to realize we were not alone, because the Lord saw us through the darkness of our situations. We became stronger as we learned important lessons through adversity. Today's scripture reading tells us how the Lord's compassions fail not and are new every morning.

Webster's dictionary defines compassion as "to bear, to suffer, sympathetic consciousness of others distress together with a desire to alleviate it". Just imagine, we can interpret this definition as the Lord suffers with us; He understands and is sympathetic to our distress and He desires to alleviate it once his plan for us is fulfilled. His compassion is new every morning! The Lord feels this way toward us every morning.

As children of God we can claim the promise that the Lord draws near to us everyday of our lives. As a result of His caring and love for us, we can say and sing "great is thy faithfulness".

Point: Everyday we receive a fresh supply of compassion and strength from our heavenly Father. We can walk with confidence to face whatever life brings our way.

Prayer: Thank you Lord for your faithfulness toward us. You are always near to us and understand everything about our lives. Help us to truly believe you walk beside us in the valleys and on the mountaintop. Praise your name for being just a prayer away.

Practice: Invite the Lord Jesus to be apart of your life everyday. You will experience the peace and comfort of the Holy Spirit and know that you are not alone.

Today's Reading:
Exodus 13-15; Mark 11

January 27

Who Is Jesus?

By Scott Kalevik

John 8:58-59 *"I tell you the truth," Jesus answered, "before Abraham was born, I am!" 59 At this, they picked up stones to stone him, but Jesus hid himself, slipping away from the temple grounds.*

When Jesus says, *"Before Abraham was born, I am,"* He clearly declares Himself to be God. How? Not only does Jesus claim to be around before Abraham was born, but when Jesus ends His statement with the words *"I am"*, He refers directly to Exodus 3:14: *"God said to Moses, "I AM WHO I AM. This is what you are to say to the Israelites: 'I AM has sent me to you.'"*

When the crowd hears Jesus refer to Himself as, *"I am,"* they know He is calling Himself by the same name that God identified Himself with in Exodus 3:14. You can tell they make the connection because they immediately pick up stones to kill Jesus. Claiming to be God was considered blasphemy and punishable by death.

It didn't matter to the people that Jesus had routinely done what only God can do. The blind could see. The deaf could hear. The dumb spoke. The lame could walk. Demon possessed people had been restored to their right minds. Storms had been stilled. Water turned to wine. Sparse morsels of bread and fish had fed thousands. Still the crowd chose to ignore the facts. Instead of falling at His feet in worship, they tried to kill Him.

Jesus confronts us with the truth of who He is even today. Like the people listening to Him in ancient Palestine, we are forced to deal with His claims. His claim that He is God still stands today. Do you believe it or not? As C.S. Lewis once said, "Jesus is either a liar, a lunatic, or Lord." In other words, Jesus is either lying to us, or He's crazy, or He's telling us the truth.

Answering the question, "Who is Jesus?" is the most important thing we ever do in our lives. Our eternal destiny is determined by whether or not we believe what Jesus claimed about Himself. How do you answer? Who is Jesus?

Point: Jesus clearly claims to be God. Do you believe His claim?

Prayer: Lord, I acknowledge the truth of your statements. I believe and submit to You.

Practice: Today I will meditate on this question: Do I live like Jesus is God?

Today's Reading:
Exodus 16-17; Mark 12-13

January 28

Like Filthy Rags
By Mike Scheimann

Isaiah 64:6 All of us have become like one who is unclean, and all our righteous acts are like filthy rags; we all shrivel up like a leaf, and like the wind our sins sweep us away.

We all have at least one pile of dirty rags in our house. Usually they are kept in the garage, or the shed and are used for changing the oil in the car, or cleaing up really gross messes. Now think about this. If you were to have company for a nice fancy dinner, would you put out those dirty, filthy rags for your guests to use as napkins? Would you use them to wash your kid's faces? Of course you wouldn't.

Unfortunately there are many people, both Christians and non-Christians, who think they can fool God by "dressing up" in their filthy rags of righteousnes. I often hear people say: as long as you are a pretty good person, and help the poor and needy every once in a while; as long as you don't rape, murder, and steal; or as long as you write a check in church on Sunday, then God will say "come on in to heaven" when you die. They say that God is a God of love, and would never cast someone into hell just because they made a few mistakes. These people are badly, and sadly mistaken.

There is no one on earth who is good enough to get into heaven on their own merit and acts of righteousness. God doesn't say the good enough shall have eternal life. He tells us that only the pure and righteous will inherit His Kingdom. There has only been one person on this planet who fits that description, Jesus Christ. The rest of us have all sinned and fallen short of the glory of God (Rom 3:23). No matter what good deeds we do, or how much money we give, or how nice we are to others, and how many trees or whales we save, we'll never be good enough to pass judgement before the Almighty. There is only one way to become pure and righteous enough to enter heaven and that is by letting Jesus wash you truly clean with His blood, and by being made pure through His righteousness.

Point: God is a holy and righteous God, and expects us to be holy and pure before Him through Christ.

Prayer: Jesus, thank You for making us clean.

Practice: Tell others you can never be good enough on your own; you need Jesus.

Today's Reading:
Exodus 18-20; Mark 14

January 29

I'm Singing In The Jail

By Scott Kalevik

Acts 16:24-25a *Upon receiving such orders, he put them in the inner cell and fastened their feet in the stocks. 25a About midnight Paul and Silas were praying and singing hymns to God ...*

The world must think we're nuts. Christians are repeatedly instructed throughout Scripture to rest in the sovereign will of God even when outward circumstances are horrible. The Bible goes so far as to tell us to rejoice and consider our troubles with an attitude of joy in our hearts:

Phil 4:4 *Rejoice in the Lord always. I will say it again, Rejoice!*

James 1:2 *Consider it pure joy, my brothers, whenever you face trials of many kinds,*

Matthew 5:11 *blessed are you when people insult you, persecute you and falsely say all kinds of evil against you because of me. 12 Rejoice and be glad, because great is your reward in heaven, for in the same way they persecuted the prophets who were before you.*

Paul and Silas illustrate this principal in Acts 16. They're praying and singing hymns while shackled in jail. Their circumstances are horrible, but their hearts are praising God.

How can they do that? They understand with every fiber of their beings that God has not abandoned them. In fact, just the opposite is true. God has allowed them to experience jail in order to glorify His name and accomplish His purpose. Paul and Silas trust the Lord. They sing because they know He has everything under control! They're not nuts ... they're exactly where God wants them and rejoicing about it!

Sure enough, the Lord delivers them from jail, but not before bringing salvation to the jailer and his household. The Lord is glorified, the jailer is saved, and God's sovereign love is demonstrated.

Whatever your circumstance today, you cannot be separated from the love of Christ. Continue to surrender your heart to Him and sing His praises. Rejoice and rest knowing that He is working out His plan for your life. It's time to sing!

Today's Reading:
Exodus 21-22; Mark 15-16

January 30

IN THE MIDST OF DISAPPOINTMENT

By Peggy Kalevik

Psalm 107:29 *He stilled the storm to a whisper; the waves of the sea were hushed.*

In this section of Psalm 107 we see how even the merchants of the sea must give testimony to the power of God. Verse 24 says *"They saw the works of the LORD, his wonderful deeds in the deep."* They saw they could do nothing to hold back the hand of God; for when He spoke and stirred up a tempest, all they could do was cry out to Him for mercy. Then He brought them out of their distress.

This Psalm brings us lessons learned from those who believe on His word. It recounts the many reasons we have to give thanks and praise. The last verse is a kind of invocation of wisdom, it tells us that 'the righteous will become wise by understanding and living according to the word of God, living in and through the great love of the Lord in every aspect of their lives'.

Here is a place to come for comfort and rest in the midst of our trials and disappointment. Give thanks to the Lord for He is good. In the middle of the today's crisis', or at the loss of a loved one, or when caught in a place of sin in your life, or buried under the financial pressures of living above your means, heed the word and power of God and *"Give thanks to the Lord for He is good: His love endures forever."* In the midst of your trials and disappointments look up to the heavens and praise Him.

Point: In the midst of the disappointments of life, don't lose sight of the Lord's blessings. Praise Him!

Prayer: Lord, don't let me get so caught up in living that I forget to walk in Your light and praise You.

Practice: Remember to praise God every day for what He has done for you personally.

Today's Reading:
Exodus 23-25; Luke 1

January 31

DISPUTABLE MATTERS
By Scott Kalevik

Romans 14:1-2 *Accept him whose faith is weak, without passing judgment on disputable matters. 2 One man's faith allows him to eat everything, but another man, whose faith is weak, eats only vegetables.*

Some Christians have decided it's best to worship on Saturdays. Others say Sunday is the 'right' day to worship. Still others say any day is fine. Some say there are certain foods that should not be eaten (like bacon for instance). Others say any food is ok. Some Christians say you should never drink a glass of wine with dinner. Others say drinking wine with dinner is fine as long as you don't get drunk. Some Christians insist that the King James Version of Scripture is the only one that should be used. Others disagree. And on and on it goes.

So who is right? The answer is: Nobody's right and everybody's right! If there is no Biblical text which, when interpreted responsibly, directly addresses an issue, then the Bible calls that issue a "disputable matter." We are instructed to each follow our conscience without judging someone who disagrees when it comes to disputable matters.

Instead of fighting or dividing over disputable matters, Paul says: Ro 14:19 *"Let us therefore make every effort to do what leads to peace and to mutual edification.* We are called to keep the peace and build our brothers and sisters up in the faith rather than dividing regarding "disputable matters."

To be sure, many issues in Scripture are crystal clear and beyond dispute. We don't practice tolerance when it comes to Jesus' deity or the resurrection. These truths are essential to our faith and so clear in Scripture they are indisputable.

But love and tolerance rule the day when it comes to disputable matters.

Point: No one is right and everyone is right when it comes to disputable matters. Keeping a clear conscience before God while acting in love towards those who disagree takes top priority.

Prayer: Lord, please help me make every effort to do what leads to peace when it comes to disputable matters.

Practice: Read Romans 14. If you recognize that you've judged other believers over disputable things, what can you do to act in love instead of judgment?

Today's Reading:
Exodus 26-27; Luke 2-3

February 1

How Do You Consider Others?

By Scott Kalevik

1Peter 3:7 *Husbands, in the same way be considerate as you live with your wives, and treat them with respect as the weaker partner and as heirs with you of the gracious gift of life, so that nothing will hinder your prayers.*

One day the generous husband told his wife he would make dinner. He told her he wanted her to go to the store and buy steaks, potatoes, and salad. When she returned home, he asked her to prepare a special sauce and marinate the steaks. Then he requested she bake the potatoes in the oven while he got the grill started. So, after making the sauce and marinating the steaks, she prepared the potatoes and put them in the oven while he pulled his lawn chair over to the grill and sprinkled lighter fluid on the coals.

As he tossed the match onto the coals he reflected on what a considerate husband he was. He bet none of his buddies were making dinner for their wives. The flame grew hot and so did he. He called to his wife and asked her to bring him an iced tea. After she brought him the iced tea, he realized the sun was bearing down on him. So he yelled to his wife to bring him some sunscreen and his favorite hat.

The coals were finally hot enough, so the generous husband sweetly requested that his wife bring the steaks out to him so he could put them on the grill. Upon her arrival he perceptibly evaluated her demeanor. He could tell something was bothering her. Although he wasn't sure what she was upset about, he trusted that all of his effort to make her this beautiful dinner was bound to cheer her up.

As he flipped the steaks over for the last turn and plopped back into the lawn chair, he called to his wife and told her the steaks were almost done. She should get the salad made and the table set so everything would be ready when he was done making dinner. He noticed his glass was empty and politely requested a refill for his iced-tea. His wife was noticeably angry as she poured his refill.

How ungrateful he thought. I finally take the time to make dinner for her and all I get is attitude. In case you're not getting this: THIS IS NOT THE WAY TO TREAT YOUR WIFE! God values her so highly that your prayers are likely to be hindered if you don't show her consideration and respect.

Point: Our prayers may be hindered by our behavior towards others.

Prayer: Lord, help me treat others with consideration and respect.

Practice: Consider how others are impacted by your actions. Are you self-centered?

Today's Reading:
Exodus 28-30; Luke 4

February 2

No Surprises!

By Herb Hubbard

John 6:5-6 *5 When Jesus looked up and saw a great crowd coming toward him, he said to Philip, "Where shall we buy bread for these people to eat?" 6 He asked this only to test him, for he already had in mind what he was going to do.*

Have you had someone set up a surprise for you? Maybe a special dinner or a night out on the town? The evening may have been a complete surprise for you, but it wasn't for the person who planned the event. You would have to trust the person and know that what they had in mind was for your good, not harm.

In our scripture today we see Jesus asking Phillip how they were going to feed the mulitude which was approaching. Our response to the question may have been alot like Phillips'; we'd look at our natural resources and feel hopeless.

It is reassuring in our spiritual journey to know nothing comes into our lives that is a surprise to our Lord. He already has in mind a plan for our lives if we will surrender our complete life and will to Him and trust that he has our best interest at heart. He will accomplish His will for us and His will for us is to give glory to the Father.

Point: Jesus knows his plan for our lives. There are no surprises to him.
Prayer: Lord help me to have the mind of Christ to glorify the Father
Practice: Lord help me to have the mind of Christ to glorify the Father

Today's Reading:
Exodus 31-32; Luke 5-6

February 3

WHAT IS "TRUE LOVE"?
By Mike Scheimann

John 15:13 *Greater love has no one than this, that he lay down his life for his friends.*

February is often known as the month of love, and even has it's own special day dedicated to celebrating our love for the special people in our lives. But lost among the cards, the flowers, the gifts, and the candy, is the true meaning of love. We celebrate love without knowing what it really means. You may love someone enough to buy them gifts, but do you love them enough to willingly die for them?

How many of us could honestly answer that question with an unhesitating "YES"? Well, Jesus not only told us that this is how He defines the true meaning of love, but He also proved it by His action, laying down His life for us.

Point: Flowers wilt and die, candy is sweet for only a moment, and the luster of jewelry fades with time. But to love somebody enough to die for them, means you love them more than self.

Prayer: Dear precious Savior, thank you so much for proving how much you loved us by giving up everything, to become nothing by losing all you had, including your life, so that we may find life in you.

Practice: Make it a point to tell your loved ones that you love them, not just on Valentine's Day, but everyday. Prove it to them through your actions and sacrifices, both big and small, on a daily basis.

Today's Reading:
Exodus 33-35; Luke 7

February 4

STANDING ON THE SIDELINES
By Mike Scheimann

1Timothy 6:18 *Command them to do good, to be rich in good deeds, and to be generous and willing to share.*

For the first year after we joined the church, we did what a lot of new members do; we basically stood on the sidelines and watched. We showed up at 10:29 for church on Sunday morning, wrote our check, and left pretty much as soon as church was over. That was our obligation and duty to God for the week. However, as we slowly began to grow and mature in Christ, the Holy Spirit began to convict us that that wasn't enough. He told us in order to really grow in His word, to become strong prayer warriors, and to be useful servants for Him, we needed to do more. We needed to start making friends in the church, and start plugging into bible studies and other activities. That's when we started getting involved in the Wednesday night prayer group, and then later the Sunday night prayer group. After that we joined the choir, and started to go to more and more functions. We slowly began to feel more connected to our brothers and sisters in the body of Christ, as well as to our Lord and Savior.

As we studied and prayed more, our faith grew, and so did our love for Jesus and for the church body. Now we feel like the church is indeed our home, and the members are indeed our true brothers and sisters. We face accountability with them when we mess up, or start skipping meetings, and we help keep others accountable.

We finally felt a sense of belonging and meaning. We hurt when one of you is hurting. We have prayed for others, and have been prayed for by others, through many storms. In fact, in many ways, we are much closer to our brothers and sisters in Christ, than we are to some of our own family and friends.

Point: How about you? Do you feel like you are part of a big family, or do you feel like you are watching from the sidelines, observing the show?

Prayer: Heavenly Father, help each of us to get off the sidelines, and get involved in growing in you, and serving you and others.

Practice: Start growing in Him and serving Him by getting involved in one of the bible studies or prayer groups.

Today's Reading:
Exodus 36-37; Luke 8-9

February 5

SELF GIVING LOVE THAT FULFILLS GOD'S LAW
By Peggy Kalevik

Ruth 4:10 10 *I have also acquired Ruth the Moabitess, Mahlon's widow, as my wife, in order to maintain the name of the dead with his property, so that his name will not disappear from among his family or from the town records. Today you are witnesses!"*

Love and the law, the two seem to have little in common. But here in the story of Ruth we see the two come together to fulfill God's law. Ruth is a story of selfless devotion, kindness and generosity. As you read this beautiful story keep in mind that Ruth is not an Israelite, but a Moabite. Even so, her actions reflect the wonderful love of God.

Throughout the Bible (Lev 19:18; Matt 19:19; Mark 12:31, 33; Rom 13:9; Gal 5:14; and James 2:8), God tells us *"love your neighbor as yourself."* God rewards obedience to His word. In Ruth 2:12 Boaz says to Ruth *"may the lord repay you for what you have done"*. In essences He blesses her, because she has been a blessing to Naomi. His blessing also concerns her acceptance of the God of Israel. Note how Ruth did not for a moment consider going back to her family in Moab. Instead, in chapter 1:16b-17, she makes a vow to Naomi saying, *"Where you go I will go, and where you stay I will stay. Your people will be my people and your God my God. 17 Where you die I will die, and there I will be buried. May the LORD deal with me, be it ever so severely, if anything but death separates you and me."* This is a complete and utter denial of her people and their gods. She is vowing to be loyal to Naomi, her people and her God until death. Naomi is the recipient of this great love. Ruth too received a great blessing from her acts of love to Naomi. This is the same kind of love which transformed Israel from desperation at the death of Eli to peace and prosperity in the early days of Solomon through the selfless devotion of David, a descendent of Ruth.

God uses this non-Israelite to show us a picture of how taking part in the coming of God's Kingdom is not decided by ones blood and birth right, but by living our lives according to the will of God through obedience that comes from faith and love.

Point: Be a blessing to someone today. Show love selflessly.

Prayer: Dear Lord, help me to be a blessing to someone today, without expecting anything in return.

Practice: Today I will take every opportunity to do something to help someone in need.

Today's Reading:
Exodus 38-40; Luke 10

February 6

THE OPULENT COW CATASTROPHE!
By Scott Kalevik

Amos 4:1 Hear this word, you cows of Bashan on Mount Samaria, you women who oppress the poor and crush the needy and say to your husbands, "Bring us some drinks!" 2 The Sovereign LORD has sworn by his holiness: "The time will surely come when you will be taken away with hooks, the last of you with fishhooks.

We live in comparative opulence when measured by the standard of living endured by eighty percent of the world. Take food for instance. Most of us don't decide to eat because we're hungry. We decide to eat because it's time to eat. We don't wonder about whether or not there will be food to eat. We ponder what kind of food we want. There's a grocery store every few blocks and it's packed full of food. Our restaurants throw out enough food every day to feed thousands of people in destitute countries. But in this country, even those who are "down and out" can eat three meals a day if they work the system well.

God has blessed us abundantly but with blessing comes accountability. God calls the ladies of Bashan cows. The cows of Bashan were arguably the best breed of cattle in Canaan. Pampered and privileged, these cows usually spent all day eating. Apparently these ladies of Bashan were experts at satisfying any culinary desire that crossed their minds. But their hearts were never mooooved with compassion towards those who had nothing. God uses Amos to tell them they've oppressed the poor. They've crushed the needy ... and they still want more!

Then God tells them about judgment. There's a catastrophe coming because these cows were totally self-indulgent. Verses four and five speak about how they continued to offer sacrifices to God and fulfill their religious duties. But they never shared what they had with the poor. Thinking of none but themselves, they spent God's blessings on themselves. God hated it.

Who are we sharing our abundance with? God expects us to care for the poor and oppressed. We will either obey Him by doing what we can to share our abundance or we'll be rightly accused of oppressing the poor and crushing the needy. Hoarding abundance leads to catastrophe.

Point: We are called to care for those who have less than we do.
Prayer: God, help me share Your blessings with others.
Practice: What has God blessed you with that you can share with others?

Today's Reading:
Leviticus 1-2; Luke 11-12

February 7

Who Comes First?

By Scott Kalevik

Proverbs 3:9-10 *Honor the LORD with your wealth, with the firstfruits of all your crops; 10 then your barns will be filled to overflowing, and your vats will brim over with new wine.*

"I lost my focus and I stopped giving my tithe." The lady that called me with this news said a relative had convinced her she couldn't afford to give money to God anymore. She relayed how since she stopped giving to God, her finances had sunk to new lows and it seemed like her financial hole was deeper than ever.

As she struggled, the Lord reminded her that He comes first. By faith, she began to give again. Even though her call was long-distance, she sounded radiant as she began praising God for His goodness! Since she put God first in her finances, her whole financial picture had improved. It was funny to hear her try to explain it. She couldn't really point to one thing which had changed. All she knew was since she started honoring God with her money, she was able to give to God, pay her bills, and still have some money left over!

God teaches us how to handle our money. He promised repeatedly that if we make Him our first priority and honor him with our wealth, He will respond by supplying all our needs.

God gives us the choice. We can either run our own financial lives, put ourselves first, and depend upon ourselves, or we can obey His word and honor Him by giving our best back to Him. What choice are you making?

I heard a preacher once say that all of us could evaluate the true priorities of our lives by looking at how we spend our money. What does your checkbook register tell you?

Point: Putting God first when it comes to finances brings His blessing.
Prayer: God, help me use whatever resource you've given me for your glory.
Practice: Begin giving and see what God does!

Today's Reading:
Leviticus 3-5; Luke 13

February 8

THE STUMBLING BLOCK

By Peggy Kalevik

1 Corinthians 1:22-23 *Jews demand miraculous signs and Greeks look for wisdom, 23 but we preach Christ crucified: a stumbling block to Jews and foolishness to Gentiles,*

The Greek word *"skandalon"* Paul uses here explains the problems (the lack of acceptance) the gospel presented to the Jews, the Greeks and the Romans of Jesus' day. The Jews, Paul said, seek for "miraculous signs", the Greeks seek "wisdom" and in this way they hope to find the answers to the mysteries of God.

The Greeks and the Romans saw the people who were crucified as the lowest of criminals. So, how could one who was crucified be the Messiah or the Savior? To them Christ was a "stumbling block" because His teachings and His sacrifice were not logical. They had trouble understanding how a god, being spirit, could become human and provide atonement for the sins of all mankind. He was foolishness to some because they were on their way to being lost.

What are our stumbling blocks? Is there something about Christ we simply can't accept? I know a pastor who is fond of saying "You can believe the moon is made of cheese, but that doesn't make it so". We can form our own opinions of God but that won't make them true. If we find there are things about Jesus and what He's done for us we can't accept because they don't make sense to us, it won't change Him or what He's done. We can accept it or not, it's our choice.

Don't let your own wisdom condemn you to a life without Christ. Remember what Paul says in verse 18: *"For the message of the cross is foolishness to those who are perishing, but to us who are being saved it is the power of God"*.

Point: Gain greater understanding of Christ and what He has done for you. Lean not on your own understanding, walk in the spirit.

Prayer: Lord, help me to stand firm on Your word and trust and not faint.

Practice: I will read and study the Bible and ask questions when I don't understand something I have read. I will attend a Bible Study to strengthen my faith and understanding.

Today's Reading:
Leviticus 6-7; Luke 14-15

February 9

Don't Give the Devil a Foothold

By Mike Scheimann

Ephesians 4:27 *and do not give the devil a foothold.*

Advanced and daring rock climbers can climb a cliff that looks impossible to climb. They carefully go up or down the face of the cliff, looking for small little ledges or cracks they can get a fingerhold or toehold into, and carefully work their way along, one hold at a time. All a good climber needs is a small crack or crevice to gain a hand or foothold on the cliff. In much the same way, the devil looks to gain footholds with believers, so he can lead us astray.

Often times we tend to look at other Christians and think to ourselves, wow, they really have it together. What could the devil possibly do to cause them to sin, or to lead them to stray from the straight and narrow path? However, the devil looks at these people, especially if they are in the lime light of the Christian community, and thinks to himself; the bigger they are, the harder they will fall. He keeps chinking away at them and finds a small crack he can use as a foothold to cause them to sin.

Often times we see high profile Christians on TV, or read about them in the newspaper, and marvel at how somebody who seemed like such a rock for Christ, could have such flaws. But before we get too judgmental, we only need to look in the mirror to realize that the devil attacks us one and all, not just the big, but also the small.

But there is hope. Once we are children of God, the devil can no longer permanently defeat us. He may find a chink and cause us to sin, but Christ has already defeated Satan and sin, once and for all.

Point: Ephesians tells us if we have an area in our lives which consistently causes us to sin, we need to pray. Then we need to make a conscious effort through the power of the Holy Spirit to get rid of that foothold, and eliminate the pattern of sin

Prayer: Dear Jesus, give us the strength and the determination to make the effort to weed out areas of sin in our lives, and to take away the devils footholds.

Practice: Pray to Jesus and ask the Holy Spirit to convict you of the areas in your life that you know are causing you to sin, and which are making the devil's job a lot easier than it should be. Work to get rid of anger, malice, and other things in your

Today's Reading:
Leviticus 8-10; Luke 16

February 10

Drop It! (An Illustration)

By David Fundenberger

Ezekiel 18:30 30 *"Therefore, O house of Israel, I will judge you, each one according to his ways, declares the Sovereign LORD. Repent! Turn away from all your offenses; then sin will not be your downfall.*

When I was stationed along the rock bound coast of Maine I would watch the waves crash on shore at Schoodic Point. On Sunday afternoons we'd go there and feed the seagulls scraps of bread. We'd toss bread into the air and the seagulls would catch the bread in flight.

One day we were feeding the gulls and everybody ran out of bread. One resourceful dude decided to tear a little piece of foam rubber from his worn out pick up truck seat. He tossed it up and a seagull caught it and after tasting it immediately dropped it. Another gull dived for it and after tasting it also dropped it. One by one the gulls would catch, taste and drop the worthless foam.

What a picture, I thought. This is the way a Christian should respond to sin. As soon as we recognize it, we need to drop it immediately!

Point: As we move along in life we occasionally grab something bad that we think will be good, but we must drop it immediately.

Prayer: Dear Lord, help me be just like that seagull and drop a bad thing just as soon as I know it's bad.

Practice: Today I will instantly drop anything that I realize isn't pleasing to you.

Today's Reading:
Leviticus 11-12; Luke 17-18

February 11

THE SAME GOD YESTERDAY, TODAY, AND TOMORROW
By Mike Scheimann

James 1:17 *Every good and perfect gift is from above, coming down from the father of the heavenly lights, who does not change like shifting shadows.*

As young children in Sunday School, our teachers taught us lessons about the miracles and mighty works of God. We learned how God used plagues and miracles to bring the Jews out of Egypt. We all remember how Israel marched around the walls of mighty Jericho, blowing their trumpets, and God made the walls come tumbling down. We often think to ourselves, if God still did miracles and mighty works like that, then all the earth would have no choice but to believe in Him. We read about the miracles of healing in the New Testament, and say to ourselves, I wish God would just miraculously heal this person like He did back then. Sometimes we pray and pray to God, and wonder if He even hears us. We wonder if He is really in us and around us, or if He is far away in Heaven, sitting on His throne, waiting to send judgement upon us as written in Revelation.

Rest assured God does hear every prayer, every word, and even every thought you think. Also know our God of today, is still the God who did the mighty works of the past. He still has the same powers, and still demonstrates his powers through miracles here on earth on a daily basis. We hear praises about healing, and financial miracles all the time in chruch and in our prayer groups. God is still and will always be a mighty and powerful God, who can do anything He wants, according to His purpose and His perfect timing.

Point: Be confident that God is never changing, and is still large and in charge.

Prayer: Almighty Father, King of kings, and Lord of lords. We praise you, and stand in awe of you. We thank you that you are the same God today as you were when you created the heavens and the earth; and as you will be when you return triumphant at the end of the earth. In a world of constant change, thank you for being our rock and our foundation.

Practice: Sit down and make a list of some of the miracles God has worked in your life. Thank Him for what He has done in your life so far, and continue to seek Him and pray to Him; knowing He will hear and answer you.

Today's Reading:
Leviticus 13-15; Luke 19

February 12

The LORD drove back the Sea

By Peggy Kalevik

Exodus 14:21 Then Moses stretched out his hand over the sea, and all that night the LORD drove the sea back with a strong east wind and turned it into dry land. The waters were divided,

A miracle is an event or action that appears to be contrary to the laws of nature and is regarded as an act of God. Something that is totally amazing, extraordinary and unexpected. Imagine looking at a rough raging sea, and seeing it part and all the water rolled up into two walls facing each other. Then imagine you, walking between the two walls of water. That would be pretty amazing, extraordinary and unexpected. If you can envision that scene, then you know what the children of Israel felt like on that awesome day.

The LORD tells the Israelites to turn back and camp in a place that the Egyptians would assume they were either confused (maybe lost) or their God had stopped protecting them. But God understood exactly what He was doing. He knew that He had hardened pharaoh's heart and that Pharaoh would come after the Israelites. When he did God would show him and all of Egypt that He was the LORD!

There are scientists who believe that the parting of the Red Sea occurred due to some natural phenomena. I wonder if scientist know who controls natural phenomena. God arranged this event to show his power, to glorify Himself and to make a point. Moses stretched out his hands and all night the LORD drove back the sea with a strong east wind. What an intimidating awesome sight. In Deuteronomy 4:35 Moses tells the Israelites that they were shown these things so that they might know that the LORD is God; besides Him there is no other. These "things" that God has done to free them from Egypt are the greatest events in all of history. From the creation of the world until now no where on the earth has such a miraculous event occurred.

Point: The LORD is God in heaven and on the earth below. Who is like the LORD?

Prayer: LORD You are my rock, my fortress and my deliverer; in You I take refuge.

Today's Reading:
Leviticus 16-17; Luke 20-21

February 13

GIVE US A SECURITY BLANKET
By Peggy Kalevik

1Samuel 8:5 *They said to him, "You are old, and your sons do not walk in your ways; now appoint a king to lead us, such as all the other nations have."*

Israel went into a period of desperation at the death of Eli the priest and his sons. They made some terrible errors in judgment, sending the Ark of the Covenant into battle and losing it to the Philistines. As Samuel started to age they wanted a King. Interfering with God's plan and desires, they broke God's heart with their rejection of Him. The Almighty God has a broken heart because of mans rejection, imagine that.

God's desire was for a people who would abide in the wisdom of His word and provision. But the people wanted to be like all the nations around them. They wanted a permanent military leader who would raise up a great army. But wasn't God always with them? Hadn't he delivered them from Egypt; protected them in the desert for forty years, and most recently, even though they'd lost the Ark, hadn't God returned it to them. How could they not understand that God was their King? The earlier patriots recognized that God was the ultimate King of Israel, that he possessed absolute power and authority over Israel (Exodus 15:6; Judges 5:3-5).

Can we relate to this feeling of insecurity as we look back and remember how we felt on September 11, 2001? Many of us experienced a sense of insecurity, that we'd never felt before. Well, that is probably how the people of Israel felt; at least our government structure was still intact. Things were a little worst for them, their previous leader was dead and their current leader was getting old and his sons were not godly men; the people were afraid. God gave them what they wanted but he did not hurry His plan He gave them Saul, and continued to wait for His own timetable to bring David. Are we looking for a security blanket too, or are we willing to accept that God has already provided.

Point: Be careful what you ask for, God sometimes gives us what we want even when it's not good for us.

Prayer: Lord, help me put Your desires ahead of my own.

Practice: In the midst of current world struggles, I will rest in the security of God.

Today's Reading:
Leviticus 18-20; Luke 22

February 14

THE LOST ART OF PURITY!

By Scott Kalevik

Matthew 5:8 *Blessed are the pure in heart, for they will see God.*

Our society has largely abandoned the ideal of purity. If you seek purity these days, the world says you're inexperienced or naïve or old-fashioned. If you're sexually pure, for instance, the world calls you a prude. If you don't laugh at the dirty joke, the world calls you 'stuck-up' or judgmental. If you refuse to obey the boss when you're told to cheat the customer, you may be fired.

God doesn't see it that way. He values purity of heart more than you and I can comprehend. Living with a wholehearted, single-minded devotion to God, having been washed clean by faith in Jesus, is a marvelous life in God's eyes.

Jesus promises that the pure in heart will see God! If we could sit on that hillside and listen to Jesus speak these words, we'd see a shocked reaction among those who knew the Old Testament. Undoubtedly some recalled these words: Exodus 33:20 *But," he said, "you cannot see my face, for no one may see me and live."* Yet, Jesus promised that the pure in heart will see God.

How can we be pure in heart? Ps 119:9 *How can a young man keep his way pure? By living according to your word.* Obeying God's word leads to purity. How important is it to God? Heb 12:14 *Make every effort to live in peace with all men and to be holy; without holiness no one will see the Lord.* Make every effort.

As you consider purity, it's important to understand what direction your decisions are taking you. Some have the attitude that it's ok to pursue evil desires as long as they don't get discovered. If that's you, repent. God wants us to be pure in heart. God has made our purity possible through Christ. Walk in the Spirit today. Forsake evil.

Point: The pure in heart experience the favor of God and will see Him.
Prayer: Lord, I want to live a pure life in Your sight.
Practice: Examine your attitudes and actions. Is your life characterized by single-minded devotion to pleasing God in purity, or not?

Today's Reading:
Leviticus 21-22; Luke 23-24

February 15

Is Meek Weak?
By Scott Kalevik

Matthew 5:5 *Blessed are the meek, for they will inherit the earth.*

Blessed are the meek. They will inherit the earth. But if I'm really meek, do I have to take any and all offenses without comment or complaint? No, being a doormat for others is not the point of meekness. Meekness doesn't mean passively submissive to any offense. Rather, a meek person is humble, gentle, and not aggressive on their own behalf.

Moses is described in Numbers 12:3 like this: *(Now Moses was a very humble man, more humble than anyone else on the face of the earth.)* Moses wasn't stepped on by anyone. Pharaoh found that out the hard way. But Moses was meek. He is described as more humble than anyone else on earth. Instead of operating with the idea that he had the gifts and talents to deliver Israel, Moses served the Lord knowing that everything depended on the Lord's wisdom and strength and not on his!

Jesus exhibited meekness as well: Matthew 11:29 *Take my yoke upon you and learn from me, for I am gentle and humble in heart, and you will find rest for your souls.* Jesus was perfectly yielded to the will of the Father. He set aside His own rights to accomplish the purposes of the Father. Yet, when confronted with the travesty of corrupt commerce at the temple, Jesus forcibly removed the moneychangers with a whip (John 2:15). He wasn't a doormat. But His aggression was motivated by righteousness on behalf of God's will. His aggression was never the result of His defending Himself.

A meek person understands that the Lord is in charge and yields his or her will to the Lord. Humbleness, gentleness, and lack of aggression characterize meekness. The world we live in tends to look at a meek person as weak. The meek know that the Lord is their strength. Jesus says the meek will inherit the earth.

Point: Jesus promises that meek people will inherit the earth.

Prayer: God, teach me to trust You and react with godly gentleness the next time I am hurt by the words or actions of another.

Practice: Are you constantly defending or justifying yourself to your friends or boss? Today seek the Lord's strength and practice meekness.

Today's Reading:
Leviticus 23-25; John 1

February 16

Missing The Obvious!

By Scott Kalevik

John 1:10 *He was in the world, and though the world was made through him, the world did not recognize him.*

Our culture has declared that we have the right to decide what's right for ourselves. Truth is no longer true unless we decide it's true. As lords of our own moral universes, we are told we can pick and choose whatever we want as our truth. Such blatant idolatry has caused us to miss the obvious.

The Bible is crystal clear: God came to this world as the man Jesus; Jesus made this world; This world did not recognize Him. There's no doubt that Jesus claimed to be God: Mt 26:63 *But Jesus remained silent. The high priest said to him, "I charge you under oath by the living God: Tell us if you are the Christ, the Son of God." 64 "Yes, it is as you say," Jesus replied. "But I say to all of you: In the future you will see the Son of Man sitting at the right hand of the Mighty One and coming on the clouds of heaven."* Or Jn 8:58 *"I tell you the truth," Jesus answered, "before Abraham was born, I am!"* or Jn 17:24 *"Father, I want those you have given me to be with me where I am, and to see my glory, the glory you have given me because you loved me before the creation of the world.* Yet, very few people believe Him.

There's no doubt Jesus did miracles only God can do. He made the blind see, the dumb talk, the lame walk, the sick were healed, the dead were raised, demons cast out, the wind was stilled. Yet, very few believe.

How can the creature not recognize the Creator? The answer in one word: sin. Sin blinds us. Sin separates us from God and renders us unwilling to submit to obvious truth. Sin deceives us into believing that we can decide what's true for ourselves. Sin kills.

Don't miss the obvious. Jesus is God. He created the world. He loves you. Jn 1:12 *Yet to all who received him, to those who believed in his name, he gave the right to become children of God—*

Point: Sin keeps me from recognizing the obvious truth of Who Jesus is.

Prayer: Jesus, please break through the hardness of my heart so that I can recognize You.

Practice: Have you believed that you decide what's true? Look to Jesus for truth.

Today's Reading:
Leviticus 26-27; John 2-3

February 17

CARE FOR THE NEEDY

By Peggy Kalevik

Jeremiah 22:16 *He defended the cause of the poor and needy, and so all went well. Is that not what it means to know me?" declares the LORD.*

We see lots of charity organizations in our communities anymore. Churches and private entities serve the community by helping those who can't help themselves. Deuteronomy 15:11 says *"There will always be poor people in the land. Therefore I command you to be openhanded toward your brothers and toward the poor and needy in your land."* The Bible is clear that we need to help the poor and our country does a fairly good job, but there is room for improvement. We give food, clothing and even shelter; what we are slow to give is our time and our hearts. We can provide food and clothing but we don't have time to talk with them, to teach them. Fellowship is important.

You may know someone who thinks, "It's America and you can become anything you want to be if you work hard enough. If you don't make it it's because you didn't try hard enough; you were lazy, you weren't smart enough." In some cases that might be true, but sometimes it doesn't make any difference how hard you try, or how smart you are, you can't seem to get out of the hole. When you're living below the poverty line things done just happen for you no matter how hard you try. It seems as though some of us can't accept that sometimes people need help. Sometimes it takes a hand from above to help lift a brother or sister up. God uses the hands of those who have to help those who have not. After all He provided for those who have so that they are able to help.

In today's passage God is speaking of Josiah who defended the cause of the poor and needy (2 Kings 23:25). James 1:27 uses this same kind of analogy to describe a proper relationship with God. *"Religion that God our Father accepts as pure and faultless is this: to look after orphans and widows in their distress and to keep oneself from being polluted by the world."* (James 1:27)

Point: God desires and expects us to help the needy. He says that's what it means to know Him.

Prayer: Father, help us to know you better by reaching out a helping hand to those in need. Show us how you want us to serve your people.

Practice: Make an effort to reach out to the people in your Church body and community who need assistance.

Today's Reading:
Numbers 1-3; John 4

February 18

WILL YOU GIVE IT ALL UP?

By Peggy Kalevik

Matthew 10:37-39 *"Anyone who loves his father or mother more than me is not worthy of me; anyone who loves his son or daughter more than me is not worthy of me; 38 and anyone who does not take his cross and follow me is not worthy of me. 39 Whoever finds his life will lose it, and whoever loses his life form my sake will find it.*

In America we are all well aware of our rights, our freedoms; our right to be angry, happy, married, single, to have freedom of speech, protections under the law, to own a hand gun, to vote, and they go on and on. We think we should be able to do whatever we want, whenever we want. And we don't care or consider our neighbors, or Jesus. In today's political environment, we may loose some of these rights with the stroke of congress' pen. But Jesus presents us with a challenge. We must be willing to give up all these things if we are to follow him.

Do we honestly think about loving Jesus more than our mother, father and children? This is what He is asking of us. He is saying that we should love Him more than anything or anyone in our lives; and that we love Him supremely. He's not saying don't love your spouse and your children. He is not saying that you must die or that you must be a martyr for Him, although that's not out of the question and many have been martyred. This is not a call to gloom and doom, but a call to discipleship. He reflects on the cross and crucifixion, He's asking us to die to self, to let go of our own agenda and take up His. Dying to self can be a painful experience, however Jesus tells us that those who live (lose) their life for His sake will find it in the age to come and those who are living for themselves in this life will lose it in the life to come.

The question is are we willing to give up the "things", "the rights" and "the freedoms" in our lives that we hold dear if keeping them means we don't follow Christ.

Point: Live your life for the cause of Christ to the glory of God.
Prayer: Father please help me to die to self for Christ.and live
Practice: Today I will consider the needs of someone else

Today's Reading:
Numbers 4-5; John 5-6

49

February 19

WHAT DOES MATURITY IN CHRIST LOOK LIKE?
By Scott Kalevik

Romans 12:9-14 *Love must be sincere. Hate what is evil; cling to what is good. 10 Be devoted to one another in brotherly love. Honor one another above yourselves. 11 Never be lacking in zeal, but keep your spiritual fervor, serving the Lord. 12 Be joyful in hope, patient in affliction, faithful in prayer. 13 Share with God's people who are in need. Practice hospitality. 14 Bless those who persecute you; bless and do not curse.*

Are you mature in Christ? As you walk in the power of the Holy Spirit today, see how you measure up as we examine these verses:

1) Love must be sincere: no faking! Love others from the heart.
2) Hate what is evil: If God hates it, you should too.
3) Cling to what is good: Hold on to those things God loves!
4) Be devoted to one another in brotherly love: Are you?
5) Honor one another above yourselves: this really takes humility.
6) Never be lacking in zeal: are you excited about serving God?
7) Keep your spiritual fervor: Burn out be gone!
8) Serving the Lord: Are you serving Him today? How?
9) Be joyful in hope: Is your heart joyfully anticipating what God has promised?
10) Patient in affliction: Are you waiting where God has put you today?
11) Faithful in prayer: Have you prayed today? Do you pray regularly?
12) Share with God's people who are in need: What have you shared lately?
13) Practice hospitality: Who's come over for dinner lately?
14) Bless those who persecute you: Can you love those who hurt you?
15) Bless and do not curse: Stated twice so we can't misinterpret it.

The list goes on for five more verses. Paul ends his list in verse 21 by saying: Ro 12:21 *Do not be overcome by evil, but overcome evil with good.* None of us can muster up this kind of behavior on our own. Surrender to Christ and He will mold you into His image!

Point: The Bible describes maturity in Christ and it comes through surrender.
Prayer: God, please give me the desire and strength to mature in You.
Practice: Examine this list. What areas are your strengths? Where do you need to grow? Pick one area and pray about it. What needs to change?

Today's Reading:
Numbers 6-8; John 7

February 20

REFUSING TO DO WHAT WE KNOW IS RIGHT

By Peggy Kalevik

James 4:17 *Anyone, then, who knows the good he ought to do and doesn't do it, sins.*

Here James gives a warning to Jewish Christians who are arrogant enough to make plans without considering the will of the Lord. John gives a similar warning in John 9:41 *"If you were blind, you would not be guilty of sin; but now that you claim you can see, your guilt remains."* The people to whom James directs his comments would be covered by this verse from John. They are people who claim to know and have accepted Christ. Their attitudes and behaviors however, says that they are self-sufficient and confident in their own knowledge and strength.

Today's scripture is particularly penetrating in that it gets right to the hard of the matter. If we insist on doing what is wrong, when we are fully aware of what is right, we sin. Many people think what harm can one little white lie do? Maybe it will have no impact on the situation in which it was told. But God knows that we have told a little lie and it impacts our relationship with Him. He knows that you knowingly said what was not true and He is offended. If He is concerned about a little white lie, how much more is He concerned when we make our life plans without considering Him and His plan? Genesis 4:6 says: *"If you do what is right, will you not be accepted? But if you do not do what is right, sin is crouching at your door; it desires to have you, but you must master it."* We master sin by resisting temptations and doing what is right in all situations.

Point: Consider God's plan when making your plans.

Prayer: Father, help me to rely on You in every circumstance and always consider you in my life decisions.

Practice: Today I will consciously consider God in even the most insignificant decisions I make.

Today's Reading:
Numbers 9-10; John 8-9

February 21

A Position of Power and Influence
By Peggy Kalevik

Colossians 3:23 *Whatever you do, work at it with all your heart, as working for the Lord, not for men,*

Looking for the perfect career: a position of power and influence; or of menial task and trivial non-sense? The answer may not matter; it may be all about how you represent God in the place He plants you. Have you considered the career that God has designed especially for you? God has created all of us for a purpose, maybe it's not a career filled with glamour or a six figure income, but it's where He wants you.

Today's scripture comes from Paul's rules for the servant as he serves his master. As we are servants of Christ it is a fitting way to start the search for that great career. Where can we fulfill our need for employment that meets our financial goals and serves God's purpose? Martin Luther King once said, "If you take a job as a garbage collector, be the best garbage collector you can be." Paul wants the servant to see his work as a service rendered to God, not to man. So if you find yourself working in a menial position you can feel great joy at doing the job in a way that glorifies God. While we may not know where and what specific job or career God intends for us today, it might be that we can pursue any career as long as we are representing Him well, reflecting His love, and being obedient before the world. Who knows what powerful influence we can have in a world that seems to have forgotten honest, truth, love and integrity? If we can perform the tasks of our employment and exhibit these traits, we can be great evangelist without speaking a word.

Point: No matter what your job or career; work at it as though you were reporting directly to God, because if you are a Christian you are reporting to Him. Keep that in mind when you're having a bad day at work.

Prayer: Lord, I am Your servant. I want to serve you with honor and dignity. Let me represent You well before my supervisor(s) and co-workers.

Practice: I will seek God first in all my career decisions and for guidance with my everyday work habits.

Today's Reading:
Numbers 11-13; John 10

February 22

Will a Man Steal from God?

By Peggy Kalevik

Malachi 3:8 *Will a man rob God? Yet you rob me. But you ask, 'How do we rob you?' "In tithes and offerings.*

Stealing means to take unlawfully or furtively (to take or get something secretly). Is that what we do when we don't tithe? Malachi asks the question, will a man rob God? If not paying our tithe means we are stealing from God, the answer is yes. Many of us do not pay our tithe for one reason or another.

When Malachi made these statements in today's reading, failure to bring in your tithe was considered robbery. It was considered stealing to keep what belonged to someone else, in this case God. Today as we live our day to day lives we don't worry about being called a theft or robber if we don't give our tithe; no one says a word, but God knows. Verse 9 says that *"the entire nation is under a curse because you rob me."* We rob God of more than money we rob Him of our time and talent.

2 Corinthian ask New Testament Christians to excel in the grace of giving (8:7), as we remember that Jesus made Himself nothing to save us from our sin. We should give with gratitude and joy, because we understand what Jesus has done for us. The scripture goes on to say *"I am not commanding you, but I want to test the sincerity of your love by comparing it with the earnestness of others.* And in chapter 9 Paul goes on to tell us that *"the Lord loves a cheerful giver,"* and if we give generously, grace will abound for us and we will have all that we need.

Point: Make up your mind to give generously, whether financially, with your talents, or time and God will be blessed, so will you!

Prayer: O Lord, as I bring in my tithe I will praise Your name and glorify You with thanksgiving for the many blessings You have given me. I am blessed to be able to give back to You.

Practice: If you have not given a tithe to God, I challenge you to read Malachi 3 and any related scriptures and act accordingly.

Today's Reading:
Numbers 14-15; John 11-12

February 23

ASLEEP ON DUTY
By Mike Scheimann

Luke 12:40 *You also must be ready , because the Son of Man will come at an hour when you do not expect Him.*

There is a popular song by the Christian group Casting Crowns, that speaks about how the world, especially Israel, was sleeping the night that Jesus came to earth the first time. The song then asks will it be the same way when He comes the second time? Especially in America? The difference will be that this time when Jesus comes, it will not be as a little baby to save the world; it will be as a King coming to pass judgement and deliver justice to the world. Scripture tells us that no one will know the hour or the day that He is coming back, so we had better be prepared at all times. Many of you were in the military and know what it is like to pull a guard duty shift over night. You also were made well aware of what would happen should an officer or NCO come by and find you asleep on duty. It is a reality that the consequences for being asleep on duty when Jesus returns will be much harsher and will last for all eternity.

Point: When we are not actively serving God, obeying His commands and trying to grow in our relationship with Him, we are "asleep on duty". God has given you a gift, and or has called you to serve in a particular ministry.

Prayer: Dear Jesus, our King and our Lord. We eagerly await the day that we will be reunited with you in heaven for all eternity. Help us to stay awake spiritually and to actively seek to serve you and minister in whatever way you have called us, while we are still on this earth.

Practice: How is your walk with Christ? Are you ready to stand confidently before Him at the throne, should He return right now? Are you actively serving Him and doing what He has called you to do?

Today's Reading:
Numbers 16-18; John 13

February 24

The Extent of Our Faith
By Peggy Kalevik

James 1:6 *But when he asks, he must believe and not doubt, because he who doubts is like a wave of the sea, blown and tossed by the wind.*

To doubt, to feel unconvinced or uncertain about something, or think that something is unlikely. Is that how we demonstrate the extent of our faith? Do we face a circumstance wandering if, or worst, doubting that God will move on our behalf? James says that if our faith is in that condition we *"should not think he (we) will receive anything from the Lord"*.

There are times when our faith will waver, doubts will creep into our mind, but that should be fleeting and over turned in favor of trust and hope in the Lord. If we spend too much time wavering we loose our confidence in the Lord. God is not so much interested in the circumstance in which we find ourselves as He is in how we respond to the situation. He measures the extent of our faith by our level of sincerity, and purity of heart. Do we come to Him in prayer confident of His power to do what is best for us, and free of any un-confessed sin? Or do we enter into prayer before the Lord, thinking I'll never get through this, God will not help me. And sometimes knowing that we have un-confessed sin in our lives. We must come to Him with confidence knowing that He has the power to do all things. In Matthew 21:21 Jesus says, *"I tell you the truth, if you have faith and do not doubt, not only can you do what was done to the fig tree, but also you can say to this mountain, 'Go, throw yourself into the sea,' and it will be done..."*

Imagine the sea raging, and tossing itself back and forth, is that how we characterize our faith? If so, God is not pleased. We need to focus our faith on the power, and person of Jesus.

Point: In all things trust and do not doubt, there is nothing too hard for God.
Prayer: Father, let me remember the trails you have already brought me through and increase my faith.
Practice: Today I will trust and not doubt.

Today's Reading:
Numbers 19-20; John 14-15

February 25

THE WONDERS OF FORGIVENESS!
By Scott Kalevik

1 Samuel 12:20 *"Do not be afraid," Samuel replied. "You have done all this evil; yet do not turn away from the LORD, but serve the LORD with all your heart.*

Israel had really blown it. They wanted to have a king like the rest of the nations. In essence they had rejected God to His face. They willfully traded divine leadership for human. Saul was installed as king. They had sinned against God. Finally willing to admit their sin, they asked Samuel, their spiritual leader, to pray for them. 1Sa 12:19 The people all said to Samuel, *"Pray to the LORD your God for your servants so that we will not die, for we have added to all our other sins the evil of asking for a king."*

Samuel's response to their request is a snapshot into the loving character of God. Samuel encourages them not to turn away from the Lord. He tells them to serve the Lord with their whole heart.

Does that make sense to you? Remember when Adam and Eve sinned? They deliberately hid themselves from God. Why? They were ashamed to face Him knowing that they had gone against His word. Sin separates us from God

But Samuel tells the people of Israel specifically, DO NOT TURN AWAY FROM THE LORD. You've messed up. You've done evil. But don't turn away. Serve the Lord with all of your heart.

So if you're feeling like God can't forgive you today, remember that His instruction to you is: don't turn away; serve the Lord with all of your heart! But before we think that God doesn't mind our sinful behavior and complacency seeps into our actions, we should remember how this section ends: 1Sa 12:24 *But be sure to fear the LORD and serve him faithfully with all your heart; consider what great things he has done for you. 25 Yet if you persist in doing evil, both you and your king will be swept away."*

Point: God is quick to forgive the sinner who repents.
Prayer: Lord, thank You for forgiving me. Help me serve You wholeheartedly.
Practice: No slinking back because of sin! Confess, repent, and serve Him today!

Today's Reading:
Numbers 21-23; John 16

February 26

Facing Consequences
By Peggy Kalevik

Genesis 42:22 Reuben replied, "Didn't I tell you not to sin against the boy? But you wouldn't listen! Now we must give an accounting for his blood."

In the world of Christian writers a lot of time has been given to the subjects of forgiveness and unforgiveness. They are topics of importance in our walk with Christ. Christ shed His blood that we might be forgiven of all our sin and inherit eternal life. It is a debt we can never repay. However sometimes we have great difficulty forgiving ourselves, especially when we commit a sin that has physical or tangible consequences? The Bible (Rom 3:23) says all have sinned and fall short. Everyone has told at least one lie; most have exceeded the speed limit; and a few have taken something from work that they shouldn't have.

In Genesis 42, Joseph has already forgiven his brothers, but he wanted to point up to them the wrong they had done. Accountability is crucial in our walk with Christ. The young men start to feel the pinch of guilt even though they have no idea the man they are talking to is the brother that they betrayed so long ago. Reuben voices the important **Point:** "now we must give an account for his blood." We must give an account for our actions. Sometimes it is hard to forgive yourself for an unimportant little white lie, much less a failure that results in a terrible consequence. Regardless of the consequences we must face for our actions, if we confess our sins, he is faithful and just and will forgive us our sins and purify us from all unrighteousness (1 John 1:9). So no matter how awful the act, if you confessed and repented (turned away), God has forgiven you. All you need to do is endure the consequence and forgive yourself.

Point: No sin is so great that God will not forgive you, if you come to him. And if you feel you can't forgive yourself, it means you don't believe that God has or can forgive you.

Prayer: Father, Create in me a pure heart, O God, and renew a steadfast spirit within me. Restore to me the joy of your salvation and grant me a willing spirit, to sustain me. (Psalm 51:10-13)

Practice: I challenge you to find biblical support for refusing to forgive yourself. Self-condemnation does not make us pleasing to God, He is not impressed.

Today's Reading:
Numbers 24-25; John 17-18

February 27

Violating The Conscience!

By Scott Kalevik

Acts 24:16 So I strive always to keep my conscience clear before God and man.

Have you ever thought about the value of physical pain? Most of us try to avoid pain at every turn. Still, pain serves a vital function. If it weren't for pain, how would you know you hit your thumb with the hammer? If it weren't for pain, how would you know you were burning your hand on the oven rack? Pain alerts us to physical injury and calls us to take immediate action.

Just as physical pain alerts us to physical injury, so the conscience alerts us when we do damage to our souls by sinning against God. When we rebel against the commands of God, our conscience sounds the alarm. We feel guilty. We feel shame. We know we need forgiveness. God uses the conscience to bring us to repentance.

It's possible, however, to stop the conscience from doing its job. How? Repetitive, unrepentant sin will eventually short-circuit the conscience. It's called searing the conscience. A seared conscience can commit atrocities against God and humanity without alerting the person to the fact that they are condemning their soul.

Think of it this way. Piercing your ears hurts. But with the repetition of putting your earrings through the hole, the pain subsides. Soon skin covers the wounded area. Eventually, it doesn't hurt at all.

Violating the conscience works the same way. Telling that first lie produces an alarm of self-destruction from the conscience. But the 2nd lie is easier to tell. The third lie rolls off the tongue. Soon the lies are told without any response from the conscience. The seared conscience leads to spiritual death.

Is your conscience seared? Can you sin against God without any reaction from your conscience? Confess your sin to God. Ask God for forgiveness and ask Him to make your conscience sensitive again. Godliness with a clear conscience is a joyful life!

Point: The conscience alerts us when we damage our souls.

Prayer: Lord, please give me a sensitive conscience and help me not violate it.

Practice: Am I violating my conscience? What action is needed?

Today's Reading:
Numbers 26-28; John 19

February 28

Our Daily Bread
By Peggy Kalevik

Matthew 6:31 *So do not worry, saying, 'What shall we eat?'*
or 'What shall we drink?' or 'What shall we wear?'

From the earliest days of American society, men have been head of the household. He is the bread winner; he brings home the bacon. That's what my generation was taught. What about all the American families that don't have a man to bring home the bacon. Who provides for them?

When I was a child my mother (a single mom) always told us there was no need to worry, God is still on the throne as though it was the answer for everything. She never worried about having food in our home; we didn't always have lunch money when we went to school, so some days we were hungry until we got home. But God provided for us, as mother knew he would, she had no doubts, seeking Him continually in prayer. On occasion we would laugh at her because we thought she was talking to herself, it turns out she was talking to God.

In Matthew 6 God is asking us not to worry about anything. He wants us to understand that he has already given us much more important things: life and body. These are more important than food and clothing. He is not saying that we don't need to do anything to provide for ourselves. Even the birds go out of the nest to find food, but God has provided the food for them to retrieve. He is saying worry may most likely shorten the life you're trying to prolong and that these matters are ultimately in His hands. He provides even for those things in His creation that have no way of being productive, such as the lilies and flowers of the field. So, how much more will He care for us.

Point: God will take care of you, He will provide for all your needs, and He knows the difference between your needs and your wants.

Prayer: God help me to know the difference between my needs and wants. Give me the wisdom to ask you to supply my every need.

Practice: Today is a good day to stop running after an abundance of things that I don't need and find a way to live that helps someone in need.

Today's Reading:
Numbers 29-30; John 20-21

March 1

A Marathon, Not A Sprint!

By Scott Kalevik

Hebrews 12:1 *Therefore, since we are surrounded by such a great cloud of witnesses, let us throw off everything that hinders and the sin that so easily entangles, and let us run with perseverance the race marked out for us.*

Sprinters and marathon runners train differently. Sprinters measure success in hundredths of seconds. Marathoners measure success in hours and minutes. Sprinters never slow down to eat or drink during the race. Marathoners absolutely must refuel their bodies. If they don't, they risk total collapse.

The Christian life is a marathon, not a sprint. We're told to persevere and run the race marked out for us. It's a race that will take you the rest of your earthly life to finish. Running your spiritual marathon wisely is a must!

No marathoner in his right mind would try to run the race with a forty pound ball strapped to his ankle. Yet how many of us try to run with Christ while dragging extra things with us? What hinders you? TV? Entertainment? Lifestyle? Sports? Financial gain? Food? Relationships? Anything in our lives that is more important than our walk with Christ will hinder us. We must seek the Lord's strength to keep Him as our main priority in life. Our passage today tells us to *'throw off everything that hinders.'*

We're called to abandon the sin that entangles us. You can't expect to run the spiritual race while toting your sins with you. If sin is keeping you from running your race well, confess it and ask God for strength, then turn away from it.

Any marathon runner can tell you about the wall. When your legs, ankles, knees and muscles scream to stop, you know you've hit the wall. Successful marathon runners persevere and run through that wall of pain. The only way we can persevere as Christians is through the day by day discipline of walking in the Spirit. Without abiding in His strength, we'll never finish.

One last thing: Successful marathon runners rest. They let their bodies recover. Take some time today to rest in the Lord.

Point: We must deliberately remove what hinders and walk in the power of the Spirit to finish our spiritual marathon well.

Prayer: Lord, I want to unload those things in my life that hinder.

Practice: What do you do that works against your walk with Christ? How can you nullify those behaviors so that Christ is your main priority?

Today's Reading:
Numbers 31-33; Acts 1

March 2

Fear of the Lord

By Peggy Kalevik

Proverbs 1:7 *the fear of the LORD is the beginning of knowledge, but fools despise wisdom and discipline.*

We come in reverent fear of the Lord, bowing in awe of His greatness, power and mercy. We come not in paralyzing dread of our Father. We know that He loves us, but we also know that we must submit to His will. These are characteristics of a true believer, a true worshiper, and they are expressions of knowledge.

How often we have read the words *"The fear of the LORD is the beginning of wisdom."* Yet, most of us think of it as dreadful fear, that we should be afraid of our Lord in the same way we would be afraid of being killed by a terrorist. That is not what the Bible is trying to convey. We should have reverent fear of our Lord, which is a feeling of profound respect and/or awe. God does not want us to come to him trembling in fear, but in humble, grateful submission; knowing that He loves and cares for us, that He always wants the best for us.

On the other hand, there are those who have no knowledge and make no effort to attain wisdom. They are prideful and careless in their speech; they are immoral and refuse to be corrected, they despise God's wisdom and discipline. The Bible calls these people "fools". These people see wisdom as worthless.

We have a choice, we can choose to be filled with the knowledge of our creator; or we can refuse His knowledge and correction.

Point: Come to the Father in humility, reverence and awe. Blessed is the man whom God corrects.

Prayer: Father, give me a heart that is humble before you, let me bow in reverence before you, and receive Your knowledge and wisdom.

Practice: In your quiet time with God ask Him to show you where you have not relinquished your will to His.

Today's Reading:
Numbers 34-35; Acts 2-3

March 3

WISDOM: LISTEN AND LEARN!
By Scott Kalevik

Proverbs 10:8 *The wise in heart accept commands, but a chattering fool comes to ruin.*

The book of Proverbs is a treasure chest of wisdom. It's a collection of sayings written by King Solomon, the wisest man on earth. There are 31 chapters to the book of Proverbs. It's a great exercise to read one chapter per day. Like taking your 'wisdom' pill along with your vitamins.

Today's verse explains one characteristic of wisdom. Wise people accept commands. Wise people are willing to learn and change. There's a certain humility that goes with being taught. If you think you know everything already, you're unlikely to accept instruction from another. It's even more unlikely that you'll accept commands.

Mom used to point out that I had two ears and one mouth. She encouraged me to live proportionately by listening twice as much as I spoke. That's wisdom. Listening and learning can't happen if we don't stay quiet long enough to hear.

By contrast, a foolish person just keeps chattering away when instruction comes. The fool gives no credence to new knowledge because he's blabbing away. The fool is unteachable because he's self-absorbed. The proverb teaches us that chattering fools come to ruin. If we're unwilling to learn and adapt, we can never grow.

God has issued commands. If we're wise, we will accept His instruction from the heart and steer our lives to live by His word. If we're fools, we'll chatter on. Are you wise or foolish?

Point: The wise listen, learn and obey sound instruction. Fools don't pay attention.

Prayer: Lord, I want to accept your commands from my heart. Help me not act foolishly by ignoring your instruction.

Practice: Are you teachable? Or, are you so convinced of your superior position that you chatter on like a fool?

Today's Reading:
Numbers 36-Dt 2; Acts 4

March 4

FAITH THAT RESTS ON GOD'S POWER

By Peggy Kalevik

1 Corinthians 2:4-5 *My message and my preaching were not with wise and persuasive words, but with a demonstration of the Spirit's power, so that your faith might not rest on men's wisdom, but on God's power.*

The believers in the church at Corinth were impressed with the teachers of their day. Many had come to faith through the ministry of Peter, Paul and Apollos. They were new in the faith and had the tendency to rely too heavily on those who had taught them. It is a malady that we still see in the church today. Paul wanted to stem this trend by teaching the believers the true foundation of their faith. Healthy spiritual growth, faith should be rooted in Christ. They should not strive to rely on their teacher but to become mature spiritual peers to them.

The key to this issue that Paul addresses is that those being taught were looking at the messengers, and not the power of the message. The people were focusing on the speech and the person who gave it; their style and ability to present; and yes their brand of wisdom. Paul came without eloquence of speech, but with the power of the message as given by God. He wanted them to see that salvation does not come from being persuaded by human style, ability, or wisdom, but the simple message and the power of God.

Remember these things that Paul tried to teach the Corinthians: The power of God, 1 Corinthians 2:5; God's power to resurrect, 6:14; The power to reign, 15:24; The power to reveal, 2 Corinthians 4:7; and the power to restore, 2 Corinthians 12:9.

Point: Our faith rest on the power and wisdom of God, not on man's wisdom.
Prayer: Father I will approach Your altar with confidence in Your power and wisdom, giving thanks for the salvation You have given me.
Practice: Strive to understand and grow in what you believe, and not rely completely on those who are responsible to teach God's word.

Today's Reading:
Deuteronomy 3-4; Acts 5-6

March 5

PRACTICAL REALITY

By Peggy Kalevik

Ecclesiastes 7:25 *So I turned my mind to understand, to investigate and to search out wisdom and the scheme of things and to understand the stupidity of wickedness and the madness of folly.*

While we might all agree that the problem of evil is unsolvable or incapable of being explained or justified; there are realities of our modern world for which we can take responsibility. God did not intend that we would do all of the horrible things that are now happening in our world. God knew that we would be disobedient and participate in immoral acts. But it was not His intent: the killing of the innocent; human bombs; children starving to death in nations of plenty and in nations of poverty. We brought these things into God's creation, we are responsible.

Solomon, after much searching and investigation came to the conclusion that *"God made mankind upright, but men have gone in search of many schemes"* (7:29). He was resigned to believe that we cannot blame God for this; the fault lies in our misuse of the freedom God gave us. In today's scripture we see that Solomon resolves to investigate and study the stupidity of wickedness and the madness of folly. He discovers that a wise man is rare and even rarer, a wise woman.

Solomon's findings are based for the most part on his experience with his one thousand wives and concubines. How unfortunate, if only the wisest man who ever lived could have found "one" good/wise woman, maybe there would not have been the other 999. And it seems that Solomon's search for a good woman turned out to be more than just folly, it was also disobedience to God. Solomon like the rest of us got into this place of disobedience through misuse of the freedom to choose that God gave him. The practical reality is that Solomon made bad choices. Have you made a few bad decisions?

Point: The foolishness of God is wiser than man's wisdom, and the weakness of God is stronger than man's strength.

Prayer: God fill me with the knowledge of Your will through all spiritual wisdom and understanding, that I may live a life worthy of You and may please You in every way.

Practice: Be obedient to the will and word of God, and trust His wisdom to have a life filled with blessing and be a blessing to others.

Today's Reading:
Deuteronomy 5-7; Acts 7

March 6

COPING MECHANISMS THAT MAKE A DIFFERENCE!
By Scott Kalevik

2 Timothy 2:8-10 *Remember Jesus Christ, raised from the dead, descended from David. This is my gospel, 9 for which I am suffering even to the point of being chained like a criminal. But God's word is not chained. 10 Therefore I endure everything for the sake of the elect, that they too may obtain the salvation that is in Christ Jesus, with eternal glory.*

My guess is that you've had a bad day in the past. Maybe you're having one today. The apostle Paul served Christ faithfully, yet he spent many years of his ministry in jail! He was beaten several times. He had to run for his life on more than one occasion. He tells Timothy and he tells us how to get through anything.

First, Paul instructs us to remember Jesus Christ. What do you focus on when you're in trouble? Most of us can't stop thinking about our circumstances. But Paul teaches us that we should focus on the fact that Jesus Christ is alive!

If Jesus is alive, we have an advocate with the Father. If Jesus is alive, He will hear us when we pray. If Jesus is alive, we are able to lay whatever is troubling us at the feet of the One who loves us. He will work everything out according to His purpose. We can rest in Him. God is right next to you in your trouble.

Secondly, we cope best if we're suffering for the right reasons. Paul is suffering for the gospel. If you and I find ourselves suffering because we've sinned, there will be no peace without repentance.

Thirdly, we cope by focusing on the big picture of God's purpose. Paul, even in his suffering, remembers that God's word is not changed. God is still accomplishing His purpose even though Paul's life isn't exactly how he'd like it to be. Can you see God's big picture in your circumstance?

Fourthly, we cope by focusing on others. Paul can endure everything for the sake of the elect. Thinking about, caring for, and praying for the needs of others in the midst of our trouble are extremely effective ways of coping.

God never said life would be easy. But He gave us tremendous tools to endure anything that comes. You can cope with anything!

Point: Coping is accomplished by focusing on specific truths!
Prayer: Lord, help me learn to endure everything by following your direction.
Practice: When hard times come, deliberately focus your heart on the above.

Today's Reading:
Deuteronomy 8-9; Acts 8-9

March 7

What's Your Choice?

By Scott Kalevik

Proverbs 16:16 *How much better to get wisdom than gold,*
to choose understanding rather than silver!

We all have our priorities. What's the most important thing in the world to you? For many in our culture, making money is the immediate answer to that question. Even for some Christians, making money is supreme. Some have one, two or even three jobs, and, consequently, don't have time to study scripture, pray or attend church. Income has become the number one priority.

Don't get me wrong, it's important for us to pay our bills and live responsibly within our means. We need to work. In fact, it's a blessing from God to be able to work. But we as followers of Jesus Christ are called to evaluate our priorities in light of what God teaches us in His word. Proverbs tells us that acquiring wisdom is to be preferred over acquiring gold. In case we didn't get it, the writer goes on to teach us that we should choose understanding over silver!

What? Wisdom should take a higher priority in our lives than money? Understanding is more valuable than silver? Yep! God's instruction to you and I is to seek wisdom and understanding as a higher priority in our lives than making money.

How do we change our priorities? First, we look at how we spend our time. Do you have a time set each day when you study the scripture and pray? If your answer is that you pray at stoplights, you need to reevaluate your priorities. This is a crucial step in your spiritual growth. It is one of the most important steps to gaining wisdom and understanding from God.

Second, do you really need to earn more? Perhaps you need to spend less. God has promised to supply all of our needs. Do we really need big screen televisions, cable, bigger houses and more shoes? So, what's your choice? Wisdom or gold? Silver or understanding? Set your priorities to reflect God's priorities and watch Him bless your life!

Point: God knows that wisdom and understanding are worth more than money.

Prayer: Lord, help me examine my life and set my priorities to reflect my love for You. Forgive me for placing income ahead of You.

Practice: If you haven't already, start a daily quiet time with God. Examine your finances in terms of needs and wants. Can you make changes that will lighten your financial load?

Today's Reading:
Deuteronomy 10-12; Acts 10

March 8

The Cure For H.H.S.!

By Scott Kalevik

Proverbs 3:7 *Do not be wise in your own eyes; fear the LORD and shun evil.*

Has anyone ever told you that you tend to be stubborn and have a hard head? If so, did you agree or argue? If you argued, I'm afraid you proved that you have H.H.S. or, Hard Head Syndrome.

People with H.H.S. are usually easy to spot. When the doctor tells them to take their medicine, they refuse and say that doctors don't know what they're talking about. When the boss says she wants things done in a certain way, the person with H.H.S. will disobey the instructions knowing their way is best. One suffering from H.H.S. usually chooses to stay in bed on Sunday rather than go to church because they believe that attending "Bedside Baptist" with Pastor Sheets is just as pleasing to God as the corporate worship at their Church.

The writer of Proverbs gives us three steps to freedom from H.H.S. First, do not be wise in your own eyes. In other words, consciously adjust your opinion of yourself. Most of us simply don't have the strength to accomplish this in ourselves. God is extremely good at using the painful circumstances in our lives help us understand that we are limited creatures made of dust. If you want to be cured from H.H.S., you must humble yourself before God and acknowledge that He knows more than you.

Second, fear the Lord. Be afraid of God! Perhaps you're thinking that God is your loving Father and that you don't have to fear Him. While it's true that He loves you and cares for you, it's also true that we can't even conceive of the power and might and strength possessed by God. He created all that is. We should always approach Him in reverent fear. He may be a gracious King, but He's still King! We're the clay. He's the Potter. Obey.

The third step in overcoming H.H.S. is to shun evil. Many of us flirt with evil. God asks us to turn away from it and refuse to entertain it. Shun means to disdain. Do you hate evil? H.H.S. leads to foolishness and destruction.

Point: We must be cured from H.H.S. to follow God wisely.

Prayer: Please adjust my opinion of myself to match with Your opinion of me, O God. Give me the wisdom to fear you and to turn away from evil.

Practice: What areas of life are you trying to control yourself? Will you submit them to the Lord?

Today's Reading:
Deuteronomy 13-14; Acts 11-12

March 9

BE SURE YOUR SIN WILL FIND YOU OUT
By Peggy Kalevik

Psalm 38:4-5 *My guilt has overwhelmed me like a burden too heavy to bear. My wounds fester and are loathsome because of my sinful folly. My wounds fester and are loathsome because of my sinful folly.*

In Numbers chapter 32 the Reubenites and Gadites come to Moses and ask permission to make their home on the east side of the Jordan. They would not take any of their inheritance on the west side of the Jordan. However, they agreed to go across to help their brothers acquire the land that God had promised. Moses grants their request, but he admonishes them to help their brothers fight for their inheritance in the Promised Land; he warned them: *"if you fail to do this, you will be sinning against the LORD; and you may be sure that your sin will find you out".* (Num 32:23) Number 32:22-23 serves as a declaration of the agreement the men of Gad and Reuben made in the presence of God, Moses and the other Tribes. They are bound to keep it, or they will have sinned against God.

If these Israelites do not keep their word they will be consciously committing a sin, or being foolish. When one is guilty of knowingly committing sin, being foolish, it can cause mental, emotional and spiritual upheaval and unrest, sometimes physical pain. In this Psalm we see David experiencing just such anguish. He has committed some offense against God and now he suffers the consequences. David of all people knew that he would experience the wrath of God for his offense, yet he somehow has done something he knew he should not. We all need to remember, we have no secrets from God. After much lamenting, David ends the Psalm with *"do not forsake me"*, *"come quick to help me"*.

If our conscious is doing its job this is what happens to us when we act foolishly and yield to temptation or willfully commit sin. Moses was so right; *"your sin will find you out"*. When I was growing up the old people were fond of saying, "a hard head makes for a soft behind". I don't think that needs an explanation.

Point: If we conceal our sins we continue to be foolish; wisdom confesses and renounces sin and finds mercy.

Prayer: May I be so busy praising You Lord that I won't have time to contemplate folly.

Practice: Always think well of God, He is the best good; understand that sin is evil: resist the devil and he will flee from you. (James 4:7)

Today's Reading:
Deuteronomy 15-17; Acts 13

March 10

God's Way To True Riches!
By Scott Kalevik

Proverbs 22:4 *Humility and the fear of the LORD bring wealth and honor and life.*

Our culture tells us that the way to be rich is to climb the ladder. Even if you have to step on a few people on the way up, you can be rich and have a great life if you get ahead of all your competition by using all of your abilities to win.

Scripture says something completely different. Humility and fear are the characteristics described as bringing wealth and honor and life.

What's humility? Humility is the opposite of pride. It's the knowledge that our worth and our abilities are rooted in what God has given us. Humility is NOT believing that we are worthless and without any ability. Rather, humility recognizes that everything we have, and all that we are, have been given to us by God. Humility depends on God for everything. Why? Because humility recognizes the need for God's guidance, supply, strength and ability. Humility submits to God. Pride tries to control. God gives grace to the humble, but He opposes the proud (James 4:6).

What does 'fear of the Lord' mean? Fearing God is knowing at the core of our beings that He is all powerful and almighty and that we are not. Our fear of Him puts us on the road to obedience because we understand that God has all power, wisdom, strength and that His desire for us is the best. When we fear God we obey Him knowing that He is right!

Submit to God in humilty. Fear Him and obey. Depend upon God's power, wisdom and strength and not your own. That's God's way to the "good life."

Point: Humility and fearing God leads us to wealth, honor and life.

Prayer: God forgive me for seeking to get rich without seeking you. Today I acknowledge that You are the source of all of my blessings and all of my abilities. Please help me serve you in humility and the fear of the Lord.

Practice: Examine your attitudes about success. What do you find?

Today's Reading:
Deuteronomy 18-19; Acts 14-15

March 11

How Long Is Your Fuse?

By Scott Kalevik

Proverbs 12:16 *A fool shows his annoyance at once,*
but a prudent man overlooks an insult.

When I was a child I learned the phrase, "Sticks and stones may break my bones, but words will never hurt me." Unfortunately, growing older taught me that there is no truth to that saying. Verbal assaults can leave emotional wounds that don't heal easily.

Ever been called a derogatory name? Maybe the bully at school used you as his verbal punching bag. Perhaps your brother or sister insulted you just to get under your skin. Or, worse yet, were your parents verbally harsh with you when they disciplined you?

Most of us have experienced the sharp end of someone's tongue. Although we can't control what people say to us, we can control how we react. Proverbs teaches that a prudent man overlooks an insult. In other words, wisdom considers the source of the remark and walks by. No retaliation necessary.

Can you see yourself being insulted and letting it roll off of you like water off a duck's back? Easier said than done. But it's imperative to realize any insult that may attack you is rooted in the person doing the insulting, not in you. If you understand that 'hurt people hurt people', it will be easier to realize that the insult resides in the one hurling the remark. It only impacts you if you let it. A wise person overlooks an insult.

A wise person also lives in the humility of knowing that they belong to God and that God will defend His own. The greatest example of this is Jesus himself. As he hung on the cross, they hurled insults at him. He never condemned. In fact, he was dying on the cross to save the very ones that were insulting him.

On the other hand, a fool reacts to an insult immediately. Proverbs says he shows his annoyance at once. It's the pride of the fool that erupts in retribution when insulted. "When insulted, fight," is the motto of the fool. The fool has a short fuse that can be ignited with the smallest spark.

How long is your fuse? Are you wise or foolish when it comes to being insulted?

Today's Reading:
Deuteronomy 20-22; Acts 16

March 12

LEVEL WITH ME!

By Scott Kalevik

*Psalm 51:6 Surely you desire truth in the inner parts;
you teach me wisdom in the inmost place.*

A certain man was plagued by guilt because he had cheated on his taxes. Years were spent with sleepless nights and a guilty conscience. Finally, in desperation, the man wrote to the IRS. In his letter he confessed that he had cheated on his taxes. He then went on to enclose a check for $500.00 to the IRS. He concluded his letter with the following line: "If, after sending you this $500.00, I find that I still feel guilty and cannot sleep, I'll send you the rest of the money I owe you!" That is NOT the way to repent!

Psalm 51 records David's prayer after he committed adultery and murder. He confesses his sin to God. He begs God for mercy. And then he delivers one of the most profound truths in scripture. The Holy Spirit shows David that God wants truth in the inner parts.

So much of religion these days is about the show. Fancy churches with robed clergy litter the landscape. Do you think God cares about the size of your church building? Preachers may pray long emotion packed prayers. But their prayers may not matter to God at all if it's just for show. Choirs may sing great worship songs. But, again, their worship may not matter to God. You may look great on the outside when you go to church this Sunday, but are you clean on the inside?

God wants us to be pure from the inside out. His priority is not how we look but who we are. God desires truth in the inner parts. In other words, God wants us to be completely honest with Him about who we are and what we've done. He wants us to level with Him.

David confessed everything before God. God restored him. Yes, David still spent years suffering through the consequences of his sin. His family fell apart. He experienced heartache after heartache. But God forgave him and restored him and allowed him to continue as the King. Why? Because David gave God what He wanted: sincere complete truth from the heart.

If you allow yourself to be totally honest before God about who you are and what you've done, God will bring wisdom to your heart. He will teach you.

Today's Reading:
Deuteronomy 23-24; Acts 17-18

March 13

There Is No Condemnation In Christ!
By Scott Kalevik

Romans 8:1 *Therefore, there is now no condemnation for those who are in Christ Jesus,*

No condemnation! NO CONDEMNATION! Have you ever felt guilty or worthless or like a failure before God? The apostle Paul wrestled with his inabilities: Ro 7:21 *So I find this law at work: When I want to do good, evil is right there with me. 22 For in my inner being I delight in God's law; 23 but I see another law at work in the members of my body, waging war against the law of my mind and making me a prisoner of the law of sin at work within my members. 24 What a wretched man I am! Who will rescue me from this body of death?*

Right after declaring himself to be wretched and asking who will rescue him from this body of death, Paul declares that there is now no condemnation for those who are in Christ! Why? Because no matter how we may feel about ourselves and our failures, the truth is that Jesus' work of forgiveness on the cross eternally overcomes our inability!

But notice the qualifier. No condemnation is available to those who are IN CHRIST. Without the work and power of Christ, our sin will certainly condemn us. But if we are in Christ, His power will forgive our sins and bring us through the judgment of God clothed in His righteousness!

God has chosen to look at all who come to Jesus Christ through the lense of Calvary. He forgives the repentant sinner. He adopts the believer into His family. There is no condemnation for those who are in Christ Jesus! Will you take your comfort here?

Point: If you are in Christ, you will not be condemned.

Prayer: God, thank you for allowing me to live life knowing that despite my failures, You have saved me through faith!

Practice: Today, if I feel like I'm unable to meet God's standard, I will remind myself that God has rescued me from this body of death through Jesus and that because of Him, I will not be condemned.

Today's Reading:
Deuteronomy 25-27; Acts 19

March 14

Making Decisions!
By Scott Kalevik

Proverbs 12:15 *The way of a fool seems right to him, but a wise man listens to advice.*

What makes the wise person wise? What makes the fool foolish? One answer lies in the way they approach making decisions.

The fool does not seek counsel when making decisions. Why not? Who needs counsel when you already know you're right? The fool lets his own emotion dictate direction. The fool doesn't want to be confused with the facts. You can't tell the fool anything because his ears can't hear it. He's convinced that he is more than able to consider all aspects of any problem and make a great decision. This approach to life usually ends in disaster. As Proverbs 16:25 confirms: *There is a way that seems right to a man, but in the end it leads to death.* Or, again in Proverbs 26:12, *Do you see a man wise in his own eyes? There is more hope for a fool than for him.*

The root of the fool's problem is pride. It takes humility to accept advice. It takes humility to think that someone knows more about life than you do. Fools don't have that kind of humility: *The sluggard is wiser in his own eyes than seven men who answer discreetly* (Pr 26:16).

Wise people, on the other hand, seek out and listen to advice. Notice this passage does not say that a wise person does whatever someone else advises them to do. But a wise person does have a teachable attitude. A wise person listens. Listen to this: *Listen to advice and accept instruction, and in the end you will be wise* (Pr 19:20).

So, who do you listen to for advice? Scripture provides a wonderful ocean full of advice to listen to. Do you listen to the Holy Spirit as you pray? Do you have friends or family you seek out when making a big decision? Wisdom listens.

Point: Wise people seek advice and listen to it.
Prayer: Lord I want to be wise. Please help me listen to Your advice.
Practice: Next time you're making a big decision, ask another's opinion.

Today's Reading:
Deuteronomy 28-29; Acts 20-21

March 15

Why is Wisdom calling to us?

By Peggy Kalevik

Proverbs 1:20 *Wisdom calls aloud in the street, she raises her voice in the public squares;*

Proverbs teaches us the ways of God and shows us how to apply those ways to our daily lives. Solomon starts Proverbs by speaking about attaining wisdom and discipline. If we can't see the realities of everyday life, then we are probably not wise. A wise person sees life as it really is, they are not living in a fantasy. The decisions of a wise person are based on the reality of the situation, not on what they suppose, or would like things to be. The life path or direction of a person who possesses wisdom is prayerfully laid out with guidance from God. Proverbs also tells us the life consequences of the unwise. (Also Isaiah 5:21-25)

Proverbs 1:20 gives us a picture of a woman standing in the street calling out to the ignorant and the scornful to listen, for fear of the consequences of refusing to grasp wisdom. It is more than a call. It is an excited exhortation, an urgent plea. She is on a public street to make known to all, because wisdom is available to all. In verse 22, wisdom asks, how long will the simple, the mockers and the fools remain in their ways? If only they would respond to the rebuke of wisdom, she would make known to them her ways. But because they would not listen, she says: *"Then they will call to me but I will not answer; they will look for me but will not find me. Since they hated knowledge and did not choose to fear the LORD".* But for those who do listen and seek wisdom: *"...they will live in safety and be at ease, without fear of harm."* Wisdom is calling to us to save us from a life of frustration and destruction. Why seek wisdom? So that we can traverse life situations as they come to us, and interpret trails and circumstances from God's eternal perspective.

Point: If we ignore the call of wisdom life becomes difficult, unmanageable, and very, very dangerous.

Prayer: Father, give me a desire to seek your wisdom, let me not become wise in my own eyes.

Practice: Find counsel in God's word and be prayerful about every decision, wait on the Lord today.

Today's Reading:
Deuteronomy 30-32; Acts 22

March 16

THE HEARTBREAK OF FOOLISHNESS
By Peggy Kalevik

Proverbs 10:1 *A wise son brings joy to his father, but a foolish son grief to his mother.*

What a wonderful joy to have a child. In many instances husbands and wives have prayed for years to have that bundle of joy. Once the child is born the parents do everything in their power to help the child grow into a special person. They sacrifice and save, they attend every event the child has in school they make sure they are well provided for and nurtured. All in the hope of producing that great: doctor, teacher, lawyer; basketball or soccer player. Parents want to be proud of their children.

But what if the child doesn't turn out to be all that we want them to be? What if, in spite of all the preparation and nurturing, the child is not the brightest candle on the cake? Proverbs 17:25 says that a foolish sons brings grief to his father and bitterness to the one who bore him. Parents are grief stricken if their children grow up to be foolish. They will continue to love them anyway, but their heart will be heavy. They are terribly disappointed. The Bible describes a fool as one who has no knowledge and makes no effort to attain wisdom, they are prideful and careless in their speech; they are immoral and refuse to be corrected, they despise God's wisdom and discipline (Prov. 10:14, 21; 14:3; 15:5; 20:3; 24:7; 26:5; 27:22).

What can a parent do if the child grows into a foolish adult? The parents, particularly the father, should have disciplined the child. Proverbs 1:8 says the father should tell the child to: *"Listen, my son, to your father's instruction and do not forsake your mother's teaching."* And if the child heeds his father's instructions: the instructions and teaching will be a garland to grace his head and a chain to adorn his neck.

Point: He who loves his son is careful to discipline, to instruct, pray for and love him.

Prayer: Father, You know that love for my child is my motivator; I pray that You give me the strength to disciple and discipline this child that he/she will be strengthened in their faith and seek Your wisdom.

Practice: One of the greatest things we can do for our children is to learn how to say "no" when it's appropriate.

Today's Reading:
Deuteronomy 33-34; Acts 23-24

March 17

Do You See The Light?
By Scott Kalevik

Job 15:8 Do you listen in on God's council? Do you limit wisdom to yourself?

One dark and foggy night the ship's Captain was informed of a light shining on the distant horizon. Thinking another ship was on a collision course with his own, the Captain ordered a message flashed across the sea. "Turn to the South immediately!"

The reply came swiftly, "You turn to the South immediately." The Captain was outraged. He sent another message: "This is the Captain of a U.S. Battleship. Turn South immediately or be sunk."

The surprising reply was equally swift, "This is the Lighthouse. YOU turn to the South immediately or be sunk."

Sometimes we believe we understand what's true about a situation when in reality, we are mistaken. Knowing the TRUTH is absolutely imperative if we want to avoid crashing into the rocks. The question is: "How do we know the truth?"

God has provided truth for us in the person of Jesus Christ. He has provided truth for us in His revealed word, the Bible. We know the Truth when we live in relationship with Jesus Christ and obey His word. Like a lighthouse warning us of the rocks, the Lord will guide us away from those things that would shipwreck our lives.

The tragedy of it is that many of us choose to ignore God's light. We sail straight for the rocks all the while thinking that we are wise. We limit our truth to our own opinion. When disaster strikes and our life is sinking, we are quick to ask God why He let such a catastrophe happen to us. God puts His arms around us and lovingly asks us why we didn't follow Him. He's provided the light of His Son and His word. Will we rely on our own opinion, or will we follow the light of His truth?

Point: Our lives must be guided by God's truth.

Prayer: Lord, please divorce me from my opinion and help me live by your truth.

Practice: Do the decisions of your life today match up with God's truth?

Today's Reading:
Joshua 1-3; Acts 25

March 18

WANTING THE RIGHT THINGS!

By Scott Kalevik

2 Chronicles 1:12 *therefore wisdom and knowledge will be given you. And I will also give you wealth, riches and honor, such as no king who was before you ever had and none after you will have."*

If God told you He'd give you anything you desired, what would you ask for? Would you ask for money? Fame perhaps? Power? Health? Better relationships? Would you ask God to give you a spouse? Children? What would it be?

This very scenario played out in 2 Chronicles 1:7 That night God appeared to Solomon and said to him, *"Ask for whatever you want me to give you."* Solomon could have requested anything he wanted.

Solomon chose to answer with the following request: 2Ch 1:10 *Give me wisdom and knowledge, that I may lead this people, for who is able to govern this great people of yours?"*

Solomon asks God for wisdom and knowledge. He wants to do a good job of governing God's people. He wants to be able to discern right from wrong. His request is rooted in his desire to serve God well.

Imagine that! Solomon didn't ask God for material blessings. He simply asks for wisdom. It sounds to me like Solomon was already wise before he asked God for wisdom. I wonder who among us would have been able to give Solomon's answer.

Once Solomon told God his answer, God not only blessed him with discernment, but also gave him all the wealth and material blessings imaginable. Solomon wanted the right things and God responded by giving him everything.

This principle is echoed by Jesus in the New Testament: Mt 6:33 *But seek first his kingdom and his righteousness, and all these things will be given to you as well.*

So, what do you want out of life? Desire to please God. Desire to live by the wisdom of God. Everything else you need will be added.

Point: If we want what God wants, the storehouses of heaven will open as God meets our other needs.

Prayer: Lord, help me get out of my selfishness. Allow me to want your will.

Practice: Examine your praying. What are you telling God you want?

Today's Reading:
Joshua 4-5; Acts 26-27

77

March 19

CORRUPTING WISDOM
By Peggy Kalevik

Ecclesiastes 10:1 *as dead flies give perfume a bad smell,*
so a little folly outweighs wisdom and honor.

Sometimes the writings of Solomon may seem like the mindless scribbling of a mad man. You have to ponder them a while to understand where he's coming from. Solomon was constantly trying to understand the purpose of our existence. Why are we here? What is our purpose? In Chapter 9 Solomon is analyzing why we should strive to do the right thing, to be good, to be wise. I don't know that he found the answers he was looking for, but I know that the Bible says that there had never been anyone like him; nor would there ever be (1 Kings 3:12). He was a wise and discerning man. In chapter 9:13-18 Solomon tells of a poor man who saves the town in which he lives, when the town is threatened by a powerful King and his army. The man saves them with only his wisdom. However the people quickly forget what the man did for them and he is forgotten as well. The people were embarrassed to admit that they were saved by a 'nobody', so they simply forgot about the man and his good deed. Should the man have kept silent and not helped the town? Should we not do the right thing for fear that we won't be given credit or praise? No, God expects us to do the right thing even if we know before we act that no one will thank us for what we do. Solomon concluded that: Wisdom is better than weapons of war, but one sinner destroys much good.

This verse is a caution for us to not allow the wisdom that we do have to be corrupted by apparently insignificant, unwise behavior. The dead flies in a bottle of perfume will undoubtedly ruin the fragrance, the same as behavior unbecoming a wise man will ruin the impact of the things he does.

Point: Be aware that the occasional bad behavior or bad attitude can destroy the good that you strive to do.

Prayer: Father let my desire be to I live and serve to worship You, not the praise or approval of man.

Practice: If ever I feel myself enjoying the praise of man for what I do in God's service, I will repent.

Today's Reading:
Joshua 6-8; Acts 28

March 20

THE WISDOM OF LISTENING
By Peggy Kalevik

Acts 16:14 *One of those listening was a woman named Lydia, a dealer in purple cloth from the city of Thyatira, who was a worshiper of God. The Lord opened her heart to respond to Paul's message.*

There is great power in the ability to really listen. This business woman of ancient culture, who was a worshiper of God, sat down one day to listen to the speech of a missionary and her entire family was changed. If we take the time to really listen our lives will be changed as well.

How many of us can remember the topic of last weeks sermon or any of the scriptures referenced? Do you remember what you read from the Bible yesterday? God always speaks to us for our benefit, if we listen with our heart not just our ears, we can hear what He's trying to tell us and we will remember. This woman had every human reason not to listen or to hear. She is living in a culture where women are not highly valued. Carrying on a business in this kind of environment would be taxing enough, but then to listen to this new concept of God and invite these missionaries into her home, not an easy task. Yet she listened to God's word, received Him and shared what she knew about him with others.

This is a simple story about a woman who heard the voice of God calling to her. Do we hear God when He speaks to us, or do we get so caught up in our busy lives that we can't hear? In John 10:27 God says: *"My sheep listen to my voice; I know them, and they follow me."* Remember that those who won't listen cannot be taught, will not grow and as a result have no wisdom. If you want to have relationship with God, listening is essential. If you don't listen how will you hear his voice? Keep in mind that God will use whom ever He chooses to bring His message, don't be surprised if He uses someone you have trouble listening to, to bring His message to you. Sometimes, God likes to challenge us; He wants to see if you are listening and if you will recognize His voice.

Point: The Word of God has truth for you. Listen and you will receive.

Prayer: Father, from heaven may I hear Your voice, be guided, protected and gain wisdom.

Practice: Today make your prayer time a time to speak a little and listen a lot.

Today's Reading:
Joshua 9-10; Romans 1-2

March 21

ARE YOU BILINGUAL?
By Herb Hubbard

John 8:43-44 Why is my language not clear to you? Because you are unable to hear what I say. You belong to your father, the devil, and you want to carry out your father's desire. He was a murderer from the beginning, not holding to the truth, for there is no truth in him. When he lies, he speaks his native language, for he is a liar and the father of lies.

At Living Hope we have a unique opportunity to be exposed to two languages every Sunday. Our sister church Iglesia Esperanza Viviente speaks Spanish while we at Living Hope speak English. When I walk by the Spanish service I can often feel the presence of the Lord in their worship and yet I can't understand what is being said because it's in Spanish and I only know English. In our text today Jesus is talking to the Jews. He asks them *"Why is my language not clear to you?"* And then he answers his own question by telling them they can't hear what he says because they belong to their father the devil. Jesus goes on to tell them that the devil was a murderer from the beginning and when he lies he is speaking his native language. We by nature are born into sin and so our native language would be that of lies and deceit. I am not saying we lie all the time but I know I have bent the truth when it has served me to do so. Lying is one of those sins that I don't think we label as being really bad, but look what Jesus says of the devil, *"He was a murderer from the beginning not holding to the truth."* The devil used lies and deceit to trick Adam and Eve and so cause the downfall of mankind he was a murderer from the beginning with his native language.

Revelation warns us in Chapter 21:8 that liars will have their place in the fiery lake of burning sulfar. We need to honor God by speaking the language of truth.

Point: Jesus is the truth and his followers we must live and speak the truth all the time.

Prayer: Lord help me to be a true disciple and to know the truth so the truth can set me free from my native language of lies and deceit.

Practice: Always tell the truth even when it would benefit you to bend the truth just a little.

Today's Reading:
Joshua 11-13; Romans 3

March 22

POSITION AND POWER

By Peggy Kalevik

Ecclesiastes 4:13 *Better a poor but wise youth than an old but foolish king who no longer knows how to take warning.*

The power of listening is sometimes lost to us through our fears and insecurities. When we find ourselves becoming insecure about our ability to do the things at which we were once very capable, we become frustrated. We start to doubt the loyalty of those around us and we are unable to trust anyone. This is an issue that is particularly troubling in Kings, Presidents and any government officials.

In this section of Proverbs chapter 4, Solomon speaks about the frustration of politics. Here in verse 13 he talks about the value of wisdom and the ability to listen to the voice of reason or logic. It appears that the old King refuses to heed any advice or warning. In his quest to maintain his position, the King fights all opposition and ignores the warnings of his advisors. Thus he is overtaken by his successor. Solomon's point here is that advancement is also meaningless, because even though the King may have come to power through poverty or mediocrity, he too will one day lose his position to someone else. It is the natural order of things. Our fears of the inability to function as we once did do not give us license to put everyone else at risk or in danger. When we can no longer make good decisions or operate in a given position or role in life, we need to have the humility and wisdom to let go. While the young, poor but wise youth may have come to power through his many triumphs and has a great following, he too will succumb to the pressures and foibles of lost confidence, illness and or aging and have to let go of his position or role in life.

Point: The person who will not listen is un-teachable, cannot grow, and is without wisdom.

Prayer: Father let mine be a heart that listens to you. Teach me, O LORD, to hear Your voice and follow Your way; give me understanding, that I may obey Your will with all my heart.

Practice: Today you will have opportunity to speak with someone who is trying to tell you something, take the time and make the effort to really listen.

Today's Reading:
Joshua 14-15; Romans 4-5

March 23

WHERE DOES WISDOM START?
By Scott Kalevik

Proverbs 9:10 *The fear of the LORD is the beginning of wisdom, and knowledge of the Holy One is understanding.*

What a simple phrase: The fear of the Lord is the beginning of wisdom. Want to be wise? Fear the Lord. What does it mean to fear the Lord? According to the International Standard Bible Encyclopedia the fear of the Lord is the feeling of reverent regard for God, tempered with awe and fear of the punishment of disobedience.

Reverent regard for God means we approach God knowing that He's the boss. Most of us have experienced a job with a human boss. The boss may be our friend. The boss may be loving and nice. But even our human boss commands our respect.

God is better than any human boss. He really cares for us. He loves us. He wants to guide us and nurture us and develop us into the image of Christ. If we're willing to obey Him, He's willing to supply blessings in abundance. Just look at what God promises to those who fear Him:

Pr 10:27 *The fear of the LORD adds length to life, but the years of the wicked are cut short.*

Ps 128:1 *Blessed are all who fear the LORD, who walk in his ways.*

Ps 34:9 *Fear the LORD, you his saints, for those who fear him lack nothing.*

Ps 85:9 *Surely his salvation is near those who fear him, that his glory may dwell in our land*

Want to be wise? Want life? Want God's blessings? Want God's supply? Want God's salvation? Fear the Lord.

Point: Fearing the Lord is the first step to godly wisdom.

Prayer: Lord, I fear you. Help me live each moment knowing that You're eye sees all.

Practice: Do you fear the Lord? List five areas of your life (relationships, finances, walk with Christ, employment, etc) How do you fear Him in each area?

Today's Reading:
Joshua 16-18; Romans 6

March 24

The Prudent Man

By Peggy Kalevik

Proverbs 12:23 *a prudent man keeps his knowledge to himself, but the heart of fools blurts out folly.*

What is a prudent man? He is one who uses "good sense" when dealing with practical matters, he uses good judgment, considers the consequences and acts accordingly. The ancient Asian culture has a proverb which I think stresses the same meaning as our scripture for today. It is entitled "The Ancients were attuned to Heaven" and it states: Knowing the way is easy; refraining from speaking of it brings one in Accord with Heaven; to know and to speak brings one in accord with human kind.

Like the Asian proverb our scripture directs us to use discretion when speaking. If we speak too abruptly, or without understanding we may find that we are portraying a fool. People know and hear the difference between wisdom and foolishness. The prudent man "keeps" or conceals his knowledge; it doesn't mean that he never speaks, it means that he uses discretion. He knows that there is no need to run to display his wisdom. Sometimes it is better to be quiet. One of my favorite responses when people around me are talking about things that maybe they shouldn't is "some things are best left unsaid". Not that we don't all at some time say things we wish we hadn't. It's a human thing to do. Spiritual maturity and growth will help us with that.

Point: Remember that discretion can be the better part of valor. Think and pray before you speak.

Prayer: Father, teach me, and I will be quiet; show me where I have been wrong, that I may correct my behavior.

Practice: In your prayer time today ask yourself if you have spoken unwisely recently? Then pray for a heart of discernment.

Today's Reading:
Joshua 19-20; Romans 7-8

March 25

Anticipating The Rainy Day!
By Scott Kalevik

Proverbs 21:20 *In the house of the wise are stores of choice food and oil, but a foolish man devours all he has.*

When I was young I played Little League Football. I was a defensive tackle in charge of stopping the run. One time our opponents had hiked the ball and started an end run right at me when the referee blew his whistle. The ref called off sides and penalized them five yards. They lined up for the next play. Little did I know that the next play would stay with me the rest of my life.

They ran the exact same end run they had tried before. Their guard pulled out, blocked me, and their runner ran for a touchdown. I was run over by the play. We lost the game.

The reason that play has stuck with me for forty years is because I failed to anticipate. I remember walking home that night asking myself why in the world didn't I think far enough ahead to anticipate a play I could have easily known was coming my way.

Do you ever try to anticipate what might happen? Proverbs tells us that wise people have stores of choice food and oil. Why is that the case? One reason for their abundance may be their earning ability. But another is their ability to anticipate. Wise people look down the road and prepare for what may be coming. Even though the pantry is stocked full today, a wise person saves some food in anticipation of leaner times.

A fool, on the other hand, does not anticipate reversals. He devours all he has. A fool never anticipates the rainy day. He lives like there's no tomorrow. When tomorrow comes, the fool has nothing.

We live in a world that encourages us to spend every dime (or even MORE than every dime) we make. Credit is easy. We're told not to save but rather to buy. Our debt threatens to strangle us as we live pay check to pay check. One little bump in our financial road can easily lead to our ruin. Perhaps we should reevaluate our lives in terms of what's wise. The wise anticipate coming trouble. Save something today.

Today's Reading:
Joshua 21-23; Romans 9

March 26

REJECTION OF THE REVELATION OF GOD
By Peggy Kalevik

Romans 1:20 *For since the creation of the world God's invisible qualities—his eternal power and divine nature—have been clearly seen, being understood from what has been made, so that men are without excuse.*

This verse from Romans 1 relays the understanding and purpose of God's "natural revelation". Natural revelation provides clear testimony of the power and existence of our creator God. This revelation distinguishes itself from the special revelation of the Scriptures. It is constant testimony, but limited in that it reflects God in certain aspects: His eternal power and divine nature. We must go to the scripture to see and understand God's love for us. But this natural revelation is evident to all, so that we have no excuse.

Those who discount the natural revelation of God are simply looking for a reason not to believe. They see clearly as the scripture says but some how they choose not to accept what they see. This revelation is sufficient to make all of mankind responsible for their rebellion, although by itself, it is not enough to bring them to salvation. That is the purpose of the special revelation we receive through scripture. How wise are we that we refuse to see what is right before us each and every day? We continually prove that our worldly wisdom is not wisdom at all.

Point: Through our own wisdom we did not come to know God. We are saved by His grace.

Prayer: Lord, may I not be one who sets Your grace aside in favor of my own wisdom. Christ died for me; let me humble myself before You.

Practice: Examine the way you live your daily life, do you respect and accept, or reject the evidence of God in creation.

Today's Reading:
Joshua 24-Judges 1; Romans 10-11

March 27

RESISTING THE RIGHTEOUSNESS OF GOD
By Peggy Kalevik

Romans 1:18 *The wrath of God is being revealed from heaven against all the godlessness and wickedness of men who suppress the truth by their wickedness,*

Until we understand that we are in a "lost condition", we will not be concerned about being delivered from it. We will not make any effort to understand the salvation and grace that God offers. So, Paul lays out for us our lack of righteousness, that we may stop resisting the righteousness of God.

It is interesting that Paul explains the relationship of God's righteousness and God's wrath, both are revealed by God. Paul tells us that wrath belongs to the current era that it is being revealed as history unfolds. We may frown at the notion of wrath from God because we view wrath as being fueled by revenge, anger or temperament. However God's wrath is not like the anger or need for revenge that human kind has cultivated. God's wrath is righteous. It is concerned with the godlessness (lack of reverence: neglect and rebellion); and wickedness (injustice: as it relates to our treatment of others), of man. Men suppress the truth by their wickedness; that is when the truth of God is brought to mind by their conscience, they suppress it, and they deny it. If we consciously suppress it, it means we understand we have knowledge, we convict ourselves. This points us to the fact that we have no righteousness of our own. Then we must recognize our position and accept that we lack the righteousness that God requires.

Point: Our worldly wisdom can cost us our place with God in eternity if we are not careful. Stop resisting God's righteousness and embrace it.

Prayer: Father let mine be a heart that bows to your will for me, understanding that you require righteousness and accepting the grace that you offer.

Practice: When you bow in prayer today let go of all your worldly wisdom.

Today's Reading:
Judges 2-4;Romans 12

March 28

WHAT IS WORSHIP?
By Scott Kalevik

Psalm 96:9 *Worship the LORD in the splendor of his holiness; tremble before him, all the earth.*

While most of us understand that Christians worship God, how many of us can clearly define what worship means? What's the difference between Old Testament worship and New Testament worship? What's the difference between our private individual worship and the corporate worship of the church? What roles do posture and song and prayer and fasting, and service, and giving play in worship?

Clearly, there is no greater task in life than to become someone who worships God in a way that pleases Him. Believers will spend eternity worshipping the Lord.

So, let's start with a definition: *Worship is an ACTIVE response that declares God's worth* (Worship, Rediscovering The Missing Jewel by Allen & Borror, pg.16). To worship God is to celebrate God for who He is and what He does! Worship requires participation. We must actively respond to God if we are to worship Him. In other words, worship is not a spectator sport.

Think about Sunday morning with me. We meet together for what we call a "worship service". Based on our definition of worship, this is a time for us as a group to actively celebrate God for who He is and what He does! We declare His worth!

Have you ever attended on Sunday morning without really participating? Maybe you didn't feel like singing because you were tired. Perhaps you thought the sermon was boring and you mentally "checked out". If so, the service was not a worship service for you. Instead, it was simply time spent sitting in a room with believers. In other words, it's more than possible to sit among a group of people who are worshipping God without worshipping God yourself.

Worship is your individual active response to God. As we study worship this month it's critical for us to assess our attitudes and actions when it comes to how we respond to God in worship. Passivity is not an option.

Today's Reading:
Judges 5-6; Romans 13-14

March 29

The Sacrifice
By Peggy Kalevik

Genesis 22:5 *He said to his servants, "Stay here with the donkey while I and the boy go over there. We will worship and then we will come back to you."*

Today's scripture comes from one of my all time favorite Old Testament stories: the sacrifice of Isaac. It is the single most awesome yet terrifying act of worship in the Old Testament. In my mind, it is second only to the Crucifixion. It begs the question, how many parents today would do what Abraham did, and trust God?

This verse really tells us all we need to know. *"We will worship and then we will come back to you"*. Knowing as he did, that God wanted him to sacrifice his son, Abraham still has great faith in the God he serves. He knew in his heart that he and his son would be back. In verse 8 Abraham tells Isaac that "the Lord will provide the lamb", another indication of his faith in God. As we read our Bible we know that God was testing Abraham, but he didn't know that, he "simply" trusted God.

How about us, can we let go of everything and trust God? Can we let go of our possessions, our habits, how we feel about our children, and simply worship God. We normally don't think of worship as the way we live our lives everyday. But the way we live is all about our worship unto God. If we love Him, everything we do should reflect that love. That reflection of His love in our daily lives is our worship unto Him.

Point: Does your life reflect the love of God? Do you know that the Lord will provide?

Prayer: Lord, make my life a mirror that reflects Your love, let it be a blessing to You.

Practice: Be obedient, pray, and listen twice as much as you speak.

Today's Reading:
Judges 7-9; Romans 15

March 30

THE POWER OF EXAMPLE!

By Scott Kalevik

Ruth 1:16-18 *But Ruth replied, "Don't urge me to leave you or to turn back from you. Where you go I will go, and where you stay I will stay. Your people will be my people and your God my God. 17 Where you die I will die, and there I will be buried. May the Lord deal with me, be it ever so severely, if anything but death separates you and me.*

Naomi had suffered a lot since she moved to Moab. Her husband had died. Ten years after moving to Moab, both her sons died. How much was one person expected to take? Naomi was now ready to jettison both daughters-in-law and head back to Bethlehem as an empty and bitter widow. But a strange thing happened.

Her first daughter-in-law, Orpah, agreed with Naomi's plan and left her. But Ruth, Naomi's second daughter-in-law, refused to go along with the plan. Even though Naomi told Ruth to stay in Moab three times, Ruth refused.

As Naomi suffered loss after loss, Ruth must have been watching. Unbeknownst to Naomi, impressions were made. Ruth had not only gleaned a deep love for Naomi through the suffering, but she also knew that Naomi served the one true God. She watched as God carried Naomi through tragedy after tragedy.

Perhaps you're wondering if there's any purpose to your own suffering. Do you think God has turned against you like Naomi thought? Let me encourage you that nothing escapes the plan of God. If you're suffering today, God knows all about it. He even has purpose for it regardless of whether or not you understand His purpose.

Ruth surrendered her life to God through Naomi's example. Ruth was king David's great-grandmother and in the bloodline of Jesus (Mt. 1:5). None of it would have happened without Naomi's example. And none of it would have happened without the pain. Don't give up – be the example God asks for whatever your circumstance. You never know what He's doing through you!

Today's Reading:
Judges 10-11; Romans 16-1Corinthians 1

March 31

What's In A Name?

By Scott Kalevik

Matthew 1:21 *She will give birth to a son, and you are to give him the name Jesus, because he will save his people from their sins."*

God teaches us a lot about Himself through His names. In the modern world, names normally function simply as identification. But in the ancient world, names referred to someone's characteristics or to qualities or circumstances in his or her life. When God inspires the writers of Scripture to call Him by a specific name, He is telling us a little more about Himself.

When the angel reassured Joseph that staying with Mary, despite her mysterious pregnancy, was God's will, he told Joseph to name the baby Jesus. Then the angel defined one of the purposes for Jesus' life by defining His name. He said, *"because he will save his people from their sins."*

The name 'Jesus' comes from the Hebrew name "Joshua" and means "Yahweh is salvation." God sent His Son to save. Some say Jesus was a good teacher or a healer or a good preacher, but His name tells us that His mission was to bring salvation. Jesus Himself said it this way: Lk 19:10 *For the Son of Man came to seek and to save what was lost."*

Paul reiterates Jesus' mission in his letter to the Thessalonians: 1Th 5:9 *For God did not appoint us to suffer wrath but to receive salvation through our Lord Jesus Christ.* Jesus is the Savior. Jesus saves all who believe because He received the punishment for our sin when he willfully suffered crucifixion and died. God can justly receive us into His kingdom because our disobedience has been punished on the cross of Jesus Christ. Jesus saves us from God's wrath!

As you call on the name of Jesus today, thank Him for saving you from the wrath of God. Ponder the great love God has for you. He Himself died so that you, through faith in Jesus, will live forever with Him!

Point: Jesus' name teaches us that He is the Savior.
Prayer: Lord, thank you for loving me enough to take my punishment.
Practice: Praise God today! Tell somebody that Jesus is the Savior today!

Today's Reading:
Judges 12-14; 1Corinthians 2

April 1

Considering Who We Worship!
By Scott Kalevik

Psalm 96:9 *Worship the LORD in the splendor of his holiness; tremble before him, all the earth.*

You're sitting here trying to start your quiet time with the Lord. Where should your thoughts be? Scripture repeatedly encourages us to focus our attention on the Lord's deeds and character as we actively respond to Him in worship.

The psalmist tells us to worship the LORD in the splendor of his holiness. In other words, we are called to celebrate God's splendor and character when we worship Him. Consider His holiness or how 'set apart' He is from us. God is pure – He's righteous – He's just – He's everywhere at once – He's magnificent – He's all powerful – He knows all things – He can do all things – He's merciful – He's kind – He's longsuffering – He's gracious – He created all things – He is love - all these things plus much more make up the splendor of His holiness. To worship God well, we need to focus our attention on two basic things: 1) Who the Lord is and 2) What the Lord has done and is doing.

When we celebrate and meditate on the Lord, our hearts will be greatly encouraged. No earthly problem seems too big when we realize how big our God is! As Paul tells the Corinthians: 2Co 4:17 *For our light and momentary troubles are achieving for us an eternal glory that far outweighs them all.* Trouble can only be light and momentary if we realize and focus our attention on the power and love of the Lord.

The Psalmist tells us to tremble before Him. Worshipping God is more than just knowing a bunch of details about Him. Knowledge is great, but submission to God is greater. To worship God is to take all we know about Him and combine it with a reverent awe – a trembling fear – humble acknowledgment and submissive obedience as we bow before Him. The Bible portrays people kneeling, lying prostrate, and falling face down before God. Raised hands symbolically signify surrender. We surrender to Him when we worship.

The Psalmist further commands all those in the earth to worship God. Shouldn't all of creation adore the Creator? Our culture's idea that people should be able to decide for themselves what's true for them is completely abolished in the Bible. God says the whole world – that means everyone on the planet – should rightfully worship Him and Him alone!

Today's Reading:
Judges 15-16; 1Corinthians 3-4

April 2

'I Love You Lord'

By Peggy Kalevik

Psalm 116:1-2 *I love the LORD, for he heard my voice; he heard my cry for mercy. Because he turned his ear to me, I will call on him as long as I live.* Psalm 142:1-2 *I cry aloud to the LORD; I lift up my voice to the LORD for mercy. I pour out my complaint before him; before him I tell my trouble.*

Do you have a song which just lifts up your heart to God? When you sing it you know God is listening to you. 'I Love You Lord' was once that song for me. I didn't choose it; it just came to me at a time in my life when I was crying out to God for help and understanding. Back then, I spent a lot of time on my knees praying and crying. One day during my prayer time I starting singing that song and right before me was the face of God! I couldn't say to Him all I thought I wanted to say; I just sang the song and found peace and comfort in His presence. During this long period of trial in my life I'd experienced being in His presence before; but I'd felt He was unhappy with me. This time He was smiling down at me as I was at His feet in worship. It was an awesome experience! It changed my life forever! It was so awesome I relayed the story to a friend, who is somewhat of an artist, and he drew what I told him I saw during these prayer/worship times with God.

I suppose I should have chosen a Psalm about singing a new song, there are a number of them (Psalm 33:3; 96:1; 98:1; 144:9); but that's not what this is about. This is about lifting up your voice in worship when you are troubled and in need of His care and attention. After all, He is our Father; no one can comfort us in our time of need like our Creator. I sing in my sleep. When I'm sitting somewhere in silence, in my head I'm singing a song. The song 'I Love you Lord' at that point in my life brought me face to face with God. If you can worship God in the midst of your trial or circumstance your heart will be blessed and so will God. Sing a song of praise in your heart to God in your time of need, it will help to comfort and strengthen you.

Point: God is listening, sing a love song to Him. He will be blessed and so will you.

Prayer: Lord, my heart will sing joyfully to you; I will declare Your glory, for you are great and mighty.

Today's Reading:
Judges 17-19; 1Corinthians 5

April 3

Personalized Worship

By Peggy Kalevik

Genesis 17:1 *When Abram was ninety-nine years old, the LORD appeared to him and said, "I am God Almighty; walk before me and be blameless."* James 2:23 *And the scripture was fulfilled that says, "Abraham believed God, and it was credited to him as righteousness."*

Sometimes when we worship corporately we are so focused on the words of the songs, or what the speaker is saying, we forget why we're in church. Sometimes we're lost in thought; we don't hear or see anything that's happening around us. Our focus is misplaced. We are mentally and visually occupied. Imagine knowing God so well you can hear His voice as clearly as if you were face to face staring into His eyes as He speaks to you. If we knew Him like that, I don't think we'd lose sight of our reason for being in church!

Abraham had such a relationship. He was God's friend (2 Chronicles 20:7; James 2:23). Abraham was to walk before God blamelessly. Being blameless meant He would do nothing to corrupt God's ways. Abraham's worship was rooted in his relationship with God, it was "personal". Is our worship personal? When we sing the words of the songs, pray the prayers of the Bible or read the Bible, do we make a personal connection? Can we sing the words "living every day; in the power of Your love" and think about how the love of God has taken us through many trials? Then worship God for who He is to us as individuals. Our personal worship should be a source of strength for us and our families. If it is rich enough it can enrich our corporate worship, making our worship service a spiritual celebration feast.

Point: Worship is personal, we need to come to church prepared to lift God up, to say we love Him with our hearts, and proclaim His righteousness.

Prayer: Father, may I walk before You blameless, and worship You with everything in me.

Practice: When you're sitting in your seat at church, focus on your relationship with God, participate with your heart and mind. Don't just sing and watch; lift up your spirit and worship!

Today's Reading:
Judges 20-21; 1Corinthians 6-7

April 4

Let Us Worship
By Peggy Kalevik

Psalm 95:6 *Come, let us bow down in worship, let us kneel before the LORD our maker.*

The Lord is our King; therefore we should worship and bow down before Him. This psalm, unlike the others within Book 4 (Psalms 90-106), is not clearly a psalm addressing the kingship of the Lord, it is however, in harmony with the spirit of the book. Verses 1-7 of this psalm make up a hymn and an invitation to worship. Verse 6 is a "call to worship".

Worship is a physical, spiritual, mental and sometimes emotional act of respect and reverence for someone or something. As Christians we "worship" the God of the Bible, the one true God. Our bowed head and heart is an act of obeisance; it is a tangible act of respect, love, adoration, and even humility. We worship God because He is our Maker, Creator, and Father, the Lord of Lords. Verse 7 says, *"For He is our God and we are the people of His pasture, the flock under his care."* What can we say to Him that He does not already know? What can we give Him? The one who parted the Red Sea, raised Lazarus from the dead, and rose from the grave; what can we render unto Him? We can give Him our body and our soul. That's all we can give, and that's what He wants.

Point: Let us surrender our lives, and our hearts to the Lord, and then He will be worshiped.

Prayer: Let me worship with a bowed head and humble heart that You may be blessed.

Practice: Make your daily devotional time a time of worship as well as study and prayer.

Today's Reading:
Ruth 1-3; 1Corinthians 8

94

April 5

Are You Suffering?

By Scott Kalevik

1 Peter 4:16 *However, if you suffer as a Christian, do not be ashamed, but praise God that you bear that name.*

There are lots of ways to suffer. There's physical pain when things go wrong with our bodies. There's emotional pain when we're sad or depressed. There's relational pain when there's conflict or abandonment amongst our friends and family. There's financial pain when we can't pay the bills. But have you heard of spiritual pain? It's the suffering of persecution.

Peter speaks of suffering as a Christian. That means to suffer because you are walking with God and following Him – because you'd rather obey God than please people. The suffering of persecution may involve all of the other types of suffering. Christians around the world are suffering physical, emotional, relational and financial pain today because of their faith. I know we've all experienced suffering. But have you ever experienced suffering for your faith?

Peter tells us to PRAISE God if we suffer as Christians. Maybe Peter recalled how his friends Paul and Silas reacted to being imprisoned for their faith in Jesus: Acts 16:25 *"About midnight Paul and Silas were praying and singing hymns to God, and the other prisoners were listening to them."* We are to praise God because we bear that name. In other words, it's much better to belong to Jesus and suffer than it is to not belong to Jesus and have a nice easy life.

So remember, if you suffer today in whatever setting you may find yourself, take some time out and praise God. Worship Him in the midst of the pain. Know that it is better to be His child with hardship than it is to be without Him in ease. As the song goes, "It will be worth it all when we see Jesus."

Point: Suffering as a Christian is better than ease without Christ.
Prayer: Lord, I praise You regardless of any circumstance in my life because You are worthy of praise no matter what I may be going through.
Practice: Consciously focus away from suffering and praise God instead.

Today's Reading:
Ruth 4-1Samuel 1; 1Corinthians 9-10

April 6

WE SERVE A JEALOUS GOD!

By Scott Kalevik

Matthew 4:10 *Jesus said to him, "Away from me, Satan! For it is written: 'Worship the Lord your God, and serve him only.'"*

As we explore worship, one of the pressing questions we need to answer is, "What kind of worship pleases God?" There is a right way to worship God and a wrong way to worship God (think Cain and Abel in Genesis 4). God is pleased and well honored when we worship Him according to His desire. So, what kind of worship does God desire?

First and foremost, God desires and requires EXCLUSIVE worship. In other words, God is jealous. He doesn't share worship with anything or anyone. If we want to worship God in a way that pleases Him, we must worship no one and nothing other than the LORD!

Do you remember the first commandment given to Moses on Sinai? Exodus 20:3 *"You shall have no other gods before me."* Do you remember the second commandment? Exodus 20:4 *"You shall not make for yourself an idol in the form of anything in heaven above or on the earth beneath or in the waters below. 5 You shall not bow down to them or worship them ..."* Want to worship God in a way that pleases Him? Worship only Him!

Now the idea that we should have no other gods before God seems simple enough. Most of us will acknowledge that God is the only One worthy of worship. But making no idols is a command most of us violate routinely. Oh, we might not carve pieces of wood or stone into statues that we worship, but idolatry can be much more subtle. Idolatry seeks to replace worship of the true God with worship of something other than God.

We may never bow down to our televisions, but when television consistently receives forty hours of our time every week while God gets ninety minutes on Sunday, if that, we've declared by our actions that television is more important to us than God. When our time is consumed by making money to the exclusion of time with God, repentance is needed. Time for the web but no time for God?

God is jealous. If we've replaced Him with something else, if He's become second or third or fourth place in our hearts, our worship cannot please Him. Worship the Lord and Him alone.

Today's Reading:
1Samuel 2-4; 1Corinthians 11

96

April 7

Worship in Silence
By Peggy Kalevik

Matthew 6:2 *So when you give to the needy, do not announce it with trumpets, as the hypocrites do in the synagogues and on the streets, to be honored by men. I tell you the truth; they have received their reward in full.*

Our culture loves to recognize those who have performed good deeds. We give plaques and certificates of achievement; we love to recognize the good deed doer. But it seems that God is not necessarily fond of the recognition of man for his service. He knows we have performed a service or good deed for some reason and he will reward us if the deed is worthy. In today's scripture, Jesus assumes His disciples will give to the needy because he says "when" not "if"; this is what he expects them to do.

While there is a lot that can be said about this scripture, for the purpose of this reading we will stick to the issue of hypocrisy? Jesus is addressing those people who think that by performing good deeds they are doing something for God and the community, plus, they get to look good while they do it. They can receive the praise of man for their good works. The Pharisees were noted for their love of receiving praise from others. Giving with this kind of attitude may receive the praise of man but not the praise of God.

There is a poem by Ruth Harms Calkins which I love. It expresses so well, how God is calling us to worship through our service. In this excerpt from the poem you'll get the picture of what I mean: "You know, Lord, how I serve You with great emotional fervor in the limelight… But how would I react, I wonder, if You pointed me to a basin of water and asked me to wash the calloused feet of a bent and wrinkled old lady. Day after day, month after month, in a room where NOBODY SAW AND NOBODY KNEW"

Point: We can worship God through our service to others without the need to let the world know we're doing it. Serve in silence to the best of your ability. God knows and He is glorified and blessed by it.

Prayer: Father, give me a heart that stores up treasures, not on earth but in heaven, that I my dwell with You for all eternity.

Today's Reading:
1Samuel 5-6; 1Corinthians 12-13

April 8

HE PROCLAIMS HIMSELF
By Peggy Kalevik

Psalm 19:1 *The heavens declare the glory of God; the*
skies proclaim the work of his hands.

In the beginning God created the heavens and the earth. The Bible says: *"For by him all things were created: things in heaven and on earth, visible and invisible, whether thrones or powers or rulers or authorities; all things were created by him and for him."* (Colossians 1:16). We understand from the Bible that everything comes from God; everything lives by His will and His power and exists for His purpose. Through these things He declares His glory. So, why are we here?

It appears we were created for His purpose and His pleasure, to do with as He pleases. We are here at the will and discretion of God our Father. 1 Peter 2:9 says: *"But you are a chosen people, a royal priesthood, a holy nation, a people belonging to God, that you may declare the praises of him who called you out of darkness into his wonderful light."* We exist then, as part of His creation to give glory to Him; to proclaim His righteousness and glorify His name (Rom 15:7-9). Isn't that worship? But does He really need us? No! God doesn't need us to do anything for Him. He chooses to use us to declare His glory and to worship Him. He made it easy for us; all we need to do is look around to understand we should worship Him. The heavens already declare His glory; we don't need anyone to explain their beauty and majesty. How can we not worship Him?

In today's verse David uses the words declare and proclaim to express the continuous revelation of God through His creation. As we look at God's creation we get a glimpse of God's great power. Not that we should worship His creation, but we should understand He alone has the power to create life and the heavenly bodies. Can man with all his technological advancement create such magnificence?

Point: Who is like the Lord? He is worthy of our praise and our worship!!
Prayer: Father, give me understanding that I may worship You simply for who You are and not what You can do for me.
Practice: Look around and praise God for the works of His hands; His love and mercy.

Today's Reading:
1Samuel 7-9; 1Corinthians 14

April 9

THE RIGHT CONCLUSION – THE RIGHT RESPONSE!

By Scott Kalevik

Matthew 14:33 *Then those who were in the boat worshiped him, saying, "Truly you are the Son of God."*

The storm was over. Moments earlier the disciples had been cowering in a boat being tossed about by the wind and the waves. Experienced fishermen feared for their lives. In the midst of their terror they witnessed Jesus stand up. The Carpenter from Nazareth issued the command for the wind to stop. To the astonishment of the disciples, the wind obeyed. The waves died down. The storm stopped. The forces of nature had been neutralized by a word from Jesus. In utter amazement, the disciples found themselves floating on a calm sea!

Their minds must have been racing. "Who is this man that controls nature with a word?" Like the bright sunrise of a new day, the only possible answer dawned on them. God is the only one who commands obedience from wind and waves. God is sitting next to us in this boat in the Person of Jesus!

Their conclusion about Jesus was correct and so was their response. Once they understood God was in the boat, they worshiped Him. They acknowledged Jesus as God. Interestingly, the text gives no indication that Jesus tried to stop their worship of Him. Jesus clearly understands He is God and receives the worship of His disciples rightfully and willingly. Just another indication in the New Testament that Jesus claimed to be, and was, God in the flesh.

The New Testament drives you and I to accept the same conclusion the disciples came to: Jesus is God. But to come to the right conclusion is not enough. Had the disciples recognized Jesus was God and done nothing, they would have missed the point. The right conclusion requires the right response. Jesus is God and, therefore, worthy of all of our worship!

Have you come to the right conclusion? If there's any doubt in your mind about who Jesus is, read your New Testament again. The claim is clear. If you've come to the right conclusion, are you displaying the right response in your life? Do you worship Jesus?

Today's Reading:
1Samuel 10-11; 1Corinthians 15-16

April 10

ARE YOU BLINDED BY RELIGION?
By Scott Kalevik

Matthew 2:2 *and asked, "Where is the one who has been born king of the Jews? We saw his star in the east and have come to worship him*

Abram was called by God to leave his homeland and go to a land the Lord would show him. God led him to Canaan, changed his name to Abraham, and gave him a son. Thus, the Jewish nation began. God's people received God's revelation as they followed Him through centuries of time and experience.

Moses wrote the Law. Psalmists wrote Psalms. Prophets wrote prophecy. Centuries went by. The history of the Israelites was recorded. The coming Messiah was predicted. The hope of every follower of God was to see His Redeemer come.

Yet, despite being God's chosen people, despite the predictions, and despite centuries of study, God's people, for the most part, completely missed Jesus' birth. They had become so used to carrying out the duties of their religion that they were no longer listening to or looking for God.

Instead, in God's sense of humor, a group of wise men from Persia saw a star and understood that a King was to be born in Palestine. This group of pagan idolaters packed their bags full of fine gifts and traveled to Bethlehem to worship the coming Messiah.

Sometimes it's so easy to fall into the ruts of religion. We begin to "go through the motions" of religious life while in our hearts we've disconnected from seeking the Lord with all of our hearts. When we replace our relationship with God with the ritual of religion, we stop listening to and looking for God.

Worshipers act like the wise men from Persia. They look for God. They try to go where God is. When they find Him, they bow, give their best, and worship Him. Just going through the motions today? Look for the Lord! Listen for Him! Worship Him and give Him your best.

Today's Reading:
1Samuel 12-14; 2Corinthians 1

April 11

Preparing for Worship

By Peggy Kalevik

1 Chronicles 16:29 *Give unto the LORD the glory due unto his name: bring an offering, and come before him: worship the LORD in the beauty of holiness. (KJV)*

Sunday morning is a time to relax and read the paper as you have a leisurely breakfast, right? Well, if you have five kids to get ready for church it's far from relaxing. If you have to unpack all the gear and set up the chairs before you have a worship service, it can be a little taxing, and yes, frustrating. But some how we need to find time to prepare our hearts and minds for worship. We need to come to a place of calm within, to quiet our sprit in a way which opens our soul to the presence of God.

The scripture reference for today is quoted from the King James Version (KJV) because the New International Version (NIV) translates the Hebrew phrase in a way which shifts the emphasis from the worshipers to God. The use of this particular Hebrew phrase makes it difficult to determine if it should read "the beauty of holiness" or "the beauty of His holiness." I've chosen the KJV here because it conveys more closely what I'm trying to relate; that we (the worshipers) should come to worship before our LORD adorned in holiness; clothed in a spirit of holiness.

During our daily devotions we should include a little time to talk with God about our personal worship; asking him to lead us in how we should honor Him. If we give a little of our time in worshiping Him every day in our personal life, it will make our corporate worship richer for us and more glorifying for Him. Prepare your heart to let go of all the worries of life and honor Him with your whole heart, soul, body and mind.

Point: Prepare yourself; your hearts, and your mind, take the time in your daily routine to worship Him.

Prayer: Lord, give me the desire and determination to prepare myself for worship this week, and every week there after.

Practice: Read an extra Psalm everyday this week; take time to pray and sing a praise chorus each day.

Today's Reading:
1Samuel 15-16; 2Corinthians 2-3

April 12

WHY SHOULD GOD BE PRAISED AND WORSHIPED?

By Peggy Kalevik

Psalm 99:5 *Exalt the LORD our God and worship at his footstool; he is holy.*

The LORD reigns, let the nations tremble; he sits enthroned between the cherubim, let the earth shake. Great is the LORD in Zion; he is exalted over all the nations. Let them praise your great and awesome name — he is holy (Psalm 99:1-3). The sovereignty and glorious reign of the Lord "over all the nations" should be enough to make every living creature tremble and fall to their knees in worship. Oddly, for some it is not enough. Some of us need more proof.

God has given us a book full of proof and yet we question. One of the great proofs of our need to worship is again found in the Bible in Romans 1. God shows us clearly how he knew we would come to this age in which we currently live; cultivating and even celebrating depravity. He inspired Paul to write about it.

We can go through the Bible and find plenty of reasons to praise and worship God. We can praise God for His great power (Exodus 14:21-22; John 11:43-44); praise God for His holiness, mercy, and justice (2 Chronicles 20:21, Psalm 99:3-4); praise Him for His grace (Ephesians 1:6); praise Him for His goodness (Psalm 135:3); praise Him for His kindness (Psalm 117); praise Him for His love (John 3:16); and we can praise God for His salvation (Ephesians 2:8-9). The list could go on!

As we've said a few times this month, His creation speaks volumes, and the Bible tells us over and over of His love for all of us. May our Father receive from us the praise and worship He so richly deserves!

Point: Our God is "God". He is worthy of glory and honor. Give Him the praise; worship Him!

Prayer: I worship You O Lord for You are worthy to receive glory and honor and power, for you have triumphed gloriously over evil and have already won the victory for me. I thank You and I worship You.

Practice: Research a few of these verses today to reinforce what you believe and increase your faith. Then worship God!

Today's Reading:
1Samuel 17-19; 2Corinthians 4

April 13

Worship From The Heart!
By Scott Kalevik

Matthew 15:8 *"These people honor me with their lips, but their hearts are far from me. 9 They worship me in vain; their teachings are but rules taught by men."*

God complained about His people in Isaiah 29:13: The Lord says: *"These people come near to me with their mouth and honor me with their lips, but their hearts are far from me. Their worship of me is made up only of rules taught by men."* In our passage today from the New Testament, Jesus repeats God's complaint. In both passages people think they are pleasing God with their religious activities while God thinks they are worshiping Him in vain.

These passages should scare us. They both point to the idea that we can be deceived. It's possible for us to believe we're pleasing God as we perform our religious duties when, in fact, God is not pleased at all. What if our worship of God is in vain?

Both passages focus attention on the attitude of our hearts. Vain worship is characterized by saying the right things without meaning them from the heart. Vain worship seeks to keep the rules of God without having relationship with God. Vain worship looks good on the outside but is not genuine.

True worship loves the Lord from the heart. As Joshua warned: *"So be very careful to love the LORD your God"* (Joshua 23:11). God wants us to obey Him out of love instead of obligation. God desires relationship with His people. To think that we gain God's favor by rule keeping is to miss God's point. He wants to know us. He wants to walk with us through this life. Even if we do godly things, if we do them without hearts full of love for the Lord, we fool ourselves.

Let's examine our hearts today. Do we love the Lord with all of our heart? Do we serve wholeheartedly? Or are we simply going through the motions of religion without relationship with Jesus?

Point: God is not impressed with the vain worship of religion.

Prayer: Father, help me examine my heart. Please allow me to serve you and follow you motivated by love in my heart for you.

Practice: Think of all the 'religious' things you do each week. Do you do them out of obligation to God or out of love from the heart?

Today's Reading:
1Samuel 20-21; 2Corinthians 5-6

April 14

Praise and Worship
By Peggy Kalevik

Psalm 150:1 *Praise the LORD. Praise God in his sanctuary; praise him in his mighty heavens.*

Let everything that has breath praise the Lord! We've heard it so many times, but do we ever stop to think about what it really means? All of God's creation that has breathe, particularly humankind, is called to praise the Lord. So, do we understand the difference between "praise" and "worship"?

We understand the definition of praise is to speak well of someone or some thing. We all do it; we praise our children, other people, our pets, our cars, and many other "things" in our lives. We also praise God. We say He is wonderful; an awesome God. Praise is an acknowledgement of God's excellence through speaking, singing, and/or praying about God. Thanksgiving is an expression of gratitude for something God has done for us.

Praise and thanksgiving are to express gratitude and admiration; to compliment, applaud and extol. They are outward expressions; they compliment each other and are almost always expressed together. Probably our greatest expression of praise to God is our acceptance of Him as our Lord and Savior.

Worship differs from praise and thanksgiving in that it is to speak, sing, and/or pray to God. We do not work up to worship, we must enter into it. True worship is the heartfelt acknowledgment of God and all His power and glory in the things we do. When we worship we go beyond the outward oral expression of thanks and admiration and enter into worship of Him for who He is. Worship is to glorify and exalt God; to show our love, faithfulness and adoration to our creator God, our heavenly Father. Worship is an attitude of the heart, an expression of reverence toward our Lord.

Point: Let your offering be your body, soul, heart and mind presented as living sacrifices, holy and pleasing to God.

Prayer: Lord, I want to be Your vessel, cleanse my body, heart and mind of all worldly behaviors and attitudes, that I may worship You.

Practice: Commit today to give more attention to your personal worship.

Today's Reading:
1Samuel 22-24; 2Corinthians 7

April 15

LIVING THE LIFE OF WORSHIP!

By Scott Kalevik

Romans 12:1 *Therefore, I urge you, brothers, in view of God's mercy, to offer your bodies as living sacrifices, holy and pleasing to God—this is your spiritual act of worship.*

Many people think of worship as something you do on Sunday mornings at church. But that's not how the Bible describes worship. According to Romans 12:1 we are called to offer our bodies to God as living sacrifices. We are called to be holy or set apart from this world. We are called to be pleasing to God. We are taught that this is our 'spiritual act of worship'.

When an animal was offered as a sacrifice in the Old Testament, its physical life was sacrificed. Similarly, to be a living sacrifice means we must die – but not physically – no, we must die to self. Jesus said it this way: Lk 9:23 *Then he said to them all: "If anyone would come after me, he must deny himself and take up his cross daily and follow me. 24 For whoever wants to save his life will lose it, but whoever loses his life for me will save it."* Taking up your cross and becoming a living sacrifice are one and the same. The life of the disciple is laid down before God so God can lead that life wherever and whenever He chooses.

Wow! To live like that means we worship God 24/7. Every thought, word, and action is offered to God as an act of worship. Our dreams and ambitions in life are laid down at His feet in order that we might accomplish His dreams and ambitions and will for our lives.

As people in love with Jesus, our whole lives should be lived in worship. Each thought captive to the will of God. Each deed dedicated to Him. We are called to live the life of worship.

Point: Dying to self is our spiritual act of worship.
Prayer: Lord, I want what you want more than I want what I want. Help me live each moment of the day as a living sacrifice.
Practice: Make the commitment before God to live as a living sacrifice. Then live the life of worship.

Today's Reading:
1Samuel 25-26; 2Corinthians 8-9

April 16

LOSING SIGHT OF PRIORITIES!
By Scott Kalevik

1 Samuel 15:22 *But Samuel replied: "Does the LORD delight in burnt offerings and sacrifices as much as in obeying the voice of the LORD? To obey is better than sacrifice, and to heed is better than the fat of rams.*

The Christian Booksellers Association convention was held in Washington, D.C. Addressing the convention, Priscilla Shirer spoke about what it means to truly experience God in a real and personal way. She said, "In the first century in Palestine, Christianity was a community of believers. Then Christianity moved to Greece and became a philosophy. Then it moved to Rome and became an institution. Then it moved to Europe and became a culture. And then it moved to America and became a business. We need to get back to being a healthy, vibrant community of true followers of Jesus."

We so easily get our priorities mixed up. To follow God is about having a relationship with Him. We obey Him out of love, not obligation or manipulation. Following God is not a philosophy. Living a "Christ-centered" life is not about belonging to an institution. Worshiping God is not rooted in culture. The location, size, and effectiveness of a church building is not God's first priority. Read your Bible all you want. If walking with God is not your first priority, you're simply educating yourself.

Samuel tells King Saul that the Lord would rather have him obey than do 'religious' things like sacrifices. Saul failed to obey God. Saul was rejected as king. Saul tried to do the right things in his own wisdom, but he never obeyed God from the heart.

God wants us to walk with Him in obedience. That's His top priority. Jesus died to make it possible. Is relationship with God your top priority?

Point: Walking with God in obedience is God's top priority for us.
Prayer: Lord, help me love you most of all.
Practice: What is your top priority in life? What should it be?

Today's Reading:
1Samuel 27-29; 2Corinthians 10

April 17

Curing the Down Day!

By Scott Kalevik

Psalm 100:2 *Worship the LORD with gladness; come before him with joyful songs.*

This will most likely sound too simple. Psychology probably doesn't agree. But I'm going to share a secret with you. A secret that will change your mood every time! Next time you're feeling down, hopeless or blue, start singing songs to the Lord. Sing! Sing songs of gladness. Sing songs of joy. Sound silly? Have you ever tried it?

What's that? You say you don't feel like singing when you're down? Think of the age-old question: Which came first, the chicken or the egg? Ask yourself: "Which comes first, the song or the glad heart?" Start singing even if you don't feel like it and see what happens.

If you really want to experience a wonderful day, think about the God you're singing to while you sing. Put your heart into it. Praise Him! Think about all the things He's done for you. Think about all the things He's doing for you. Think about all the things He's promised to do for you in the future! Sing it to Him!

The heart is lifted when singing songs of praise. Singing songs of praise can refocus our attention onto the very facts that the Psalmist encourages us to consider when he continues in Psalm 100:3 *Know that the LORD is God. It is he who made us, and we are his; we are his people, the sheep of his pasture. 4 Enter his gates with thanksgiving and his courts with praise; give thanks to him and praise his name. 5 For the LORD is good and his love endures forever; his faithfulness continues through all generations.* Try it!

Point: Worshiping God with songs of gladness will encourage us.
Prayer: God, forgive me for wallowing in my problems. Help me sing praise to You.
Practice: Start singing next time you're down. Call you pastor and tell him what happened!

Today's Reading:
1Samuel 30-31; 2Corinthians 11-12

107

April 18

Do You Want Proof?

By Scott Kalevik

Matthew 27:42 *"He saved others,"* they said, *"but he can't save himself! He's the King of Israel! Let him come down now from the cross, and we will believe in him.*

I have a friend who insists that he cannot believe; he says God hasn't 'proven Himself' to him. It reminds me of those gathered around the cross watching Jesus die. Like my friend, they knew something of Jesus, but they missed the point.

First, they said, "He saved others." And they were right. Jesus showed mercy to tax collectors, prostitutes, demon possessed people and every person who genuinely believed. Even the thief hanging next to Jesus received mercy when he called on Jesus. Jesus saved others! The observers understood correctly.

But the crowd showed their ignorance when they said, "But He can't save Himself." During His arrest, Jesus let His disciples know that He could have stopped this whole thing: Mt 26:53 *Do you think I cannot call on my Father, and he will at once put at my disposal more than twelve legions of angels?* Jesus could have saved Himself. But He chose NOT to.

The crowd was right when they said, "He's the King of Israel." Just a few days before Jesus' crucifixion another crowd had gathered to hail Jesus as King and to lay palm branches before Him as he rode a colt into Jerusalem. Jesus accepted their acknowledgment.

But as Jesus hung from the cross, the crowd decided to believe in Him only if He came down. In other words, they agreed to believe if God met their requirements. Like my friend, they decided God would have to 'prove Himself' to them before they would believe.

How ironic that as the Savior hung bleeding as the sacrificial Lamb of God, God was giving absolute proof to them but they couldn't see it. Like my friend, they wanted more proof. They wanted God to jump through their hoops.

Why is it many require "proof" from God when God has already demonstrated His love by dying in our place? Who loves you enough to die for you? As we meditate on the cross this Easter season, remember that God already has proven His eternal love for us. We don't need more proof. We need to surrender.

Point: God has given us more than enough proof. We need to surrender.
Prayer: God forgive me for being hard hearted. Help me surrender all to You.
Practice: Are you asking God to prove Himself to you? Consider the cross.

Today's Reading:
2Samuel 1-3; 2Corinthians 13

April 19

FIGHTING THE OPPOSITION!
By Scott Kalevik

Exodus 12:31 *During the night Pharaoh summoned Moses and Aaron and said, "Up! Leave my people, you and the Israelites! Go, worship the LORD as you have requested".*

If you really choose to walk with Jesus and offer your whole life to Him, you will most likely be met with opposition. Jesus spoke about it: Jn 15:18 *"If the world hates you, keep in mind that it hated me first. 19 If you belonged to the world, it would love you as its own. As it is, you do not belong to the world, but I have chosen you out of the world. That is why the world hates you."*

The important thing to remember if you are persecuted for your faith is that God is not only with you, but He's also at work in the midst of your trouble. You don't need to fight back. God will defend you. Simply trust and obey.

Moses had told Pharaoh to release the Hebrews. Moses told Pharaoh repeatedly. Pharaoh steadfastly refused to let the Hebrews go and worship God. Moses simply did whatever God told him to do. The plagues kept coming. Pharaoh kept refusing. Finally, God sent Pharaoh a message he would listen to. The first-born males of Egypt were killed by the Angel of death. Pharaoh was convinced. He woke Moses up in the middle of the night and told him to go.

Nothing can stop you from following God. There is no opposition strong enough to derail you. Perhaps, like Pharaoh, the opposition may be stubborn and hard-hearted. But God will overcome. Hold on. Follow. Worship Him. He will deliver you.

Point: No opposition is strong enough to keep us from worshipping the Lord.
Prayer: God, help me faithfully obey as YOU defeat my enemies.
Practice: Instead of retaliating against your enemy, pray for them.

Today's Reading:
2Samuel 4-5; Galatians 1-2

April 20

HUMBLE BUT TRIUMPHAL ENTRY
By Peggy Kalevik

Matthew 21:10 *When Jesus entered Jerusalem, the whole city was stirred and asked, "Who is this?"*

When Jesus entered Jerusalem that Palm Sunday, the people were wondering; who was this man causing so much excitement? It must have been a dramatic and (for those who didn't understand what was happening) confusing event. We call it the Triumphal Entry, but he rode in on a donkey. Shouldn't a triumphant victor come into the city riding on a stallion of some kind? Zechariah 9:9 says: *"Rejoice greatly, O Daughter of Zion! Shout, Daughter of Jerusalem! See, your king comes to you, righteous and having salvation, gentle and riding on a donkey, on a colt, the foal of a donkey."*

The Jews understood Zechariah 9:9 to be a reference to the Messiah, the son of David. Did Jesus use this event to disclose His true identity? He says to the disciples who He dispatched to acquire the donkey and colt to tell anyone who asks that "the Lord" needs them. These two things point to His identity: the donkey with its colt; and He called Himself "the Lord". The Hebrew word used here for Lord means "commander" or "official." The ride on the colt symbolized peace and humility. To those Pharisee and Sadducees who understood the scriptures, the secret was out. This should have erased all their doubts about His true identity.

Jesus could have come to Jerusalem on a big white stallion, but He needed to fulfill the scripture. In Zechariah 9:9, Zechariah describes the character of the one he's writing about saying that He is righteous, He brings with Him salvation, He is gentle (or humble) and riding on the colt of a donkey. He does not come on a stallion; and His own people reject Him and His peace. Then why is it a triumphal entry? Because, as in everything, Jesus did what the Father wanted (John 8:29).

Point: He came in humility, not weakness, doing the will of the one who sent Him.

Prayer: Father, let me be humble in the victories You give me, and give all the glory to You.

Practice: Praise God in joy and sorrow, in triumphs and failures; understand that He loves a humble heart.

Today's Reading:
2Samuel 6-8; Galatians 3

April 21

Elohim

By Peggy Kalevik

Genesis 1:1 *In the beginning God created the heavens and the earth.*

Through this verse we meet the Creator God, the God of our Fathers and of the covenant at Sinai. In this, the very first verse of the Bible, we are given a clear understanding that all that exists in the universe owes its origin and existence to God; He alone is eternal. By identifying God as the strong creator, a vital difference is noted between the God of the Fathers and the god of the nations or idols. Through these distinctions, and His eternal existence, we know our Creator God and Father is God.

The Hebrew name used for God in this verse is Elohim "*lohiym*" (one of the primary names of God). This name for God focuses on several characteristics: power, strength and creativity. Elohim is used clearly in scripture to indicate: the relationship of God to man in creation (Gen 2:7-15); the moral authority of God over man (Gen 2:16-17); the one who controls man's earthly relationships (Gen 2:18-24); and the one who redeems man (Gen 3:8-15, 21). (The word Elohim is used almost universally to describe deity, even idols.)

Here is where we begin the "beginning" of the story of God and His people. God starts the journey with His people by announcing that He is God, (the strong one, or more effectively the strong creator). He alone has all creative power; He alone is without beginning and without end. He is omnipotent, He is accountable to no one, and He swears by Himself; He is God.

Point: Who is the Creator of the universe and all that exists? Elohim – the supreme being; the creator; the eternal one. Our God is all these things and more.

Prayer: Father, give me wisdom and understanding about who You are, and in particular, help me to appreciate You for all that You are.

Practice: Start researching today to understand more about "Elohim" and El. There is much more to learn.

Today's Reading:
2Samuel 9-10; Galatians 4-5

April 22

JESUS: THE LIVING WATER!
By Scott Kalevik

John 4:4 *Now he had to go through Samaria.*

Did Jesus really HAVE to go through Samaria? Jesus was traveling North from Judea to Galilee. Jews and Samaritans typically hated each other and, therefore, travel routes had been established that could get a person from Judea to Galilee without journeying into Samaria. But our text tells us Jesus HAD to go through Samaria. Why did He have to go through Samaria?

Read the gospels and one thing becomes crystal clear about the life of Jesus. Jesus doesn't discriminate against anyone based on race, gender, ethnicity, color, political viewpoints, educational background, legal or economic status. Jesus saves all who come to Him on His terms. Jesus HAD to go through Samaria because an outcast needed Him.

Jesus meets a woman by the well at Sychar. This woman had already gone through five husbands and was living with a sixth man. We're told she went to the well to draw water at the sixth hour. That's about noon. The only people that choose to draw water in the heat of the day are the people that don't want to encounter others. She was just the kind of person society rejects.

Jesus breaches custom and begins a conversation with this woman at the well. He tells her about her family life even though she never mentions it to Him. Jesus offers her "Living Water." When she asks Him where to get this living water Jesus tells her that He is the source of living water - He is the Messiah. The woman believes!

To this unsuspecting outcast of society, Jesus reveals Himself as Messiah and offers the opportunity to start fresh. Society's reject comes to Jesus and receives forgiveness and new life. She goes on to tell her whole town about her Savior!

There is no sin so great that Jesus will not forgive. He's not worried about your gender or race or ethnicity or age or education or past. Jesus offers each of us the opportunity to come to Him if we'll come on His terms. If we receive Him by faith, repent of our sins, and obey Him, we will know what it's like to drink living water! Jesus HAD to go through Samaria!

Today's Reading:
2Samuel 11-13; Galatians 6

April 23

THE RESURRECTION AND THE LIFE

By Scott Kalevik

John 11:25 *Jesus said to her, "I am the resurrection and the life. He who believes in me will live, even though he dies; 26 and whoever lives and believes in me will never die. Do you believe this?"*

The mortality rate for human beings has been running at 100% for thousands of years. Most of us have attended a funeral. Death is a fact of life. Why? God says we die because we choose to go our own way instead of obeying Him. We sin. Ro 6:23 *For the wages of sin is death, but the gift of God is eternal life in Christ Jesus our Lord.*

Despite our disobedience, God mercifully decided to give us the opportunity to live with Him. He sent His Son Jesus. Jesus did not deserve to die on the cross. Jesus never disobeyed God. Jesus never sinned. Yet, in obedience to His Father, He willingly died as a substitute for us. Our sin was punished by His death so that we can live in Christ even as God's judgment against sin is satisfied.

In John 11, Jesus declares Himself to be the resurrection and the life. In other words, Jesus declares Himself to be the One who actually has the power to conquer death. Jesus gives sinners undeserved life instead of eternal death. To prove His claim, Jesus called four-day-dead Lazarus out of the tomb. In obedience to God's command, Lazarus came back to life and walked out of the grave.

"He who believes in me will live, even though he dies and whoever lives and believes in me will never die. Do you believe this?" Do you want to escape eternal death and live forever? The Resurrection and the Life calls you to submit your heart to Him today. Do you already believe? Rest. Rest in the fact that no matter what difficulty life has brought you today, Jesus has promised you that He has overcome your greatest adversary – death itself is defeated. Jesus is Lord! Serve Him well today! Hallelujah!

Point: Jesus has the power over death.
Prayer: Lord, thank You for conquering death that I may live by faith in You.
Practice: Perspective check! Are you down today? Remember that Jesus has overcome death on your behalf. Rejoice and again I say, rejoice!

Today's Reading:
2Samuel 14-15; Ephesians 1-2

April 24

THE BLOOD OF JESUS

By Beth Nelson

Hebrews 9:14 *How much more, then, will the blood of Christ, who through the eternal Spirit offered himself unblemished to God, cleanse our consciences from acts that lead to death, so that we may serve the living God!*

You cannot possibly be alive without blood in your body. Even in ancient times, people understood the significance of blood. Around 3500 years ago, Moses wrote this in the book of Leviticus, "For the life of a creature is in the blood." Blood distributes life-giving nutrients to all parts of the body and without it, there would be no life. Today we have blood banks and we have blood drives when the supplies are low. And though scientists are trying to create a blood substitute, there's still no substitute for the real thing.

Blood figures into God's economy, too. If we ask the question of where we get the power to overcome sin, Satan and eternal death; the answer lies in the blood sacrifice of Jesus Christ. God's justice demands a payment for sin. Every sin separates us from God and ultimately will bring destruction and death, which is Satan's goal. In Old Testament times, this payment cost something - the sacrifice of a life; not a human life, but the life of an animal. And because it was an animal, it was a temporary and imperfect payment and had to be repeated regularly, because we sin and are separated from God regularly. So the shedding of blood was required to bring the sinner back into the presence of God.

However, it was never God's ultimate solution for our situation. And, because we were always on God's heart and he yearns to have us close to Him, he had a plan to bring down that dividing wall of sin once and for all. It cost us nothing. But it cost him everything.

The message God wants us to receive from him is that we were redeemed, we were bought with the precious blood of Christ, a lamb without blemish or defect. And to all those who believe on his Name, the blood of Jesus, God's Son, purifies us and frees us from all sin. (1 Pet 1:19; 1 Jn 1:7; Rev 1:5)

Let us treasure the life we have with God, life that is made possible through the blood Jesus shed on the cross for us. For it is that blood that cleanses us and breaks the bonds of all of our sins.

Point: The blood of Christ, the only perfect one, cleanses us from all sin.

Prayer: Thank you, oh Lord, for paying the ultimate price to free me from my sins.

Practice: Realize that you are dead to sin and alive to God. Ask Him how you can serve Him today.

Today's Reading:
2 Samuel 16-18; Ephesians 3

April 25

Yahweh

By Peggy Kalevik

Exodus 20:7 You shall not misuse the name of the LORD your God, for the LORD will not hold anyone guiltless who misuses his name.

The Israelites were very careful about speaking the names of God, especially the four letter name for God "YHWH"; or as we pronounce it "Yahweh." To the Jews, it is the distinct personal name for God. It is a name they would neither speak nor read out loud. There is power in the name of God! The proclamation of the mouth should profess true love and adoration for God. To speak this name was such a profession.

In this passage of scripture, one of the Ten Commandments, we need to understand that the name of God stands for more than simply pronouncing a title. It tells us of His nature, being and person; His teaching or instruction to us concerning His doctrine; and the moral and ethical teaching which He's laid out for us. The Jewish people believe if we use the name lightly, we are taking the name in vain; thus, we violate the commandment. Think about that the next time you use it as an expression.

In Exodus 3:14, when Moses asks God what he should say if asked who sent him, He answers Moses with: *"I AM WHO I AM. This is what you are to say to the Israelites: 'I AM has sent me to you.'"* God tells Moses *"I will be with you."* God's answer to Moses is *"I am for I am will be present"* with you. This "I AM" is the God of Abraham, Isaac, and Jacob and He was sending Moses. This was to be His name forever; His name was His person, His character, His authority, His power, and His reputation.

This is the same God we serve; He is with us in all our trials, pain, triumphs, and failures. He loves us through our greatest sorrows, and tears. He is with us just as He was with Moses. In Joel 2 it is written: *"And everyone who calls on the name of the LORD will be saved…"* We have salvation only through this name, Yahweh. (See also Acts 4:12)

Point: You shall not misuse the name of the LORD your God!
Prayer: Father, help me to hold Your name in great esteem; with love and adoration will I speak Your name, knowing all that it means to me.
Practice: From this day forward we should speak the name of our Lord with great esteem and love. Each time you speak His name, think about what you are saying.

Today's Reading:
2Samuel 19-20; Ephesians 4-5

April 26

Son Of Man

By Scott Kalevik

Daniel 7:13 *In my vision at night I looked, and there before me was one like a son of man, coming with the clouds of heaven. He approached the Ancient of Days and was led into his presence.*

If you study your New Testament you'll see that the title 'Son of Man' is used 29 times in Matthew. The shocking part is that the ONLY person that calls Jesus the 'Son of Man' is Jesus Himself. Mark uses the title 12 times – always used directly from Jesus' lips about Himself except 8:31 when the narrator describes what Jesus called Himself. Luke uses 'Son of Man' 25 times and, again, every occurrence comes from Jesus' own lips. John uses 'Son of Man' 12 times – again all from Jesus except 12:34 when the crowd repeats 'Son of Man' because Jesus had used the term of Himself.

In other words we find 76 instances in the gospels where Jesus refers to Himself as "Son of Man" with 2 additional instances of 'Son of Man' coming from sources referring to what Jesus said. Why does Jesus use 'Son of Man' so much?

Daniel 7:13 refers to the coming one as the 'son of man.' The Son of Man will come on the clouds. Reading further we find that this one like a son of man is actually divine! Da 7:14 *He was given authority, glory and sovereign power; all peoples, nations and men of every language worshiped him. His dominion is an everlasting dominion that will not pass away, and his kingdom is one that will never be destroyed.*

Every time Jesus calls Himself 'Son of Man', He refers to His divine nature. Instead of using the title to tell us He's born as a human, He uses it to tell us He has all authority, glory, and sovereign power. He wants us to know that people from every nation will worship Him. That His dominion is everlasting! Jesus unmistakably claims that He is God by referring to Himself as Son of Man.

Point: Son of Man is used by Jesus alone referring to His divine nature.
Prayer: Lord Jesus, I worship You.
Practice: Do you believe Jesus is God? Surrender to Him and follow His word.

Today's Reading:
2Samuel 21-23; Ephesians 6

April 27

Immanuel

By Scott Kalevik

Matthew 1:23 *"The virgin will be with child and will give birth to a son, and they will call him Immanuel"—which means, "God with us."*

The name Immanuel means, "God with us." When Matthew applies this title to Jesus, he's telling us that Jesus is, "God with us."

Most religions of the world are characterized by people striving for enlightenment or trying to get to God. Christianity is the story of God coming to us in the Person of Jesus. What an amazing truth. Jesus, God in the flesh, divested Himself of heaven. He agreed to interrupt His face-to-face communion with the Father so He could be with us. Paul described it to the Philippian church like this: Php 2:6 *Who, being in very nature God, did not consider equality with God something to be grasped, 7 but made himself nothing, taking the very nature of a servant, being made in human likeness. 8 And being found in appearance as a man, he humbled himself and became obedient to death— even death on a cross! 9 Therefore God exalted him to the highest place and gave him the name that is above every name, 10 that at the name of Jesus every knee should bow, in heaven and on earth and under the earth, 11 and every tongue confess that Jesus Christ is Lord, to the glory of God the Father.*

Jesus taught us that even after completing His mission on the cross and rising from the dead He was willing to be with us: Jn 14:23 *Jesus replied, "If anyone loves me, he will obey my teaching. My Father will love him, and we will come to him and make our home with him.*

So today as you face whatever circumstances life throws at you, remember that Jesus has not only come to earth to save you by dying in your place on the cross, but He is still Immanuel. He makes His home with all who believe and obey Him. If that's you, you have no reason to fear no matter what circumstance may confront you. God is with you!

Point: "God with us" applies both to Jesus' earthly life and to believers now.
Prayer: Lord Jesus, please help me commune with You today through my obedience to Your word.
Practice: Whenever you feel overwhelmed, call upon Him knowing that God is with us!

Today's Reading:
2Samuel 24-1Ki 1; Philippians 1-2

April 28

From Everlasting to Everlasting

By Peggy Kalevik

Psalm 90:2 *Before the mountains were born or you brought forth the earth and the world, from everlasting to everlasting you are God.*

Yes, our God is infinite, He is immeasurable, and He is exceedingly great. He was "in the beginning", He is now, and He forever will be. He is "El Olam", the "Everlasting God." (El is GOD).

Our God is mysterious; He has no beginning and no end. He is omnipresent, omniscient, and omnipotent. The psalmist says "from everlasting to everlasting you are God" and in doing so affirms God's kingship over the earth, His unchanging nature and His eternal endurance.

In Genesis 21:33 Abraham plants a tamarisk tree in Beersheba and calls upon the name of the LORD; the Eternal God. He plants the tree as a sign of his covenant with Abimelech then prays to the Eternal God, El Olam. This prayer to the "Eternal God" is different because Abraham is experiencing, in part, the fulfillment of the covenant promise. The treaty with Abimelech gives Abraham his first claim in the land of promise, so Abraham calls on the everlasting God who is showing him His great power, protection and grace.

Abraham asked for God's protection, mercy and provision over the Promised Land for his descendants. In the same way, this Eternal God is also available to us. In the name of God is power and purpose; it's not just a name. Respect it and understand it.

Point: In your all of your circumstances call on the name of God, pray with confidence, and faith. He is with you; He is all powerful; and He will do it.

Prayer: "How great you are, O Sovereign LORD! There is no one like you, and there is no God but you..." (2 Samuel 7:22)

Practice: Take some time today to look up some of the character traits listed in today's reading, such as, omniscience, omnipresence, and omnipotent and get a greater understanding of the God you serve.

Today's Reading:
1Kings 2-4; Philippians 3

April 29

SON OF DAVID

By Scott Kalevik

Luke 18:38 *He called out, "Jesus, Son of David, have mercy on me!"*

A blind beggar sits by the road when he hears that Jesus of Nazareth is passing by. The beggar screams out, *"Jesus, Son of David, have mercy on me!"* What was the beggar saying by calling Jesus "Son of David"?

The blind beggar understood that Jesus had the lineage required to truly be the Messiah. Jeremiah foretold how the house of King David would be the house from which the Messiah would eventually come: Jer 23:5 *"The days are coming," declares the LORD, "when I will raise up to David a righteous Branch, a King who will reign wisely and do what is just and right in the land. 6 In his days Judah will be saved and Israel will live in safety. This is the name by which he will be called: The LORD Our Righteousness."* By calling Jesus the 'Son of David,' the beggar is telling Jesus that he believes Jesus is the Messiah.

The blind beggar also understood that Scripture is true. What was predicted so many centuries earlier had no come to pass in the person of Jesus. The beggar showed his faith by using 'Son of David.'

The beggar also understood that Jesus had the power to heal. No doubt he had heard stories of the miraculous works Jesus was doing throughout the region. But he also knew that if Jesus was the Son of David then God the King was listening to his plea for mercy. The blind beggar left his encounter with eyes that could see!

When we recognize Who Jesus is and plead with Him for mercy we can count on the fact that God hears our plea and He will respond according to His will and purpose for our lives. The blind beggar was ignored by almost everyone who passed by. But when God passed by, in the Person of Jesus, the blind beggar was not only heard; he saw.

Point: Jesus is the Son of David. All prophecies concerning Jesus either have or will come to pass.

Prayer: Lord, help me have the faith of the blind beggar.

Practice: Today I will contemplate how Jesus fulfills every requirement to be the genuine Messiah sent from God. No one else in history can make that claim.

Today's Reading:
1Kings 5-6; Philippians 4-Colossians 1

April 30

ADONAI: THE LORD - MASTER

By Peggy Kalevik

Genesis 15:2 *And Abram said, Lord GOD, what wilt thou give me, seeing I go childless, and the steward of my house is this Eliezer of Damascus? (KJV)*

In today's passage we observe the first occurrence of Abraham giving a verbal response to God. God has taken Abraham from Ur of the Chaldean, to Haran, to Canaan, to Egypt, and to Hebron; a distance of approximately 1300 miles; and God is leading and instructing him all the way. Through all this Abraham has obediently responded to the voice of God. Now Abraham finally speaks to God; he asks questions concerning how the promise will be fulfilled. When he speaks he calls God "Lord or Master"; in the Hebrew language the word is "Adonai." Adonai comes from the word adon, a word used to describe a master who owns slaves (one of the primary names of God). Adonai is the plural form of the word, implying Trinity. Hence, Abraham knows God to be his Lord and Master.

Abraham knows the relationship between a master and servant begins with the master. God is the master and as such He is responsible for providing for the needs of His servant; He must direct and instruct him as well. As a servant, Abraham must be obedient and follow.

We start to follow Abraham's walk with God when he leaves his father's household at God's instruction (Gen 12:1). By then he is 75 years of age; it's the first instance where we see he is living by faith in God. By Chapter 15 Abraham is probably about 84 or 85. This is based on the fact that he went to Canaan when he was 75 and had Ishmael through Hagar at age 86 (Genesis 16:3 & 16).

While in Chapter 15 it may appear from his questioning of God that his faith is faltering, he knows God is his protector and Lord. We are reminded of this in verse 6, *"Abram believed the Lord, and He credited it to him as righteousness."* Abraham believed, trusted and followed. God is Adonai to Abraham; he loves, trusts and has faith in his master for everything in his life.

Point: "Adonai" assures believers that our Master has the resources and ability to take care of us. As servants, all we need to do is trust and follow.

Prayer: Praise to You LORD, for You show Your wonderful love to me. I trust in you, O Lord. (Psalm 31:14 & 23)

Practice: Do more reading about the name Adonai.

Today's Reading:
1Kings 7-9; Colossians 2

May 1

THE FATHER - PATER

By Peggy Kalevik

Luke 2:49 *"Why were you searching for me?" he asked.*
"Didn't you know I had to be in my Father's house?"

When Jesus is found missing from the caravan his parents are traveling with, they come back to Jerusalem looking for him. When they find him they are amazed at what he was doing in the temple and his mother said to him, *"Son, why have you treated us like this? Your father and I have been anxiously searching for you."* (Luke 2:48) Jesus replies, why were you looking for me, didn't you know I would be in my Father's house, as if he were surprised about the fact that they were even looking for him. As if to say where else would a son be except in his father's house doing his father's business. His parents did not understand what he was talking about. But he went with them in obedience. Jesus Father took priority over the desires of his earthly parents; he was doing what his Father sent him to do.

All who are saved enter into a spiritual family; we have a spiritual kinship with each other and with God our Father. John 1:12 says that we are "children of God", (KJV: "sons of God"). Because of this relationship we call God, Father. When we bow in prayer we are not praying to a strange and unknown person or idol of stone but a loving, caring, wise and just Father. This New Testament name for God, gives the believer intimate relationship and access to God's presence. We have fellowship with Him and we receive guidance and security from Him. Maybe the most wonderful thing we receive from our Father is our inheritance, all the riches of the Father will one day be ours. Romans 8:17 says: *"Now if we are children, then we are heirs—heirs of God and co-heirs with Christ, if indeed we share in his sufferings in order that we may also share in his glory".*

I grew up without an earthly Father. God is the only Father I have ever known, He's provided for me, protected me, taught me, disciplined and loved me. He is my Father.

Point: God is our Father if we have accepted Christ as our Savior and are living by faith in Him.

Prayer: Praise be to the God and Father of our Lord Jesus

Today's Reading:
1Kings 10-11; Colossians 3-4

May 2

Jesus Is My Righteousness

By Scott Kalevik

1 Corinthians 1:30-31 *It is because of him that you are in Christ Jesus, who has become for us wisdom from God—that is, our righteousness, holiness and redemption. 31 Therefore, as it is written: "Let him who boasts boast in the Lord."*

Jesus is called our righteousness. It points to the substitution God provided on the cross. When we stand before God on judgment day it will be the righteousness of Jesus that allows believers to escape God's wrath.

Why do we need Jesus' righteousness? Because you and I are not pure in and of ourselves. We can never meet God's standards on our own. If we have to be approved by God based upon our righteousness, we are doomed.

But today's text reminds us that Jesus is our righteousness. In other words, Jesus is our pure standing before God. When God looks at believers on judgment day, He will see all who are "in Christ" through the righteousness of Jesus Christ. 2Co 5:21 *God made him who had no sin to be sin for us, so that in him we might become the righteousness of God.* Believers stand absolutely pure before God because they are in Jesus - the One who is absolutely pure!

Our standing before God does NOT depend on our ability to be perfect in and of ourselves. We are made righteous in God's sight because we surrender our lives to Jesus through faith. Ro 10:4 *Christ is the end of the law so that there may be righteousness for everyone who believes.*

Today is a glorious day! Our right standing before God rests completely in the Person and work of Jesus Christ. God will welcome us into heaven on judgment day because all of our sin has received its just punishment on the cross and because we are clothed in the righteousness of Jesus through faith.

This great truth is precisely why the "holier than thou" attitude of some believers is so misplaced. None of us are "holier than thou." All of us who come to Jesus Christ and surrender our lives by faith are made pure before God by the righteousness of Jesus. We have no room to boast.

Today's Reading:
1Kings 12-14; 1Thessalonians 1

122

May 3

Jehovah Rophe
By Peggy Kalevik

Exodus 15:26 *He said "If you listen carefully to the LORD your God and do what is right in his eyes, if you pay attention to his commands and keep all his decrees, I will not bring on you any of the diseases I brought on the Egyptians, for I am the LORD, who heals you."*

The LORD showed Moses a piece of wood (King James says, "The LORD showed Moses a tree), and Moses threw it into the water and the water became sweet, they drank. The LORD healed the waters of Marah. This healing of the bitter water may be a symbol of the LORD's ultimate healing power. The tree may be undrestood to symbolize the Cross which heals us of all our infirmities, physical, emotional, spiritual, and even social.

The LORD allowed the Israelites to go three days without water just after they walked through the parted waters of the Red Sea, to test them. This is not the same as the testing at Meribah (Ex 17), or at Sinai (Ex 20), or even Taberah (Nu 11:3; 13:26-33) but this testing concerned the promise he made to them. *"If you listen carefully to the voice of the LORD your God and do what is right in his eyes, if you pay attention to his commands and keep all his decrees, I will not bring on you any of the diseases I brought on the Egyptians, for I am the LORD, who heals you."* If you read closely you see that there is a condition for this healing. Do we "listen carefully to the LORD, and do what is right in his eyes"? Do we "pay attention to his commands and keep all his decrees"? The LORD has the power to restore the health of those who are sick with diseases or injury. He is after all the "LORD" who heals.

Point: We must listen and do what is right, pay attention to His commands, and we must demonstrate a measure of self control.

Prayer: LORD, give me patience and self-control that I may be able to receive all that you have for me.

Practice: If you have habits in your life that could cause you illness or harm, ask the LORD to deliver you.

Today's Reading:
1Kings 15-16; 1Thessalonians 2-3

May 4

Jehovah Shammah: The LORD Is There

By Peggy Kalevik

Psalm 139:7 *Where can I go from your Spirit? Where can I flee from your presence?*

Our Lord is always with us, it's a quality we have a difficult time understanding. However, it is true. This does not mean that He spreads Himself out so much that we only have part of Him and other parts are somewhere else. No, All of God is here with you all the time.

The Psalmist is saying that God is everywhere; there is no way to hide from Him. There is no place to hide from Him, and why would we want to? We are surrounded by His "presence" And He understands all things in all places at the same time. The Psalmist says, *"If I go to the heavens, You are there; if I make my bed in the depths, you are there"* (Psalm 139:8). The hand of the Lord protects us wherever we are, even in our distress. The darkness is not dark to God; the Psalmist says that even the night will shine like the day, for the darkness is as light to God (v 12). So even when we find ourselves in the darkest place in life, God is there with us. And if we open our eyes in the dark He will bring light.

In Genesis Chapter 16, Hagar said of the LORD, *"you are the God who sees me"* (Beer Lahai Roi). Even in her distress the LORD followed her as she tried to run away from her mistress. Hagar was in a state of disobedience, running from a mistress who was mistreating her, but even then the LORD was with her. He spoke to her with wisdom and correction; He sent her back to her mistress. So, even when we are in a state of sin, the LORD is there, He sees all. The LORD is always with us. He is omnipresent. He is Jehovah Shammah!

Point:　After Salvation, maybe the second greatest gift from the LORD is the gift of His presence in our lives. *"And surely I am with you always, to the very end of the age"*. (Matthew 28:20)

Prayer:　LORD, thank You for Your presence in my life. Thank You for watching over me and turning me back when I am going the wrong direction. May You be blessed by the life You have given me.

Today's Reading:
1Kings 17-19; 1Thessalonians 4

May 5

THE LAMB OF GOD!

By Scott Kalevik

John 1:36 *When he saw Jesus passing by, he said, "Look, the Lamb of God!*

Why is the Most High, All-Knowing, All-Powerful, Almighty God of all existence called a Lamb? Aren't lambs weak and defenseless and vulnerable? Can't any wolf kill a lamb? Then why does Scripture refer to Jesus as a Lamb?

The answer takes us back to Exodus 12 when God is preparing to deliver His people out of the hands of the Egyptians. Ex 12:3 *Tell the whole community of Israel that on the tenth day of this month each man is to take a lamb for his family, one for each household.* Before the last plague came, God commanded each Hebrew household to slaughter a lamb. Ex 12:7 *Then they are to take some of the blood and put it on the sides and tops of the doorframes of the houses where they eat the lambs.* Ex 12:13 *The blood will be a sign for you on the houses where you are; and when I see the blood, I will pass over you. No destructive plague will touch you when I strike Egypt.*

The blood of the lamb on the doorposts spared the Hebrews from the death of their firstborn sons as God struck Egypt with the plague of death. Passover began as the celebration of God 'passing over' those people whose doorposts were covered by the blood of the lamb.

Just as God delivered His people from the bondage of Egypt by the blood of lambs, so God delivers all who believe from the bondage of sin through the blood of Jesus. Jesus is called the Lamb of God because He allowed Himself to be sacrificed in weakness for the sins of the world. Isa 53:5 *But he was pierced for our transgressions, he was crushed for our iniquities; the punishment that brought us peace was upon him, and by his wounds we are healed.*

Almighty God has chosen the imagery of a weak, defenseless, slaughtered lamb to communicate the price He paid for our sin on the cross of Jesus. But make no mistake. The Lamb of God who provides forgiveness for all who surrender to Him will be worshipped in glory for eternity. Rev 7:17 *For the Lamb at the center of the throne will be their shepherd; he will lead them to springs of living water. And God will wipe away every tear from their eyes."*

Today's Reading:
1Kings 20-21; 1Thessalonians 5-2Thessalonians 1

May 6

I AM WHO I AM
By Scott Kalevik

Exodus 3:14 *God said to Moses, "I AM WHO I AM. This is what you are to say to the Israelites: 'I AM has sent me to you.'"*

Imagine walking through the desert minding your own business when you see a bush on fire. Upon further investigation you notice that the bush is not consumed by the flame. It's just burning. As you step a little closer you see a heavenly figure in the flame and you hear a voice calling you by name and telling you to take off your sandals because you're standing on holy ground. The voice identifies Himself as God. God then tells you that He wants you to go to the most powerful leader of the most powerful kingdom on earth and demand the release of that leader's money making labor force – namely the Hebrew people. I don't know about you, but I would be feeling completely overwhelmed by such a morning!

This exact scenario confronted Moses in Exodus 3. As Moses stands before God processing the moment, he tries to take a giant step backward. He asks God to please find someone else. God assures Moses that He will be with him.

Then God tells Moses His name: "I AM WHO I AM." By using the name "I AM WHO I AM," God essentially tells Moses that He exists without the help or necessity of anyone or anything else in all existence. God exists by His own power. He is self-existent. There is nothing else living in all of existence that can make such a claim. All of creation depends on the Creator to exist and to survive, but the Creator depends only on Himself.

In one name, therefore, God reassures Moses, that He and He alone controls all of life. Moses has nothing to worry about! I AM WHO I AM is overseeing every step. I AM WHO I AM can never be defeated. I AM WHO I AM has the power to deliver His people. I AM WHO I AM is Lord of all!

Today as you face whatever trouble may come your way, remember that I AM WHO I AM did exactly as He promised and delivered His people from Egypt through Moses. Remember that His power to love and care for His own is unequaled. If you've surrendered your life to I AM WHO I AM, you may live today in faith and confidence that His purpose will be accomplished with your life!

Today's Reading:
1Kings 22 - 2Kings 1-2; 2Thessalonians 2

May 7

A Child of Blessing

By Kathy Bryant

Psalm 127:3 *"Sons are a heritage from the Lord, children a reward from him"*

The subject of motherhood has many connotations associated with it. The first things that come to mind are child bearing or child rearing. One of the first commands in Genesis is *"Be fruitful and increase in number, fill the earth and subdue it"* (Gen 1:28). What happens when a woman is unable to fulfill this command? In Old and New Testament times the women who could not bear children were ridiculed and teased by other women. To be childless was a threat to the welfare of a woman in her old age. It was even a common practice for wealthy women in the ancient times to offer female slaves as surrogates in order to get children from their husbands. Several women in the Bible shared this common condition. They were barren or childless. The Bible tells us that in many cases God closed their womb. The following women and their sons shared this condition but God uses their children to glorify Himself or to fulfill a plan: Sara/Isaac (Gen 16:1-2), Rebekah/Esau and Jacob (Gen 25:21), Rachel/Joseph (Gen 30: 1-2), Manoah's wife/Samson (Jud 13:2-3), Hannah/Samuel (1Sam 1:2-6), Elisabeth/John the Baptist (Luke 1:7). These women suffered the ridicule of family and friends; prayed to God and waited, sometimes years, before God blessed them with a child. The child arrived at the right time to fulfill God's purposes. Christian women, who have been frustrated by the condition of childlessness, should remember that God makes no mistakes. God's plan for our lives will sometimes supersede our dreams or our wants in this life. In Jeremiah 18: 3-4 *"So I went down to the potter's house and saw him working at the wheel. (4) But the pot he was shaping from the clay was marred in his hands, so the potter formed it into another pot, shaping it as it seemed best to him".* We are pots in the Lord's hand. If the role of motherhood is not given to a woman, it doesn't mean she can't be useful for the Lord. It just might mean God has another job for her for which He needs her entire focus. God loves us and wants the best for us (Jeremiah 29:11). Sometimes we might need to set aside our own wants in order to be used by God.

Today's Reading:
2Kings 3-4; 2Thessalonians 3-1Timothy 1

May 8

I'm So Glad My Mother Prayed for Me
By Peggy Kalevik

1Samuel 1:13 & 15c *Hannah was praying in her heart, and her lips were moving but her voice was not heard. Eli thought she was drunk "… I was pouring out my soul to the LORD."*

Many women, who want to be mothers with everything in them, have spent days in prayer before the Lord. Here in 1Samuel Hannah does just that. A woman barren all of her life, wanted badly to have a son. Where can she turn but to God?

Hannah had intimate relationship with the Lord, evident by her prayer. Verse 12 tells us that Hannah prayed to the Lord; verse 13 that she prayed in her heart; and her voice was not heard, (she prayed in silence). So, her prayer for this son came from the relationship she had with God, she is not speaking to a god she does not know. She is pouring out her heart to her Father. God was not surprised by her approach, he knew His daughter. All these years God watched and waited, saw the anguish and bitterness of heart and still he did nothing to change her situation. But on this day at worship, she pours out her heart and He answers her. All things are done according to God's time.

In the same way, He answers the many mothers who pray for the children that they already have, the one who rebels and the one who loves. I have listened at my mother's bedroom door as she prayed for me and my siblings. It was sometimes very frightening and often spiritually moving. And one night I sat on the floor outside that same door and listened to my mother pray and cry at the death of my sister. It was heartbreaking and inspiring; she prayed that the Lord would give her strength to endure. She never asked why, never spoke of the pain; she only asked that He would see her through. She said: the Lord gives and the Lord takes away, blessed be the name of the Lord.

Point: Prayer changes things, know that you mother is praying for you.

Prayer: Lord, bless the mothers who are on their knees in prayer for their children.

Practice: I will be a blessing to my mother.

Today's Reading:
2Kings 5-7; 1Timothy 2

May 9

LORD Jehovah

By Peggy Kalevik

Genesis 32:9 Then Jacob prayed, "O God of my father Abraham, God of my father Isaac, O LORD, who said to me, 'Go back to your country and your relatives, and I will make you prosper,'

Jacob was confronted by angels at the eastern border of the Promise Land on his return to the land of his father Isaac in Canaan. He is now praying for God's protection and maybe deliverance from of all people, his brother. He calls on the name that God most often calls himself LORD. Jacob was already concerned about how his brother would receive him. Now that He knows that his brother is coming to meet him with 400 hundred men, he is distressed. So, it is from this distress that he prays to LORD Jehovah, the self-existent-One.

The Old Testament is littered with occurrences of LORD Jehovah (one of the primary names of God). It appears at least 1472 times in the King James Version. The first occurrence is Genesis 2-4; today's reading is from Genesis 32. It is the name that God Himself makes known to Moses. In Exodus 6:2-3 God tells Moses: *"I am the LORD. I appeared to Abraham, to Isaac and to Jacob as God Almighty, but by my name the LORD I did not make myself known to them."* Yet Jacob called on Him using that name. Jacob prays for safety and his appeal to God is founded in God's promise made earlier (Genesis 31:3). Why does Jacob use this name? Well the name itself may hold the answer. The LORD (standing before the word Jehovah or Yahweh) comes from the Hebrew verb (hayah) that means to be or to become. So the name means the One who exists in Himself and the One who reveals Himself. Maybe Jacob had revelation in his heart or maybe he understood the Hebrew language. In any case, he called on the LORD Jehovah and his prayers were answered.

The emphasis of this chapter is Jacob's almost miraculous accumulation of wealth, and the restoration of relationship with his brother. Esau's anger from our perspective may be well founded but Jacobs' prayer was crucial in changing the outcome of their meeting. Jacob prayed to a sovereign God who does whatever pleases Him.

Point: The next time you're in prayer, pause give reverence, then use His name with confidence having faith in an all powerful self existing God.

Prayer: O LORD my God, I take refuge in you; because of your unfailing love, you are the one I praise.

Today's Reading:
2Kings 8-9; 1Timothy 3-4

May 10

Your Blessing Is In Obedience
By Scott Kalevik

Luke 5:4 When he had finished speaking, he said to Simon, "Put out into deep water, and let down the nets for a catch." 5 Simon answered, "Master, we've worked hard all night and haven't caught anything. But because you say so, I will let down the nets for a catch.

The guys had been out fishing all night. That was typical. The untypical was that they had caught nothing. So, tired with nothing to show for the night's work, they headed back for shore. As they approached land they were summoned by Jesus to let Him sit in their boat and preach to the people on the shore.

When Jesus was done preaching He told Simon to go back out to deep water and put down the nets. Simon had a choice to make; should he obey or not? After all, Simon was the one who knew about fishing. He'd done it all his life. Wasn't Jesus a carpenter by training? Wasn't there tomorrow night to try fishing again? Wouldn't the crew rather go to bed? Common sense was banging in Simon's brain, "Just tell Jesus that we'll fish again tomorrow night."

Instead of following human inclinations, Simon decided to obey Jesus. They went back to deep water and let down the nets. Luke records what happens next: *Luke 5:6-7 6 When they had done so, they caught such a large number of fish that their nets began to break. 7 So they signaled their partners in the other boat to come and help them, and they came and filled both boats so full that they began to sink.* Every fisherman in the boat knew a huge catch NEVER happened in mid-day heat. But it happened at Jesus' command.

Simon chose to obey Jesus rather than to rely on his own expertise. Simon chose to obey Jesus rather than making up excuses about why he should delay. Simon obeyed Jesus in the face of facts contrary to Jesus' command. And Simon received a bountiful blessing, so many fish that the boats were in danger of sinking.

Simon had enough money to leave and follow Jesus after a catch like that. Simon also had the unmistakable assurance that Jesus truly was the Christ.

Our obedience to God's leading is more valuable to God than our expertise. Your blessings are in obedience!

Point: God doesn't need my expertise. I need to obey and watch His power.

Prayer: God help me rely on you instead of relying on what makes sense to me.

Practice: Do you feel like your expertise in life is valuable to God? Submission and obedience are worth much more!

Today's Reading:
2Kings 10-12; 1Timothy 5

May 11

Start Walking!

By Peggy Kalevik

Luke 17:17 *Jesus asked, "Were not all ten cleansed? Where are the other nine?*
18 Was no one found to return and give praise to God except this foreigner?"
19 Then he said to him, "Rise and go; your faith has made you well."
Heb 11:1 *"Now faith is being sure of what we hope for and certain of what we do*
not see". Jesus encountered ten lepers while traveling near Samaria one day. Since the
beginning of history, people with leprosy have been cast out of everyday society. But Jesus
willingly loves the outcast. These ten lepers ask Him to have pity on them. The text tells
us that they called from a distance. The lepers understood that no one wanted to come
near them.

Jesus told them to go show themselves to the priest. Showing yourself to the priest was the normal procedure AFTER you had been cleansed from a disease (Lev. 14). Jesus is asking these ten to start walking to the priest as if they had already been healed. A leper with common sense could have argued that there was no reason to go see the priest because they still had leprosy. But, by faith, all ten lepers obeyed Jesus. As they were walking to the priest, they were healed.

One came back to thank Jesus. Only one! And he was the Samaritan. Remember that Samaritans were traditionally viewed as 'half-breeds' by the Jews. Disdained and disenfranchised, nonetheless, the Samaritan leper was so overjoyed at the healing God had blessed him with that he had to return to praise God for the gift of health. Jesus asks where the other nine went. He tells the Samaritan leper that his faith has made him well. His willingness to believe Jesus and obey Jesus restored his life.

We have to step out in obedience to what Jesus commands if we want to see God work. If the lepers hadn't started walking in response to Jesus' command, they would not have been healed. But they believed and obeyed. They were all healed. God's blessings come when we start walking in obedience to His truth. Today is the day to start walking by faith in obedience. You will see God work. Don't forget to be one who comes back to give Him thanks.

Point: When we start walking in obedience and faith, Jesus does His work in our lives.

Prayer: God, please give me faith that moves at your command

Today's Reading:
2Kings 13-14; 1Timothy 6-2Timothy 1

May 12

I HAVE DELIVERED JERICHO
By Peggy Kalevik

Joshua 6:20 *When the trumpets sounded, the people shouted, and at the sound of the trumpet, when the people gave a loud shout, the wall collapsed; so every man charged straight in, and they took the city.*

When God summoned Moses to Mount Sinai to receive the tablets of stone, Moses sat and waited six days in the cloud cover and on the seventh day the LORD spoke to him (Exodus 24). When Ahab went out to battle against the King of Aram, they camped opposite each other for seven days, on the seventh day the battle was joined, and Ahab was victorious (1 Kings 20). Here in Joshua chapter 6 there are seven priests, seven trumpets and on the seventh day after marching around the city seven times the walls fall down. I think that we can safely say that this was no ordinary battle, it was a divine event.

At the time this event occurred Jericho was an important Canaanite city in the Jordan valley. However, it was directly in the path of the Israelites, who had just crossed the Jordan River (Joshua 3:1-17). God had promised this land to the Israelites. Now the city of Jericho was shut up tightly because they heard how the LORD had dried up the Jordan before the Israelites and like all the people they were terrified. So they sat in their homes in the walled city and wondered what those Israelites were doing, walking around the city every day for a week. It was the end of the harvest (Joshua 3:15), they had all the food they needed, and the city had a stream of fresh water within its walls. Still they must have been completely beside themselves when the Israelites gave a shout and the walls came down.

A study of the site by archeologist shows that all but a portion of the north section of wall fell down. And of course, scientist think there was some natural phenomena that caused the wall to collapse. But they agree that the timing would have been too perfect. God told Joshua in 3:7, *"Today I will exalt you in the eyes of all Israel"*, and He did. In 6:2 He tells Joshua, *"see I have delivered Jericho into your hands…"* and He did. Joshua said *"cursed is the man who undertakes to rebuild this city, Jericho"*. And cursed he was, read all about it in 1Kings 16:34.

Point: God is true to His word! Joshua was obedient to the will of God and he was blessed!

Prayer: LORD, I know that my obedience is more pleasing to You than sacrifice, that listening to You is much better than any sacrifice we can make. Give me a heart that is obedient to You.

Practice: Be obedient to His voice; consider His will in all you do today.

Today's Reading:
2Kings 15-17; 2Timothy 2

132

May 13

BE STILL MY TONGUE

By Peggy Kalevik

Numbers 12:10 *When the cloud lifted from above the Tent, there stood Miriam—leprous, like snow. Aaron turned toward her and saw that she had leprosy;*

God in his infinite wisdom shows us again that He alone is all powerful and omniscience. Miriam the recipient of God's wrath in this story is punished for her verbal attach against her brother Moses because of jealousy and yes racism. In their jealousy of Moses prophetic gifts and his apparent marriage to a Cushite woman, the two siblings rouse God's anger, and He defends Moses. (The Bible takes this opportunity to tell us about the great humility of Moses.) God gives them a good talking to and lets them go; it is only after He leaves them that they realize Miriam has been afflicted with Leprosy.

Leprosy is caused by the organism Mycobacterium leprae. It is not very contagious, but the Mycobacterium leprae multiplies very slowly and the incubation period of the disease is about five years. Symptoms can take as long as 20 years to appear (World Health Organization). What scientist can explain, how Miriam could go out of the tent of meeting to speak with God having no symptoms, and in a few minutes have the full blown disease. It just doesn't happen that way, we cannot understand it.

Some Bible scholars believe that Miriam was singled out for this punishment because she was the principal offender, and because of "who" she was in God's plan. She had literally preserved the life of the infant Moses, by watching over him when he was left among the reeds on the bank of Nile. And it was Miriam who made it possible for Moses' mother to become his nurse (Ex 2:4 &7). She also sang the first Psalm as recorded in Exodus 15. She played an important role in God's ministry to His people, which made the attack against Moses a great act of rebellion against God and Moses. But God is gracious, He forgives and restores, and true to His Word, in seven days He restores Miriam. Discipline completed!

Point: We should be careful in how we speak about God's people and always remember we will give an account on the Day of Judgment for every careless word we have spoken. (Mt 12:36)

Prayer: Father, let me not attempt to speak with pride, contempt or arrogance against the righteous.

Practice: Moses Cushite Wife – http://www.americanbible.org/brcpages/ blacksantiquity and God's Sovereignty – http://www.theopedia.com/ Sovereignty_of_God

Today's Reading:
2Kings 18-19; 2Timothy 3-4

May 14

Praise God for Problems!

By Scott Kalevik

Matthew 14:20 *They all ate and were satisfied, and the disciples picked up twelve basketfuls of broken pieces that were left over.*

Have you ever thought about the role your problems play in your life? They are vital to your spiritual health! No problem equals no growth. No problem equals no opportunity to learn how to trust God. And the bigger the problem, the bigger the potential lesson in just how powerful and loving God is.

Jesus forced His disciples to learn the value of a problem one day out in the middle of nowhere. He tried to go to a remote place for some solitude. But the crowds found him. Thousands of people literally followed him wherever He went. Counting women and children, over ten thousand people were out in the wilderness following Jesus.

It was time for dinner. Peter whipped out his cell phone and called for three thousand pizzas to be delivered immediately. No, not really. They had no way to get enough food to feed all the people. Even if they could find that much food, they had no money. The disciples told Jesus to send them away. Here is Jesus' solution to the problem: Mt 14:16 *Jesus replied, "They do not need to go away. You give them something to eat."*

What would you do if Jesus told you to feed them? Jesus deliberately puts His disciples in the middle of an impossible problem. Why? To see the power of God!

Mt 14:17 *"We have here only five loaves of bread and two fish," they answered.* They tackled their problem by totaling their resources. Five loaves, two fish. There would be a lot of hungry people left over. Jesus asks the people to come to Him. He blesses the food they do have. He commands that the bread and fish be passed out to the people. Twelve baskets full are collected after all have eaten.

The disciples' contribution to the miracle consists of two basic things. They offered what they had to God. They obeyed God's instruction. God did the rest.

Maybe we should look at our problems as gifts from God. Perhaps God is asking us to offer Him what we have and follow Him through the problem so that He can demonstrate His power in our circumstance. Without the problem, there'd be no opportunity to witness the power. Praise God for the problems!

Practice: Write down your three top problems. Are you offering God your resource, no matter how meager? Are you listening to His leading as you walk through?

Today's Reading:
2Kings 20-22; Titus 1

May 15

Jealousy and Envy
By Peggy Kalevik

Numbers 16:31-32 *As soon as he finished saying all this, the ground under them split apart 32 and the earth opened its mouth and swallowed them, with their households and all Korah's men and all their possessions.*

The rebellion that brings on this awesome scene is brought about by a cousin of Moses and Aaron (Exodus 6:16-22). This Levite, Korah and three Reubenites – Dathan and Abiram, and On, along with 250 other men of various tribes, became insolent and rose up against Moses. Jewish tradition holds that Korah had been discontent for sometime. Though appointed to the service of the tabernacle, he had become dissatisfied with his position and aspired to the dignity of the priesthood. That tradition further believes that Dathan and Abiram whose tents were near to Korah, descendants of Reuben (Jacobs' eldest son), they felt that they should be in control of the civil authority of the Israelites. (Patriarchs and Prophets) Korah particularly objected to Aaron and his sons being the only ones who could perform the function of offering incense at the LORD's Tabernacle.

"*They came as a group to oppose Moses and Aaron and said to them, "You have gone too far! The whole community is holy, every one of them, and the LORD is with them. Why then do you set yourselves above the LORD' assembly?*"" (Numbers 16:3) They did not accept or understand that the God of the covenant was their leader, and that veiled by the pillar of cloud, the presence of God went before them. It is from Him that Moses and Aaron received all their directions. After Moses pays homage to God He tells the men to come tomorrow with their censer before the Lord and that God will show everyone who he has chosen. Dathan and Abiram refuse to come. (Jewish tradition infers that On withdrew his objections.) At the appointed time the men took their place at the entrance to the Tent of Meeting and Dathan and Abiram stood outside their tents. God shows up and tells Moses and Aaron to move the assembly away from these men. After a traumatic speech by Moses the ground opens and swallows the men, their tents, their families and everything they own. And fire came out from the LORD; it consumed the 250 men who were standing at the Tent of Meeting with their censers burning.

Point: Don't let jealousy and envy, lead you to an act of rebellion against God. Don't make God angry!

Prayer: Lord, may my hands be clean, let my heart be pure; that I may serve you without jealousy or envy.

Today's Reading:
2Kings 23-24; Titus 2-3

May 16

DO YOU WANT TO GET WELL?

By Scott Kalevik

John 5:6 When Jesus saw him lying there and learned that he had been in this condition for a long time, he asked him, "Do you want to get well?"

What a question. This guy had been lying by the pool of Bethesda for 38 years! THIRTY-EIGHT YEARS! Local superstition believed that an angel would stir up the water every now and then. First one in the pool got the healing. But this guy couldn't move! Helplessly he waited day after day. Wouldn't you assume that someone in that position would want to get well?

Listen to the man's answer to Jesus' question: *Jn 5:7 "Sir," the invalid replied, "I have no one to help me into the pool when the water is stirred. While I am trying to get in, someone else goes down ahead of me."* The man offers Jesus his excuses instead of his faith.

Many times you and I do the same thing with God. We have problems. Instead of asking God for help and exercising our faith by obeying His leading, we offer Him our excuses about why we are stuck in our problems.

The invalid man didn't recognize the power of Jesus. He didn't ask Jesus for help. He gave Jesus his excuse. He was so used to being a victim in his circumstance that he didn't see the freedom standing right in front of him in the Person of Jesus. Jesus heals him anyway.

Do you want to get well? Jesus challenges each of us with that question. He asks us if we're willing to trust Him to change our lives. Are we willing to leave the old patterns and habits and walk in the freedom of truth?

Jesus clearly demonstrates His ability to overcome any problem. The man jumps up and walks away after thirty-eight years of lying there. Jesus has the power to overcome whatever it is that has us stuck as well. He can and will change us. The question is, "Do you want to get well?"

Point: Jesus has the power to change our lives. Do we want to change?

Prayer: Lord, help me not wallow in my problems. Help me trust You to change. I want to get well.

Practice: Examine your life. Are you giving God excuses instead of submitting to Him?

Today's Reading:
2Kings 25-1Chronicles 1-2; Philemon

May 17

AND THE WATERS PART, AGAIN

By Peggy Kalevik

2 Kings 2:14 Then he took the cloak that had fallen from him and struck the water with it. "Where now is the LORD, the God of Elijah?" he asked. When he struck the water, it divided to the right and to the left, and he crossed over.

Two of God's great prophets stand at the banks of the Jordan one day and one of them like Moses at the Red Sea, parts the waters of the Jordan. God displays His power through these two men and He blesses their loyal faithful service. Add to all that Elijah departs this earth in a blaze of glory on a chariot of fire and Elisha parts the waters of the Jordan as well.

Elijah is on his last mission in the service of his God. He is taking his aid (student) Elisha along on his last journey in this life. This must be like a final exam for Elisha. Elijah is about to leave Gilgal and go to Bethel to visit the prophetic school, he tells his aid to stay here, but Elisha refuses. From Bethel they set off for Jericho and from Jericho to the Jordan. Each time before they set off, Elijah tells Elisha to stay, and each time Elisha refuses, saying, "as surely as the Lord lives and you live, I will not leave you". At every stop the prophets who are there ask Elisha if he knows that the Lord is going to take his master today. Elisha' response is the same each time, *"yes I know, but do not speak of it".*

It is an awesome glorious event that Elijah is taken up into heaven in the chariot of fire, but that is not the point. The point is the testing of this prophet who will inherit the mantle from Elijah. Will he see clearly what God wants him to see on this day and understand? In Matthew 13, Jesus says in answer to a question concerning the parables: *"…Though seeing, they do not see; though hearing, they do not hear or understand."* Jesus explains that he speaks in parables because the people are spiritually insensitive. But He has chosen His disciples to understand the mysteries. In his test of Elisha God is doing this same thing. He is showing both of these prophets that Elisha is sensitive to the spirit and does have the understanding to carry the mantle that Elijah is leaving. In verse 10 Elijah tells Elisha, *"yet if you see me when I am taken from you, it will be yours—otherwise not."* If Elisha had stay behind at any point on this day he would have missed God's blessing, and the one thing he wanted, "a double portion" of his master's spirit.

Prayer: Father, let me see and understand clearly your intent for my life, that I may serve you well.

Today's Reading:
1Chronicles 3-4; Hebrews 1-2

May 18

Faith That Doesn't Quit!
By Scott Kalevik

Mark 2:3-5 Some men came, bringing to him a paralytic, carried by four of them. 4 Since they could not get him to Jesus because of the crowd, they made an opening in the roof above Jesus and, after digging through it, lowered the mat the paralyzed man was lying on. When Jesus saw their faith, he said to the paralytic, "Son, your sins are forgiven."

It's so easy to give up. All you have to do is stop trying. Leave hope at the door, let go of your dreams, and quit – that's all it takes. After that you just need to come up with your excuses about why you quit so you can explain yourself to others.

The paralytic in Mark 2 refused to quit. He had obstacles in his life that most of us never encounter. But he refused to quit. He believed Jesus could heal him, but he couldn't move. So he had his friends carry him. He knew he had to get in front of Jesus, but he couldn't get into the house because of the crowd. So he had his friends carry him up to the flat roof. Once there, he had his friends dig a hole through the adobe roof and lower him into the presence of Jesus. This paralytic would not quit!

When Jesus saw him, he forgave his sins. How would you feel if you went through all of the trouble to see Jesus so that He could heal your body and then you heard him forgive your sins? If we think about it, the forgiveness of our sins impacts our eternity. The condition of our bodies impacts our life only here on this earth. In other words, by forgiving his sins, Jesus met the paralytic's most desperate need first.

But just to prove that He had authority to forgive, Jesus commanded the paralytic to stand up, pick up his mat, and walk. The crackling of the bones could probably be heard through the whole room. Muscles materialized. Tendons connected. Strength flooded the paralytics body and he stood up. Healing of soul and body inundated his life.

The paralytic didn't quit despite the odds being stacked against him. He believed so strongly that he was willing to overcome any obstacle in his way to be with Jesus.

Jesus is still the same. If we seek him with all our hearts and don't quit, He will be found and He will meet our every need! Don't quit! Do all you can to be with Him.

Point: Seek Jesus with ALL your heart, soul, mind, and strength. He'll answer.
Prayer: Lord, forgive me of losing sight of your power and giving up. Strengthen my faith.
Practice: What obstacles are you letting stop you from meeting with Jesus today?

Today's Reading:
1Chronicles 5-7; Hebrews 3

May 19

THE TOUCH OF FAITH!

By Scott Kalevik

Matthew 9:20-22 *Just then a woman who had been subject to bleeding for twelve years came up behind him and touched the edge of his cloak. 21 She said to herself, "If I only touch his cloak, I will be healed." 22 Jesus turned and saw her. "Take heart, daughter," he said, "your faith has healed you." And the woman was healed from that moment.*

Twelve years of being sick and tired came to an end one day with a simple touch. Twelve years of doctors appointments and isolation were finished when a woman believed that if she simply touched Jesus' garment, He would heal her. She had suffered physically by bleeding, but she had also suffered emotionally. She was constantly 'ceremonially unclean' due to her constant bleeding. It meant she could rarely, if ever, participate in the normal worship routines with the others.

God rewards faith. She wholeheartedly knew that Jesus could and would send His healing power through her body if she could only touch Him. The day came. Nervously she prepared to follow through with her plan. As Jesus walked down a crowded street, she pressed through the crowd and touched Him.

She immediately felt power go through her. From head to toe she was healed. But to her great dismay, Jesus stopped. He wanted to know who touched Him. His disciples didn't understand the question. People were packed all around Him. He had been touched by dozens. But Jesus knew one touch had been the touch of expectancy.

One touch had been the touch of faith. When Jesus met her, He told her that her faith had healed her.

James 4:8 *come near to God and he will come near to you…* Whenever we decide to look to God for our answers, He responds. The woman in our story understood that the only One who could help her was the Lord. She initiated a plan to touch Him. Her faith drove her to action. And as she touched Him, He transformed her.

Do you have a plan to draw near to God today? Are you praying? Do you really believe that God has the power to deal with whatever circumstance confronts you? Put all your faith in Him. Draw near to Him. He still responds to the touch of faith.

Point: Jesus responds to faith.

Prayer: Lord, thank you for this woman's experience with You. Please allow me to put all my faith in you and to take action accordingly.

Practice: What action can you add to your faith today?

Today's Reading:
1Chronicles 8-9; Hebrews 4-5

139

May 20

How Do We Know The Truth?
By Scott Kalevik

1 John 5:20 We know also that the Son of God has come and has given us understanding, so that we may know him who is true. And we are in him who is true—even in his Son Jesus Christ. He is the true God and eternal life.

Ever asked the big questions? "Why are we here?" "Where did all this come from?" "What's the meaning of life?" "Do I have a purpose?" Some say there are no answers to these questions. Others make up their own answers. But God, in His love for us, has given us true answers. He has told us the truth about life by telling us the truth about Himself. When God shows us Who He is, and what He's done, and what He wants, He is telling us the truth about this life and the life to come.

God has shown Himself to us – and God has revealed Himself to us in many ways - through scripture, through creation, through nature, through our consciences, through fulfilled prophecy, through angels, through dreams, through visions, through appearances, through history, and, greatest of all, God has told us about Himself through the coming of His Son, Jesus.

Read today's verse again, please. Notice how many times John refers to truth in today's passage. It is God's desire that we understand what's true about life. In fact, John tells us how to understand. *"...the Son of God has come and has given us understanding."* Understanding truth comes through personal relationship with Jesus Christ. *"He is the true God and eternal life."*

What greater quest could you and I embark on than to know the truth about life? We dare not put our trust in things that God has not promised. We dare not fall for the lies of the devil. But if God has revealed the truth, then we can put all of our faith in it and live by it! Are you believing what's true?

Point: Truth about life is rooted in knowing Jesus Christ.
Prayer: Lord, help me make my decisions today based upon Your truth and not my opinion or the world's ideas. Give me strength to follow You.
Practice: Are you nurturing your relationship with Jesus today? How?

Today's Reading:
1Chronicles 10-12; Hebrews 6

May 21

GOD, MY FRIEND

By Beth Nelson

2 Corinthians 5:19 God was reconciling the world to himself in Christ, not counting men's sins against them.

The first man and woman who ever lived had an extraordinary relationship with God. Being made in his image, God spoke and they could understand. They could share anything with him and not feel judged. God loved spending time with them and they loved being with God. For Adam and Eve, it was exhilarating. They felt ALIVE.

But this joyful friendship ended one day when man and woman sinned. God didn't swoop down and zap them when they sinned. Satan planted fear in their hearts so that the first thing they did was to run behind some trees and try to hide from God. Satan no doubt whispered to them that they were so bad that God couldn't be their friend anymore; that He only loved them when they were perfect.

And people have been afraid of God ever since. Sin clouds our thinking. Because we don't take the time to find out for ourselves, we continue to believe lies about God. We believe the current thinking that he's aloof from the world he created; that he doesn't care about people when they suffer; that he doesn't love us because he's too busy being angry with us.

But God longs to have the friendship with us that he had with the first man and woman. Though we as people moved away from him, he initiated a plan to reach out to us and bring us back as his friend. Jesus came willingly to the earth to live with sinful, suffering people just like you and me. In his short life here on the earth, he lived a life of compassion, tenderness and love for the people that he had created. He even took the punishment that we deserved for all of our sins, so that all we would have to do would be to reach out to him and invite him into our lives. In some of his final words to his disciples, he says that he no longer calls them servants, but friends (Jn 15:14-15). Would you like to know that you are Jesus' friend? It doesn't take perfection. Just step out from whatever your "tree" is and reach out to God.

Point: Admit your fears to God. Ask him to help you so that you can experience the joy and peace and comfort that come from friendship with him.

Today's Reading:
1Chronicles 13-14; Hebrews 7-8

May 22

Believe The Truth

By Scott Kalevik

Mark 12:24 *Jesus replied, "Are you not in error because you do not know the Scriptures or the power of God?*

When I was a child somebody told me the moon was made of green cheese. At the time I had no information available to me to prove them wrong. I'd never been to the moon. It didn't really look green to me, but it could be. Ah, but then Neil Armstrong took one small step for man and, even as a child, I believed that the moon was made of rocks – not green cheese. Although I still haven't been to the moon to see for myself, I put my faith in what Neil Armstrong claimed because his was a credible claim. He told the truth with evidence.

I have a choice. Even though Mr. Armstrong brought rocks back from the moon, I can still choose to believe that the moon is made of green cheese. I can believe it sincerely. I can be earnest and tell others. But no matter how much earnestness and sincerity I muster, I'm wrong. The truth doesn't support my belief. My belief is false.

People all over the world believe a whole range of things about God and spirituality. But all of those beliefs cannot all be true. It can't be the case, for instance, that Jesus' is the only way to God (as He claimed, Jn. 14:6), and that the popular belief that any road leads to heaven are both true. Simple logic dictates that at least one of those beliefs is false. And, although someone may be sincere and earnest about his or her belief, if the belief is not true, eternity is at stake.

Jesus confronted the Sadducees one day. They didn't believe that people arose to life after death. Jesus doesn't comfort them and tell them that if they are sincere and earnest, everything will be fine. No! Jesus tells them that what they believe is false. They are badly mistaken because they do not know the Scriptures. They are badly mistaken because they do not know the power of God.

Knowing God's Word and knowing God's power is where truth is found. As we examine what we believe, we must continually ask ourselves, "Is what I believe true?" In other words, have we believed God's Word? This requires honest, diligent effort and study.

Jesus said He is the truth: Jn 14:6 *Jesus answered, "I am the way and the truth and the life. No one comes to the Father except through me.* There is more than enough credible evidence to support His claim. Believe the truth.

Today's Reading:
1Chronicles 15-17; Hebrews 9

May 23

THEY SAID IT WOULDN'T LAST!
By Peggy Kalevik

Matthew 5:18 *I tell you the truth, until heaven and earth disappear, not the smallest letter, not the least stroke of a pen, will by any means disappear from the Law until everything is accomplished.*

Even the great scholar Gamaliel thought that nothing would come of this new "Way" if they just left the apostles alone. He told his fellow Pharisees to consider carefully what they were doing in trying to punish or execute the apostles for their evangelical efforts. He reminded them that there had been others like Theudas and Judas who had appeared and gathered a great number of people around them to bring about a new way, belief, or just plain revolt. In time these men were killed and their followers were scattered. *"Leave these men alone! Let them go! For if their purpose or activity is of human origin, it will fail. But if it is from God, you will not be able to stop these men; you will only find yourselves fighting against God."* (Acts 5:38-39)

Gamaliel was right about one thing, you can not stop the power of God. In today's scripture, Jesus is confirming the authority of the Old Testament even down to the smallest individual stroke of the Hebrew language. He has the utmost respect and regard for the entirety of the Old Testament Scriptures. And to top it off He assured everyone listening that it will endure forever. He tells them that until heaven and earth disappear and the entire purpose of all that is prophesied in the Scriptures comes to past, not one single stroke of the pen will disappear. Jesus is telling His listeners that God has already revealed His salvation or redemptive power in the Old Testament. That in him is God's fulfillment and accomplishment of the Old Testament prophesies. Jesus is the introduction of God's eschatological Kingdom; and God will one day complete that kingdom. God is from everlasting to everlasting; His word will live for ever. No man can stand against Him. He is unstoppable!

Point: God reveals His power, purposes, wisdom and presence again and again in His word.

Prayer: Great is Your Word O LORD! Your kingdom is an everlasting kingdom, and Your dominion is from generation to generation. (Dan 4:3)

Practice: Research the word Eschatology

Today's Reading:
1Chronicles 18-19; Hebrews 10-11

May 24

His Majesty and Glory

By Peggy Kalevik

Psalm 8:1 *O LORD, our Lord, how majestic is your name in all the earth! You have set your glory above the heavens.*

How majestic is Your name; Your name O LORD speaks of Your power and strength, mercy, kindness and love. The Lord has displayed His glory in the heavens and on the earth. We can only bow in reverent awe.

Consider that an all powerful God has taken the time and power to create such a complete and beautiful environment for man, whom He also created. Why? Did He do it just because He loves us? Did He do it because He wanted us to understand who He is? Our Father, the creator God, made us ruler over all the works of His hands and gave us dominion over all living creatures on the earth. We rule as His partners, we must look to Him for guidance and wisdom. We are not alone as rulers of the universe; we must depend on Him, obey His will and submit to His Lordship in all things.

The purpose of this Psalm is to praise God for His creation. It is a "hymn of creation praise". It is not an expression of worship or joy in creation apart from God; instead it praises God as the good Father, creator, ruler and sustainer of the universe. This Psalm exalts God as the Redeemer King of Israel. It praises Him for the works of His hands, His glory is established and no one can overpower Him. We worship and adore Him, not His creation, but in this creation we see His great power, majesty, glory and His dominion. His creation offers conclusive proof of His existence. Who can set the sun and moon in the sky? Who brings the rain and the snow? What man or woman can hold back the ocean if it decides to overflow? Praise His glorious name!

Point: Our God is God!! How majestic is His name in all the earth!

Prayer: Father, we bless Your name, we give you all the glory, for You alone are worthy of glory and all praise.

Today's Reading:
1Chronicles 20-22; Hebrews 12

May 25

TIME

By Beth Nelson

Luke 10:41-42 *"Martha, Martha," the Lord answered, "You are worried and upset about many things, but only one thing is needed. Mary has chosen what is better and it will not be taken away from her."*

Have you ever heard the phrase, "How do children spell love? Children spell love 't-i-m-e'." Children need us to form relationships with them, and to do that requires our time. Isn't that true of any relationship? When my (future) husband and I were dating, we spent as much time together as possible – almost every day and every evening. And as we spent that time getting to know each other, we formed a solid relationship that our love was built on.

Because God is a person, the only way to get to know him is to spend time with him. A few years ago, Robert Foster wrote a booklet entitled, *7 Minutes with God*. Since most of us lead very busy, even hectic lives, we feel that we don't have any extra time to spend reading the Bible or talking to God. I've felt like that many times in my life. So when my children were young, I often set my alarm to go off before anyone got up; then before I did anything else, I sat down with my Bible and asked God to speak to me and to help me with my day. God met me and poured his truth and love into my heart, even if I only had 7 minutes.

Mary and Martha ran a busy household. Martha was so hospitable that she invited Jesus and his disciples to come and stay with her. It required a lot of work to get everything ready. Instead of helping her sister, Mary took the time to sit still and listen to the Lord. I can't imagine ignoring my sister as she frantically bustles around with all of the preparations! Yet Jesus said that Mary had made a better choice in how she spent her time than Martha. With my earthly eyes, it doesn't make sense. However, from God's point of view, what he has to share with us outlasts this moment. It warms our hearts and enlightens our minds long after the last piece of pie has been eaten. The time we spend with him literally carries our souls to heaven.

Point: If only we would long for love like children. Then perhaps we would think twice about taking on another thing, and instead, set aside some time to be with the lover of our souls. What we gain there can never be taken away from us.

Today's Reading:
1Chronicles 23-24; Hebrews 13-James 1

May 26

Victorious Kingship

By Peggy Kalevik

Psalm 29:3-4 *The voice of the LORD is over the waters; the God of glory thunders, the LORD thunders over the mighty waters. 4 The voice of the LORD is powerful; the voice of the LORD is majestic.*

In this Psalm of praise to the king of creation, the Lord of the entire universe, the Psalmist focuses on the rule and power of God over all known forces of creation. He praises His victory, His power and His redemptive ability. The Lord has triumphed over all his foes. He has made known His omnipotence, and omnipresence. Our God is sovereign over all the forces of the earth, the universe!

As a child, I remember seeing pictures of the mushroom cloud that was the result of the first explosion of the atomic bomb over the desert in New Mexico in 1945. It was horrifying to read of its devastating power, how it had the potential to kill all life for 100 miles around the site of the explosion. I had never heard of such a bomb or anything that had such great power. Many years later I learned that the code name for the project was "Trinity". How ironic, who thought of that? It's as though we try to mock God with the knowledge He gave us.

Even the great power of the atomic bomb pales in comparison to our God, whose power is much greater. He created the universe that this bomb has the power to destroy. He created the men who created the bomb and all its components. And He gave them the wisdom and understanding to put it together. How much more in awe should we be of our LORD! And why did He allow man to create such a thing? We may never know the answer to that question but we can rest in the fact that He is still more powerful than that bomb and anything else in our universe. Isaiah 40:13 sums it up for us, *"who has understood the mind [or spirit] of the LORD, or instructed him as his counselor?"* This is a question we can answer with a resounding "no one".

Point: To whom can we compare the Lord? Because of His great power and strength all of the earth holds together and not one star is out of place.

Prayer: There is none like You, O LORD! No one else has the power or love to do what You do. LORD, we thank You!

Today's Reading:
1Chronicles 25-27; James 2

146

May 27

God Moves His People
By Beth Nelson

1 Chronicles 28:9 *for the Lord searches every heart and understands every motive behind the thoughts. If you seek him, he will be found by you;*

God wants for us to find him. So if you're searching for God, he'll use any means necessary to reach back to you. My friend Lisa was living in a troubled marriage. Her husband was an alcoholic; they had three children and one on the way. She began studying Mormonism in an attempt to find answers for her life. Then one day, a Christian woman moved into the house across the street where they lived. The Lord spoke to her and told her, "You have something that Lisa needs." So she brought some cookies over and introduced herself. God used that neighbor to show Lisa that God wanted to be her friend, to be let into her heart and life so that he could help her through those hard times. Lisa became a Christian, and her spirit-filled life has overflowed to many, many others around her.

There's a similar story recorded in Acts 17. The people of Athens were searching for answers to the questions of life. It says that all of the people living there spent their time discussing the latest ideas. They were obsessed with worshipping and had many, many idols, yet still thought that they may have left some unnamed one out.

God must have seen their hearts because right at this time, Paul made a stop in Athens while he waited for some friends to join him. Seeing all of the idols troubled him so he struck up conversations with some of the people there. As he told them about the one true God, God brought him to people that were truly searching and a number of believers were born into the kingdom that day. Was this by chance? I don't think so. For when a soul is seeking, God delights in being found by them.

Sometimes in our ignorance, we don't even know what we need. We only know that we are needy. It is in those dark times of need, when we cry out to God, that he moves heaven and earth and even his own people to come to us.

Point: Never underestimate the power of God to reach even one hungry soul that reaches out to him.

Today's Reading:
1Chronicles 28-29; James 3-4

May 28

STRIKE THE SHEPHERD AND THE SHEEP WILL SCATTER

By Peggy Kalevik

Zechariah 13:7 *"Awake, O sword, against my shepherd, against the man who is close to me"! declares the LORD Almighty. "Strike the shepherd, and the sheep will be scattered, and I will turn my hand against the little ones."*

Zechariah takes us to a time when all of the followers of the Messiah will fall away, scattered because the Shepherd is rejected by his people. To understand this oracle we must go to the striking down of the Shepherd in Matthew 26. All the disciples are scattered because Jesus is arrested and crucified. We remember Gamaliel' words from Act chapter 5: *"In time these men were killed and their followers were scattered."* Gamaliel was concerned with the current situation which he and the Pharisees were trying to resolve. But our passage for today has eternal significance.

In Matthew 26 Jesus quotes from Zechariah's oracle. He knows that the disciples are going to abandon him and although it is a very human irresponsible thing to do God knew that they would. Even this failure is not outside the great plan of our God. It is part of His plan. Zechariah's oracle pictures most of the followers (sheep) perishing, but one third are left, and after being refined they will become God's people. God has a plan that is so great it contains room for our failures. If this quoting of Zechariah by Jesus assumes this scattering of His disciples as the fulfillment of Zechariah's oracle then the disciples may well be a part of the scattered sheep who will be Gods people. And they may also be part of the one third who will survive. If they are Zechariah says in verse 9 - *This third I will bring into the fire; I will refine them like silver and test them like gold. They will call on my name and I will answer them; I will say, 'They are my people,' and they will say, 'The LORD is our God.'"* Most amazing in all of this is that it is the hand of God that wields the sword that strikes the Shepherd down, because that too is part of His great plan. If he is not stroke down how will he be lifted up?

Point: From among the fallen He redeems His people; The LORD will purify and refine His people.

Prayer: Father, You are an awesome God. Even when we fail You, You do not abandon us. Blessed be Your name O LORD!

Today's Reading:
2Chronicles 1-3; James 5

May 29

SPECIAL MESSENGERS

By Beth Nelson

Hebrews 1:14 *Are not all angels ministering spirits sent
to serve those who will inherit salvation?*

The Bible tells a lot of stories about people that were visited by angels. Many times they brought special messages from God. God sent an angel to Zechariah to tell him that his barren wife would become pregnant with a son - a son who would be used by God to turn the hearts of the people toward the Lord; God sent an angel to Mary to tell her that she would miraculously bear a child that would be called the Son of the Most High; God sent an angel to John to show him what was soon to take place. And John recorded all that the angel revealed to him in the book of Revelation.

Angels are more active today than we may think. When I was reading the book, Jesus and the Eskimo, I was surprised to read the following story. Around 1887 in a remote village in Alaska, an angel appeared to a young Eskimo couple. They had become very unhappy with the oppressive, controlling shamans of their village. Though they had no contact with the outside world, they wondered if there was a better way to live. Suddenly a very bright, robed man appeared in the room near them. He spoke to them and said that soon someone would be coming to tell them about "the father of us all. " A few weeks later, a man traveling by dog team, arrived in their village and told them about Jesus. Realizing that this must be the message that the angel had relayed to them, they gladly gave their lives to Christ. They and their family became missionaries to their own people. Eventually more Christians arrived to continue the work of spreading the gospel and 60 years later, my parents also went to Western Alaska to continue the work that God had begun there many years before, the work that had started with the message of the angel.

Have you seen an angel? I haven't, or at least I don't think that I have. But I believe that they're all around us; beings sent by God to minister to his people, and sometimes to bring special messages straight from the heart of God.

Today's Reading:
2Chronicles 4-5; 1Peter 1-2

May 30

A Spirit of Wisdom and Revelation
By Peggy Kalevik

Ephesians 1:17 *I keep asking that the God of our Lord Jesus Christ, the glorious Father, may give you the Spirit of wisdom and revelation, so that you may know him better.*

Paul intercedes for the followers of Christ in Ephesus. He prays for their continued growth in Christ; that they may get to know Him in a deeper more meaningful personal relationship. Paul is teaching us that we need to intercede on behalf of our brothers and sisters in Christ. Christ is the focus of our faith, and that faith in Christ is expressed in love towards others.

Galatians 5:6b tells us that *"The only thing that counts is faith expressing itself through love."* Faith is not simply intellectual conviction. True faith is rooted in the love of God and that love being expressed in our actions and interactions with everyone we come in contact with. When we pray for our brothers and sisters in the faith we lift them up before the Father by name. We pray for wisdom and understanding, for God's revelation in their lives. Paul gives us a list of things that he prays will be accomplished in these believers and this is why he prays for them. He wants them to know Christ. He prays that: 1. they be given the Spirit of wisdom and revelation (insight and discernment); 2. The eyes of their heart may be enlightened (inner awareness from the Holy Spirit); 3. They may know the hope to which he has called them (the "blessed hope" of eternal glory); 4. That they receive the riches of his glorious inheritance promised to all the saints (an inheritance in heaven); and 5) His incomparable great power for us who believe (the power of God as directed toward and/or on behalf of believers).

When we pray for members of the body of Christ we should pray in a manner that is in accord with the will of God. If we pray for someone in a way that is not in line with the word of God we pray in vain. We must not let our prayers be worldly centered. God reveals Himself to us and others through our Christian experience in this way.

Point: Our prayers reflect our understanding and wisdom of God. Are you praying for believers?

Prayer: Teach me, O LORD, give me understanding, that I may obey Your will.

Practice: Pray in faith believing that God is able to do all that He says He will.

Today's Reading:
2Chronicles 6-8; 1Peter 3

May 31

Staying Alive!
By Scott Kalevik

Matthew 4:4 Jesus answered, "It is written: 'Man does not live on bread alone, but on every word that comes from the mouth of God.'"

Jesus had been without food for 40 days when He rebuffed Satan with these words. The gnawing pain of hunger must have been intense. Satan uses the occasion to tempt Jesus. Satan tries to get Jesus to make bread out of stones. What's wrong with that if you're really hungry and you have the power to change stones into bread? A guy's got to eat doesn't he?

Jesus understands the root of this temptation: He is being asked to rely on Himself and His own strength instead of relying on His Father's provision. He refuses to sin against the Father in this way. Instead, Jesus quotes Deuteronomy 8:3 where the Israelites are reminded that God provided manna from heaven for them when they were hungry as they wandered in the desert.

Jesus basically tells Satan that eating is not what actually sustains life. God's word gives life. Think about that for a minute or two! Sure, we need to eat to live, but eating cannot create or give life. It can only maintain life. Any hospice worker can tell you that a terminally ill patient can eat bread all day and still die from an illness. Bread doesn't give life. Bread won't defeat an illness. Bread will simply maintain life that is already there.

The point? We live and die according to God's word. He gives life. He sustains life. He gives us bread so that we can maintain the life He's given. His word is more important than food when it comes to staying alive.

Point: God's word gives life. Food simply maintains life.
Prayer: Father, help me understand the absolute necessity of your word in my life.
Practice: Study, study, study God's word. Need help? Attend a local Bible Study!

Today's Reading:
2Chronicles 9-10; 1Peter 4-5

June 1

READER BEWARE!

By Scott Kalevik

Hebrews 4:12 *For the word of God is living and active. Sharper than any double-edged sword, it penetrates even to dividing soul and spirit, joints and marrow; it judges the thoughts and attitudes of the heart.*

Most read the Bible to learn about God. The Bible tells about God's love for us and about how He sent His son Jesus to die for our sins. The Bible helps us understand the grace, mercy, and compassion of God. The Bible also tells about the history of His people and how God accomplished His plan of salvation. But the Bible does more than these things.

When we honestly read what God has said in His word, something happens to us. It's like the giant light of truth and righteousness shines down on our lives and examines us. The writer of Hebrews tells us that God's word is alive. It's active. In other words, we can't read it without being actively confronted by the truth it contains. It challenges us to live in a way that God has declared pleasing.

The Bible penetrates its reader like a double-edged sword. God's word evaluates our thoughts, attitudes, and lifestyles to tell us whether we are living obediently to His truth. In other words, while it's true that the Bible teaches us about God, it's also true that the Bible teaches us about ourselves.

For example, the Bible tells me I need to confess my sin to God. If I have confessed and repented of my sin, I experience peace, forgiveness, rest, and gratitude to God as I read. However, if I refuse to admit and confess my sin before God, I experience fear, guilt or a sense of dread when I read the Bible. As King David wrote: Ps 32:2 *Blessed is the man whose sin the LORD does not count against him and in whose spirit is no deceit. 3 When I kept silent, my bones wasted away through my groaning all day long. 4 For day and night your hand was heavy upon me; my strength was sapped as in the heat of summer. Selah* David knew about the double edged sword of God's word.

Reader beware! Each day you open your Bible to learn about God, God will be opening your heart to shine the truth of His word into your life and let you know where it is you need to change to conform to His will. No need to fear. Obey and experience the joy of a clear conscience as you follow the Lord!

Today's Reading:
2Chronicles 11-13; 2Peter 1

June 2

TEACH ME, O LORD

By Peggy Kalevik

Romans 15:4 *For everything that was written in the past was written to teach us, so that through endurance and the encouragement of the Scriptures we might have hope.*

As we read the Bible we see that Ezra wasn't alone in his desire to study the scriptures. Daniel read about the coming desolation of the Temple in Jerusalem, and Paul used the scripture as a legal defense to prove the case for Christ. Paul is making it clear to his students that the main purpose of the scripture is to instruct, to give us understanding that will strengthen us and get us through life's journey.

Not surprisingly Jesus loves to quote the scriptures; He uses it as a sword, as comfort, and to disarm His foes. He understands all that is written in it and shows us that we are to live by it and through it. It is His greatest teaching tool; He uses the parables to unfold the mysteries of God to us. The Scriptures were meant to teach us, to mold us, to bring conviction, to give us comfort and encouragement.

The Scriptures teach us how to worship and praise God, they give us the strength to endure, to continue on when we face the impossible. When we are at our lowest it seems that the scripture has the power to lift us up. We can read them and see that God's people have endured hardships that we can not fathom. We know that we have not yet shade our blood as Jesus did for us, so we can keep on keeping on. We can make it because Jesus has died that we might live. Praise be unto God, that He left His word for us, praise be unto God! *Your word is a lamp to my feet and a light for my path.* (Ps 119:105)

Point: If teaching God's Word is your passion, study the Bible diligently and pray for God's guidance. God will bless the heart that truly wants to teach His people.

Prayer: Teach me, O LORD, to follow your path; then I will follow to the end.

Practice: Don't be discouraged by the enormity of the Bible, there are many tools to help deepen your understanding of the Word. Get a good reference book, attend a Bible Study and spend more time studying on your own.

Today's Reading:
2Chronicles 14-15; 2Peter 2-3

June 3

The Glue That Keeps Us Together

By Herb Hubbard

Ephesians 4:2-3 *Be completely humble and gentle; be patient, bearing with one another in love. 3 Make every effort to keep the unity of the Spirit through the bond of peace.*

In high school I had a shop teacher. His name was Crane Biberstein. He had a very demanding way of teaching. He expected nothing but the best from each and everyone of his students. One of the first things he taught us was the various tools used in wood working. His favorite saying was "Everything has a place and everything in its place".

He also taught the proper techinques for working with wood. One of the areas was wood preparation particulariry if the wood was going to be bonded to another piece by using wood glue. Each piece had to be straight and clean with a good smooth edge which usually required sanding which I didn't like to do. So I would do as little as possible and then try to make up for it with extra glue. The results always showed my lack of discipline. Glue drips would be evident from overuse and gaps would show because the pieces were not properly fitted together.

Today's text tells us to make every effort to keep the unity of the Spirit through the bond of peace. And like a good teacher, Paul gives us the tools to do that. By being completely humble, gentle, patient, bearing with one another in love. That may sound easy but just like bonding two pieces of wood together both pieces have to be smooth and prepared before the bond can set and hold them firmly together. When we struggle with fellow believers in the area of unity of the Spirit we should always make sure we are doing our part of being humble, gentle and patient bearing with one another in love so the bond of peace will hold fast.

Point: We have to do our part to ensure the unity of the Spirit

Prayer: Lord help me to demonstrate the bond of peace in my life as I deal with others.

Practice: Look at your attitudes towards others, check for humbleness and gentleness and patience.

Today's Reading:
2Chronicles 16-18; 1John 1

June 4

WHERE WOULD WE BE?

By Beth Nelson

Hebrews 9:14 *How much more, then, will the blood of Christ, who through the eternal Spirit offered himself unblemished to God, cleanse our consciences from acts that lead to death, so that we may serve the living God!*

If Jesus had not come, we would still be dead in our sins.

If Jesus had not come, we would be loaded down with guilt.

If Jesus had not come, we would be serving ourselves and Satan.

The truth is, we would be lost, confused, and damned if Jesus had not come.

BUT because Jesus came, his life, death and resurrection hold the power to make us alive and to free us from all sin.

Because Jesus came he frees us from all guilt. Our burdens of guilt and shame are taken away.

Because Jesus came, the way has been provided for us to serve the living God.

Praise be to God for his awesome and unspeakable gift! We are no longer estranged from God, but are brought near by the blood of Christ. Let us now humbly and gratefully serve the living God!

Today's Reading:
2Chronicles 19-20; 1John 2-3

June 5

TRUTH AND FREEDOM
By Beth Nelson

John 18:37b&c *"for this reason I was born, and for this I came into the world, to testify to the truth. Everyone on the side of truth listens to me." "What is truth?" Pilate asked.*

"What is truth?" is a question we should all be asking. Many countries only allow their citizens to be exposed to one "truth," whether it's Hinduism, Islam, or atheism. In the United States we are blessed in that we are free to learn about any religion under the sun. But in a country where we have such freedoms, do we really take advantage of our freedom to learn more about truth?

John declared that Jesus was full of grace and truth. Jesus himself said, "I am the way, and the truth and the life."

It is ironic that in a country where we have incomparable personal freedom, Satan is working hard to put us and to put our children in prisons. Prisons of the mind, of our emotions, of our behavior. Once there, we have great difficulty breaking free on our own.

Jesus shows us the way out of our prisons. He says that if we hold to his teaching, we will know the truth, and it is the truth that will set us free. He alone has the power to free us from our bondage.

Do you have something that you're struggling to be free of? Immerse yourself in God's truth. Learn as much as you can. Obey what he teaches you. Draw near to the Savior and trust Him to set you free!

Point: Jesus alone is the Truth

Prayer: Dear Jesus, I ask you to reach in to my life and to free me from this prison that I find myself in. I cannot do it by myself. I want to follow you. Help me in my weakness.

Practice: As we are honest and truthful about ourselves, and ask the Lord for help, He can free us.

Today's Reading:
2Chronicles 21-23; 1John 4

June 6

JESUS AND THE HEART OF GOD
By Beth Nelson

Luke 19:10 *For the Son of Man came to seek and to save that which was lost.*

What is on God's heart? The lost world. He has paid the ultimate price to bring the lost world back to him – coming to the earth as a man, Jesus, living like us, loving us and dying for us. All so that we would come back to Him. And so that we would turn around and invite our brother to come to Him, too.

God the Father, full of compassion, sent Jesus, knowing that without Him we are without hope, without direction, lost. He came as a shepherd, looking for that one sheep that had wandered away and was lost. He came as a father whose heart is still full of love and pity for the son who had turned his back on him and on all that he stood for.

Today he earnestly seeks lost souls all around the world, precious souls that will come to him. Every man, woman and child, is equally precious in his sight. This is difficult for us to understand because it includes not only every Martin Luther King, Jr. and Billy Graham out there, but every jihadist, every molester, everyone who plots murder. And just as Jesus so loved the world, we his "found" children are to love the world just like he did. It is love that draws the lost person to the Lord. It is love that brings a spark of hope to a hopeless world. It is love that changes things. All of our well-intentioned programs will not bring about change that will last. It is only when God places a lost soul in our life and then pours His love through us into that person, that real and permanent change begins to take place.

The heart of God has not changed. Jesus is the only hope for the lost world. Let us allow the love of the Father to open our eyes to the lost ones around us. Then let us be his hands, his feet, his words that will love that lost one to Him.

The last words of Jesus: "Go and make disciples of all nations…and surely I am with you always."

We are not doing any of this alone. God the Father is working all around us. The Spirit is drawing people to God. Ask God to open your eyes to see the lost souls in your life. Then have courage and speak the good news to that person. Jesus is with you.

Today's Reading:
2Chronicles 24-25; 1John 5-2John

June 7

Jesus, Full of Grace
By Beth Nelson

John 1:14, 16-17 The Word became flesh and made his dwelling among us. We have seen his glory, the glory of the One and Only, who came from the Father, full of grace and truth...From the fullness of his grace we have all received one blessing after another.

Imagine living with someone who treats you with unlimited kindness and mercy even when you don't deserve it. John, the man who wrote these words, did live with just such a person. The words, "full of grace and truth" weren't empty words. John was fully and continually washed clean by the grace and mercy of Jesus, day after day after day. The grace of Jesus flowed like a continuous cleansing stream to the people that lived with him.

The truth is, as Christians we do live with this same person. We hold Jesus in our very hearts and minds as he walks with us in our daily lives. His kindness and mercy wash over us continually whenever we go to him. And oh how I need it! Oh how you need it! There is nothing so freeing, so exhilarating, so rejuvenating as knowing that God accepts us and loves us just as we are. So often I beat myself up, or worse yet, try to justify and rationalize my sins rather than seeking his kindness, mercy and forgiveness.

When is the last time you felt the forgiveness of God flood over you like a fresh rain, a cleansing baptism, bringing joy to your heart? He's longing to wash us clean, to lavish blessing after blessing on us, as John wrote. When we are honest about ourselves with God, letting go of fear and drawing near to him, we will be washed, cleansed, filled up with blessings.

The songwriter/singer Todd Agnew no doubt had experienced the grace of the Lord when he wrote these lyrics, "Hallelujah! Grace like rain falls down on me. Hallelujah! All my stains are washed away, washed away." (from Grace Like Rain)

Point: Jesus lived a life full of grace and truth.
Prayer: We bow before you . Thank you for giving us your grace in unending measure. We are so undeserving of it.

Today's Reading:
2Chronicles 26-28; 3John

June 8

JESUS THE CREATOR

By Beth Nelson

John 1:2, 3 He was with God in the beginning, … and through him all things were made. Heb 1:2 ..in these last days he has spoken to us by his Son, whom he appointed heir of all things, and through whom he made the universe.

The Bible is clear that one of the attributes of the Son of God is his creativity. A number of scriptures refer to Jesus as the creator of the universe. Col 1:16 says that *"by him all things were created; things in heaven and on earth, visible and invisible whether thrones or powers or rulers or authorities; all things were created by him and for him."*

The Genesis account of creation displays a methodical, intelligent, well thought-out process. It's not random or sloppy, but shows a creation that's arrived at by stages. And at each stage, throughout the whole process, God the Son surveys what he has done, evaluates it and when it satisfies him, the scripture says over and over, "And God saw that it was good."

Scripture is also clear that man and woman, being made in God's image, have the same capacity for creativity. In fact, in Gen 2:19-20, God incorporates man into the creative process. He brings each animal and bird to Adam to see what he would name it and whatever he called it, that was its name. Adam's very first task is to use his God-given creativity and to name these creatures. And through the following centuries, mankind has continued to create; sometimes out of necessity, sometimes simply for the joy of creating or of expressing a God-given talent or gift. We don't often see the creative process as a spiritual act of worship. But whenever we create, we are expressing an aspect of God.

I believe that when the Spirit of God gives us a desire to create, that we should not ignore it. Realize that God has gifted you so that you can bless others. Give your efforts to God. Ask him to make these creative offerings shine for his glory and to use them to expand the kingdom of God on this earth. Since our Creator God made you, he will bring it about.

Point: Just as Jesus created us, we have the capacity to create in ways that are specific to us.

Prayer: Dear God, thank you for this gift you've given me.

Practice: Ask God to make it shine and to use it for His glory.

Today's Reading:
2Chronicles 29-30; Jude-Revelation 1

June 9

Jesus the Revolutionary
By Beth Nelson

Matthew 10:38-39 "..anyone who does not take his cross and follow me is not worthy of me. Whoever finds his life will lose it, and whoever loses his life for my sake will find it."

In our current culture, there's not much to really get excited about. Not much that we'd be willing to die for. Contrast that with the life Jesus urges us to be willing to live. God wants to grab us and infuse us with a vision for the work that he's doing, equip us with armor and with the Spirit, then unleash us to do the improbable and impossible.

Jesus was the ultimate example of conviction, confidence and courage. He was fearless. Jesus locked horns with the Jewish officials, those highly feared and respected leaders of their day. No one else dared to cross them. Jesus called the Pharisees an evil bunch of snakes. (Matt.12:34) He socialized with prostitutes and known sinners. Coming upon some self-righteous men gathered to stone a woman caught in adultery, he dismissed the stone-throwers and gently restored the woman's conscience and dignity. He didn't care what people thought about him or said about him because he was very clear about his mission.

Jesus said that if there is anything keeping us from being sold out to him, to get rid of it, give it away, cut it off, then come and follow Him. Following Him might mean not having a place to call your own. Following the call of God is more important and long-lasting and far more exciting than any earthly pursuits.

We need to understand and embrace the whole truth about who Jesus was. His life was anything but boring. And he invites us to join with Him in advancing the kingdom. But we do need to count the cost, for He asks nothing less than that we lose our lives for his sake. But what we gain is far greater than anything that we can imagine.

Point: We often only emphasize the meek and mild Jesus who came to love us and forgive us. The truth is, he was this but so much more. He was a true revolutionary, a man of ultimate conviction who knew exactly what God wanted Him to do.

Today's Reading:
2Chronicles 31-33; Revelation 2

June 10

JESUS IS GOD

By Beth Nelson

John 14:10 *I am in the Father and the Father is in me.*

Have you ever wondered what God is like? Though we can never fully understand or know God, if we learn who Jesus Christ was, we also learn about God. For God the Son is the very expression of God the Father. At one point some Jews asked Jesus, "Who are you? Tell us plainly."

He replied, "I am God's Son, the one whom the Father set apart and sent into the world. The Father is in me and I in the Father." And again, "I and the Father are one."

And why did God the Son come to the earth? 1) To reveal to us God the Father. For he was not simply God-like, he was God Himself. 2) To reconcile the world to Himself. In the person of Jesus, God came all the way to us for our salvation. This is a God who reaches out to us before we even seek Him.

Sometimes we Christians in America are, let's face it, ashamed to speak boldly and honestly about Jesus Christ. We easily talk about God, since "God" can mean many different things and is used by many different religions. It's more politically correct than speaking of Jesus. The person of Jesus has been divisive ever since he came.

Why do we care more about what people think of us than of what God thinks of us? Man can only kill the body. God can kill both the body and the soul. Jesus said that whoever disowns him before men, he will disown before the Father in heaven. (Mt 10:33) And later, he said, *"If anyone is ashamed of me and my words in this adulterous and sinful generation, the Son of Man will be ashamed of him when he comes in his Father's glory."* (Mk 8:38) Satan plants fear of man in our minds because he knows that Jesus is the power of God unto salvation. There is great power in the name and person of Jesus, and Satan will do all that he can to keep that knowledge from spreading.

What do we have to be ashamed of? God the Son perfectly embodied and demonstrated the love, compassion, wisdom, power and righteousness of God. What awesome truth! Let's not keep it to ourselves.

Point: Jesus is God. Jesus and God are one
Prayer: Jesus, we bow before you and we worship you as God. We thank you for showing us who God is.
Practice: Let us speak boldly the truth that Jesus Christ is God in the flesh.

Today's Reading:
2Chronicles 34-35; Revelation 3-4

June 11

Jesus is Lord

By Beth Nelson

Matthew 7:21-23 *Not everyone who says to me, 'Lord, Lord,' will enter the kingdom of heaven, but only he who does the will of my Father who is in heaven. Many will say to me on that day, 'Lord, Lord, did we not prophesy in your name, and in your name drive out demons and perform many miracles?' Then I will tell them plainly, 'I never knew you. Away from me, you evildoers!'*

I sometimes have difficulty when someone else tells me what to do. My fleshly pride rises up in indignation and false superiority. We in America pride ourselves on being fiercely independent and for the most part, we can run our own lives as we wish. That's why we often resist or conveniently gloss over the biblical teaching that not only is Jesus our Savior, but He's our Lord.

However, if we think that we're the master of our own fate, we're believing one of Satan's lies. The Bible clearly teaches that each person is a slave to something. Either to sin, which gives us pleasure for only a short time, or to righteousness. Sin is defined as being all in word, thought or deed that is contrary to the will of God. Sin ultimately disappoints and makes us fall short of the victorious life that God wants for us. Though God in his graciousness, gives us the free will to choose what path we will take, it is only for a time.

The dictionary defines "lord" as "a person who has authority, control, or power over others; master or ruler." Jesus, in the gospels, has plenty to say about how we are to conduct our lives. He also makes it crystal clear that if we love Him, we will obey his teaching. The more we give up our own lordship and bow to Him, the more God lives in us and pours his love into our lives. (Jn 14:23) If we read his words with our minds and hearts bowing to his authority over our lives, he presses us closer and closer to Himself and calls us his friend.

We do not control our own lives. We are all slaves to something. The choice is ours: either we choose to follow Jesus and to take his teachings to heart or we become slaves to sin. Come to Jesus now, bow before his lordship in your life, and he will most certainly bless you.

Point: Dear Lord, I humbly bow before you, acknowledging that my own way is sinful and leads to death. I want to embrace your teaching, for it brings blessing and leads to life. Help me in my weakness and lead me I pray. Amen.

Today's Reading:
2Chronicles 36-Ezra 1-2; Revelation 5

June 12

How To Kill Your Prayer Life!

By Scott Kalevik

Isaiah 1:15 *When you spread out your hands in prayer, I will hide my eyes from you; even if you offer many prayers, I will not listen. Your hands are full of blood;*

God is supposed to listen to us when we pray right? Then why does He inspire Isaiah to pen today's verse? The Lord is clearly telling His people that He will no longer hear them. Even if they pray a lot, the Lord is done listening to them!

What has killed their prayer life? Chapter one of Isaiah answers this question with one word: SIN! Sin shuts the ears of the Lord. But it's not just any sin. The people pretend to serve God by going through the motions of their religion yet, in their hearts, they refuse to obey His commands.

Verse two of this fascinating chapter speaks about the people rebelling against the Lord. They refuse to do what He asks. God says His people don't understand. They're loaded with guilt. Even when disciplined, they won't do right. And they've been decimated by their unwillingness to turn to the Lord.

Despite their rebellion, however, they still act religious. They attend synagogue and they sacrifice ... they have religious festivals and they pray. They go through the motions of life with God. But they will not yield their hearts to obey God.

The Lord tells them their religion stinks. He's more than just unhappy about it – it makes Him sick to see them going through the motions of religious life without loving Him enough to obey Him. He finally tells them that He will no longer listen to them when they pray. He's had enough of their hypocritical show!

The solution? Isa 1:16 *wash and make yourselves clean. Take your evil deeds out of my sight! Stop doing wrong, 17 learn to do right! Seek justice, encourage the oppressed. Defend the cause of the fatherless, plead the case of the widow.*

First, ask for forgiveness. Second, act right. Do those things God has asked and stop doing those things God hates.

Sin can shut God's ears to our prayers. But make no mistake. God's ears never close to the one who seeks His forgiveness. The Lord always graciously hears and answers the repentant sinner's prayer. No, the sin that kills a prayer life knows what the Lord asks but continually refuses Him - all the while pretending nothing is wrong.

Today's Reading:
Ezra 3-4; Revelation 6-7

June 13

THE ELEMENTS OF PRAYER: 1(A). OUR FATHER
By Peggy Kalevik

Matthew 6:9b *Our Father in heaven, hallowed be your name, (NIV)*

It was after Jesus came, that man started to think and speak of God as "Father". Other than a few occurrences in Isaiah and Malachi, the Old Testament doesn't often refer to God as "Father". Its use is simply not that common in the Old Testament. The Word implies a close, special relationship. The use of the word "Abba" was also rare. The Jews considered it to be disrespectful to God. In Mark 14:36 Jesus uses it because He held a unique place with God.

Jesus often uses the phrase "our Father" to include Himself with His disciples (and all believers). But He is particularly careful to use the phrase "your Father" when He speaks about sin or the forgiveness of sin. And we understand why - He had no sin! As He teaches this prayer to His disciples He starts with "our Father" because He intends this prayer to be prayed with others, not in solitude. It's a means of sharing the communication to God with others of the same belief; to share in the fellowship of believers.

Jesus starts the prayer by acknowledging to whom we pray, and where He resides. We're praying to our Father, God who resides in Heaven. He has transcended the earth, moon and the stars. He is independent, and exists above and apart from the material world. He is sovereign; He is the supreme authority, with supreme power, and with all knowledge. This opening also tells us the kind of God to whom we're offering the prayer. We have a special relationship with God because He is our Father; we are his children, sons and daughter. "Hallowed be your name" is not saying He will become Holy (He is Holy) but He is to be regarded and treated as Holy. We treat Him with respect and adoration.

Point: God is our Father, as such we love and adore Him, and we obey and submit to Him.

Prayer: Lord, Teach me to pray with a greater understanding of who You are and to give you the honor and respect you deserve.

Today's Reading:
Ezra 5-7; Revelation 8

June 14

THE ELEMENTS OF PRAYER: I(B).
ADORATION AND THANKSGIVING

By Peggy Kalevik

*Isaiah 63:16 but you are our Father, though Abraham does
not know us or Israel acknowledge us; you, O LORD, are our
Father, our Redeemer from of old is your name.*

In praying to "our Father" we are expressing our understanding of who God is to us; we're saying we love Him for who He is. By asking that His name be "hallowed" we thank Him. We're saying we also know what He has done and that is why we treat and regard Him as Holy. We adore and thank Him for being our Father. Isaiah says He is "our Father; our redeemer from of old is His name".

An important trait of the word Father is the implication of "a close" relationship. In Isaiah 63, as the prophet prays he pleads with God for tenderness and compassion. He prays to "our Father". Isaiah is filled with an intense awareness of the sins of God's people and His pleas are on Zion's behalf. Please note, verse 7 (the beginning of the prayer) is an acknowledgement of all that God has done for his people. Like the prayer in Matthew 6, he begins by acknowledging and thanking his "Father". He doesn't start out by making a request.

How do we adore and thank Him in prayer? We acknowledge Him, His deeds, His power, His greatness, and His holiness. We tell of His goodness to us and to others, in other words we give our testimony and thank Him for all His wonderful blessings. We acknowledge He alone is worthy of our praise. The first element of prayer as given in Matthew 6:9b is adoration and thanksgiving to God our Father.

Point: Through our praise and adoration, our testimony and thanksgiving, God, "our Father" will be glorified.

Prayer: Father we love you, we will worship and adore you. We will glorify Your name in all the earth.

Today's Reading:
Ezra 8-9; Revelation 9-10

June 15

THE ELEMENTS OF PRAYER: 2. AFFIRMATION
By Peggy Kalevik

Matthew 6:10 *Your kingdom come, your will be done on earth as it is in heaven.*

The second element of prayer as recorded in Matthew 6 is the "affirmation". In this section of the prayer we are agreeing with and submitting to God's will. We are praying God's will be done or accomplished right now on earth as it is being done right now in heaven. We are agreeing with Paul that God's will is good, pleasing and perfect (Rom 12:2). We declare His will is true, and so we submit.

When we pray for God's Kingdom to come we're asking for the extension of His sovereign rule. His Kingdom is already here, it started its journey with Jesus' ministry. It is not and will not be consummated until the end of this age. So, we are asking for the extension of His rule and the consummation of His Kingdom.

We often hear the phrase "God is sovereign" and understand it means He can do whatever He wants whenever He wants. But it means a little more than that. Its meaning includes the fact that He is self-ruling, "the" supreme authority and power, and excellence is His standard. His will not only involves His righteous requirements but also His fixed purpose to bring about certain events that will afford salvation for all those He wants to include in the salvation plan.

The prayer Jesus teaches His disciples is not just a group of words to be learned by rote with no understanding. It is a commitment of ones heart to the desires of God: "Your Kingdom come, Your will be done". Father, I give up my will for Yours, even if it hurts.

Remember these things about this section of the **Prayer:** 1) God's righteous requirements and fixed purpose be accomplished. 2) That His will be fully accomplished or done on earth as it is in heaven.

Point: Affirm and proclaim His Kingdom! May His Kingdom come and His will be done. Are you ready to enter His Kingdom?

Prayer: O God, be gracious to us and bless us, make Your face shine upon us. (Psalm 67:1)

Practice: Daniel 2:44; 7:14; Matthew 3:1-2; 4:17; 25:34.

Today's Reading:
Ezra 10-Nehemiah 1-2; Revelation 11

June 16

THE ELEMENTS OF PRAYER: 3. PETITION AND INTERCESSION

By Peggy Kalevik

Luke 11:3 *Give us each day our daily bread.*

In Exodus 16 God provides daily for His people in the wilderness. He provides physical food for the nourishment of their bodies. Here in Luke and in Matthew 6:11 Jesus may be speaking of more than simply physical nourishment for our bodies. He may be speaking of spiritual nourishment. The wording is difficult to understand because the meaning of the Greek word used for daily (*epiousios*) is obscure when translated. The NIV Lexicon records only two uses of this word in all of the New Testament: this verse in Luke of course, and the corresponding verse in Matthew 6. The word could mean "every day", or "day by day", or "for tomorrow", or "God's provision when the Kingdom comes (eschatological bread)", or maybe it means "provide sufficiently for us". In any case, Jesus is telling us to pray for our needs, not our wants. He wants us to understand we need to be dependent on God everyday. God provides what is sufficient for all our needs everyday.

Among the elements of prayer this is the place to make your request and to "intercede" on behalf of others. The Israelites trusted God for food when they were in the wilderness, they had no choice. While there is an abundance of food in America there are still people who have none. We too must trust God. If we are to survive in this world we need to obtain understanding of His word, His word is our food. This will give us strength to live a life pleasing to Him everyday until He returns to take us home.

There are many scripture verses to help you pray in this section during your own personal prayer time. I believe God loves to hear His word spoken back to Him; what better way to speak to Him than with His own words. The other benefit derived from using His word when you pray is when used correctly you know you are praying in His will. Make your prayer time more comforting and reassuring, by using God's word. It will help you to understand His will for your life. It will bring you a greater level of peace and satisfaction to know He sees your willingness to please Him. And above all, pray for your needs and not your worldly desires.

Point: Be dependent on God for everything, He provides for all your needs everyday.

Prayer: LORD, O LORD, forgive my iniquity, though it is great. Instruct me in the way You have chosen for me. (Psalm 25:11& 12)

Today's Reading:
Nehemiah 3-4; Revelation 12-13

June 17

THE ELEMENTS OF PRAYER: 4. CONFESSION
By Peggy Kalevik

Luke 11:4a *Forgive us our sins, for we also forgive everyone who sins against us.*

True confession is an earnest acknowledgement or declaration of sin to God. It is an admission of guilt, not just with the mouth but with heart and soul. We must confess our sins before we can ask God to forgive us our sin. Psalm 32 concerns thanksgiving and wisdom; in it David thanks God for His gift of forgiveness. In verse 5 He writes: *"Then I acknowledged my sin to you and did not cover up my iniquity. I said, "I will confess my transgressions to the LORD"— and you forgave the guilt of my sin."* David understands the compassion and grace of God; therefore He is willing to confess.

David notes when he kept silent about his sin, his bones wasted away; God's hand was heavy upon him. He says his strength was all gone, but when he acknowledged and confessed his sin God forgave him. If we go on to read verse 6 we can only conclude we must confess our sin. It does us no good to hide our sin from God, He already knows. And the longer we try to avoid admitting our sin to God, the longer we will suffer under the weight of guilt. Let us be quick to admit/confess when we have committed sin. God is waiting to forgive.

This verse also tells us we must forgive others when they sin against us. We have all had difficulty forgiving someone at some point in our life. We find it difficult to forgive when someone hurts us. But God expects us to forgive. In Matthew 18 Jesus tells Peter we should forgive a brother who has offended us, not seven times, but seventy-seven. Jesus is not saying we should forgive them 77 times but seventy times seven. The message is really to forgive without number or beyond measure; because we have all been forgiven more times than we will ever forgive someone else.

Point: Confess your sins to the Father and forgive your brother when he offends you. Don't allow un-confessed sin and un-forgiveness to keep your prayers from reaching the Father's heart and ear.

Prayer: *Have mercy on me, O God, according to your unfailing love; according to your great compassion blot out my transgressions.* (Ps. 51:1)

Today's Reading:
Nehemia 5-7; Revelation 14

June 18

THE ELEMENTS OF PRAYER: RENEWAL
By Peggy Kalevik

Matthew 6:13a *And lead us not into temptation, but deliver us from the evil one*

The Greek word for temptation (*peirasmos*) in this scripture can be interpreted in many ways. Its typical use is to convey temptation from the perspective of trials or testing; although, it can mean temptation from the perspective of being enticed. Jesus isn't asking God to let us avoid testing or trials. Neither is He speaking about being enticed. The Bible says we will have trials. He instead asks God to not let our escape from the trials or from the testing be too difficult to endure. Just as God can not be tempted and does not tempt us; we will not be without trials and testing. (John 16:33; 1 Peter 4:12; James 1:13-14).

The other word to understand in this verse is "deliver" (*rhyomai*). This is a simple clear cut Greek word that has two meanings, deliver and rescue and all their variations (deliverer, delivered, rescued, and rescues). Jesus is asking our Father to withhold/ spare us or "deliver" us out of any and all evil. Depending on the construction of the text preceding the word, this could mean deliver us from evil or, from the devil. But this is not necessarily about the devil or, only the devil. (Matthew 4:1-11, the writer is speaking specifically about the devil (*diabolos*), and not any evil.)

This portion of the prayer is for the renewing of our mind and spirit; to bring us back to a place of peace and right standing with Him. We're asking God to give us new life in Him or, restore our spirit to a place of peace that is pleasing to Him. Or, we're asking Him to replace our tired run-down spirit with a fresh burst of His power and energy. It seems to be something you can only ask after confessing and repenting. I don't know how He can hear this part of our prayer if we approach it with un-confessed, un-repented sin in our lives. How can we be renewed if we won't confess or repent? This is a very necessary part of the prayer. It covers a multitude of struggles in life. For Jesus told us: *"In this world you will have trouble. But take heart! I have overcome the world."*

Point: Jesus knew that we would have trials and/or face temptations, thus He taught us to pray for God's wisdom and protection in coping with them.

Prayer: Father, spread Your protection over us who love your name that we may rejoice in you.

Today's Reading:
Nehemia 8-9; Revelation 15-16

June 19

THE ELEMENTS OF PRAYER: CLOSING
By Peggy Kalevik

Matthew 6:13b *For thine is the kingdom, and the power, and the glory, forever. Amen.* (KJV, NKJV & NASB)

This final verse of what we know as the Lord's Prayer is believed to have been added by the early Church. While Bible scholars agree it is spiritually and biblically appropriate, they dispute whether this was part of the original manuscript. It was probably added to give closure to the prayer and offer praise to God.

We have become so accustomed to using this closing we would have a hard time dropping it; like so many things we have added to God's Church. However, this phrase made its way into many versions of the Bible and we know the Bible has gone through much scrutiny* to emerge in the form we enjoy today. Luke's prayer does not include this part of the verse. Even so, the commentators have not written anything beyond the fact that it was not included in the original manuscript with very few explanations of its purpose.

Most of us would agree however, it is appropriate to praise God in our prayer time. Use the words of scripture to praise Him in your prayer time. Scripture gives us many examples of the fact that God is in control of, and has all the power and the glory, forever: 1 Chronicles 29 says *"Yours, O LORD, is the greatness and the power and the glory and the majesty and the splendor, for everything in heaven and earth is yours. Yours, O LORD, is the kingdom; you are exalted as head over all."* Psalm 150 says we should praise Him for His mighty acts and His marvelous deeds. Beyond all that, we know we are dependent upon Him for our very life.

Point: He is worthy of our praise!
Prayer: Great are You, LORD, and most worthy of praise. (Psalm 48:1)

Today's Reading:
Nehemia 10-12; Revelation 17

June 20

PERSISTENT PRAYER
By Beth Nelson

Luke 18:1 *Jesus told his disciples a parable to show them that they should always pray and not give up.*

I believe that there are times when God would love to grant us the desires of our hearts, if only we would think to ask Him. Jesus said, *"Ask and you will receive, and your joy will be complete"* (Jn 16:24).

Israel's last great judge may never have been born had his mother not asked the Lord for a son. The Bible says that Hannah poured out her soul to the Lord out of her great anguish and grief. Her unusual demeanor caught the attention of Eli, the priest, and he told her that God would grant what she had asked of Him. Hannah conceived and bore a son and then gave that son back to the Lord, as she had promised.

Another person of faith, the prophet Elijah, knew first-hand of the great power of God. He wasn't afraid to called on God to act if he knew that the result would be pleasing to God. One day he prayed to God for the dead son of the widow in whose home he was living. It says that in desperation, he cried out to the Lord, *"O Lord my God, have you brought tragedy also upon this widow I am staying with, by causing her son to die?"* (1Kings 17:20) Three times he lay across the boy and cried out, *"O Lord my God, let this boy's life return to him!"* And God heard him and had compassion on them and restored the boy's life.

Do we always know that God will answer our prayers the way we want? No. There are times when God's will isn't clear, but Jesus invites, even commands us to pray about everything. David was a man after God's own heart. When his child became ill, he pleaded with God to heal his sick child, even fasting and weeping and lying on the ground; but after seven days God took the child home.

The Bible says that we don't have because we don't ask. If you know that you're asking with pure motives, ask. And ask again. Pour out your deepest desires to the Lord. It may or may not be in His will to grant your prayer, but if you don't ask, you may never know.

Point: Don't give up praying for something that God has laid on your heart. Pour out your soul to God and watch to see how He will answer.

Prayer: Dear Lord, thank you for allowing me to come to you with everything and for welcoming all of my prayers.

Today's Reading:
Nehemiah 13-Esther 1; Revelation 18-19

June 21

THE HOLY DWELLING

By Peggy Kalevik

1 Corinthians 6:19 *Do you not know that your body is a temple of the Holy Spirit, who is in you, whom you have received from God? You are not your own;*

Among the many definitions for the word temple, my favorite is "a place where something holy or divine is thought to dwell, e.g. the body of a holy person". This definition comes under the heading a "holy dwelling". We don't often think of ourselves as a "Holy Dwelling". But it's one of the ways God sees us. We are His holy dwelling because the Holy Spirit lives within us.

In my opinion Jesus explains this best in John 14:16-17. Jesus is giving His disciples comfort and instruction in the ways of the Father, then he starts to tell them of the coming Holy Spirit: *"And I will ask the Father, and he will give you another Counselor to be with you forever— the Spirit of truth. The world cannot accept him, because it neither sees him nor knows him. But you know him, for he lives with you and will be in you."* Jesus goes on to tell us He will never leave us as orphans. And, we are not alone. The Father sent the Holy Spirit to be with us, and in us. We have our own private counselor as we travel through our life journey. The word "counselor" here is very interesting and meaningful, it is the Greek word "parakletos" which means "a person summoned to ones aid". Jesus came in the flesh to teach us the ways of God the Father. His presence here on earth was that of a representative of the Father so we might know how to live. The Holy Spirit does the same, He functions as a representative of God to us as Christians or believers. He never leaves us alone because "He dwells within us".

In our verse for today Paul is making the point that, as Christians, we have received the Spirit of God through the work of Christ on the cross. We now belong to Him, our bodies are not our own, He bought us at a high price. We have no right to abuse or misuse our bodies because they house the Holy Spirit. And this is how Paul is telling us we should view our bodies, as a holy dwelling place, the place where God, the Holy Spirit resides.

Point: If you have received Christ as your Savior, you are God's holy dwelling, the temple of God.

Prayer: Thank You Lord for cleaning me that I may be Your vessel. Let me represent You well, that You may be glorified.

Today's Reading:
Esther 2-4; Revelation 20

June 22

NEVER ALONE AGAIN

By Beth Nelson

Hebrews 13:5 *God has said, "Never will I leave you; never will I forsake you."*

Have you ever been abandoned? Unfortunately, in this sin-sick world, abandonment is rampant. Even if we haven't experienced it ourselves, we all know people who have been abandoned. Husbands and wives break their vows and abandon each other, fathers abandon their children, friends drift apart, never to speak again. Many are scarred by it, filled with anger and rage, emotionally crippled, not daring to trust again.

It is into this selfish, self-righteous, sinful world, in the midst of broken and abandoned people, that God the Father comes. He is waiting with open arms for us to come to Him with our deepest hurts. When a spouse that once loved us leaves us, He is there beside us, whispering His deep and abiding love for us; when a father disappears or dies, He is there to hold us close; when a dear friend turns his back on us, He is there as the friend that sticks closer than a brother. He whispers, "Take heart. I will never, ever leave you or forsake you. You are of infinite worth to me. I died for you and I would have died for you alone, just so that you would be with me forever." He patiently and gently calls us to come to Him so that He can comfort our deepest hurts and fulfill our deepest longings.

When we become new in Christ we inherit so many riches, the greatest of which is the deep and abiding presence of God Himself. As God's forever children, we are never abandoned again for He Himself is with us always, to the very end of the age.

Ps 68:5 *A father to the fatherless, a defender of widows, is God in his holy dwelling.*

2 Cor 6:18 *I will be a Father to you, and you will be my sons and daughters, says the Lord Almighty.*

Mt 28:20 *And surely I am with you always, to the very end of the age.*

Point: You who have been abandoned, come to Him now, with all of your hurts and scars. He is reaching out to you, ready to comfort you and to replace your sorrow with singing. And for those of you who have abandoned someone, there is no sin that God cannot

Today's Reading:
Esther 5-6; Revelation 21-22

June 23

DEVELOPING COPING SKILLS!
By Scott Kalevik

Lamentations 3:21 *Yet this I call to mind and therefore I have hope:*

Ever felt like you couldn't take it anymore? Ever been to the end of your rope? Here's a powerful tool to experience great relief if you're in that circumstance! THINK ABOUT THE LORD!

Jeremiah spends the book of Lamentations lamenting the fact that his nation has been carted off to exile. The judgment of God is upon him and his nation. People are suffering everywhere. Jerusalem is in shambles. The temple is no longer functioning. Starvation is rampant. Life has been turned upside down! God has hidden His face from them.

How does Jeremiah cope? He disciplines his thought life. He starts to think about the character of the Lord. He calls things to mind. This change in his thinking leads him to hope.

Jeremiah remembers in verse 22 that God still loves him. He knows that's why they have not been consumed. He remembers that God's compassions never fail. In fact, they are new every morning. Jeremiah reminds himself about the great faithfulness of God.

Jeremiah starts talking to himself! He tells himself that the Lord is his portion. Jeremiah will wait on the Lord. In other words, Jeremiah surrenders all of his current circumstances to the control of God. He rests in the midst of disaster knowing that God is watching. God is in control. God is compassionate. God is faithful. God is loving.

And because of Jeremiah's focus on the person and character of God, Jeremiah has hope in his heart instead of depression. Has anything in his physical circumstance really changed? No! All the suffering is still there! Then why is Jeremiah experiencing relief? Because he's taken his thought life away from the disaster of his circumstance and begun thinking about God!

Today, if you're having trouble coping with life, why not use the technique Jeremiah is teaching? Take some time to read your Bible and reflect on the person and character of God!

Today's Reading:
Esther 7-9; Matthew 1

June 24

Little Children
By Beth Nelson

Matthew 11:25 *I praise you, Father, Lord of heaven and earth, because you have hidden these things from the wise and learned, and revealed them to little children.*

Can children understand the deep spiritual truths in the Bible? Jesus' words on the matter are crystal clear, *"I praise you, Father, Lord of heaven and earth, because you have hidden these things from the wise and learned, and revealed them to little children."* Mt 11:25 Can a teenager really know God and set an example for even older Christians to follow? I Tim 4:12 says, *"Don't let anyone look down on you because you are young, but set an example for the believers in speech, in life, in love, in faith and in purity."* Young people are often times more able to grasp spiritual truths than adults.

Children have a special place in the heart of God. There's a story in Mark about some parents who brought their children to Jesus so that he could touch them. The disciples, who were trying to protect the master and his valuable time, told them to go away. When Jesus found out about it, he wasn't just unhappy, he was indignant. He told the disciples, *"Let the little children come to me, and do not hinder them, for the kingdom of God belongs to such as these. I tell you the truth, anyone who will not receive the kingdom of God like a little child will never enter it."* After he said this, he took each child one by one into his arms and blessed them. Mk 10:13-16

We need to take Jesus' example seriously and begin to teach the precious children that are in our lives, the truths in God's Word. Then we need to humble ourselves like little children and receive the Word with meekness and gratitude.

Point: God places high value on children for their willingness and ability to understand spiritual truths.

Prayer: Dear Lord, forgive me for overlooking the children around me. Help me to invest my time and resources to bring the truth to them.

Today's Reading:
Esther 10-Job 1; Matthew 2-3

June 25

NEW EYES TO SEE

By Beth Nelson

John 9:25 *"One thing I do know. I was blind but now I see!"*

God created us with eyes to see, but far more important than having good eyesight is that we have spiritual eyes to see His truth more clearly. One day Jesus healed a man who had been born blind, which caused a huge stir among the Pharisees. They argued so much over this that they ended up throwing the man out of the synagogue. When the man found out that Jesus, who had healed him, was the Son of God, he immediately believed in him and worshiped him. Then Jesus said, *"For judgment I have come into this world, so that the blind will see and those who see will become blind."* (John 9:39) What a paradox! The Pharisees, who had studied the scriptures all of their lives were spiritually blind, but the poor blind beggar who had never seen the scriptures, had spiritual eyes and could see clearly!

A number of years ago there was a woman who had great spiritual insight. She had been blind since infancy, but she had such a heart for God that she could see spiritual truths with crystal clarity. Her name was Fanny Crosby, and she wrote over 8,000 gospel hymns, supplying us with more beloved hymns than any other person in history, hymns that we still sing today. Hymns such as, Take the World But Give Me Jesus, He Hideth My Soul, and Praise Him! Praise Him! Jesus, Our Blessed Redeemer! One day someone asked her if she could have had one wish at birth, what would she have wished for? She replied that she would have wished to be blind so that when she got to heaven, the first sight to gladden her eyes would be that of her Savior! What an example she was of someone who truly saw what was most important in life!

Point: Dear Lord, help me to more clearly see . . . beauty in nature and in the people around me the potential in a child the bigger picture a hungry soul your truth to the heart of a matter the lost who cannot help what they do.

Today's Reading:
Job 2-4; Matthew 4

June 26

THE LIGHT

By Peggy Kalevik

Matthew 5:14 *You are the light of the world. A city on a hill cannot be hidden.*

In both the Old and New Testaments light is most often the symbol of purity, truth, knowledge, and the divine revelation and presence of God. Yet Jesus says to His disciples, *"you are the light of the world"*. Though Jesus took the disciples away from the crowd to instruct them with these beatitudes, they are words for all of us to understand and live by. God says we are His light in this world.

The Jews saw themselves as the light of the world; after all they were God's chosen people. But Christ is the true light of the world, the light that came into the world but the world rejected (John3:19). Christ says whoever believes in Him will never walk in darkness (John 8:12). Because He is the light, we who believe and have accepted Him as Savior are tasked to reflect His light into a world of darkness. He came to teach us how to live. Now as His faithful followers we are to live like Him, for Him. If we live for Him, our light will shine in a way that reflects Christ's love.

As Christians we should be the "city on the hill". Our light should illuminate our environment. In the days of Jesus, cities built on hill tops were often carved out of white limestone. So they gleamed in the sunshine during the daylight hours and the reflection of light from lamps at night lit-up the sky in the dark. Just imagine God sees us as that kind of light, illuminating the world. Are we that kind of light; do we share Gods word with others? Are we hiding our light because we're afraid to tell people about God? God wants us to give our light away or at least share it. Everyone has to make the choice to be what God wants them to be, or go their own way. If God sees you as the light, why would you want to be anything else? Today, act as God's presence in every place, and every conversation in which you're involved. Don't find yourself in the dark!

Point: You are the light of the world; don't turn off your light!

Prayer: Father, teach me Your word, so I can shed more light in my environment. Help me to stop hiding my light because of fear or lack of understanding. Give me Your wisdom and knowledge to be a brighter light.

Today's Reading:
Job 5-6; Matthew 5-6

June 27

GOD IN US
By Beth Nelson

John 14:20 *On that day you will realize that I am in my Father, and you are in me, and I am in you.*

Have you ever gone into an empty church when you've been distressed, in an attempt to reconnect with God? I've done that in the past, back when churches used to leave their front doors unlocked. Sometimes the traditional church setting, with its stained glass windows and lofty ceilings makes us feel that God is near.

God will certainly meet us there. But Acts 17:24 says that, *The God who made the world and everything in it is the Lord of heaven and earth and does not live in temples built by hands."* The truth is that he will meet us wherever we are, because he's interested in dwelling within us, rather than dwelling in a building.

Jn 14:20 states that Jesus Christ is in God, he is in us and we are in him. 1 Jn 3:24 says that, *"Those who obey his commands live in him, and he in them. And this is how we know that he lives in us: We know it by the Spirit he gave us."* All who believe in him for salvation are filled by the Holy Spirit. This is a daily filling, a continual filling as we personally connect to God through Bible reading and prayer.

I eventually learned that when I am distressed, all I have to do is to find a quiet room and go to God directly. And wherever I am, he is there, also. What a glorious mystery! What a profound reality! Christ in you, Christ in me, the hope of glory. (Col 1:27)

Point: Because Christ is in me, I can go directly to him.

Prayer: Thank you, Father, for living in me through your Spirit.

Practice: I need to be continually filled with the Holy Spirit on a daily, even moment by moment basis.

Today's Reading:
Job 7-9; Matthew 7

June 28

COMMITMENT TO GOD'S WILL

By Peggy Kalevik

Psalm 40:8 *I desire to do your will, O my God; your law is within my heart."*

Commitment is a big word; it has more than a few meanings. It can mean responsibility, loyalty, or a previous engagement, a referral of some type, a court order or institutionalizing someone. But today in this reading we'll be talking about loyalty. David offered himself to God as a devoted offering, set aside for the Lord. It was a wholehearted devotion to change his ways for the will of God, as God willed in his word. He dedicated himself to the way of the Lord.

You will recall the tribe of Levi was set aside for God. Their entire purpose in life was, and is, to serve God. They hold a unique place in the history of Israel.

Hannah dedicated Samuel to the Lord in 1 Samuel 1:28: *"So now I give him to the LORD. For his whole life he will be given over to the LORD.' And he worshiped the LORD there."* Samuel is one of the few people in the Bible about whom there is nothing negative recorded. He was a faithful servant of God his entire life. This kind of commitment to God today is very uncommon. But God wants us to make that kind of commitment to Him.

In Psalm 40 the Old Testament concept of sacrifice gives way to an attitude of submission to God's will. David tells God in v6 *"Sacrifice and offering you did not desire, but my ears you have pierced, burnt offerings and sin offerings you did not require."* David understands God is no longer interested in the continual sacrifices the Priests make at the Temple. Because they will never be enough, they must be made over and over again! In His own time, God would make the ultimate sacrifice for us. However, we need to submit our whole self, heart, mind, body and soul to God, because this is really all we have to offer and this is really what God desires. What else can we offer? He has everything.

Point: Make yourself a living sacrifice to our Father today. Are you willing to make the sacrifice?

Prayer: Lord, this day I make myself available to You. All that I am is Yours. All You have given me, I give back to You. My will I give to You; use me Lord.

Today's Reading:
Job 10-11; Matthew 8-9

June 29

Obedience That Comes From Faith

By Peggy Kalevik

Romans 1:5 *Through him and for his name's sake, we received grace and apostleship to call people from among all the Gentiles to the obedience that comes from faith.*

This letter, originally written to the Church at Rome, served multiple purposes. Paul wanted of course to spread the gospel message, but he also wanted to help the population understand the relationship between Jews and Gentiles in God's plan of redemption. In addition, he wanted to pave the way for his visit to Rome. With the gospel message as his new life calling, it is not surprising that as part of the letter's introduction, he speaks about obedience which comes from faith.

Paul starts today's verse by making known his purpose in Christ, that of an apostle. He explains we (himself and the other apostles?) have received grace and apostleship from Christ. And, because of this undeserved grace, they are tasked to call people from among the Gentiles to the obedience which comes from faith. Paul believed his purpose in life was to teach the gospel to all gentiles. He was to help them understand their need for a savior, and that the savior is Jesus Christ. Paul's expectation was that they would respond to this teaching by accepting Christ. Obedience which comes from faith is the correct response to the gospel message. If we believe the gospel message, then by faith we must become obedient to it.

The recipients of the message are not being called to be apostles; they are called to belong to Jesus Christ, to be "saints". By receiving and accepting the message, they are set free from sin by God's grace, they are saints. Like Paul and the apostles, as believers we have all been "set apart". Those who accept the message are sanctified, freed from sin and made holy. For all of us who were not there to see the resurrection, this is only by faith. Webster's Dictionary has eight definitions for faith; one of them says faith is belief that is not based on proof. The Bible has a slightly different view: *"Now faith is the substance of things hoped for, the evidence of things not seen."* (Heb 11:1 KJV)

Point: Your faith should be fueling your obedience. To obey God is to love God.

Prayer: Father I have found in Jesus the righteousness that I could not achieve on my own. Thank You for sending Him, and for giving me faith that I might believe on Him; from that faith may I be obedient to You.

Today's Reading:
Job 12-14; Matthew 10

June 30

THE IMPORTANCE OF YOUR EXAMPLE
By Peggy Kalevik

Psalm 37:31 *The law of his God is in his heart; his feet do not slip.*

Have you considered that the second best reason to walk obediently before the LORD is to set a good example for your children and their children? The first reason of course is to keep yourself pure before God and to maintain your relationship with Him. The second reason is to ensure your children understand they too must walk in purity and humility before a Holy God, that He will accept nothing less. There is no darkness in His presence and we know this because the Bible tells us in 1John 1:5, *"This is the message we have heard from him and declare to you: God is light; in him there is no darkness at all.*

In Psalm 37, David says he has never seen the righteous forsaken nor their children begging for bread. The righteous are generous, they lend or give freely. Their children are blessed. The righteous will inherit the land and live in it forever. On the other hand, he says the offspring of the wicked will be cut off. The Lord loves His people; those who love Him and obey His word. The Lord loves those who have a reverent fear of Him and are submitted to His will. He loves those who speak with wisdom and do not slip because of envy or jealousy; they are not doers of evil.

These are the things God is looking for in those of us who follow Him. Thus, we are responsible to teach our children so they will not be cut off. His heart would rejoice in seeing you and me on our knees teaching our children to pray. He has "shown" us the way, but we "tell" our children they should pray and think that is enough. We would be surprised at the impact actually praying with our little children has on them, instead of simply telling them to pray. The same is true of all our actions. Children learn from watching the adults in their lives. If we tell them to pray but they never see us praying, they won't be inclined to pray at all.

The thrust of today's verse is simply this: Those who love the Lord will not slip because they have not given into evil; they are grounded in the Lord and His ways. They teach their children the ways of the Lord and He will not forsake them or their offspring.

Point: Keep your mind, heart, and behavior on the Lord, and "teach" your children His will and His ways.

Prayer: *The LORD is my shepherd; I shall not be in want. Even though I walk through the valley of the shadow of death, I will fear no evil, for You are with me.* (Psalm 23)

Today's Reading:
Job 15-16; Matthew 11-12

July 1

RETURN TO GOD

By Peggy Kalevik

James 4:8 *Draw nigh to God, and he will draw nigh to you. Cleanse your hands, ye sinners; and purify your hearts, ye double minded. (KJV)*

How well we remember the story of David and Bathsheba. David in his lust for this woman kills her husband. We can easily see that it is the wrong thing to do but it is the perfect example of what can happen when we allow our desire to rule the direction of our life. David was acting out of lust not the will of God. Yet God knew him and said he was a man after His own heart.

What makes us do things we know are wrong? Sometimes our desire for something is so strong we will do anything to get it. We are still human. The point James is trying to make for us in chapter four of his book is: we "kill and covet" and cannot have what we want, because we go after it in the wrong way. We do not ask God. We lust and fight rather than pray. (I would add that we sometimes want things that are not in God's will.)

In today's verse James calls God's people sinners because they have set their hearts on their own pleasure. Though they still consider themselves to be God's people they have, through their actions and behavior, become estranged from God. In verse 4 James says their unfaithfulness is a direct result of the devil's (the world's) influence. *"But God gives us more grace,"* therefore come back to Him. *"Submit yourselves, then, to God. Resist the devil and he will flee from you"*. There is no greater reason to draw near to God than the fact that we are living in a world filled with temptation and hardship. It is easy to fall away from God, we must be careful everyday. We must read His word and pray for His guidance every day, otherwise we "will" fall prey to the temptations of the world.

Today's scripture gives us re-assurance of His love for us. God yearns for the devotion of His people. He calls us to "wash our hands", in other words, make our conduct pure; and to "purify our hearts" by purifying our thoughts and motives. Then as we come near to Him, He will come near to us.

Point: Don't allow the world to lead you away from God.
Prayer: I draw near to You; You draw near to me. I call on Your name, I need You my God. Let me hear You speak to me Lord. (Darlene Zschech)
Practice: Read the Bible every day, saturate your mind with God's word.

Today's Reading:
Job 17-19; Matthew 13

July 2

DENYING YOURSELF TO GAIN SOMETHING MORE
By Beth Nelson

Matthew 10:37-39 *Anyone who loves his father or mother more than me is not worthy of me; anyone who loves his son or daughter more than me is not worthy of me; and anyone who does not take his cross and follow me is not worthy of me. Whoever finds his life will lose it, and whoever loses his life for my sake will find it.*

The call of Jesus to those who follow him has not changed. In Guatemala a few years ago, a successful businessman and his wife were working hard and enjoying the material rewards for their labor. God met them through a miraculous healing of their sick little girl and they became believers. Seeking to find out what the Lord wanted them to do He led them to become the pastor of a church and work with a large children's ministry in a poor section of the city. A few years later, God called them to leave their homeland and to come to pastor our Spanish-speaking congregation in Aurora. Though by no means as affluent as they had been in their earlier days, I have never heard them look back with regret.

We may think that back in Jesus' day, it was much easier to leave your work behind to follow Him than it would be today. But at least one man, Matthew (also called Levi) gave up a lot to follow Jesus. He was a successful man with a lucrative, secure job. It says in Luke 5:27,28 that Levi was hard at work one day in his tax booth when Jesus invited him to leave his job and his life as he knew it behind. I must think that Jesus saw a readiness in Levi's spirit for something more, something truly satisfying, because Levi didn't even hesitate. He got up, left everything behind and followed him. The next thing we know, Matthew is throwing caution (and his reputation) to the wind and splurging on a huge banquet so that all of his wealthy co-workers can also meet Jesus.

The next time we hear about Matthew, he's going out on a mission with the other disciples, with no money or provisions, to preach the kingdom of God, heal the sick and drive out demons. Matthew never looked back longingly on his old life for he found new life with Christ. Before he died, he wrote one of the four great gospels of the New Testament, the book of Matthew, in which he shows clearly that Jesus of Nazareth was indeed the Messiah, the Savior of the world.

Someday we will give an account of our own response to the call of Jesus on our lives. If he asks us to give up everything to follow Him, will we do it?

Today's Reading:
Job 20-21; Matthew 14-15

July 3

What's New?

By Scott Kalevik

2 Corinthians 5:17 *Therefore, if anyone is in Christ, he is a new creation; the old has gone, the new has come!*

Paul clearly tells us that something happens on the inside of a person when they are in Christ. Those who surrender their lives to Jesus are new creations. But what's so new about someone who is in Christ? If you look at most who have come to Christ, they look the same on the outside. This month we'll take a look at the changes God makes in our hearts and minds when we come to Him.

STUDY HELP: Anytime you read "therefore" in a verse of scripture, you need to ask yourself one simple question: "What is that 'therefore' there for? Almost always the 'therefore' will be the main conclusion of the points made just before the verse. So study what came before the verse to understand the conclusion.

Look up 2Corinthians 5:17 to discover the argument that led to the 'therefore.' Prior to verse 17 Paul tells us what is new about a person who believes. Believers live by faith instead of sight (vs. 7). Believers live with the goal of pleasing the Lord (vs. 9). Believers are motivated by the fact that we will all face God's judgment (vs. 10). Believers try to persuade others to come to Jesus Christ (vs. 11). Believers serve with humility (vs. 12-13). Believers are compelled to serve out of love because Christ died for them out of love (vs. 14). Believers don't live for themselves anymore because they belong to Jesus (vs. 15). Believers don't look at anyone from a worldly point of view anymore (vs. 16). Then comes the 'therefore.'

What's new about you? If you've repented of your sin and surrendered your life to Christ, then the attitudes and actions of your life have been transformed by the Lord. You are a new creation! The old has gone and the new has come!

What? Many of these attitudes are not characteristic of your daily life? It's all about surrender. Are you letting Jesus do His work in you and through you or are you insisting on living your life your own way? If you surrender to Him, Jesus will change your thoughts, attitudes and actions! All will be new!

Point: God makes His followers NEW.

Prayer: Lord, I surrender my life to You. Have your way with me and make me new.

Today's Reading:
Job 22-24; Matthew 16

July 4

DRAWING NEAR TO GOD: DENYING MYSELF

By Scott Kalevik

Luke 9:23 Then he said to them all: "If anyone would come after me, he must deny himself and take up his cross daily and follow me.

The first step in drawing near to God can be defined in one word: Surrender! What does God demand each of us to surrender? We must surrender the idea that we are the captains of our lives! To draw near to God is to surrender the dreams, ambitions, and skills of our lives to the Lord. The Lord is Master and He leads the life of the one surrendered.

In other words, what you want out of life is surrendered to God so that Jesus may accomplish His purpose for your life! Jesus modeled this attitude for us as He prayed to the Father: *"Not my will but yours be done (Luke 22:42)."*

Scripture says a lot about our surrender to the Lord. In fact, Jesus Himself repeatedly demonstrates this attitude of surrender in His own life. Read these verses to see for yourself:

John 6:35-40 … notice verse 38
John 4:34
Hebrews 10:7-9
Matthew 26:39-42
Why did Jesus need to surrender His life to the Father?

Jesus taught us to pray with an attitude of surrender: Mt 6:10 *your kingdom come, your will be done on earth as it is in heaven.* Whose will are we taught to ask God for? GOD'S WILL – not mine – not yours – THE LORD'S! Ever been frustrated because God won't do what you want Him to do? NOTICE: God wants us to surrender our lives to Him and pray that He accomplishes what HE wants – not what we want!

In addition to demonstrating total surrender to the Father in His own life, Jesus taught about surrender on numerous occasions. Here are a few for you to study:

Luke 9:23-24
Luke 17:33
Matthew 10:37-39
Matthew 16:24-25

Today's Reading:
Job 25-26; Matthew 17-18

July 5

DRAWING NEAR TO GOD: DENYING MYSELF (PART 2)
By Scott Kalevik

Luke 9:23 *Then he said to them all: "If anyone would come after me, he must deny himself and take up his cross daily and follow me.*

The apostle Paul describes his surrender to Christ:

Gal 2:20 *I have been crucified with Christ and I no longer live, but Christ lives in me. The life I live in the body, I live by faith in the Son of God, who loved me and gave himself for me.*

Crucifixion refers to death. How can Paul say he's been crucified if he's still alive and writing to the Galatians? What's been crucified or executed in his life? Paul's desire to have life his own way has been crucified! He has totally surrendered every area of his life to the lordship and will of Jesus Christ.

Paul says, "I no longer live." Does he mean that literally? No! Paul is still physically alive. But his desire to have life his own way has been put to death.

Paul says, "Christ lives in me." In other words, Paul's life is surrendered to the direction and power of the One who has forgiven him and filled him with the Holy Spirit.

It follows naturally that Paul says the life he lives in his body (i.e. his physical existence), he lives by faith in Jesus. In other words, every decision, every direction, every day, is submitted and surrendered to the will of God.

Look these up to learn more about living the surrendered life:

Galatians 5:24; Romans 6:5-14; Colossians 3:1-10; John 14:20-24

Do you want to live your life totally surrendered to Jesus? Commit yourself to these steps:

1) Ask God to forgive you for trying to live life your own way.

2) Tell Jesus that you surrender your life to Him in every area and ask for His strength and guidance to live the surrendered life.

3) Believe that God leads your life from here as you surrender each decision and direction to His guidance. In other words, live by faith!

If you're like me, you'll have to take these steps EVERY DAY! But if you honestly surrender your whole life to Christ, nothing will ever be the same! God will draw near to you.

Write a paragraph or two answering this question: Is my life surrendered to Jesus?

Today's Reading:
Job 27-29; Matthew 19

July 6

DELIGHT IN AND MEDITATE ON HIS WORD
By Peggy Kalevik

Psalm 1:2 *But his delight is in the law of the LORD,
and on his law he meditates day and night.*

The words delight and meditate aren't often used together in our culture. To delight is to enjoy or take pleasure in. To meditate is to empty your mind of all thought in order to concentrate or focus your mind on one thing in the hope it will enable you to develop (grow) mentally or spiritually. So why should we delight in and meditate on God's word? As Christians God's word gives us instruction and guidance in how to live in agreement with God's will. We should not only take joy in reading and thinking about God's word, we should be living it out every day.

In the early days of the Christian Church the Bible was not compiled as one book as we know it today. The believers were unable to pick up their Bible and look-up scriptures. They were taught in their meetings from the available scrolls and letters. They memorized the scriptures they were being taught and meditated on them. Imagine a child being taught the scripture as soon as he/she is able to speak. Every day the child is taught a verse until the age of 18. If taught the scripture, along with the proper reinforcements, the child later as an adult will be filled with the word of God without ever having a Bible in His hand. We can't imagine life without a Bible now. With all the distractions of our world we would never learn anything about the Bible if we had to rely solely on what we heard at the Sunday morning worship service. Our attention span and capacity to stay focused enough to remember what we've heard has diminished dramatically since the birth of the Christian Church. But God has blessed us with His book. We must read it, study it, understand it, memorize it, and meditate on it. And we should take great joy in doing so. Empty your mind and meditate on today's scripture verse or this week's memory verse. Think about His greatness and how He has left nothing to chance. If you are struggling with something today, surely there is an answer in the book for you.

Point: The faithful believer delights in doing the will of God, and meditates on His word day and night.

Prayer: *"My heart rejoices in the LORD; my horn is lifted high."* 1 Samuel 2:1

Today's Reading:
Job 30-31; Matthew 20-21

July 7

LEARNING OBEDIENCE THROUGH SUFFERING
By Peggy Kalevik

Hebrews 5:8-9 *Although he was a son, he learned obedience from what he suffered and, once made perfect, he became the source of eternal salvation for all who obey him*

We have heard it said that we call on God more sincerely and steadfastly when we are in our greatest distress. Learning to be obedient is much the same; it is best learned through trial, struggle and sometimes failure. Jesus struggled a little with his call to go to the cross, but he never failed at anything. Yet, He suffered greatly for us. And he was made perfect by his suffering and he was obedient unto death. He was made perfect but not in the sense that he was ever imperfect. No, He became perfect in the sense of a changed relationship; the suffering he endured led to his becoming the source of our eternal salvation. Through his suffering He learned to obey, again not that he was disobedient. He learned obedience from the act of obeying. We learn better when we actually perform the task as opposed to being prepared to act. Its one thing to read about performing a heart transplant, it's an altogether different thing to actually do it.

Jesus the Son of God suffered. We would not expect the Messiah to come into the world and suffer. After all He could call down ten thousand angels to do battle for Him, but He didn't. He took on the cross alone for you and me. It is strange that today's verse starts with the phrase, "Although he was a son" because He was not just a son. He was the "Son of God". Wouldn't you think that His standing with God would get Him a go home free card? Isaiah told us it would be this way, in Isaiah 53:10a he wrote: *"Yet it was the LORD's will to crush him and cause him to suffer".*

So, Jesus endured the cross, and His suffering there was not in vain, we have all been blessed by it; saved by it. We have all had opportunity to understand and learn from what He taught us. The Bible tells us that when He was on the cross His sweat was like great drops of blood falling down to the ground (Luke 22:44). As we watched the movie "The Passion of the Christ" some of us were shocked by the violence, and found it unbearable. I found myself sitting there the only person in the theatre who wasn't crying, thinking, He could stop this anytime He wants to, but He didn't stop it He endured it all for me. God allows hardship so that we will learn and grow as a result of enduring the suffering it sometimes brings. Don't let your struggles and trials be in vain, learn from them.

Today's Reading:
Job 32-34; Matthew 22

July 8

THE RESULT OF DISOBEDIENCE
By Peggy Kalevik

Romans 5:19 *For just as through the disobedience of the one man the many were made sinners, so also Through the obedience of the one man the many will be made righteous.*

What an ominous statement. The disobedience of one man has made us all sinners. How many of us as children received punishment because one of our siblings did something wrong? Well, our entire universe can say we are all guilty of sin because our older brother was disobedient to God. Adam and Eve had no idea what they were doing when they ate the "fruit" of the forbidden tree. Because of what they did, we are all sinners and we should all receive condemnation as a penalty. But God saw fit to give us another chance; so he gave us a gift that was unlike the trespass of the one man. This gift brought justification for all who would receive it (Rom 5: 15-17). *"Consequently, just as the result of one trespass was condemnation for all men, so also the result of one act of righteousness was justification that brings life for all men"* (Rom 5:18).

This brings us to today's verse. Adam and Eve's trespass in the garden changed our status before God. Adam and Eve were tempted to taste the fruit because of a human desire to be like God. They committed this act of disobedience before the law was introduced. The law when it came, simply illuminated the trespass. God knew the answer to sin was not the law; it was by grace that we would be reckoned to Him. So, the trespass of the one man, which put us in a position of separation from God, was made right through the shed blood of another man on the cross. Adam and Eve responded to temptation with an attitude of selfishness, "let my will be done". But Jesus' response to God, when sent to die of the cross, was an attitude of humility and selflessness: *"...Yet not what I will, but what you will."* (Luke 22:42) The condemnation brought by one man's disobedience was rectified by the obedience of another man. *"God made him who had no sin to be sin for us, so that in him we might become the righteousness of God."* (2Cor. 5:21)

Point: If you are seeking to have a closer walk with God, obedience is a must.
Prayer: *"Thou, O LORD, art a shield for me; my glory, and the lifter up of mine head."* (Ps 3:3) I will walk in obedience to Your word.

Today's Reading:
Job 35-36; Matthew 23-24

July 9

THE GLORY OF GOD REVEALED!

By Kathy Bryant

Matthew 17:2 *"There He was transfigured before them. His face shone like the sun, and his clothes became as white as the light"*

During Jesus' ministry on earth he appeared as an average man. He had a family, worked, ate, felt tired, and he enjoyed companionship with his disciples. It's hard for us to imagine that under his outer appearance He was God Himself. Jesus never gave up his glory while on earth. In the story of the transfiguration, which Matthew, Mark, and Luke recorded in the gospels, it says *"His face shone like the sun, and His clothes became as white as the light* (Matt 17:1-2) In addition, Jesus talked to Moses and Elijah whom God Himself either buried or took up to heaven. (Deut 34:5-6 and 2 Kings 2:11) The transfiguration shows Jesus' majesty and the promise of life after death.

God's cloud of glory appeared to the disciples and the same words spoken in Matt 3:17 at Jesus' baptism, are spoken here in Matt 17:5: *"This is my Son, whom I love, with him I am well pleased"*. John the disciple remembered this scene again in Revelation 1:14-16, where Jesus' face is described *"like the sun shinning in all its brilliance"*. Whereas, Jesus chose not to reveal just who he was when he asks Peter *"who do people say the Son of Man is?"* (Matt 16:13). In Revelation 1 Jesus revealed he *"...was the First and the Last. I am the Living One; I was dead, and behold I am alive forever and ever..."* The last chapter of Revelation 22:12 re-states Jesus to be God again. When Jesus returns he will not come back as a man. He will come back in the Father's glory with his angels. Jesus made no secret of who he was to His inner circle (Peter, James, and John); He was God incarnate. After the resurrection many people realized they had missed the opportunity to see and know the Father. (John 14:9-10)

Today's Reading:
Job 37-39; Matthew 25

July 10

TRUSTING GOD

By Peggy Kalevik

Psalm 16:8 *I have set the LORD always before me. Because he is at my right hand, I will not be shaken.*

David was a fascinating person, with many gifts. He was a mighty warrior, a great writer and a powerful worshiper. His greatest gift might well have been his trust in God. He shows us in his writings that his confidence and loyalty was always in the Lord. When we reflect on our life we can see all that God has done for us. We trust Him because He is always with us and He never fails. In view of His love and faithfulness to us we endeavor to be like David, in that we "set the LORD always before us".

The theologians have not pinned done conclusively at what point in his life David wrote Psalm 16. They speculate that it was written at a time of peace and quiet. Regardless of when David wrote it, it is a confession of his confidence in God and expresses the great trust that he placed in his LORD. Not only is his trust in God while he lives but even in death, for he says in verse 10, "because you will not abandon me to the grave". Hallelujah!!

Read through this Psalm and understand the devotion that is expressed. He confesses that there are people in the land who are practicing in idol worship, but he acknowledges the importance of those in the land who are consecrated to the Lord. He praises God for the blessings in His life. By day David says the Lord gives him counsel, by night the Lord instructs him. *"I have set the Lord always before me. Because He is at my right hand, I will not be shaken".* If we allow the Lord to be our foundation and shield like David we will not be shaken. If God is for us, who can be against us? No power on earth can defeat Him. In him we put our trust, in Him we rest.

Point: Let go of all the things in your life that seem impossible. Turn them over to God, He can handle it.

Prayer: I worship You Lord. There really is none like You. You are my shield and deliverer, in you I will trust.

Today's Reading:
Job 40-41; Matthew 26-27

July 11

THE ANOINTING

By Peggy Kalevik

1 John 2:27 *As for you, the anointing you received from him remains in you, and you do not need anyone to teach you. But as his anointing teaches you about all things and as that anointing is real, not counterfeit—just as it has taught you, remain in him.*

In our modern day worship services we occasionally hear the word or phrase "the anointing", but we almost never hear an explanation for it. It is assumed everyone understands what it means. The word means to literally rub oil or ointment on a person, animal or thing. It can also mean to install, ordain or appoint someone to a position. The Bible uses it mostly when speaking of rubbing oil on for the purpose of ordaining priests, and kings, or cleansing the temple. The word anointing is used 31 times in the NIV, only three instances are found in the New Testament, the remaining 28 are in the Old Testament.

In this passage John uses it in his effort to convey to the believers of his day that what they have received from the word of God, the message Jesus himself gave, is sufficient. Those who teach anything contrary or add to what Jesus has taught are false teachers. In fact he labels them the "antichrist". The anointing referred to here is of course the Holy Spirit. The Anointing is one of many names for the Holy Spirit. For when we accept the teaching of the Gospel and acknowledge Christ as our Lord and Savior we are endowed with, or receive the Holy Spirit. You could say we are "anointed" with the Holy Spirit.

The Spirit leads us in our growth in the faith. It is this anointing that helps us to understand the scripture and causes us to learn spiritual truths. In verse 20 John tells his readers they have an anointing from the Holy One and they know the truth. In today's scripture John is saying the divine anointing, God's gift of the Holy Spirit (which came by means of the word of God through Jesus) now abides in those who have accepted Jesus as their savoir. If they continue to live according to the word they were taught and according to the Holy Spirit who dwells in them, they need not believe or be taught another Gospel. When we receive Christ the anointing will be with us forever just as Jesus says, *"And I will ask the Father, and he will give you another Counselor to be with you forever—"* (John 14:16)

Today's Reading:
Job 42-Psalm 1-2; Matthew 28

July 12

ANGER MANAGEMENT – 101

By Kathy Bryant

1 John 1:9 *If we confess our sins, he is faithful and just to forgive us our sins, and to cleanse us from all unrighteousness.*

Have you ever experience high frustration, a mini meltdown, or an emotional nuclear explosion. I have experienced varying degrees of the above, I've learned that I have a weakness towards anger. After all, only a few of us have not derived some pleasure in speaking our mind, lobbing a verbal assault against someone else. When the words hit their mark, and either crush someone's spirit or elicit an angry response, it can feel good. Usually, these feelings are temporary for God's children. Immediately, feelings of remorse (conviction) from the Holy Spirit and shame (condemnation) from the evil one are sure to follow. If that wasn't bad enough, you then feel the overwhelming need to ask for forgiveness.

As Christians we are told to repent and confess our sins to be forgiven. How many times do we begin a cycle of outburst, conviction, condemnation, and then repentance? I believe that proactive anger management could be an answer to this dilemma. In Galatians 5:22-23, one of the fruits of the Spirit is gentleness. Our path to gentleness may go through the valley of anger. Thus, we need to recognize the stimuli that cause the angry response. We can get help dealing with our responses through seeking help from the Holy Spirit and prayer. We can begin to learn not to give in to sin and move toward becoming gentle with true repentance by not becoming a repeat offender.

Point: We do not need to be lead by our emotions.

Prayer: Lord Jesus, help us to recognize our weaknesses which hinders our attempts to achieve the fruits of the Spirit. Holy Spirit help us to confess and truly repent, so we can live in freedom instead of shame.

Practice: Learn to recognize the things that trigger a response from our sin-based nature, and then seek help from the Lord Jesus.

Today's Reading:
Psalm 3-4; Mark 1-2

July 13

A New Position

By Beth Nelson

Ephesians 2:4 *But because of his great love for us, God, who is rich in mercy, 5 made us alive with Christ even when we were dead in transgressions—it is by grace you have been saved. 6 And God raised us up with Christ and seated us with him in the heavenly realms in Christ Jesus, 7 in order that in the coming ages he might show the incomparable riches of his grace, expressed in his kindness to us in Christ Jesus.*

When we become a new creation in Christ, we assume a brand new position. God seats us with Christ in the heavenly realms! The story is told in the Old Testament of a poor, crippled man who was brought to the king, King David. This poor man was trembling with fear, for he was part of the previous king's family and he knew that the new king had the power to kill him. Humbling himself before the king, he said, *"What is your servant, that you should notice a dead dog like me?"* (2Sam. 9:8) But instead of killing him, King David loved him for he had made a covenant with this man's father. David said, *"Don't be afraid, for I will surely show you kindness for the sake of your father Jonathan."* (2Sam. 9:7) He elevated this man to a high level, so that from then on, he ate at the king's own table. He received land and for the rest of his life he had servants to take care of his every need. What a contrast, from living in fear that he might be killed to now being treated like the king's own son!

What a perfect illustration of what God does for us when we accept Christ! It is not because of anything we have done. All of our attempts at righteousness are like filthy rags. Much as we may try to clean ourselves up on the outside, we are who we are. Our hearts are still full of sin and rebellion and we don't deserve the king's favor.

But God! God who is rich in mercy, loved us while we were still sinners. He raised us up and seated us with Christ. He took off our filthy rags and clothed us in Christ's pure righteousness. He made us part of His family. We feast daily at His table on the bread of life and our hunger is satisfied. We drink from the living water, and we never thirst again. Our lives are the living illustration of God's incomparable kindness and grace. Praise be to God!

Today's Reading:
Psalm 5-7; Mark 3

194

July 14

THE FAMILY OF GOD
By Peggy Kalevik

John 1:13 *Children born not of natural descent, nor of human decision or a husband's will, but born of God.*

Many people believe that we are all children of God, whether we have accepted Him or not. In a sense they are right, God did created us all. But God is more than just our creator. He is our Father if we have believed or received Him. John is giving us an insight into the heart of God, that we may understand how He sees us, how much He loves us. If we have believed His word and received His son as savior then He, through the work of Jesus makes us members of His family, the family of God.

John tells us that the children of God are not His children because of natural human birth. No, we have become children of God by being born of God. We have experienced a change that is neither of man nor the work of man. This change is spiritual, not physical or biological. In John 3:6-8 Jesus tells Nicodemus that to enter the kingdom of God requires an internal change that must be a direct act of God. The new life of one who has received Christ is as unexplainable as the direction of the wind. It is unpredictable, yet it is undeniable. The person who is born of the spirit experiences new life in Christ, he or she is a new creation. Paul tells us in 2 Corinthians 5:17 that *"the old has passed away and the new has come!"* Paul goes on to say that through Christ God is reconciling humankind to Himself.

Through the years since He was here with us we have heard Jesus words to Nicodemus repeated over and over again, *"You must be born again"*. But have we understood what Jesus does not say in John 3:7 – I can do that for you; all you need to do is come. Whoever answers yes to Jesus will experience a re-birth and will be born of God and become a member of the Family of God.

Point: We who have accepted Christ as our Lord and Savior are the children of God, members of the Family of God.

Prayer: Father we praise You for making us Your sons and daughters, children of the most High God. You have done this out of Your love and compassion for us. Thank you for being a gracious and merciful Father.

Today's Reading:
Psalm 8-9; Mark 4-5

July 15

GROWING INTO THE FAMILY OF GOD
By Peggy Kalevik

Romans 11:17 *If some of the branches have been broken off, and you, though a wild olive shoot, have been grafted in among the others and now share in the nourishing sap from the olive root,*

The Father in His infinite wisdom decided to adopt us all; if we will come. He has given the invitation for all to be His children. And according to our confession of faith that is what we have become. For centuries the Jews have been reluctant to accept Christ as the Messiah. Yet Paul says God will redeem them as well (11:25-26). So, one day we will all be together worshiping the Father of us all.

Paul tells us about God's "cutting off of Israel" as a warning and to make us understand, God doesn't want us to repeat the mistakes of the Jews. He tells us in verse 25 that Israel experienced a hardening of their hearts only for a time so that God may bring in the full number of Gentiles. And why was this necessary; God wanted to bring in all of us! Paul uses the analogy of the olive tree to make his point. The Father broke off some of the branches because of unbelief; we could say they were dead wood. That's great for us! The wild olive branch God placed in with the cultivated olive tree and its root; we took hold and now we are one with the tree.

One of the most important things to remember here is Paul isn't trying to tell us we're more important than Israel. On the contrary, he tells us plainly in v21 not to become arrogant because of God's blessings to us. If God did not spare the natural branches He will not spare us either. Now that we've accepted Christ we are one body made up of many members. Each member is important to God and He nurtures and instructs every one of us. As a good Father He encourages and disciplines His children with patience and love. He has called us to be His own.

Point: The mercy of God is extended to all who will come. He has made room for us all.

Prayer: LORD, thank you that you have shown compassion and grace; that you are slow to anger, and abounding in love and faithfulness. Your love has saved us. (Ex 34:6 &7)

Today's Reading:
Psalm 10-12; Mark 6

July 16

I Have Purpose

By Peggy Kalevik

Psalm 138:8 The LORD will fulfill [his purpose] for me; your love, O LORD, endures forever - do not abandon the works of your hands.

When young people graduate from High School and College, they leave behind a way of life that is all they have known for twelve to eighteen years. Sometimes it's a really difficult transition and sometimes it's a long awaited, planned-for event. In the last few years we have seen a lot of young people who don't think they have a purpose in life. They're living life as if there's no tomorrow or they don't want to see tomorrow. Well, God has a plan for each and every one of them and for us. He has left nothing to chance, we just need to seek Him for our purpose, and He will show us.

The Lord is in control of and exalted in his rule of all he has created, whether man or beast. He did not create anything without purpose. If we look at the life of David we see how the Lord protected Him as he was waiting for God to place him on the throne. No matter what Saul did to try and eliminate him, God always made a way for David. God loves us just as much as He loved David. He has a plan for us as well and He'll find a way to help us accomplish that for which He created us. Like David, Paul is confident God will see the work of His hands through to its final completion (read Philippians 1:6).

In Matthew 28:19-20 God asks us to take his message to all nations, making disciples and baptizing them in His name. Throughout the Bible we see He has asked us to worship, praise and serve Him; to have no other God before Him. He asks us to care for widows, orphans, and the poor. In 1 Thessalonians 5 Paul tells us we should: *"Be joyful always; pray continually; give thanks in all circumstances"*. All of these things are our purpose. In addition, God has gifted each one of us for some individual purpose that is a part of His plan. As He purposed David to be Israel's King, He has purpose for each of us. Lay down your aspirations in favor of His will.

Point: Study God's word, pray and seek God for your individual purpose.
Prayer: Father, give me the strength to give my life to Your purpose for me.

Today's Reading:
Psalm 13-14; Mark 7-8

July 17

THREE WAYS THROUGH!

By Scott Kalevik

Romans 12:12 *Be joyful in hope, patient in affliction, faithful in prayer.*

Having trouble today? Here are three things the Lord wants you to do to survive whatever life may be throwing at you.

First – Be joyful in hope. What we think about in times of trouble will really impact our attitudes. If we let the "What ifs" begin to swim around in our brains, many times it leads us to fear or dread. We become overwhelmed by what might happen.

Instead, the Lord instructs us to focus on the hope that we have. Be joyful about that hope. God has guaranteed us life with Him forever. We know that Jesus has risen from the dead and that He intercedes for us and listens to us when we pray. We know that the Holy Spirit has indwelt us. He leads us. He guides us. He comforts us. We have a lot of hope. The Lord tells us to focus on these things.

Second – Be patient in affliction. As you know, there are a lot of things that happen in life that are simply no fun at all. Illness, accidents, problems with relationships ... this sin sick world is full of trouble. The Lord instructs us to be patient. In other words, as we cast our trouble on Him, we need to remember that He will work out the problem according to His timing. Have patience.

Third – Be faithful in prayer. So many of us feel like we really have no one to talk to about our trouble. That is never true for the Christian. We have the Lord to talk to every moment of every day. He listens and He responds. But we have to be willing to pray. If we don't engage in conversation with Him, we miss the sweet fellowship He provides in suffering. We miss the opportunity He provides to draw near in the time of need.

Are you rejoicing in the promises of God as you walk through your valley? Are you waiting patiently for the Lord's intervention? Are you praying earnestly? You can make it through whatever circumstance besets you today. The Lord has given you the tools. Will you use them?

Today's Reading:
Psalm 15-17; Mark 9

July 18

Lord, teach us to pray

By Peggy Kalevik

Luke 11:1 *One day Jesus was praying in a certain place. When he finished, one of his disciples said to him, "Lord, teach us to pray, just as John taught his disciples."*

Today's scripture verse is a Luke exclusive. It is instructive for all of us because it helps us understand how to communicate with our Father. Through the response to this question we learn how God wants us to pray to Him. Prayer is our only means of communicating with God, everyone needs to understand it. Just as through Moses God admonishes the Israelites (Deut 11:18-19) to teach their children His word and His ways. We need to teach our children not only His word and ways, but also how to pray.

Luke doesn't tell us which disciple asks Jesus the question. I believe that's because it's not as important as the fact that he asked. Praise God the question was asked. Jesus does a lot of praying in the Gospels. And there are numerous times when He tells his disciples they should pray. In Luke Jesus tells the disciples they should always watch and pray; they should pray they will not fall into temptation; and they should always pray and not give up. Prayer is an essential part of the Christian walk.

Jesus is at prayer in Luke 3:21; 6:12; 9:28, and in today's verse it's when he finishes praying that the question is asked. The disciples could see this was a regular practice for Jesus, and so the question is a natural. Their natural instinct told them if they were going to be like Jesus, they to needed to pray. In response to this question Jesus gives us an outline for how we should pray. In fact He tells them in Matthew 6:9: *"This, then, is how you should pray:"* He gives us this model for prayer so we will pray in a manner that is pleasing to God, in the will of God. In the verses following, Luke gives us five elements of a basic prayer; Matthew gives us six elements. If you want to pray in the will of God use these models. They are appropriate for every situation or circumstance. As we struggle with the questions of how to live Godly lives, here's one thing we don't have to struggle with. God has told us how to pray. Let's speak to Him the way He wants us to.

Point: God has taught us how to pray. The question came from observation; have your children asked you to teach them to pray?

Prayer: Lord, teach me to communicate with You in a manner that is pleasing to You and in Your will.

Today's Reading:
Psalm 18-19; Mark 10-11

July 19

God Loves Our Prayers

By Beth Nelson

Psalm 34:15 *The eyes of the Lord are on the righteous and his ears are attentive to their cry.*

God is our Father, and just like a father, He teaches us what we need to know and then gladly hears what we have to say to Him. I was reminded of His Fatherly love last week when I was with my brother and sister-in-law. They have one child, a daughter who is twenty years old. She is the joy of their lives and is always on their hearts and minds, even though she is living somewhere else with a friend and is trying to be more independent. They had not heard from her for two days and were beginning to miss her greatly. In fact, the day before, the friend had called on behalf of herself and their daughter, but you could tell that they were disappointed at not hearing their daughter's voice. They genuinely loved the daily communication that they were used to having with her.

Then the phone rang. My sister-in-law answered and when she heard her daughter's voice, she went off to another room to talk to her. She came back glowing and handed the phone to my brother, who also went off to talk to their daughter. He also came back glowing, recounting the fresh news that he had just gotten over the phone. I'll never forget the joy on their faces.

When we talk to God, it brings great joy to His heart. And He misses us and we miss Him when we fail to communicate. The Bible paints a wonderful picture of prayer. The prayers of God's people were represented by the incense that was offered up to God on the altar on a daily basis. It was a sweet-smelling sacrifice that was symbolic of ascending prayer and the person who was chosen to offer the incense regarded it as a solemn privilege. I'm struck by a reference in Revelation 5:8 which says that in heaven *"the elders were holding golden bowls full of incense, which are the prayers of the saints."* It shows me how precious our prayers are to our Father. They are represented by this lovely, fragrant aroma and are collected in great golden bowls. Anything that we speak or sing to God is collected there and never lost. He treasures our prayers. What an incredible picture of His love for us.

Point: Pray about everything. Pray without ceasing. It brings great joy to our Father and blessing to us.

Today's Reading:
Psalm 20-22; Mark 12

July 20

HONESTY

By Beth Nelson

Luke 18:14 *For everyone who exalts himself will be humbled, and he who humbles himself will be exalted.*

Jesus told a story about two men who went up to the temple to pray. One was a Pharisee, a knowledgeable teacher of the word of God. He began comparing his sins to everyone else's and thought he came out way ahead. He thanked God that he was who he was. The other man was a scorned tax collector, a man everyone knew was a sinner. He knew it himself. He stood off at a distance. He wouldn't even look up to heaven but bowed his head low before God. He beat on his breast in utter anguish and said, "God have mercy on me, a sinner." Jesus said that he, rather than the Pharisee, was justified before God. The Pharisee might as well have saved his time and his breath. His prayer got no higher than the ceiling. God didn't even hear him.

Sometimes I've come to God in self-righteousness. Usually I'm angry about something someone else did that in my opinion they obviously shouldn't have done. This happened to me for the first time after I'd been married for just a few weeks. (I'm married to a really great guy, by the way.) I thought that I knew God pretty well and had a handle on righteous living. I remember coming to God, just fuming about something. As I began pouring it out to God, He immediately turned it back on me. He said, "Look at you." When I looked at myself, all I could see was ugliness, anything but Christ-likeness. I was about as far away from the fruit of the Spirit as you could get, and I knew it. It was a hard lesson, but God began to do a deeper work in me beginning that day.

We cannot justify ourselves before God by comparing ourselves to other people. God will stop us in our tracks and He won't hear us. We can only come just as we are, with our pride, anger, self-pity or whatever it is and lay it at the foot of the cross. When we agree with Him about our own sin He can begin to change us. Only then does He hear us. Then our prayers reach all the way up to heaven and touch the heart of God.

Point: Be careful when you go to God in anger. He may have something to say to you.

Prayer: Lord, Have mercy on me, for I am indeed a sinner.

Today's Reading:
Psalm 23-24; Mark 13-14

July 21

Powerful Prayer
By Beth Nelson

James 5:16 *Therefore confess your sins to each other and pray for each other so that you may be healed. The prayer of a righteous man is powerful and effective.*

I would love for all of my prayers to be powerful and effective, wouldn't you? James says that the righteous person has powerful and effective prayers. Are you righteous before God? The Bible says that there is no one righteous, not even one (Rom 3:10) and that all of our righteous acts are like filthy rags. End of story?

No! This is not the end of the story. If Jesus had not come, this would be the end of it. But praise God! Though all of us have sinned and fallen far short of God's standards of perfection, yet a new righteousness, apart from the law has come to those who through faith believe in Jesus Christ. We cannot boast in ourselves and our righteous living but we can boast in the Lord. In Romans 4 Paul says that we are like Abraham, who believed God and it was credited to him as righteousness.

This passage in James does contain another key to powerful prayer. God will not hear us if we know that we are displeasing Him in some area of our lives but don't confess it and turn from it. When we come in honesty and humility before the Lord and open all areas of our lives up to Him, He shows us our sins. I find it difficult to admit my sins. It's especially hard for me to admit my sins to someone else because it's so humbling but it is powerful when I do!

So we can pray with power and great effect. First, we must know the One who is righteous. When we place our faith in Jesus Christ to save us, God counts it towards us as righteousness. Then we walk daily in the light of his word and his truth,

Point: God has placed the family of God on earth to bear each other's burdens and to pray for each other.

Prayer: Dear Lord, I confess my innermost sins to you. I desire to turn from them so that I may be healed.

Practice: May we be there to, not to criticize each other, but to hold one another up in prayer.

Today's Reading:
Psalm 25-27; Mark 15

July 22

A New Administration

By Beth Nelson

Exodus 34:10 *Then the LORD said: "I am making a covenant with you. Before all your people I will do wonders never before done in any nation in all the world. The people you live among will see how awesome is the work that I, the LORD, will do for you. 11 Obey what I command you today. I will drive out before you the Amorites, Canaanites, Hittites, Perizzites, Hivites and Jebusites. 12 Be careful not to make a treaty with those who live in the land where you are going, or they will be a snare among you. 13 Break down their altars, smash their sacred stones and cut down their Asherah poles. 14 Do not worship any other god, for the LORD, whose name is Jealous, is a jealous God.*

Sometimes I'm afraid that our thoughts about the Holy Spirit fall far short of what God's intent is. We think of having the Spirit superimposed over our lives, just adding the Spirit to who we already are. Painless, easy, but powerless. However, God is not content to be second-place. The Bible often describes God as a jealous God who is not willing to share his people with other gods; or as a husband whose heart breaks over his wayward wife. When we become Christians, the Holy Spirit takes up permanent residence in our lives, clashing with our old sinful nature. Paul speaks of delighting in God's law at the same time that his sinful nature is a slave to the law of sin (Rom 7).

No country can have two leaders. Can you imagine electing a new President, then allowing the old administration to stay in power along with the new administration? Would they be able to coexist peacefully and fruitfully? Of course not! We wouldn't think of allowing it. But I'm afraid that's what we do when we ask Him to be Lord of our lives – we give him a space in our lives but continue to cling to our old nature.

Even in the Old Testament, God ordered his people, the Israelites, to drive out the evil influences that were living among them. He told them to break, smash, and cut them down. Pretty strong language! His desire for us is nothing less than that. His Spirit gives us power to overcome beginning the moment we turn to God, away from sin. God told his people through Moses that He would do many wonders in their midst if they would just turn their hearts to Him alone. God loves to bless His people, but His blessings are often in proportion to the single-mindedness of our worship.

Praise God that we are no longer under condemnation, for the law of the Spirit of life has set us free from the law of sin and death. May be realize this truth and allow the Spirit to take control and to lead us to life and peace.

Today's Reading:
Psalm 28-29; Mark 16-Luke 1

July 23

WHO IS THE HOLY SPIRIT?

By Scott Kalevik

Luke 3:22 and the Holy Spirit descended on him in bodily form like a dove. And a voice came from heaven: "You are my Son, whom I love; with you I am well pleased."

Scripture says without question that there is only one God: Dt 6:4 *Hear, O Israel: The LORD our God, the LORD is one.* Yet, within this unity, God also reveals Himself as Three Persons: The Father, The Son, The Holy Spirit. We've come to call this the Trinity. It's a mystery that only God fully understands.

All three Persons of the Trinity are in today's passage. Jesus, the Son of God, is being baptized. The Holy Spirit descends upon Jesus in bodily form like a dove. And the Father's voice is heard from heaven saying, *"You are my Son, whom I love; with you I am well pleased."*

Our focus today is on the Person and the work of the third Person of the Trinity: The Holy Spirit. Scripture reveals much about the Holy Spirit in both the Old and New Testaments.

Honestly, some of us feel uncomfortable with the idea of the Holy Spirit. We have no trouble thinking about God as Father. We all have fathers. We can relate. Most of us identify easily with idea of Son for similar reasons. But the idea of God as Spirit is generally harder for us to conceptualize. How are we to relate to a Spirit?

The Hebrew word commonly used to refer to the Holy Spirit in the Old Testament is *Ruah*. It means "breath," "wind" or "breeze." The Greek word used in the New Testament is *Pnuema* and refers to "breath," or "wind" as well.

As we study we'll see that the Holy Spirit is revealed as God. He's a Person. He creates. He indwells the believer. He comforts. He counsels. He convicts of sin. He teaches. He intercedes on our behalf according to the will of the Father. He brings things to remembrance. He inspired the writing of scripture. He leads. He gives spiritual gifts to each believer to build up the Church.

You can't see Him, but the Holy Spirit of God is with you right now. He will lead your steps today and He will lead you into God's truth. Simply ask Him.

Today's Reading:
Psalm 30-32; Luke 2

July 24

AVAILABLE TO YOU

By Peggy Kalevik

Luke 3:16c *He will baptize you with the Holy Spirit and with fire.*

Isaiah predicted the coming of this great prophet, John the Baptist, the one who would prepare the way for the coming Messiah. God used John to open the door for Jesus to walk through and bring a world changing revival. God had been preparing His people for this since Adam and Eve took a tumble in the garden, and now we see clearly what He's been trying to tell us through His prophets for centuries.

John came baptizing with water to prepare us to receive the spiritual change to come. He preaches a basic message: repent and be saved. A humble and simple man born to aging parents; his whole life was dedicated to that for which God created Him, preaching the message of repentance for the forgiveness of sin. Jeremiah and Ezekiel both speak of God's preparation for the return of His people; John the Baptist is a part of that return to God, although, he was not the complete fulfillment of the Old Testament scriptures. We know that fulfillment is in the person of Jesus.

John told those who were present Jesus would baptize with the Holy Spirit and with fire. That is to say, Jesus will make the Holy Spirit available to all who receive Him. The Holy Spirit will have the effect of fire in that it will purge, purify and refine us. Fire in a biblical context is often used as a symbol of judgment. In this case the symbol applies. John says this one who avails the Holy Spirit to us will clear the threshing floor and gather the wheat into His barn, but will burn up the chaff with an unquenchable fire. John also exhorted the people and preached the good news, so it's evident they would receive grace as well through this one who was to come.

Point: Jesus has made the Holy Spirit available to all by the sacrifice of His life. Be baptized, in the name of Jesus Christ for the forgiveness of sin. And you will receive the gift of the Holy Spirit (Acts 2:38).

Today's Reading:
Psalm 33-34; Luke 3-4

July 25

Internal Renewal
By Peggy Kalevik

Psalm 51:11 *Do not cast me from your presence or take your Holy Spirit from me.*

Psalm 51 is a prayer of repentance and forgiveness. David pleads with the Lord for His forgiveness and renewal. He recognizes his sin and looks to God for cleansing. David's recognition of his sin is due to the revelation God gave through the prophet Nathan. It is only after God confronts him that David's conscience is pricked and the depravity of what he has done hits home and he confesses his sin. The Holy Spirit has a way of pricking our conscience, one of His purposes.

Among the many requests made by David in this Psalm is the request for God not to take His Holy Spirit from him. David understands in order to have communion with God he must be forgiven and cleansed of the sin he has committed. Along with forgiveness and cleansing he asks for wisdom, this too is essential for maintaining his relationship with God. For without wisdom how will he understand the things of God? Add to these the request for a pure heart and a renewed steadfast spirit and we see he is speaking of an internal renewal. And how do we get internal renewal? It's through the working of the Holy Spirit. Romans 8:26-27 gives us a striking view of the Spirit's working on our behalf, *"In the same way, the Spirit helps us in our weakness. We do not know what we ought to pray for, but the Spirit himself intercedes for us with groans that words cannot express. 27 And he who searches our hearts knows the mind of the Spirit, because the Spirit intercedes for the saints in accordance with God's will."* As is its purpose and nature the Holy Spirit intercedes on our behalf, He helps us when we are weak and leads us in straight paths. As Jesus said to Peter at Gethsemane, *"The spirit is willing, but the body is weak."* (Matt 26:41b). That Spirit who is willing to lead us and protect us from ourselves is also the same Spirit who gives us internal renewal when we falter.

Point: Trust the leading of the Holy Spirit in your life; be filled with contented rest only God can give.

Prayer: Father we are in awe to know that the same Spirit who raised Jesus from the dead lives in us. We thank and praise You for Your love, caring and mercy to us. Hallowed be Your name!

Today's Reading:
Psalm 35-37; Luke 5

July 26

THE CHRISTIAN HANDBOOK

By Peggy Kalevik

Galatians 2:16 … a man is not justified by observing the law, but by faith in Jesus Christ. So we, too, have put our faith in Christ Jesus that we may be justified by faith in Christ and not by observing the law, because by observing the law no one will be justified.

The one thing everyone knows about Martin Luther is that during his lifetime he changed the course of the Christian Church. Luther believed the Church had lost sight of several central truths. The most important of these is that salvation is a gift of God's grace, that we receive this gift by faith and trust in the promises of God. Through Christ's death on the cross our sins are forgiven. Man has done nothing to achieve it, nor is there anything man can do but accept the free gift. This revelation gave Luther great joy and reassurance; he found peace and freedom in this new understanding. Scholars believe Luther relied heavily on the book of Galatians in coming to his conclusions. The purpose of Galatians is to deliver this essential New Testament truth that we are justified by faith in the Lord Jesus Christ, not by works. We are sanctified not by the law but by the obedience which comes from faith in Christ.

Galatians 2:16 says we are justified or made innocent, pardoned. We are made innocent through our faith in Christ. In other words we are made "righteous" by believing and trusting in Christ's work on the cross; and we live according to the internal change made in us by the indwelling of the Holy Spirit. Therefore, we make a personal commitment to Him and we seek Him for comfort, wisdom and mercy; He is our refuge. We denounce any effort to justify our-selves through our own works. We know the works of man and the law are inadequate to bring us salvation. If we are to live up to our commitment we must let go of our sinful nature and all the acts that are part of that nature. We must rely on the grace and power of Christ and the Holy Spirit.

The "Fruit of the Spirit" is a natural product of the Holy Spirit. There are nine, but they are stated as a singular "fruit" to emphasize unity. Unlike the "gifts" of the Spirit, every Christian should possess all nine qualities of the fruit of the Spirit. (See 1Cor 12 for the gifts of the Spirit) Be prayerful as you go through Galatians 2 - 5, read it in the light of of verse 2:16; you are pardoned, set free, made righteous by the blood of Christ. As you read, evaluate yourself. Do you possess all the qualities listed in Galatians 5:22?

Today's Reading:
Psalm 38-39; Luke 6-7

July 27

The Promise of Joy
By Beth Nelson

Galatians 5:22 *The fruit of the Spirit is…joy!*

Does God owe me happiness? Listening to some preachers, you would think so. They've bought into our culture's materialism and twisted the gospel to proclaim wealth and health as evidence of God's favor. My mind keeps wandering to fellow believers living in impoverished third world countries. What about them? There's a lot of evidence that Christians in other countries, though they may live with disease and have nothing in terms of possessions, yet possess something that we are in short supply of here, namely the joy of the Lord.

Four years ago, the Evangelical Covenant Church sent a delegation to visit the Covenant Church of Congo. The Congo had been without missionaries for eight years, due to dangerous civil unrest. What they found was that "in the midst of all their suffering, the people still have joy, and the smiles on their faces radiate the love of Christ." The visitors were "inspired by the resilience and joyful faith of the believers in Congo…especially evident in the joy they express in the midst of suffering during years of turmoil." Covenant Companion, Vol XCIII p.6-7. The American Christians came away deeply blessed by their brothers and sisters in this devastated region of the world.

What the Lord offers to us is something deep and long-lasting, not dependent on outward circumstances. Ro 14:17 says "For the kingdom of God is not a matter of eating and drinking, (fleeting pleasures) but of righteousness, peace and joy in the Holy Spirit." Our joy began with the "good news of great joy" proclaimed at the birth of the Savior of the world. We are filled with indescribable joy when after asking, we receive. Jn 16:24 And we can perceptibly feel God's presence and are filled with profound joy whenever we stand alone in our witness for the Lord. Ac 5:41, 1Pe 4:13

After his sputtering start in the faith, the Apostle Peter went on to become as solid a rock as any of the first believers. As a seasoned spiritual father, he penned these lofty words, *"Though you have not seen him, you love him, and even though you do not see him now, you believe in him and are filled with an inexpressible and glorious joy, for you are receiving the goal of your faith, the salvation of your souls.* 1Pe 1:8-9 The joy of the Lord is a gift that can never be taken away.

Today's Reading:
Psalm 40-42; Luke 8

July 28

CONTENTMENT- IS YOUR GLASS FULL?

By Kathy Bryant

1 Timothy 6:6 *But godliness with contentment is great gain. 7 For we brought nothing into the world, and we can take nothing out of it. 8 But if we have food and clothing, we will be content with that.*

Let's suppose a glass represented your life and water represent the material things that we most need in this world. These items would be food, a home, a car, a job, a little ready cash, etc… Now imagine this glass is full of water in other words we have everything we need. If we add more water to the glass could it fill beyond its rim? The water would overflow and begin to waste. Similarly, material things beyond our basic needs could result in excesses or waste i.e. a bigger house, more cars, more money, and scaling the ever higher corporate ladder. If we are honest, we could not say that more things results in more sustained happiness. Some people begin to drown in excess that could lead to death.

The above passage reminds us of the potential foolishness of striving for things beyond those that the Lord has blessed us. The Lord knows what we need and He either provides or gives us the ability to provide them for our families and ourselves. We should be careful in wanting excessive amounts of things. We must keep our eyes on eternity and honoring our Lord and Savior.

Point: If we strive to become more Christ-like we can develop a sense of contentment and experience being blessed beyond measure.

Prayer: Lord heavenly Father, thank you for all that you provided for me. Help me to learn to focus on serving you. Lord guards my heart and mind from craving more material things than I need.

Practice: Learn how to be content with life's circumstances.

Today's Reading:
Psalm 43-44; Luke 9-10

July 29

THE LORD SAVES

By Peggy Kalevik

*Joshua 10:12 On the day the LORD gave the Amorites over to
Israel, Joshua said to the LORD in the presence of Israel: "O sun,
stand still over Gibeon, O moon, over the Valley of Aijalon."*

Over our Christian lives we have read much about Moses. We have seen his weaknesses and flaws, his strengths and his faith. We know of his wisdom and that God spoke to Him as a friend. But there are little things that show us his ability to discern or the depth of his wisdom that may have escaped our attention. Moses saw in Joshua great faith, courage, and a strong resolve to follow God. Seeing all these qualities in Hoshea Son of Nun Moses changed his name to Joshua Son of Nun. The name Hoshea means "salvation"; the name Joshua means "the Lord saves" its Greek form is Jesus. This change, the Lord saves, might have gone a long way in strengthening the character and determination of a young man (about forty-five years of age, Ex 17) an obedient servant of God, who was completely surrendered to the Lord.

Joshua's character was forged in the desert. The Bible never mentions anything about his life in Egypt. He comes on the scene in the desert at Rephidim when the Amalekites attack the Israelites. Moses with the staff of God in his uplifted hands stood on the hill and Joshua and the men he chose fought the Amalekites (Ex 17). At the end of the battle God told Moses to write of the victory on a scroll so that it would be remembered and make sure Joshua hears it. Joshua remained Moses' aide until Moses death, when he succeeded him. Joshua is best remembered for his bravery as a warrior and his courage. When he returned from spying out the land of the Canaanites, he and Caleb were the only two of the twelve who wanted to enter the Land in obedience to God (Num 14:6-8).

Joshua had many combat victories, the battle at Ai (Josh 8), the defeat of Jericho (Josh 5 & 6), and he made peace with the Gibeonites (Josh 9), to name a few. But I most remember him for God's great favor. During the Israelite battle against the five kings of the Amorites, Joshua prayed to the Lord: *"O sun, stand still over Gibeon, O moon, over the Valley of Aijalon."* So the sun stood still, and the moon stopped, till the nation avenged itself on its enemies, as it is written in the Book of Jashar. The sun stopped in the middle of the sky and delayed going down about a full day(Josh 10). God made the sun stand still for an entire day (24 hours). No one who is alive today or ever lived can say that except Joshua. God loved him and he was always faithful to God. After Moses death he led the Israelites into the Promise Land. God made him an aide to Moses, then a General in the Israelite army, then the leader of God's people.

Point: True surrender to God is itself a reward.

Today's Reading:
Psalm 45-47; Luke 11

July 30

HAD ENOUGH?

By Scott Kalevik

Job 17:11 *My days have passed, my plans are shattered, and so are the desires of my heart.*

Job had had enough. He lost his health, his family, his wealth, his possessions, and his livelihood. His 'friends' questioned his integrity. His pain was beyond imagination. As he says, 'my plans are shattered, and so are the desires of my heart.' Job assumed it was all over. He was finished. And yet, Job, despite how he felt about his life, was right in the middle of God's plan.

After accomplishing God's purpose for his trouble, Job was completely restored. Job 42:10 *After Job had prayed for his friends, the LORD made him prosperous again and gave him twice as much as he had before.*

Perhaps your heart is telling you to give up today. Is the test too hard? Do you feel like it's all over for you? Is depression creeping in?

In times like these it will help us to consider Job. Despite his destitution, the Lord restored him. Although Job thought things would never get better, the Lord understood exactly what to do and when to do it.

The Lord knows exactly why you're experiencing the tests you're going through today. He has a purpose. He is good. It is never too late for the Lord. Whenever He decides, everything changes.

So if you've had enough today, renew your hope in the power and love of the Lord. Ask Him for help again. Be faithful to His calling on your life. Help is on the way!

Today's Reading:
Psalm 48-49; Luke 12-13

July 31

BE AT PEACE

By Peggy Kalevik

Ephesians 2:14 For he himself is our peace, who has made the two one and has destroyed the barrier, the dividing wall of hostility,

Peace with God our creator is essential in our Christian walk. In Romans 1 we read about the wrath of God and get an understanding of the result of estrangement from God. But God found a way to heal the rift between Him and us. He has given us harmony with Him again. Once torn out of our grasp by a single act of Adam and Eve, Jesus has brought us peace with God.

Jesus is our peace. He was able to bring peace between God and man, between Jews and Gentiles and between me and you. Peace in the context of today's scripture verse is harmony in all relationships. In 1 Peter 3, Peter says we must seek peace and pursue it. How do you seek peace with someone who is stubborn and unreasonable? We face these kinds of dilemmas often in our lives. We learn how to cope, but we don't always make peace with the people in our lives. We tolerate them; we're polite we even help them out if we need to. But let's face it; there are people in our lives we simply don't like. I can honestly say I don't hate anyone, but there are people I wouldn't miss if I never saw them again. Now that's not the attitude God is looking for in me, or you. It doesn't matter that these people have been mean to me or someone I love; or that they have treated my love ones with disrespect, or have falsely accused and maligned them. No, God still wants me to live at peace with them and even love them. God knows about false accusations, lying and deception. All of those things were done to Jesus, yet He loved His enemies and tried to bring them to salvation.

God wants us to understand that His kingdom is not about how we feel when we believe we've been mistreated, it is about righteousness, peace and joy in the Holy Spirit. Yes, God cares when we are hurt by the mistreatment of others, and He will restore our peace when we bring the pain to Him. But He also loves the person or persons who hurt us. He wants us to bring our troubles, no matter how big or small to the foot of the cross and leave them with Him. He is our peace.

Point: Our peace is in understanding that Jesus is peace as well as life and hope. If you have not received Jesus, receive Him today and be at peace.

Today's Reading:
Psalm 50-52; Luke 14

August 1

Goodness – Don't give up or "What's the Use"
By Kathy Bryant

Galatians 6:9-10 *And let us not grow weary while doing good, for in due season we shall reap if we do not lose heart. Therefore, as we have opportunity, let us do well to all, especially to those who are of the household of faith.*

Do you ever wonder why people do not volunteer more often when a need arises? Some say that they are too busy, others become overwhelmed by the need, while others might be physically unable, yet others say that nothing changes so what's the use! All of these reasons can be valid but are they symptoms of weariness. When we work for the Lord, it takes a lot of effort (100%) and dedication. The Holy Spirit gives us the strength and the grace to carry on when we want to quit. We need to draw strength from our Lord through prayer and studying the word. When we rely on our own human strength we will surely burnout and grow weary. All of us have a job to do in spreading the word to the lost, showing the love of Jesus Christ to the world, and caring for our fellow brothers and sisters.

Point: When we feel that we are running on empty we can draw strength from the Lord Jesus.

Prayer: Lord, help us to have the strength to serve you and the lost in the world, and among fellow believers in your church.

Practice: Time spent in prayer and study can energize the mind and spirit for service.

Today's Reading:
Psalm 53-54; Luke 15-16

August 2

FAMILY RESEMBLANCES
By Beth Nelson

1 John 4:7 *Dear friends, let us love one another, for love comes from God. Everyone who loves has been born of God and knows God. Whoever does not love does not know God, because God is love.*

Children from the same family often have strong family resemblances. I was out with my children one day when I heard a little girl say, "Those girls have the same face." Until then, I hadn't realized how much my girls looked alike. In the same way, we who are born of God should have a strong, unmistakable resemblance to our Heavenly Father. Jesus said, *"By this all men will know that you are my disciples, if you love one another."* Jn 13:35 When asked what is the greatest commandment? Jesus replied, *"Love the Lord your God with all your heart and with all your soul and with all your mind...And the second is like it: 'Love your neighbor as yourself.' All the Law and the Prophets hang on these two commandments."* Mt. 22:37-40 It was love for mankind that caused God to send his only Son to this earth, that we might see love personified. It was love for mankind that caused Jesus to give up his position in heaven to pay for the sins that we had committed. "God is love," wrote John, the disciple closest to Jesus.

We know that it is often much easier to say, "I love you," than to act in love. 1Jn 3:18 says, *"let us not love with words or tongue but with actions and in truth."* We can't do it in our own strength, so God equips us by filling us with His Spirit of love, *"to love each other deeply, from the heart."* 1Jn 2:15,1Pet 1:22 *"He who does not love, does not know God, for God is love."* The Bible says that we are to love those who don't love us; to love those who wrong us; to love our enemies. And again, what is impossible for us is only possible in the power of the Holy Spirit.

One of the most profound demonstrations of God's love in my time was when the families of the young Amish girls that were murdered reached out in love to the family of the murderer. The world was stunned. When asked why they had done this, they said that they were simply obeying God; and since God loved them, He expected them to also act in love. To me, that is the ultimate example of love. All of my struggles to love pale by comparison. Since God loved us when we were his enemies, can we not do the same?

Today's Reading:
Psalm 55-57; Luke 17

August 3

Fill me with Your Goodness
By Peggy Kalevik

Romans 15:14 I myself am convinced, my brothers, that you yourselves are full of goodness, complete in knowledge and competent to instruct one another.

How can Paul be convinced that the brothers at the Church of Rome are full of goodness? God alone knows the heart of man, how can any of us be sure that someone is filled with goodness? In the first two verses of this chapter Paul states his case. Those who are strong in the faith, with the greatest understanding of the word, are expected to do what is best for everyone. They are to imitate Christ for the benefit of believers, especially for those who have less understanding. *"We who are strong ought to bear with the failings of the weak and not to please ourselves. Each of us should please his neighbor for his good, to build him up. For even Christ did not please himself..."* We should do what is best for the community, not what will benefit us as individuals. The goal in this case is to build up and encourage. Isn't that what God wants us to do; to build up, to edify the Church? If our faith is strong enough to do this then we should be filled with goodness.

Goodness is showing generosity to others (spiritual, material) not out of obligation but out of love in order to fulfill our commitment to Christ. We must all resist the temptation to be motivated by a desire to benefit self. Our level of generosity should be equal to our maturity in Christ. Peter tells us to *"make every effort to add to your faith goodness"* (2 Peter1:5). Goodness is an attribute of Christ; therefore, all his followers should possess it. It is a sign of mature faith and the knowledge of God.

In Romans 3 Paul quotes a verse from Psalm 14 which says no one does good, not even one. Its point is that no one does good because man ignored and turned away from God; paid no attention to the will of God; and acted in malice toward anyone who sought to serve and obey God. Jesus tells the rich young man that no one is good except God (Mark 10). Jesus is not denying he is good, but He is trying to give the young man an understanding that his only chance for salvation is to rely completely on God. So both statements point to one thing, no one does good outside their dependence on God. Our goodness is dependent on our acceptance of God, our maturity in the faith and a desire to do His will.

Point: God expects His believers to act in goodness.

Prayer: How great is your goodness, which you have stored up for those who fear you, which you bestow in the sight of men on those who take refuge in you. (Psalm31:19)

Today's Reading:
Psalm 58-59; Luke 18-19

August 4

Fighting With Truth!

By Scott Kalevik

1 Samuel 14:4-5 *On each side of the pass that Jonathan intended to cross to reach the Philistine outpost was a cliff; one was called Bozez, and the other Seneh. 5 One cliff stood to the north toward Micmash, the other to the south toward Geba.*

One of the constant attacks against faith is the question of whether or not the Bible can be trusted. Is it true? Did the stories really happen? Is it God's word? Our culture believes each individual should be able to make up his or her own truth and, therefore, the idea that one book really IS true is unacceptable. If the Bible is true, then any belief that contradicts the Bible is false.

The truth of God's word is reinforced time and time again. Today's passage tells about a battle fought by Jonathan when his father, Saul, was king. Jonathan's strategy was to ambush the enemy by climbing up a cliff between two rocky points. God blessed him with victory. In World War One a British Army Officer named Major Vivian Gilbert was stationed in Palestine. He believed the Bible was true. His brigade had received orders to take Michmash, a village that was atop a cliff on the other side of a deep valley. The name of the village struck a chord in Major Gilbert's mind. Could this be the same Micmash that Jonathan attacked? He searched the scriptures until he found this account in First Samuel. He read Jonathan's story. He took his Bible to his commanding officer and explained that the best way to attack was to climb up between the rocks of Bozez and Seneh just like Jonathan.

The Commander sent a scouting party to find the rocks described. It was just like the Bible said it was. During the night, the Brits scaled the cliff by climbing between the very rocks Jonathan went through centuries before. The Turks were defeated and the village was taken. The tactics described in God's word proved to be true and reliable (Keller, *The Bible As History*, pages 179-180).

Fight your battles today knowing that everything God says is true. When you rely on His word, you're armed with the truth!

Point: God's word is true.
Prayer: Lord, help me rely on everything you've said.
Practice: Am I putting all of my confidence in God's truth?

Today's Reading:
Psalm 60-62; Luke 20

August 5

Humble

By Peggy Kalevik

2 Chronicles 7:14 *If my people, who are called by my name, will humble themselves and pray and seek my face and turn from their wicked ways, then will I hear from heaven and will forgive their sin and will heal their land.*

This might be one of the most loved scripture verses of the entire Bible. It's certainly one of the most quoted. There are a few people in the Bible who have been able to live up to it. I wonder if we can find anyone in our lives today who genuinely lives up to this verse. This is one of my greatest concerns about the Church in America. We have little or no humility; in fact we think it's a sign of weakness. We are so proud of our accomplishments we've forgotten who allowed us to achieve them. When we were children we were taught to get on our knees and pray before going to bed at night. That was a keeper, but did we keep it? Getting on your knees to pray puts you in a humble place, it's a good thing.

In this verse God gives his requirements for receiving His blessings; the requirements for being His people. Any one who has decided to serve and worship Him must humble themselves. They must pray and seek His face; they must turn from their wicked ways. Then He will hear and forgive their sin and, in addition, He will heal their land. At a time when we're all concerned with the state of our nation these are chilling words because we can see, as a nation, we are not humble before God. God is telling us to change our behaviors, repent and seek His face. How do we get a nation, this nation, to turn back to God? We start by looking in the mirror; we change the behavior and habits of the person we see in the reflection. In our year of drawing near to God, the one person we can help to become truly humble is the person in the mirror. You don't have the power to change anyone else.

Moses was known for his humility. Jesus said of himself (Matt 11:29) that He was gentle and humble in heart. We know He had great humility because he went to the crucifixion without defense. We would never go to any legal hearing without an attorney, but He didn't even try to defend himself. When Daniel humbled himself before God, he received a quick response (Dan 10:12). Let us change the way we live, the way we think and the way we love God. Let us love Him better and worship Him better by living our lives in a way that pleases, honors and glorifies Him. Maybe, all it takes is a handful of people humbling themselves before God, praying and honoring God with their lives to turn a church, a city or a nation back to God.

Point: Humble yourself before our God and receive His many blessing.

Today's Reading:
Psalm 63-64; Luke 21-22

August 6

DEFENSE THROUGH RELIANCE!
By Scott Kalevik

Luke 12:12 *for the Holy Spirit will teach you at that time what you should say."*

What do you say when your faith is challenged? Some of us get defensive and try to argue with whomever delivers the challenge. It's like we want to prove that we are right. But God only wants us to speak the truth in love. The Lord is more than capable of defending Himself.

Others of us chose to say nothing. We justify our silence by thinking to ourselves that it is better not to have a confrontation. Still others of us live our lives so that no one could guess that we follow Jesus. If the opposition doesn't know we love the Lord, maybe they'll leave us alone. But there is a better option.

Jesus warned His disciples that they would be persecuted. A servant is no greater than his master. But the Lord also gave His disciples a tremendous truth. Jesus promised that the Holy Spirit would supply the defense for the disciple whenever necessary. In other words, the Spirit will teach the disciple and give the disciple the words to speak at the appropriate time and in the appropriate way whenever challenged.

So when it comes to answering those who oppose the gospel, our greatest asset isn't our knowledge. Our greatest asset isn't our intellectual ability. Our greatest asset by far is the Holy Spirit. We simply need to rely on His guidance and speak the words He gives us to say.

We are certainly not exempt from learning God's word and from building ourselves up in the faith so that the Spirit has more to bring to our remembrance in those times of testing. But, next time you're challenged by someone regarding your faith in Jesus, simply whisper a prayer. Ask the Spirit to guide your response and give you the words to say. He will!

Today's Reading:
Psalm 65-67; Luke 23

August 7

It's Just Not Fair!

By Scott Kalevik

Acts 12:2 He had James, the brother of John, put to death with the sword.

When things don't go the way we think they should, we are sometimes tempted to view God as being unfair. As if the Lord was acting against us in some way. Like toddlers refused ice cream, many tend to complain when God "doesn't come through" according to expectations. Consider James. He was part of the three disciples – Peter, James and John - whom Jesus routinely took aside for private lessons. He was one of a few who attended the transfiguration in Matthew 17 for instance. He was well trained and equipped by the Lord. And yet in Acts 12 Herod arrests James and kills him.

Acts 12 goes on to tell us that Herod also arrests Peter. But instead of death by sword like James, Peter receives a heavenly jail break from an angel of God. Is that fair? Why did Peter get a heavenly jail break and James get the sword? Does God care less about James than Peter?

Scripture declares clearly that God is a God of love. The Lord is sovereign. No circumstance is out of His control. Scripture tells us that He works for the good of those who love Him. We know, therefore, that God is never unfair or unloving. When we determine God to be unfair, the problem is in us, not Him.

God sees life from the perspective of His eternal plan. He knows why He's created each of us and He knows exactly when our lives will end (Psalm 139). He understands how our lives serve His purpose from beginning to end. He views death as simply the doorway from time to eternity.

We do best to transform our thinking by moving away from the idea that God needs to meet our expectations and moving toward the idea that we need to meet His. When we recognize the truth that we are the creation and the Lord is the Creator, we relieve ourselves of the burden of trying to make God meet our expectations. Instead, we can rest in the truth that our God is never unjust or unfair. He always acts in accordance with His purpose and plan.

Today's Reading:
Psalm 68-69; Luke 24-John 1

August 8

Empowered by the Spirit

By Beth Nelson

Jude 24 *To Him who is able to keep you from falling and to present you before His glorious presence without fault and with great joy —*

Imagine a poor man inheriting a large sum of money and then just letting it sit in the bank, never drawing on it to take care of his own needs. He continues to live in poverty and squalor, though right at his fingertips is the power to rise above it. Many of God's children live in spiritual poverty, believing that we are powerless to rise above the grip of fear, sin and despair. But the very same God who spoke the universe into existence, who created all that there is, has given us his incomparable Spirit, a Spirit of great power to live victoriously and to carry out His work. Jesus told his disciples, But you will receive power when the Holy Spirit comes on you. Acts 1:8 The fact is, the disciples were utterly powerless until they received the Holy Spirit at Pentecost. But after they had been filled with the Holy Spirit, it says *"With great power the apostles continued to testify to the resurrection of the Lord Jesus."* (Acts 4:33). The disciples, each one led by the Spirit, went forth and boldly witnessed to the saving grace of the Lord, casting out demons and praying over the sick in the power of the Spirit. The world was transformed.

God's children have inherited the same Spirit of power. Power to break the shackles of sin, power to overcome our fears, power to live victoriously. Paul says We are more than conquerors through Him who loved us. Rom 8:37 *The Spirit has power to conquer sin in our lives, to put to death the misdeeds of the body.* v13 *God's Spirit replaces our weakness with His strength.* I love 2Tim1:7 which says, *For God did not give us a spirit of timidity but a spirit of power, of love and of a sound mind.*

In writing to the church in Ephesus, Paul prayed that they would begin to understand the wealth of spiritual riches that were theirs. He says, *I keep asking that.. the glorious Father may give you the Spirit of wisdom and revelation, so that you may know Him better...know the hope to which He has called you, the riches of his glorious inheritance in the saints, and his incomparably great power for us who believe.*1:17-20 Let us not just believe in Jesus and stop there, as if that was all there is to the Christian life. Let us have the eyes of our hearts opened so that we may know the great hope to which He has called us, the glorious inheritance that we have. Then let us begin to draw on the incomparable riches and power that He has given us by his Spirit, and live more like children of the King.

Today's Reading:
Psalm 70-72; John 2

August 9

GENTLENESS, MEEKNESS AND HUMILITY
By Peggy Kalevik

Isaiah 66:2b *This is the one I esteem: he who is humble and contrite in spirit, and trembles at my word.*

When I first came to Living Hope, I prayed for the Church body to have humility. I prayed it because I came out of a Church where there was very little, if any, humility. In my opinion, it was the lack of humility and reverence for God's word which destroyed that body. So, I prayed it when I was alone, I prayed it at prayer meetings, I prayed it sitting in my seat during the Worship Service. I was so afraid we'd fall into the same horrible situation. Arrogant, aggressive and/or hostile behavior can destroy any group or body whether it is a Church family, work environment or your home. Blessed are the meek, for they will inherit the earth. God forgive our disrespect of Your Word.

Bible teachers say when the Bible repeats itself over and over it's emphasizing the importance of the statement. The Bible tells us many times that a meek, gentle and/or humble spirit or heart is what God wants in us. Yet, it seems in America we have the right to be as mean and cruel and rude as we can to anyone, including God, at anytime. And we enjoy doing it! However, if you read 2 Samuel 16, you can see that sometimes we should simply take the heat. When someone is just plain rude, it might be best, no matter what the situation, to say nothing. Jesus was the epitome of meek and humble. Isaiah says of him 'He was oppressed and afflicted, yet he did not open his mouth'. When I was in the worst place of my life, I repeated this verse to myself often. I prayed it. It was my life line.

Isaiah's words in today's verse are reminiscent of a time when the people trembled at the reading of God's Ten Commandments. As the Commandments were being read, there was thunder and lightning, the sound of the trumpet could be heard and the mountain was covered in smoke. The people trembled and stayed at a distance. Now, during the reading of the Bible at a worship service, we yawn and stretch and try to keep from falling asleep. What has happened to us? We don't see that this kind of attitude is an affront to God. He is disrespected and abused by our lack of humility and reverence before Him. We "must" be humble before God!

Point: I invite you to chase these three attributes through the Bible, see them from a new place of reverence, and then wear them like a treasured garment.

Today's Reading:
Psalm 73-74; John 3-4

August 10

Our most Deadly Weapon
By Peggy Kalevik

James 3:8 *but no man can tame the tongue. It is a restless evil, full of deadly poison…*

All kinds of animals, birds, reptiles and creatures of the sea are being tamed and have been tamed by man, but no man can tame the tongue. I don't know about you, but this is my greatest weakness. The gentleman who does my hair says I have an opinion about everything, and I'm not afraid to share it. He's known me for seventeen years, I think he's right. A few years before I stopped working, it started to occur to me that my opinion didn't matter to most people, so why give it? I also learned that some things are best left unsaid. Over the last four years I've gotten a little better still, because I don't want to get my husband fired. I've learned since I've stopped voicing my opinion so much, I don't have nearly as much drama and turmoil in my life. Praise God!

Self-control concerns not just our tongue, but also our mind and how we conduct ourselves. If we achieve self-control we can live out our life without becoming bogged down in things which cause us to sin. Isn't that the goal of the Christian; to walk in relationship with God in purity of heart, soul and mind?

James tells us in chapter 3 the tongue has the power to destroy and corrupt the whole person. He says it is "a fire, a world of evil among the parts of the body." This little body part can bring the world to its knees. Think about how John the Baptist met his end. A young girl "asked" for his head on a platter. If only she'd ask for a new dress! When Pilate asked the crowd "what then shall I do with Jesus", they answered "crucify him". The power of the tongue can change the course of history. However, James' point is not just about the tongue, but the mind as well. The tongue speaks what the mind communicates to it. The mind uses the tongue as an instrument. Don't miss in verse 6, he says the fire is from hell. You know that can't be good!

This scripture is set-up like a comedian's joke, except, the punch line is so poignant. Man has tamed every animal over which God has given him dominion, but he has lost dominion over himself, by the lack of self-control over his tongue.

Point: Guard, guide and govern my tongue today. Help me to be quiet before you.

Today's Reading:
Psalm 75-77; John 5

222

August 11

Who's in Control?

By Beth Nelson

Galatians 5:23 *But the fruit of the Spirit is…self-control.*

If you were to run in the Olympics, you would take off any extra weight and anything loose that could tangle you up, because, after all, you're running to win! Paul says that in the very same way, we must throw off those weights that hinder us and those sins that so easily entangle, so that we can *"run with perseverance the race marked out for us."* Heb 12:1

Often what weighs us down, what trips us up in life is our sinful lack of self-control. 1Pe 5:8 says, *"Be self-controlled and alert. Your enemy the devil prowls around like a roaring lion looking for someone to devour."* Satan is waging a fierce battle against us. He wants to master our souls, and he attacks us by appealing to our areas of weakness. Our tongue may be out of control; our appetites for food, sex or money. We may have uncontrollable anger, or an addiction. I've had several areas of weakness in my life. God began dealing with me in an area after a few years of being out of control. But not until I turned to Him in honesty and helplessness, did He step in and take over. And I've been grateful to Him ever since. That weight is gone.

We like to think that we're in total control of every area of our lives. Praise God if you are! But in this spiritual battle, our flesh is often out of control. And self-control is only possible through the mighty power of the Lord. Remember that God's grace is there for the humble. His promise is that *"The God of all grace will himself restore you and make you strong, firm and steadfast."* 1Pe 5:10 Do you want that for yourself? Admit that you are powerless to control yourself in every area of your life. Will you ask Him for help today?

Today's Reading:
Psalm 78-79; John 6-7

August 12

Got Fruit?

By Scott Kalevik

Psalm 1:3 *He is like a tree planted by streams of water, which yields its fruit in season and whose leaf does not wither. Whatever he does prospers.*

Have you ever felt like the fruits of the Spirit just weren't happening as they should in your life? No joy or peace in your life? Do you lack love for others? No patience? What's wrong?

We know that God never plays favorites. He is willing to produce godly fruit in any of us. So why don't we exhibit the fruits of the Spirit as we should?

Scripture uses the analogy of a tree planted by streams of water to describe a godly person. Have you ever walked the banks of a river and seen those huge trees that flourish near the water? Why do they get so big?

They thrive in that setting because they have all the nutrients and water necessary to facilitate their growth. Their roots are routinely soaked with life giving water. The rich mud around the banks of the river is full of those things required for growth. How simple it is for them to bear fruit.

What are your spiritual roots planted in today? Are you near the living water of God's truth? Are you sinking your roots into the daily relationship of prayer with the Lord? Are you serving faithfully as the Lord leads you and feeds your soul? If so, you will produce fruit. But if you're trying to receive your spiritual nutrition from some secular source, you'll dry up.

Many people told me that when we fasted from television in January, they felt as if they received their lives back. They had time to read their Bibles. They had time to pray. They had time to spend with their families. They talked to their friends. What happened? They planted themselves in places that truly facilitate life and growth. Instead of sitting in front of the tube – a place where there is almost no spiritual nutrition – they read their Bibles and prayed. They received the nutrition the Lord provides.

No fruit? Where are you planted?

Today's Reading:
Psalm 80-82; John 8

August 13

WHO HAS TIME FOR PATIENCE?

By Beth Nelson

Galatians 5:22 *The fruit of the Spirit is…patience.*

Who among us has not become impatient with someone who seems to take forever? I know I have. And it often leads to harsh words, anger. To be sure, we would all like to see faster results with our children, with other people, with the church. What about Jesus? Did He ever get frustrated with the twelve disciples? Oh yes. At one point, He becomes exasperated as he deals with the disciples' slowness to 'get it:' (see Mt. 17:17-20) But did he abandon them or switch them out for fresher, brighter disciples who would get it the first time around? No. They were family, His children, and even knowing their important mission, He patiently taught them and loved them to the very end. I'm afraid we would have been looking around for better prospects long ago.

Sometimes our frantic, achievement-oriented culture is the enemy of what is best in life. We have little patience for tasks that take a long time, for people that don't move quickly, for people that don't look like they're ever going to change. Patience is a fruit of the Spirit. Through patience we stick with our kids, praying over them until they 'get it.' Through patience we stick it out with our spouse, praying over them and over ourselves until we both 'get it.' Through patience we do without until God gives us the increase to take care of what we really need.

The antidote for impatience is faith in a trustworthy God who keeps His promises. Abraham and Sarah had to wait until well past child-bearing years before God gave them a child. David had to wait for years hiding from King Saul before he was crowned king. God's purposes take time – I've sometimes waited for years, not always patiently, but then I've been blessed to see God stirring, arranging circumstances, changing lives. I also know that God has been patient with my own foot-dragging, excruciating slowness to get with the program. And others have had to be patient with me, too.

The Bible tells us to *"be patient, bearing with one another in love."* Ep 4:2 To *"encourage the timid, help the weak, be patient with everyone."* 1Th 5:14 Praise God that He is so patient with us. Let us extend that same patience to the people around us.

Today's Reading:
Psalm 83-84; John 9-10

August 14

WEARING THE COAT OF KINDNESS
By Beth Nelson

Micah 6:8 *And what does the Lord require of you? To act justly, love kindness, and to walk humbly before God.*

I was with two other girls driving from Seattle to Minneapolis for our summer break from college when the car broke down in the middle of the freeway in Montana. I'm not sure what we would have done if some kind strangers had not immediately done a u-turn and come to our aid. We ended up staying with them for a week while our car was being repaired. I have never forgotten the kindness of that family.

God is unfailingly kind toward us. He is even kind to the ungrateful and wicked. Lk 6:35 In fact, it is not His wrath but His wonderful kindness that leads us toward repentance. Ro 2:4

Because God Himself is kind to all, He admonishes us also to be kind. In the OT God infused his kindness into the Israelites' code of life. The people of Israel are charged with observing kindness and justice Hos 12:6 He said to them, If one of your people should become poor, help him. Lev 25:35 Set aside a portion of your produce to give to the Levite, the alien, the fatherless and the widow. Dt 26:12 Whoever is kind to the needy honors God. Pr 14:31 Sometimes it is a kindness to tell someone the truth. David said, *"Let a righteous man rebuke me – it is a kindness."* Ps 141:5 But more often we're in need of a kind word: *"An anxious heart weighs a man down, but a kind word cheers him up."* Pr 12:25

In the NT, God continues to expects His people to shed their selfishness and to take on His kindness. "As God's chosen people, holy and dearly loved, clothe yourselves with compassion and kindness." Kindness shown to someone at a difficult time in their lives can make a huge difference for them. We may not know what hardship or pain another person is experiencing, but precisely because of that, we should show kindness always. We can treat others no less kindly than our God, whose compassion and kindness touches all.

Today's Reading:
Psalm 85-87; John 11

August 15

FAITHFUL CHILDREN OF A FAITHFUL FATHER
By Beth Nelson

1 Corinthians 4:2 *Now it is required that those who
have been given a trust must prove faithful.*

The word 'faithfulness' denotes trustworthiness or dependability. It's the glue that keeps marriages and families together, businesses in operation, the military a cohesive unit, and must be in place or a country will apart.

Our currency says, 'In God We Trust.' But what does that mean? We, as a Christian people, know that God is faithful. His trustworthiness is our stronghold. The Bible says, *"The word of the Lord is right and true; he is faithful in all he does."* Ps 33:4 *"God is faithful to fulfill all his promises."* Ps 145:13. Praise God that His faithfulness toward me isn't dependent on my perfectly unwavering faith. 2Tim 2:13 says, *"Even if I am faithless, He remains faithful, for He cannot deny Himself."* The Lord was faithful to fulfill his promise to make of Abraham a great nation, even though Abraham wavered in his faith. He fulfilled his promise to David to establish his kingdom forever (a promise fulfilled in the birth of Jesus) even though David faltered in his own commitments. *And He who began a good work in you and me will be faithful to carry it on to completion.* Php 1:6

God requires that we remain faithful to our word: our word to God, our word to others. The ability to be faithful to our commitments is the fruit of a life rooted in a faithful God. Though everything around us may change, the faithfulness of the Lord endures forever. Ps 117:2 And his love and compassions never fail. *"They are new every morning; great is your faithfulness."* La 3:22-23

Today's Reading:
Psalm 88-89; John 12-13

August 16

WALKING ON THE HIGHWAY OF HEAVEN!
By Scott Kalevik

Isaiah 35:8 *And a highway will be there; it will be called the Way of Holiness. The unclean will not journey on it; it will be for those who walk in that Way; wicked fools will not go about on it. 9 No lion will be there, nor will any ferocious beast get up on it; they will not be found there. But only the redeemed will walk there, 10 and the ransomed of the LORD will return. They will enter Zion with singing; everlasting joy will crown their heads. Gladness and joy will overtake them, and sorrow and sighing will flee away.*

You've heard of I-70, I-225, and I-25? Next time you're stuck in traffic, think about this: Isaiah tells us that in God's kingdom there is a highway called the Way of Holiness.

The Way of Holiness never has traffic jams. It's a highway reserved for those who have been ransomed and redeemed. It leads those who walk upon it to the paradise of God. We'll sing and experience everlasting joy on the Way of Holiness.

The unclean will not walk on God's highway. Wicked fools won't take one step on His highway.

Notice carefully the people God allows on His highway: those who have been ransomed and redeemed. We pay taxes or tolls to use earthly highways. To walk on God's Way of Holiness requires one to be redeemed. How are we redeemed? Through Jesus Christ! We simply believe and follow. God has paid for our redemption. He has sent His Son Jesus to die for our sins. In other words, through the work of Jesus, God has already paid our toll.

As you go through your day today, try to remind yourself to think about God's highway. Sadness may grip you today because of loss or misfortune, but God has a plan that will come to pass and through Christ, you'll someday walk on His Way of Holiness if you're redeemed.

Point: We have a great hope in Christ.
Prayer: Help me focus on your plan for my future instead of on circumstances.
Practice: Today I will consciously direct my thinking away from the traffic jams of earthly highways to focus myself on God's plan for my future!

Today's Reading:
Psalm 90-92; John 14

August 17

WHY THE PREACHER CAN'T CUT IT!

By Scott Kalevik

Colossians 3:16a *Let the word of Christ dwell in you richly...*

Let's do the math. Your preacher preaches for 30 minutes every Sunday. There are 52 Sundays every year. So, if you go to church every Sunday, you will be exposed to 26 hours of preaching God's word every year. What? You don't go to church every Sunday? How many Sundays do you miss every year? One? Two? Five? Ten? More than ten?

Let's say you miss five Sundays a year. That means you're exposed to 23.5 hours of preaching each year. So, out of the 365 days each year, you listen to God's preached word less than one day a year. (Please feel free to do your own math based on your own individual attendance).

What? You say your preacher doesn't preach every Sunday? What? Your preacher was preaching but you fell asleep? If your preacher isn't preaching, or if you fell asleep during the sermon, your exposure to the preached word is reduced again.

You say, "Pastor, I can also attend weekly Bible Study and Sunday School to gain more instruction in God's word." Yes, that's true. But do you? Even if you attend these every week, your total time in God's word would still likely be less than 3 days per year. What would happen if you decided to eat food only three days per year? Your physical body would starve to death! Is it any wonder that our spiritual lives are weak given the amount of time we study God's word?

Do you see that your daily time of reading and studying God's word for yourself is the key to knowing God's truth? Listening to the preacher is great, but the preacher can't cut it. Going to Bible study is great. But it's not enough. You need more exposure to God's word than the preacher or the study can give you. If God's word is to dwell in you richly, it's essential that you read it and study it for yourself daily. Your knowledge of God depends on your time in His word.

Today's Reading:
Psalm 93-94; John 15-16

August 18

GETTING UNSTUCK!

By Scott Kalevik

2 Corinthians 5:21 *God made him who had no sin to be sin for us,*
so that in him we might become the righteousness of God.

The phone rang at midnight. The friend on the other end of the line told me that he was tired of living like he's been living. We talked about how Jesus could change his life if he was willing to surrender to Him. But my friend was stuck. He was stuck in all the bad things he had done to others.

He kept telling me that God couldn't forgive him. He said following Jesus really wasn't for him. He thought he had done too much wrong to ever be accepted by God. He was stuck in shame and guilt.

I asked him if he thought God is a liar. He seemed shocked and said, "No, God doesn't lie."

"So if God promises to cleanse and forgive the repentant sinner, that promise applies to anyone," I continued.

"I guess so," he replied. He finally understood that God's promise of forgiveness applied to his sins too. We prayed. His new life with Christ began that night.

Jesus took the punishment for sin that you and I deserve. God made Jesus to be sin for us. In other words, God's plan of redemption involves a substitution. God punished His Son on the cross so that He could forgive anyone who put their faith in Him and surrendered their life to Him.

Are you stuck in shame and guilt? Do you sincerely believe that God can't forgive you? God wants to forgive you. He wants to give you the righteousness of Jesus. Will you surrender your life to Him? He can get you unstuck!

Point: God's forgiveness applies to all who surrender to Him and turn away from sin.

Prayer: Father, thank you for offering me forgiveness despite the evil I've done. Please help me walk in the light of your love and truth.

Practice: When guilt from the past tries to overcome me today, I will meditate on the substitution that God accomplished in Jesus' death on the cross.

Today's Reading:
Psalm 95-97; John 17

August 19

THE POWER TO CHANGE THE WORLD!
By Scott Kalevik

Romans 1:16 *I am not ashamed of the gospel, because it is the power of God for the salvation of everyone who believes: first for the Jew, then for the Gentile.*

Feeling like the world is messed up and there's really nothing we can do about it? Take heart! There is something we can do! We can stop being ashamed of the gospel!

The apostle Paul knew that the good news about Jesus was not something to hide or be ashamed of, no, to the contrary, the gospel contains the power of God to change the life of anyone who believes.

What is the gospel? Gospel is a word that literally means 'good news'. The gospel is the good news about what God has accomplished for us. In a nut shell ...

We're alienated from God by our own choices in breaking His law. Without Christ we are on course to receive the full punishment we deserve from God! God is holy. He is just. He will make sure that the wages of sin is death. But God, because of His love for us, found a way to satisfy His justice (punish every sin) without punishing us. He came to earth, born of a virgin, and lived a perfect life in the person of Jesus. Jesus, as the perfect Lamb of God, offered Himself to be sacrificed on the cross for the sins of the whole world. When Jesus died on the cross, He was punished for our sins. The good news is that if we put our faith in Jesus, the punishment that He experienced for us on the cross pays the penalty that we deserve to receive from God.

This good news of what Jesus has accomplished contains the power of God to change someone's life. The gospel is so powerful it will change the life of anyone who genuinely believes. Why do we hesitate to speak to others about such life changing news?

If I had the cure to cancer, would you expect me to share it? If I had life preservers on a sinking ship, would you want one? Most people on this planet have never put their faith in Christ because they have never had anyone lovingly explain the gospel to them! Many, many people would believe if only they knew!

Our true impact in this culture will never be through politics. The legislatures of the world will never change the human heart. Only God can change the heart! The message of the gospel has the power of God to change the heart! Change the heart and you eventually change the world. Will you share with someone today?

Today's Reading:
Psalm 98-99; John 18-19

231

August 20

GOOD FRUIT

By Beth Nelson

Galatians 5:22 *The fruit of the Spirit is…goodness.*

The first scripture that my mother had me memorize when I was a little girl was Psalm 1. I remember picking blueberries out on the tundra with the women, swatting away the mosquitos, trying hard to remember the first verses of that great psalm: *"Blessed is the man who does not walk in the counsel of the wicked or stand in the way of sinners or sit in the seat of mockers. But his delight is in the law of the Lord, and on his law he meditates day and night. He is like a tree planted by streams of water, which yields its fruit in season and whose leaf does not wither. Whatever he does prospers."* v. 1-3 What a promise – that our souls will prosper as we treasure the Word and the ways of God!

Goodness, as a fruit of the Spirit doesn't come from trying to be good or from my own effort, something I didn't understand as a child. As the psalm says, God's goodness and blessing is a byproduct of avoiding ungodly influences and spending time with the God of goodness. What we read in our spare time, the music we listen to, the kind of people we surround ourselves with (our close friends), all have an effect on us. We place deposits in ourselves. Then when life squeezes us, when disaster strikes, we draw on what we have taken the time to store up in the good times. As Mt 12:35 says, *"The good man brings good things out of the good stored up in him."*

Jesus said, *"By their fruit you will know them. Every good tree bears good fruit."* Mt 7:17 As children of a good God, we are to *"be rich in good deeds, to have a good reputation with outsiders, even to do good to those who hate you."* (1Tim 6:18;1Tim 3:7;Lk 6:27) What am I feeding on? Who do I spend time with? What kind of person am I becoming? Let us make wise choices, make good deposits, and most of all, spend time with our good God. Then the fruit that is produced in our lives will be good as well.

Today's Reading:
Psalm 100-102; John 20

August 21

Fill Up A Golden Bowl Today!
By Scott Kalevik

Matthew 6:6 *But when you pray, go into your room, close the door and pray to your Father, who is unseen. Then your Father, who sees what is done in secret, will reward you.*

Do you pray? I don't mean when the pastor says, "Let's pray" at church. Do you pray privately – a conversation just between you and the Lord? Is there time in your day devoted to talking to God? The Lord says He is watching what you're doing when no one else can see and that, when you pray privately to Him, He will reward you.

Wow! What a marvelous truth! You and I are invited – at any time we choose – to have a private conversation with the King of Kings. The Creator and Sustainer of all existence is willing to listen to your every word whenever you decide to speak to Him!

Can you call up the president of the United States and speak with him whenever you want? Is Congress ready to put you on the calendar anytime you feel like talking with them? Although the president and the congress are very powerful, they don't contain even a thimble full of power when compared to the power of God! Not to mention the fact that they aren't usually interested in what you have to say unless they're trying to get elected!

The Lord almighty has issued you an invitation and a promise. Pray in private and He will reward you. He's willing to listen. In fact, the Lord treasures His disciple's prayers to the point of saving them in golden bowls around His throne! Rev 5:8 *And when he had taken it, the four living creatures and the twenty-four elders fell down before the Lamb. Each one had a harp and they were holding golden bowls full of incense, which are the prayers of the saints.* Our prayers are like the sweet aroma of incense to our heavenly Father!

So fill up a golden bowl around God's throne today. He can't wait to hear from you.

Today's Reading:
Psalm 103-104; John 21

August 22

Joy in the face of Suffering

By Peggy Kalevik

1 Thessalonians 1:6 … in spite of severe suffering, you welcomed the message with the joy given by the Holy Spirit.

What do joy and happiness have in common? They are both good, they each conjure up bright, cheerful images in our minds. But they are different. Happiness depends largely on our circumstance. If our circumstances or bleak, we are not happy, we experience sadness. But we can experience joy in the worst of circumstances. Because our joy is in the Lord, in what he has returned to us. He has given us the means to heal our separation from God our Father; Christ has restored us to right relationship with God. Happiness can not coexist with unhappiness or sadness. But joy can coexist with great sorrow.

The Bible tells us Christ was able to look past the horror of the cross to the glory beyond. And so for the joy set before him he endured the cross. It says He scorned its shame (Heb 12:2). We must do the same. We must be able to rejoice even in our sorry, understanding that He is our peace and our joy, no matter what the circumstance. The joy in Galatians 5:22 is not concerned with just being happy according to our life circumstance. It is a never ending trust in God and the confidence of knowing that as we rely on God it's already alright. Luke tells us that Jesus was full of joy through the Holy Spirit at the return of the 72 from their time of evangelism and He gave praise to the Father (Luke 10:21). It is clear that the joy of our Lord was our Father.

Paul gives praise to God for the faith of the Church at Thessalonica. For the believers there had faced great persecution, but they stood firm in their faith. Paul rejoices that they have become imitators of him and more importantly of Christ. During this time of trouble they received the word with great joy, understanding they would face suffering as a result of their commitment to the faith (Acts 17). They became models for all believers. In our current era, Christians have not been exposed to blatant religious persecution, but it appears to be headed our way. Will we be able to stand firm with joy? Remember, joy is contentment resting in God even in the midst of suffering.

Prayer: Father please give me the strength and wisdom to maintain a spirit and heart of joy in the midst of suffering and sorrow.

Today's Reading:
Psalm 105-107; Acts 1

August 23

THE LIVING PRESENCE OF THE SPIRIT IN ME
By Peggy Kalevik

Romans 8:11 *And if the Spirit of him who raised Jesus from the dead is living in you, he who raised Christ from the dead will also give life to your mortal bodies through his Spirit, who lives in you.*

When we are involved in something that is not pleasing to God we almost always feel uncomfortable. We may try to justify what we are doing and make it seem ok for the people around us, but something in us is still uncomfortable. That's because the spirit that dwells in us can not dwell in darkness or sin. So when we are not walking in the light of Gods truth, He points it out to us. We are restless and ill at ease, we must correct ourselves.

Paul teaches us that this spirit that dwells within us as believers is the very life of God our Father, it is spiritual and eternal. While we may still have a desire to do things that might lead us into darkness we have also within us the cure for our sinful human nature. The Holy Spirit in us is a regenerating and renewing power, it gives us the strength and wisdom to continue in the path that God has for us. Through the guiding of the Holy Spirit we are able to overcome our sinful nature and live out the purpose of God in our lives. Christ's redemptive action on the cross is applied to us as believers and we are the fruit of His sacrifice.

If you believe in Christ as your Lord and Savior, then you have the Spirit in you; *"having believed, you were marked in him with a seal, the promised Holy Spirit"* (Eph 1-13). What a grand gift from God, making His presence real in us, we are never alone. We never have to worry or fear, if we trust in Him and His word. We are filled with His power and presence. We are sheltered from within.

Point: Rejoice today that God is with you and in you. He loved you enough to make His home with you.

Prayer: God, our Father, we adore You. Thank You for Your presence in me. Let walk in the light of Your love.

Today's Reading:
Psalm 108-109; Acts 2-3

August 24

View of a Servant
By Peggy Kalevik

1 Corinthians 4:4 *My conscience is clear, but that does not make me innocent. It is the Lord who judges me.*

When I was growing up in the South, ministers or preachers of the gospel were regarded as very special people. They were treated with great respect in every setting. They were given the best seat at the table no matter whose home they visited or what public event they attended. People believed everything they said was the "gospel" truth. We have come a long way from that perspective. Today 'man' has given the pulpit a black eye; a hurdle a true servant of God must bear while persevering to serve with integrity and honor.

Paul continues to state his case for the church; for them to put their faith in the message of the cross. In the first four verses of chapter four he points out to the people of the church that those who taught them God's word are servants of God, not someone God intended they should worship. They serve the body and they serve God. Yes, they have been entrusted with "the secret things of God", but now they, like all believers, are no longer slaves to sin but have become slaves to righteousness. (The responsibility of a slave is to serve his master.) Therefore their character must reflect faithfulness to God, because it is God who will judge them and all who are called to ministry. As a handler of God's truth, Paul was not concerned about what the people thought of Him, but what God thought of Him. In fact he does not even rely on his own opinion of himself or his work. He understands God has the last word about him, not the people. Paul is steadfast in his assertion of himself as having fulfilled his duty to God (Acts 23:1). In 2 Corinthians 1:12 he states: *"we have conducted ourselves in the world, and especially in our relations with you, in the holiness and sincerity that are from God."* He conducts himself at all times in a way that honors God.

Like Paul, we must all come to an understanding about our own ability and wisdom. Just because we think we're doing great things for God, or God's people, doesn't mean God agrees. In other words our opinion of ourselves or someone else is not necessarily God's opinion. God has the last word.

Point: As servants in God's ministry our obligation is to serve God, to honor Him, not man.

Prayer: Father, help me to maintain my integrity and righteousness before You and never let go of it; let my conscience be clear before You always.

Today's Reading:
Psalm 110-112; Acts 4

August 25

Jesus Is My Holiness

By Scott Kalevik

1 Corinthians 1:30-31 *It is because of him that you are in Christ Jesus, who has become for us wisdom from God—that is, our righteousness, holiness and redemption. 31 Therefore, as it is written: "Let him who boasts boast in the Lord."*

Followers of Jesus are constantly confronted by the fact that, despite our love for the Lord, we still sin. The apostle Paul defined the struggle: Ro 7:15 *I do not understand what I do. For what I want to do I do not do, but what I hate I do.* If Jesus is our holiness, as our passage today tells us, why do Christians continue to battle sin?

Jesus is our holiness: Heb 10:10 *And by that will, we have been made holy through the sacrifice of the body of Jesus Christ once for all.* All believers have been made holy. Our position before God is one of purity because Jesus has made us pure.

But the Bible also talks about the need for us to make every effort in the day-to-day practice of living holy lives. 2Pe 3:14 *So then, dear friends, since you are looking forward to this, make every effort to be found spotless, blameless and at peace with him.*

The point? Scripture speaks about the holiness of the believer in two ways. First, believers hold the POSITION of holiness because Jesus has made believers pure. Second, believers PRACTICALLY make every effort to live holy lives because God gives us the choice to disobey. If you study this verse, you'll see both our position and our practice: Heb 10:14 *because by one sacrifice he has made perfect forever those who are being made holy.*

If you've surrendered your life to Jesus by faith, God sees you as totally pure and holy today. Despite the struggle with sin, there is no condemnation for those in Christ Jesus. We wait for the day when sin will be totally abolished and our practice will align with our position. Until that day, we make every effort to be found spotless.

But praise God today! No matter how much of a failure you may think yourself to be when it comes to serving God, Jesus is your holiness! He has made you perfect forever even while you are being made holy.

Today's Reading:
Psalm 113-114; Acts 5-6

August 26

Discipleship: Loving, Learning & Living

By Scott Kalevik

Matthew 9:9 *As Jesus went on from there, he saw a man named Matthew sitting at the tax collector's booth. "Follow me," he told him, and Matthew got up and followed him.*

Lets consider what it means to be a disciple of Jesus. How does a disciple live? How does a disciple think? As each of us considers what scripture says about discipleship, I trust the Lord will shine His light of truth into our hearts and show us whether or not we are living as His disciples.

The word 'disciple' comes from the Greek word "*mathētēs*". It literally means "a learner." To be "a learner" or a disciple of Jesus means that you accept His teachings as true and that you are willing to obey. Interestingly, those called by the name "disciples" in the New Testament exhibit a broad range of responses to Jesus. Some quit. Some fail. Some succeed.

The gospel of John records that many who were willing to follow Jesus initially changed their minds and quit: Jn 6:66 *From this time many of his disciples turned back and no longer followed him.*

Peter failed the Lord by denying Him: Mt 26:74 *Then he began to call down curses on himself and he swore to them, "I don't know the man!" Immediately a rooster crowed.* But the Lord faithfully forgives and restores all who admit their wrongs and turn back to Him (read John 21 to learn how Jesus restores Peter after his denial).

All genuine disciples have one thing in common. They love Jesus with everything they have. They abandon careers and lifestyles to obey Jesus. They endure hardship and persecution to live as Jesus commands.

The New Testament also shows us that, despite human weaknesses, the Spirit of God uses disciples to revolutionize the world with the love and the good news of salvation through Jesus Christ. Thousands come to know Jesus and many are taught and healed through the ministries of those following the Lord.

As we focus on discipleship, grapple with these questions: "Does my life reflect that I am a disciple of Jesus Christ?" "Do I love Jesus with everything I have?" "Am I learning about Jesus?" "Am I living in obedience to His commands?" "Am I willing to follow Jesus wherever He asks me to go?" There is no greater quest in life than to be a disciple of Jesus Christ!

Today's Reading:
Psalm 115-117; Acts 7

August 27

The Body Sacred

By Beth Nelson

1 Corinthians 6:15-17 Do you not know that your bodies are members of Christ himself? Shall I then take the members of Christ and unite them with a prostitute? Never! Do you not know that he who unites himself with a prostitute is one with her in body? For it is said, "The two will become one flesh."

Paul's second journey as a missionary for the gospel brought him to the Greek city of Corinth. Being on a main route of travel, this city brought in trade from as faraway as Asia and Rome. It attracted throngs of wealthy foreigners from east and west. It was known for its wealth and culture, but just as much for its corruption and wickedness. The establishment of a Christian church in this city could have only been a testimony to the power of God.

After Paul left Corinth he stayed in contact with these new believers, knowing they were surrounded by a heathen population. Some time later, he received a letter from some of the Christians in Corinth, telling him that there were believers who were engaging in sexually immoral behavior. In his first letter to the Corinthians, Paul explains to them that though we have great freedom in Christ, our bodies belong to Christ. They are members of his body and Christians should never take these bodies that belong to Christ and unite in unholy union with any person outside of marriage. We become one with that person and we sin against our own bodies.

As our own culture is becoming increasingly hedonistic, we will have to be increasingly vigilant in guarding ourselves from immorality. Paul says to flee from such sin. Set your mind daily to stay away from it. The rewards for obedience are great! God's spirit dwells with those who flee temptation and draw near to God.

Today's Reading:
Psalm 118-119; Acts 8-9

August 28

THE PARADOX OF PRIORITIES!
By Scott Kalevik

Luke 17:33 *Whoever tries to keep his life will lose it,
and whoever loses his life will preserve it.*

There's a paradox of priorities in Jesus' teaching. Instead of living life with total commitment to security and happiness as most in our culture advocate, Jesus instructs His disciples that loss is what truly leads to life. The paradox is that ultimate preservation of life is only possible through loss.

Said a different way, if the point of life is self-centered satisfaction, the end of life will be eternal loss. Conversely, if the point of life is self-less, surrendered obedience to the Savior, the end of life will be eternal joy in the presence of God. Mt 10:39 *Whoever finds his life will lose it, and whoever loses his life for my sake will find it.*

Notice how this paradox provides the foundation of genuine discipleship: Lk 9:23 *Then he said to them all: "If anyone would come after me, he must deny himself and take up his cross daily and follow me.* Loss of life (he must deny himself and take up his cross daily and follow me) is mandatory to become a disciple of Jesus.

Jesus isn't speaking of literal, physical death in this paradox. He speaks about the death of self. In fact, Jesus Himself modeled selfless living for us: Jn 6:38 *For I have come down from heaven not to do my will but to do the will of him who sent me.* Jesus died to self and lived to do what His heavenly Father wanted. He lost His life serving the Father and, therefore, preserved His life.

All of us who follow Jesus must confront ourselves with the truth of this paradox. Are we willing to lay down our lives to serve the Lord? Or, are we kidding ourselves about our desire to be His disciple? Will we let the selfish desires for worldly security, happiness, and self-sufficiency be sacrificed in order to let Jesus rule our lives? Just what is your priority today? Your future depends on your answer.

Today's Reading:
Psalm 120-122; Acts 10

August 29

HAVE I MADE A MISTAKE?
By Beth Nelson

1 Corinthians 7:20 *Each one should remain in the situation
in which he was in when God called him.*

Becoming a Christian doesn't change the rules in regards to our marriage commitments. Many times I have seen Christian women struggling in marriages to non-Christian husbands. It's too difficult and they want out. If only their husband would become a Christian, they think, then everything would be different. Life would be so much easier. Those whose husbands have become believers, though there is joy in being spiritually united, the problems don't disappear overnight. They are disappointed and disillusioned.

Being a new church with no previous experience of life in Christ, the Corinthian church was under the impression that when you became a Christian, you were supposed to make radical changes in your ties with other people: cut off social ties, live lives of celibacy, or at least divorce an unbelieving spouse. Paul makes it clear that our primary allegiance is to Christ, yes, but that doesn't give us license to make major changes in our life situations. *"Each one should retain the place in life that the Lord assigned to him and to which God has called him."* 1Cor 9:17

Being naturally self-centered and impatient creatures, we may feel we can't wait for things to get better. It's natural to feel that way. And sometimes the situation warrants it. But many of us who have been blessed to be married a long time know that God is saying: If you could only see down the road you'd see the blessings I have for you. I want for you to dig deeper still; I am in the process of molding you to be more like my Son. Don't trust in your husband or wife, place your trust in Me and let me do my work.

God's best blessings come from being faithful in the position in which you find yourself. Marriage is often one of the most challenging relationships but it can also be the most rewarding. The excellent book, Sacred Marriage by Gary Thomas, says that God designed marriage not to make us happy but to make us holy. Let us not look for the easy way out, but rather, as Paul says, stay in the place assigned to us by the Lord. He has not made a mistake – and He's not finished yet!

Today's Reading:
Psalm 123-124; Acts 11-12

August 30

Changing Direction

By Scott Kalevik

Matthew 4:19 *"Come, follow me," Jesus said, "and I will make you fishers of men." 20 At once they left their nets and followed him.*

How do you like change? Not the kind that goes into your pocket, but the kind that moves your life in a different direction. Most of us prefer the rut of routine to the challenges of change. Change is unknown and scary. Status quo feels safer for most of us even when we don't really like our circumstance. For example, the Israelites wanted to return to slavery in Egypt rather than face the changes brought about by their deliverance (Num. 14:4). But the Lord seems perfectly comfortable asking us to change. In fact, the Lord requires change if we are to follow Him.

Jesus issues a call to some fishermen in Matthew 4:19. He says, *"Come, follow me."* That's the same call He issues to every one of us even today. Jesus asks us to, "Change direction. Leave the things of your life behind and follow me."

Then Jesus says to them, *"And I will make you fishers of men."* In other words, Jesus plans to override the direction of their lives if they agree to follow Him. Are you willing to change careers to follow Jesus? Are you willing to let Jesus decide what He wants you to do rather than depending on what makes sense to you? Jesus is willing to mold every one of us into people that fulfill His purpose in the kingdom of God – IF we are willing to follow Him.

Despite the natural tendency to resist change, the fishermen who hear Jesus' call in verse 20 immediately jump up, leave their nets behind, and follow Jesus. No phoning home … no auctioning the stuff to raise funds before they leave … no hesitation … no excuses – these guys immediately change the direction of their lives to make Jesus the Lord of their lives and follow Him.

It has been the same for every disciple of Jesus since the day He turned fishermen into fishers of men. Following Jesus requires change: change of heart, change of mind and change of direction. The old things pass away. Everything is new. Have you allowed Jesus to change your life?

Lk 14:33 *In the same way, any of you who does not give up everything he has cannot be my disciple.*

Today's Reading:
Psalm 125-127; Acts 13

August 31

PRAYER AND INTERCESSION
By Peggy Kalevik

Colossians 4:12b *He is always wrestling in prayer for you, that you may stand firm in all the will of God, mature and fully assured.*

In a world filled with temptations and twisted theology, it's no wonder a minister of the Gospel is on his knees in constant prayer and intercession for the body.

In this verse from Colossians Paul is speaking of Epaphras, the founder of the Church at Colosse. Epaphras was a student of Paul's who was converted in Ephesus then took the Gospel message to Colosse. Within the community there was some form of heresy which Paul doesn't pin down. He notes a number of problems but does not clearly state/name the overall issue (1:15-20; 2:2-4, 8, 9, 18, 21, 23; 3:11). However, both he and Epaphras were greatly concerned.

In this verse Paul says Epaphras is always "wrestling" in prayer. The Greek word Paul uses is *"agonizomia"* which includes in its meaning fight and struggling, and oddly, competing; leaving the reader with the impression Epaphras is engaged in battle on their behalf. Epaphras is a disciple of Christ and a firm believer in God's power. He sees what's happening in the community and knows the people whom he taught could be "taken captive" through "hollow and deceptive philosophy" based on worldly human traditions rather than on Christ (2:8). He has taught them the truth. They must be strong enough to weather the onslaught of bad theology, but now, all he can do is pray. So, he intercedes for them and asks God to strengthen and mature their faith so they can stand firm.

Like Epaphras, we must be prayerful in all things, not just a little prayer, but the prayer of a warrior. We must intercede and do battle on behalf of others, the entire Church body and the community of faith as a whole. In our society we have seen the damage that can be done by twisted theology. We have seen people who died waiting for a space craft to pick them up and take them to heaven. People killed by their pastor, who gave them all kool-aide to drink. What power do we have to stop these kinds of things from happening? We have no power, but God has all power. We must pray for God's power, presence and wisdom; that the Community of faith will be able to weather any storm.

Point: As Disciples of Christ we must be willing to stand in the gap on behalf of God's people.

Today's Reading:
Psalm 128-129; Acts 14-15

September 1

How to Read Someone Else's Mail

By Scott Kalevik

1 Corinthians 1:2 *To the church of God in Corinth, to those sanctified in Christ Jesus and called to be holy, together with all those everywhere who call on the name of our Lord Jesus Christ—their Lord and ours:*

Perhaps you've never thought about it like this, but when we read and study the book of First Corinthians, (or any New Testament epistle for that matter); we are really reading someone else's mail. The letter is written by the Apostle Paul to people who lived almost 2,000 years ago in a place called Corinth. So as we study the letter, it's important that we try to understand how the original audience would have understood the instruction given.

Consider the Corinthians. Who were these people? What was their culture like? What was their background? What was important to them and why? How had the life-changing gospel of Jesus Christ impacted their lifestyles?

Read the whole letter of First Corinthians and see if you can figure out what they were going through. If you have a study Bible, consider reading the background information supplied about Corinth and the church which bears its name.

The Corinthian church had huge problems. Division, pride, sexual immorality, disorderly worship, and idolatry are only a few of the issues addressed in this letter. But how interesting it is that Paul's instruction to those believers way back then is just as relevant and helpful to us as it was to them! It's really true: the more things change the more they stay the same!

You can learn a lot in the letter to the Corinthians about the cross and its impact on changing believers even though the world considers the cross to be foolish. You can also learn about avoiding temptation, unity, order in worship, spiritual gifts and many other topics.

Perhaps you can set your sights on reading the whole letter of 1st Corinthians. As you study this letter, I hope you will once again appreciate how great the love of God is for us – warts and all! Instead of yelling and screaming at this errant church, Paul lets them know how much God loves them and what He's done for them. He said it well in First Corinthians 1:8 – *He will keep you strong to the end, so that you will be blameless on the day of our Lord Jesus Christ.* May God bless you as you draw near to Him through study and prayer!

Today's Reading:
Psalm 130-132; Acts 16

September 2

NEVER TOO MESSED UP FOR GOD!

By Scott Kalevik

1 Corinthians 1:8-9 *He will keep you strong to the end, so that you will be blameless on the day of our Lord Jesus Christ. 9 God, who has called you into fellowship with his Son Jesus Christ our Lord, is faithful.*

The church in Corinth had a lot of problems. Idolatry, sexual immorality, incest, divisions in leadership, lack of love, disorderly worship, and doctrinal issues are only a few of the problems they faced.

Now you might think that the apostle Paul would write a very stern letter. Shouldn't he yell at them for getting so many things wrong? Doesn't good leadership mandate a good 'whoopin' to get those errant believers on track? Although later in the letter Paul will bluntly correct those in error, he begins by reminding the church of a few things about the Lord.

First, the Lord will keep them strong to the end. In other words, the church belongs to Jesus and the church is sustained by Jesus and, therefore, Jesus will supply the strength and discipline necessary to allow His church to survive. Notice our text says Jesus provides this strength so that believers will be blameless before God.

Second, Paul reminds them that God has called them into fellowship with Jesus. Paul didn't 'sell' Jesus to them. They weren't manipulated into some kind of confession of faith. God called them to be in Christ. Their goal is not to please Paul. They're called by God.

Third, God is faithful. He will supply the strength, direction, and discipline to sanctify their daily lives through and through.

If you're feeling like your life is too messed up for God today, remember what Paul says to the Corinthians. Your sanctification does not depend on your ability. God will keep you strong. Your relationship with Jesus is not rooted in your wisdom. God called you into fellowship with Jesus. God is faithful even when you're not. He will accomplish His purpose in you.

Your job? Obey and follow. Submit to the Lord. Forsake sin. His life-giving love will flood your life. Nothing you've done can cancel God's plan for you as long as you're willing to repent of your sins and obey the Lord.

Today's Reading:
Psalm 133-134; Acts 17-18

September 3

THE LIMITS OF FREEDOM
By Peggy Kalevik

1 Corinthians 10:23 *Everything is permissible"—but not everything is beneficial. "Everything is permissible"—but not everything is constructive.*

In chapter 8 Paul gives us an understanding of our freedom in Christ, and wants us to accept that our freedom should not cause others to falter in their faith. He picks up the discussion here. He wants to make the point clear, that just because something is not against the law it doesn't mean we are bound to do it. In fact even though it is lawful, it might not be good for us.

Many Christians believe it is a sin to drink liquor or wine of any kind, for any reason. Still others see nothing wrong with having a glass of wine with their pasta, or a margarita with their Mexican dinner. There are no references in the Bible saying Christians or followers of Christ should never drink liquor or wine. There are, of course, specific times and or people who should not partake of fermented drinks and or wine. But there is no place telling us it's a sin to have these things in moderation. On the other hand, the Bible frowns on over indulgence. Paul would tell those who believe it to be alright to have a glass of wine to refrain from drinking it in the presence of those who think it sinful. His goal for us to be unified is echoed here. If in our freedom we do something to offend our brother, our unity is damaged and we sin against our brother and against Christ (1 Corinthians 8:12). There is a need to consider the physical and spiritual wellbeing of others. We must not allow our freedom to hinder the faith of our brothers and sisters in Christ.

God has given us freedom in Christ, but not the freedom to damage the body. Even if we know we are right about a particular issue, we should not insist on having our way to the point of disruption. Especially concerning "disputable" matters (those things that are debatable, and don't make a difference to our salvation). God is love, He does not operate in chaos and confusion, and He desires for us to live in peace and unity. If we find ourselves constantly disagreeing over such things, we will not have peace or unity. As far as it depends on you, live in peace with everyone, don't let your right to enjoy your freedom cause you to break unity in the community of believers. (read Romans 14; 15; & 1 Corinthians 8)

Point: Don't allow your freedom in Christ to become a stumbling block to your brother.

Today's Reading:
Psalm 135-137; Acts 19

September 4

INTEGRITY BY EXAMPLE

By Scott Kalevik

1 Corinthians 4:16 *Therefore I urge you to imitate me.*

What is the impression most people have of the church today? Don't most think of us as "just a bunch of hypocrites?" Why is that? Isn't it mainly because even though we say we follow Jesus, our behavior is many times less than Christ-like?

The Lord calls us to more than new life in Him. If we truly surrender our lives to Him, we are also called to live a new lifestyle. As Jesus so poignantly said in Luke 6:46: *"Why do you call me, 'Lord, Lord,' and do not do what I say?"* He wants us to live authentically before Him by doing the things He has commanded us to do.

The apostle Paul allowed Jesus to change not only his life, but his lifestyle as well. Formerly, Paul persecuted the Lord by hurting His people. But after his conversion, Paul submits himself to living in obedience to what Jesus commands. God changed his life completely. Instead of hating people, Paul loved people with godly love. His life became an example of what it is to love God with total commitment.

In today's verse, Paul urges the Corinthian believers to imitate him. Wow! Paul's lifestyle had been so radically altered by his relationship with Jesus that he had no problems telling other believers to be like him. In fact, Paul goes on in the next verse to tell us that his life in Christ Jesus, *"agrees with what I teach everywhere in every church."* Paul isn't by any means claiming perfection when he tells others to imitate him. He knows he still sins. But he has learned how to walk with Jesus day in and day out.

Consider the power God would unleash into the lives of our families, friends, and acquaintances if we lived our lives in Christ so genuinely that we could honestly tell others to imitate our walk with Christ. Integrity matters. Blessed are the pure in heart for theirs is the kingdom of heaven. Ask the Lord to make your life one that can be imitated. He has the strength to do it. He will allow us to walk in His truth and be an example if we will obey.

Today's Reading:
Psalm 138-139; Acts 20-21

September 5

PEACE AND ORDER
By Peggy Kalevik

1 Corinthians 14:33a *For God is not a God of disorder but of peace.*

As Paul continues to bring understanding to the people of Corinth he turns from his discussion on doing all things in love to prophecy and speaking in tongues and orderly conduct in public worship. In this verse of Chapter 14 he expresses a central truth about the character of God. God is a God of order and peace. Paul is concerned that public worship, if out of control, will dishonor God; that it might damage God's reputation among the people of the world, specifically unbelievers; from reading the chapter I think especially unbelievers seeking God. (1 Cor 14)

The speaking of tongues in the church has always been a source of some contention. The issue seems to be that we can't accept the basic fact Paul lays out in chapter 14; tongues should only be used in public worship if there is interpretation. While it is a valuable gift and does edify the body, it like all the gifts should be used the way God calls us to use it. This isn't especially hard or difficult to understand but still it's an issue. The point of our verse today is to make us understand that God does not do anything in confusion and chaos. He is a God of order and peace. When we allow our gifting to be a source of disorder and confusion I think it's safe to say that God is not with us. His heart breaks when we use the gift he has given us to bring confusion into His house. Galatians 5 tells us that *"the fruit of the Spirit is love, joy, peace, patience, kindness, goodness, faithfulness, gentleness and self-control."* No where does it say the fruit of God's spirit is chaos, confusion and disorder. The next time you hear a heated discussion among God's people; ask yourself, "What would God think of this?"

In Genesis 1 God is confronted with disorder and chaos. He tells us that "Now the earth was formless and empty, darkness was over the surface of the deep, and the Spirit of God was hovering over the waters". The Hebrew word for formless used in this passage is "tohu", which includes in its meaning traits of emptiness, waste, "chaos", "confusion" "falsehood" and "worthlessness". God in his infinite wisdom deemed this uninhabitable for people. God cleaned up the chaos and emptiness by turning it into the heavens and the earth. His desire for us is order.

Point: Because He has given us peace public worship should reflect God's love, peace, and harmony.

Prayer: Father, You have called us to live in peace, grant us the hearts and minds to obey your call to live and worship in peace.

Today's Reading:
Psalm 140-142; Acts 22

248

September 6

WHICH ONE ARE YOU?

By Peggy Kalevik

1 Corinthians 12:28 — *...God has appointed first of all apostles, second prophets, third teachers, then workers of miracles, also those having gifts of healing, those able to help others, those with gifts of administration, and those speaking in different kinds of tongues.*

While serving as the outreach coordinator for a church I attended some years ago, the response I received when asking for help with an outreach to the homeless was often, "that's not my gift." I wondered what that meant. What gift is required to help someone in need? Oh, people were usually willing to give money, food, clothing, and anything I needed, anything accept their time and presence. The Bible tells us there are different kinds of gifts, service, and working, but they all come from the same Spirit, the same Lord and the same God. God has gifted us for works of service, sometimes we may feel we're out of our comfort zone, still we must serve.

As you work your way through this month's devotional, pray for Gods direction for you personally. Ask Him to allow you to feel His hand guiding you to the task He has for you at Living Hope or wherever you worship. If you know God has placed you in a body of believers, and you know He has purpose in everything He does, then you also know He has work for you to do there. The Bible tells us that some are called to teach, some to encourage and help others. Some are preachers, pastors, prophets, workers of miracles, and administrators. Which of these gifts really describes you? Prayer and humility are the keys to understanding your own gift(s). Keep your focus on God's purpose, be humble, resist evil thoughts and acts, and above all expect God to answer you. Use God's Word to help you pray in His will. I believe God loves to hear His word spoken to Him in our prayers. Pray in the spirit and He will meet you there at the point of your need.

Prayer: Father, today I come with humbly submitting my life, and my will to you. I take captive every thought to make it obedient to You I will not place my desires above Yours, I surrender all to You.

Practice: Pray, submit to the Lord and be humble before Him, resist evil, expect an answer, wait to hear from Him and accept His response, He doesn't have to communicate the way you want or expect.

Today's Reading:
Psalm 143-144; Acts 23-24

September 7

THE POWER OF GRACE

By Scott Kalevik

1 Corinthians 1:4 *I always thank God for you because of his grace given you in Christ Jesus.*

Despite all the things the Corinthian church was doing wrong, Paul always thanked God for them. Why would someone thank God for a church that is so off track? He doesn't thank God because they are 'good people' assuming that somehow they'll do better. He doesn't thank God for them because they've decided to try harder. Paul thanks God for them because he knows that God has poured out His grace on the Corinthian believers through Jesus Christ. God has given these believers forgiveness. Just like us, they didn't deserve it. They couldn't earn it. But these believers have confessed faith in Jesus Christ and, therefore, God has forgiven their sins – past, present, and future. Paul's thanksgiving to God is rooted in the character and work of God. His thanksgiving is not rooted in the character of the people.

Grace is such a powerful gift from God. Our ability to please God doesn't depend on our ability to perform. God gives His grace freely to all who believe. He's not only forgiven us, He's willing to continue to forgive us as we struggle in the flesh. Even when we sin against God after we've come to Him by faith, God continues to love and forgive as we continue to seek His forgiveness and repent.

If you're caught in sin today, remember the wonderful, bountiful grace of God. God still loves you and God is still able to deliver you from your sin. God is still willing to work in your life and use you for His glory. The requirement? Repentance and surrender! We need to admit our sinfulness to the Father and ask Him for the strength to turn away from sin.

Most believers naturally tend to distance themselves from God when we know we're wrong. God desires the exact opposite reaction. He wants us to remember His grace. He wants us to repent. Instead of distance, the Lord asks that we draw near to Him.

If you feel distant from God today, don't run from Him. Confess your sin and ask Him to restore you. Grace is a powerful thing

Today's Reading:
Psalm 145-147; Acts 25

September 8

Inconceivable!
By Beth Nelson

1 Corinthians 2:9-10 *No eye has seen, no ear has heard, no mind has conceived what God has prepared for those who love him - but God has revealed it to us by his Spirit.*

The Truman Show is a movie about a family who thought that they were living normal, happy lives, but in actuality, they were a reality show and every move that they made was being watched by millions. They were unaware that they were in a confined space, unaware of a larger world all around them. Sometimes I think that God sees us that way, as living in self-imposed spiritual limits, oblivious to all that he has planned for us. And because we don't know any better, we're quite happy to keep it that way.

For years, the nation of Israel had no king, God alone was their leader. They lived in unparalleled blessing as long as they followed after God and walked in His ways. But after awhile they became tired of what they had and traded it in for something inferior. They began to clamor for an earthly king, so they could be like the nations around them. Because of their short-sightedness, they replaced the blessings of God with earthly kings who were often greedy, corrupt, and cruel. They were led off to other countries in chains. Their lives were forever altered.

Sometimes we are very short-sighted, unable to see beyond the world that we live in, unable to conceive of God's dreams for us. Scripture says that no eye has seen, no ear has heard, no mind has conceived what God has prepared for those who love him. It also says that God will reveal it to us by his Spirit. Has God given you a vision of something greater, something out of your ordinary world? We have a choice, to focus on the people around us, to compare ourselves to them, or to look upward to the great God who is all-powerful and to begin to expand our spiritual boundaries. You may have to hold on tight. His plans are inconceivable!

Today's Reading:
Psalm 148-149; Acts 26-27

September 9

THE REASON FOR SPIRITUAL GIFTS!

By Scott Kalevik

1 Corinthians 12:7 *Now to each one the manifestation of the Spirit is given for the common good.*

I know of a church that had a group of people stand up at Bible study one night and declare that if you don't speak in tongues, you're not saved. Each in the group claimed to have the gift of speaking in tongues and claimed to be right with God because of it. This group of people caused much division in the church and eventually left the church because most of the church disagreed. Not to mention the fact that they totally disrespected the cross of Jesus. Jesus died for us and saves us through faith. Salvation does not come because we can or cannot speak in tongues.

Spiritual gifts present a terrible trap for many. It's the trap of ego and pride. Like the believers at Corinth, many of those in today's church, believing themselves to be gifted, tend to also believe that they are 'better' or 'more spiritual' than those not demonstrating similar gifts. This attitude of pride misses the whole point of spiritual gifts.

Please keep one truth in mind when it comes to spiritual gifts: The Lord bestows gifts for the sole purpose of building up His church. No exceptions. If you ever see the body of Christ dividing or fighting over the use of spiritual gifts, you can automatically know that the gifts are being misused or not present at all.

Paul instructed the Corinthians: 1Co 12:31a *But eagerly desire the greater gifts.* The Lord has also told us that He will pour out His Spirit in the last days: Joel 2:28 *'And afterward, I will pour out my Spirit on all people. Your sons and daughters will prophesy, your old men will dream dreams, your young men will see visions. 29 Even on my servants, both men and women, I will pour out my Spirit in those days.*

Two questions: Do you eagerly desire the greater gifts? Are you using your gifts to build up the body of Christ?

Today's Reading:
Psalm 150; Acts 28

September 10

GROWING UP!

By Scott Kalevik

1 Corinthians 3:1 *Brothers, I could not address you as spiritual but as worldly—mere infants in Christ.*

Growing spiritually is different than growing physically. Healthy babies are born with little arms and legs and fingers and toes and muscles and brains, etc. Given enough time and proper care, everything about a healthy infant will change automatically. The limbs and the organs and muscles all get bigger and stronger without any special attention. Growth is involuntary.

That's not how spiritual growth works. Why? Because God does not force us to grow spiritually. Instead, He invites us to grow spiritually. Our spiritual growth is tied directly to our relationship with Him. We must know Him and cooperate with Him to grow. Our growth in Him is deliberate, not involuntary. At any point, you and I have the option to decide not to obey the Lord. We stunt our spiritual growth every time we choose to live outside of His truth and guidance.

Paul calls the Corinthians 'mere infants in Christ.' And he identifies the problem – they are worldly. In other words, like so many of us, the Corinthian believers are living their lives based on the expectations of the world and what seems best to them. They are marching to the drummer of self-satisfaction and self-sufficiency rather than walking with the Lord.

Are you maturing in Christ or are you still an infant? Notice I'm not asking how long you've been a Christian. Many people have claimed to know Christ for decades and never grown significantly spiritually speaking.

Want to mature in Christ? Deliberately pursue Him! Pray, study and obey. If you are willing to draw near to Him, He will bring you to maturity and you will know the living God as never before! It's time to grow up!

Today's Reading:
Proverbs 1-2; Romans 1-2

September 11

Using Your Knee Mail

By Mike Scheimann

James 5:13 *Is any one of you in trouble? He should pray.*
Is anyone happy? Let him sing songs of praise.

In the modern age of technology and computers, our ability to communicate with others has improved dramatically. We can now IM or email co-workers, family, and friends in mere milliseconds. This has resulted in the ability to send important data and documents for business purposes, but it has also resulted in a society that no longer relies on or demands social interaction. We would rather email our co-worker 10 feet away from us, rather than get up and go talk to them. We would rather email our family and friends, than call or go visit them. We often rationalize it by saying it's quicker, and costs virtually nothing to send an email, even around the world, so it is cheaper. What makes matters worse, is that we have become a very impersonal society. How often do you find yourself forwarding emails that others have created to your friends, without ever saying a "Hi, how ya' doing?" I know I do it all the time. I rationalize it by saying I am very busy, and a little email picture or joke, or story from me, is better than not hearing from me at all.

Do we treat God the same way? Do we pray to him only when we can spare a quick moment from our busy day? Do we just tell Him generic phrases that we have said over and over, without putting any personal thought into it? Have we taken the personal, heartfelt time of fellowship and worship out of our prayer life and made it just another thing to scratch off our "To Do list"?

Point: Prayer is a time of communion with our loving Father, not a brief stop between breakfast and the shower.

Prayer: Dear Living Father, forgive us when we don't come before your throne in heartfelt prayer and adoration. Forgive us for taking you for granted.

Practice: When was the last time you got down on your knees and poured your heart out to God? Go to Him in times of trouble, and in times of praise.

Today's Reading:
Proverbs 3-5; Romans 3

September 12

Someone is Watching
By Beth Nelson

1 Corinthians 8:9; 10:33 Be careful, however, that the exercise of your freedom does not become a stumbling block to the weak…For I am not seeking my own good but the good of many, so that they may be saved.

I may think that, as captain of my ship, master of my life, I can do whatever I want. We don't like the idea of personal responsibility to others. It restricts our freedom. But the truth is, someone is watching you and me, and they're copying us. Jesus warned people to be careful not to lead little children astray. Paul picks up on the same theme. The church in Corinth had been taking license with some of their behaviors, disregarding those younger in their midst. Paul said that though they may be spiritually mature, they cannot do whatever they want. They have to impose restrictions on their behavior lest they cause a weaker brother who is watching them, to fall into sin. As we know, simply being exposed to certain behaviors opens us up to all kinds of temptations.

Children, whether biological or spiritual, emulate and copy their parents. When Ahaziah son of Ahab became king of Israel, *"He did evil in the eyes of the Lord, because he walked in the ways of his father and mother and in the ways of Jeroboam son of Nebat, who caused Israel to sin. He worshiped Baal…just as his father had done."* 1Ki 22:52-53 He clearly followed in his father's footsteps. By contrast, *"The Lord was with Jehoshaphat because in his early years he walked in the ways his father David had followed. He did not consult the Baals but sought the God of his father."* 2Chr 17:3 What a wonderful testimony to Godly influence.

People are watching. You may be mature, but be assured, someone less mature is watching. They're emulating you whether you want them to, or not. By God's grace and with His help you can be a powerful influence on others. What a privilege to lead people into the kingdom by example!

Today's Reading:
Proverbs 6-7; Romans 4-5

255

September 13

THE ROLE MODEL
By Peggy Kalevik

1 Corinthians 11:1 *Follow my example, as I follow the example of Christ.*

The man who tells people to follow his example must be pretty sure he's living a life which exemplifies God. Generations of people have read and maybe some have tried to follow Paul's example. He came from an awful beginning with God, to a glorious end. Converted by Jesus Himself and trained by His instruction, Paul is a rare Christian example. We can find few examples of weakness in his Christian armor. Although he says in 2Cor 12:7 he has a thorn in the flesh, there are no signs he ever faltered in His faith.

This verse concludes Paul's admonition to the Church at Corinth concerning the freedom of believers (10:23-33). Paul wants his listeners to follow his example, to act or live in a way that seeks the good of the body not to live in a self-serving way. It is good advice for any church body. Paul wants his readers/listeners to learn the truth and live by it, and he says it clearly - follow me as I follow Christ. Not follow me because I know I'm always right and holy, but follow me as I strive to live a life that exemplifies Christ.

As a disciple of Christ we must reflect the attributes of Christ. In Philippians 4:9 Paul tells the people of the Church at Philippi they should put into practice whatever they have learned, received or heard from him. Paul was their teacher and their example. He wanted them to remember and live by what he had taught and to pattern their lives after the way he lived among them. We must live a life which reflects to the world the truth of the Gospel. The role model for those seeking Christ is a person who understands God's Word and honors it by submitting their life to it. He/she prays in and out of season, seeks God for understanding and decision making and waits for God, never goes ahead of God. He/she reaches out a hand to help where needed, works diligently in God's garden for the good of the Kingdom and encourages and exhorts. He/she submits to Godly leadership and follows God's guidance.

Point: A true disciple of Christ will inspire those in their environment to also follow Christ and they will experience the peace and blessing of God

Prayer: I will offer God my life and glorify him with praise, gratitude and thanksgiving.

Today's Reading:
Proverbs 8-10; Romans 6

September 14

ARE YOU SERIOUS?

By Scott Kalevik

Luke 14:26 *If anyone comes to me and does not hate his father and mother, his wife and children, his brothers and sisters—yes, even his own life—he cannot be my disciple.*

Scripture clearly teaches God is love (1Jn. 4:8). Scripture tells us that love is the greatest when compared with faith or hope (1Cor. 13:13). We're commanded to love others as much as we love ourselves (Mt. 22:39). Love is repeatedly emphasized as behavior that directly reflects the character of God. God's word also instructs us to honor our parents (Eph. 6:2).

Then why does Jesus teach that if we want to be His disciple, we must HATE our father and mother? He says we must hate our spouse and children. We must hate our brothers and sisters. Jesus goes so far as to say we must even hate our very own lives or we CANNOT be His disciples! Is Jesus preaching hate?

By no means! Jesus uses a literary device called 'hyperbole' to make His point in the strongest way possible. Webster tells us hyperbole means "extravagant exaggeration." In other words, Jesus states something so radical – like hating parents and family and self – that people are struck with His real point.

And what's His point? Namely this: Jesus must be the highest priority in the life of His disciple. Loving Jesus and serving Jesus and obedience to Jesus must be more important than mother or father or spouse or children or brothers or sisters or even the disciple's own life! Anything less than absolute total commitment to the Savior precludes a person from being Jesus' disciple.

Are you serious? It is absolutely certain that Jesus is serious. To be His disciple requires a radical change of allegiance. Self must die. Jesus must reign supreme in the heart of His follower or any claim to be His follower is nullified.

If you're shocked by this truth, then Jesus' use of hyperbole has had its intended effect. He wants us to wake up and realize that following Him is more than just thinking He's a good teacher or a great leader or a wise man or a healer. To follow Jesus is to surrender every area of life to Him. Are you serious?

Today's Reading:
Proverbs 11-12; Romans 7-8

September 15

PAY ATTENTION!
By Scott Kalevik

Matthew 7:15 *Watch out for false prophets. They come to you in sheep's clothing, but inwardly they are ferocious wolves.*

Jesus warns His disciples that some 'prophets' will look totally harmless (like sheep) but, if the heart could be seen, it would be apparent that these people are actually ferocious wolves. A sheep means no harm. But a ferocious wolf intends to kill and tear apart. A ferocious wolf is even devious enough to assume a disguise to allow the prey a false sense of security before the kill.

A false prophet is someone who lies about and distorts what God has said. He or she will appear to be representing God and appear to be proclaiming what God has said, but in reality God's truth is not being taught. God has not said what they claim.

This kind of deception is not new. The devil used this trick in the garden of Eden to deceive Adam and Eve. Ge 3:4 *You will not surely die," the serpent said to the woman.* The devil openly told Eve that God's word was not true. Adam and Eve put their faith in the devil's distortion instead of in what God said. As a result, sin entered the world. Suffering and death began.

Jesus warns every disciple about this reality: The enemy's plan is to infiltrate the community of faith in order to get the people of God off track regarding the truth of God's word. Those agents of the devil will look good and appear harmless. But in actuality, the lies they teach lead to destruction.

If you are a genuine disciple of Jesus, you MUST study God's word so that you are able to discern God's truth from a false prophet's lie. If you're not familiar with what God has said in His word, a teacher who appears to be harmlessly helping you learn may instead tear you apart with destructive heresies.

Governments train their agents to recognize counterfeit money by studying valid currency so that they automatically see the flaws of the counterfeit. Likewise, disciples of Jesus must study His word so intensely that recognizing a false prophet's lie becomes second nature. Pay attention to God's truth. It will help you recognize the lies of the false prophet.

Today's Reading:
Proverbs 13-15; Romans 9

September 16

INTIMACY

By Scott Kalevik

Romans 8:15 *For you did not receive a spirit that makes you a slave again to fear, but you received the Spirit of sonship. And by him we cry, "Abba, Father."*

Sue turned from the sink with tears in her eyes and told Bob she felt like all the intimacy in their marriage had vanished. They were in a rut and she didn't like it. She desperately missed the romance they used to share.

The following Monday night Sue answered the doorbell. There stood her babysitter, Meagan. Sue knew she hadn't called Meagan. What was up? Meagan explained that Bob called her. Suddenly Bob appeared and told Sue to go put her dress on, they were going out for dinner. With glee, Sue put on her red dress and prepared for a romantic evening.

The little Italian restaurant was so quaint. Bob and Sue were seated at a romantic booth in the back. Sue found a card at her place setting. It was a hand written love poem from Bob. She thought she was dreaming. After a fantastic meal, Bob capped off the evening by presenting Sue with a purple rose! Her favorite color! Sue was on cloud nine. Their romance was back in a big way!

The next Monday night the doorbell rang again. Meagan explained that Bob had called her. Bob appeared and told Sue to put on that fancy red dress she wore last week. Sue was a little perplexed at that request, but who was she to argue with romance? Bob took her to the same Italian restaurant. They sat at the same booth. Sue received a nearly identical card with the same poem written inside. Then came another purple rose.

The following Monday night the same scenario was repeated. The next Monday night it happened again at the same time and in the same way. Sue began to dread Monday nights. Why? Because Bob had turned their intimacy into a religious routine.

As you cultivate intimacy with the Lord today are you going through the same tired religious routine? Or, are you genuinely seeking intimacy with Him? Through the Spirit of God we are allowed to refer to the Lord as "Abba" or Papa. The Lord wants to be close to you today not through routine, but heart to heart.

Today's Reading:
Proverbs 16-17; Romans 10-11

September 17

BE A LABORER IN GOD'S GARDEN
By Peggy Kalevik

1 Corinthians 3:7-8 *So neither he who plants nor he who waters is anything, but only God, who makes things grow. 8 The man who plants and the man who waters have one purpose, and each will be rewarded according to his own labor.*

Through the preaching of the Gospel we know Christ is the foundation of the Church and the head of the Church. We, as His body, are workers/servants who labor to build the Church upon Christ. Each of us brings to the body of Christ the gifts and talents God has given us. Each gift serves a purpose in the building of God's Kingdom. As servants in the body we must be able to recognize, appreciate and nurture the gifts of each member in order to bear a fruitful harvest which brings Glory to God.

Paul uses the analogy of gardening to help us understand God desires to see fruit from our labor. Our garden (church) will bear fruit if we live in obedience to God's purpose for us in His service. Each one must bring the tools God has given to the garden and work at the task God has assigned. He tells us there are things in the garden God desires and there are things He hates. Adam and Eve started in the garden and were thrown out because their behavior in the garden was unacceptable to God.

Today's Church has the same issues; there are things God loves and things He hates. The garden requires someone to make preparation for a fruitful harvest. A church should plant (preach the Gospel and evangelize); cultivate (water, weed and fertilize); teach (Bible study and prayer); and God brings the harvest! God expects us to do our part. God wants to see unity and harmony in the garden; love and nurturing; fellowship and corporate worship. One person can not and should not be responsible for all these things. God has provided people in the body with the gifts to accomplish these tasks. These things are not the sole responsibility of the "pastor". There are things in the garden God hates. God hates idle, incompatible, and incompetent workers (Matt 20:6, 11, 7). God is not pleased with workers who sit and do nothing; or engage in heated disagreements while doing His work, or teachers of His word who are unprepared and have little or no understanding.

Point: We are God's fellow workers; we are God's garden, God's building (v9)

Prayer: May Your favor rest upon us; establish the work of our hands for us—(Ps 90:17)

Today's Reading:
Proverbs 18-20; Romans 12

September 18

OH, YES! GOD IS LISTENING!

By Scott Kalevik

1 Samuel 1:10 *In bitterness of soul Hannah wept much and prayed to the LORD.*
1Sa 2:1 Then Hannah prayed and said: "My heart rejoices in the
LORD; in the LORD my horn is lifted high. My mouth boasts
over my enemies, for I delight in your deliverance.

Have you ever cried out to God in 'bitterness of soul'? Hannah was overwhelmed by the fact that she had never been blessed with children. She just couldn't take it anymore. She was at the end of her rope. She wept, prayed, and poured out her heart to God. God not only listened to Hannah, He answered! Samuel was born. Listen to her rejoice ... *I delight in Your deliverance* (2:1).

Sometimes it's hard for us to truly understand that every word we speak to God is heard. Every time we pray, God listens. He considers. When our prayer aligns with His will, He gives us what we've asked. When we're praying outside of His direction, He gives us what He knows is best. But He always answers.

He may answer with, "No." He may answer with, "Yes." He may answer with, "Wait on Me." But He always answers. Our prayers are precious to Him: Rev 5:8 *And when he had taken it, the four living creatures and the twenty-four elders fell down before the Lamb. Each one had a harp and they were holding golden bowls full of incense, which are the prayers of the saints.*

If you have reason to cry out to the Lord in bitterness of soul today, remember that He is listening to you. Dry your tears. He will answer you! Leave your burden at His feet and walk this day with the anticipation that His answer is coming. He is in control. You don't have to worry. He loves you and He knows what is best!

Point: God listens to and answers prayer.
Prayer: Lord, thank You for hearing me when I pray. And thank You for answering!
Practice: Start a prayer journal. Write your prayer on one side of the page and write God's answer on the other side of the page. You'll be amazed at His answers!

Today's Reading:
Proverbs 21-22; Romans 13-14

September 19

Transformation

By Peggy Kalevik

John 3:5 *Jesus answered, "I tell you the truth, no one can enter the kingdom of God unless he is born of water and the Spirit.*

One of the first things we learn after accepting Christ is the concept of redemption. Redemption is the act of saving something or someone from a state of corruption or decline. It means to redeem, to make the person or thing acceptable in spite of its flaws or bad qualities. Jesus came to redeem us from our lives of sin in spite of our bad habits and/or bad character. He came so we might live. But He tells us that unless we are born of water and the Spirit we will not enter the kingdom of God.

In this passage, Jesus is probably referring to John's baptism with water for the repentance of sin. John's purpose was to prepare the way for Jesus by bringing all who would come to repentance. John said: *"I baptize you with water for repentance. But after me will come one who is more powerful than I, whose sandals I am not fit to carry. He will baptize you with the Holy Spirit and with fire."* (Matthew 3:11) As we have learned, fire symbolizes purification. Not a fire that consumes and destroys, but a fire that consumes and refines.

In John 3:1-21 Jesus is speaking to Nicodemus about being born again. Of course, Jesus is not speaking of a second physical birth, as Nicodemus thought. He is speaking of a spiritual change, a spiritual rebirth. Jesus is telling us: we must be born from above; we must be able to adapt to a new way of living; we must be transformed if we are going to be a part of His kingdom in heaven. Nicodemus was doubtful, and at the same time trying to understand; longing to understand. How can a man change the way he has lived his entire life? It's a radical concept. The coming counselor, the Holy Spirit makes it possible. (*Do not conform any longer to the pattern of this world, but be transformed by the renewing of your mind.* Rom 12:2) The Holy Spirit helps us to be transformed (*...the Counselor, the Holy Spirit, whom the Father will send in my name, will teach you all things...* John 14:26).

Point: Be transformed by the renewing of your mind by the power of the Holy Spirit that dwells in you.

Prayer: *"Create in me a pure heart, O God, and renew a steadfast spirit within me."* (Psalm 51:10)

Today's Reading:
Proverbs 23-25; Romans 15

September 20

THE COUNSELOR

By Beth Nelson

John 14:16 *He will give you another Counselor to be with you forever – the Spirit of truth.*

Have you or a member of your family ever talked to a therapist? It's very commonplace these days, when we find ourselves unable to deal with life's problems by ourselves, to search out a therapist or a psychiatrist to help us. At the very least, most of us will turn to trusted friends with our problems; but too often well-meaning friends will give advise that isn't based on the truth, doesn't come from God.

The Lord knew that we would have trouble sorting out life's issues by ourselves, so He sent a Counselor, the Holy Spirit, the Spirit of truth who would teach us all things and remind us of everything that Jesus said. Jn 14:16,17,26 When you consult this Counselor with your problems, you receive not just good advise, but the best. With answers that work, results that last. The Counselor, who already knows us, brings comfort and healing and leads us in the steps that we should take to find answers. It is precisely because most of our problems have a spiritual basis, that almost all treatment centers that I've ever seen, have a spiritual component. Even if they're not religiously-based, they recognize this fact. Some will go so far as to say without equivocation that spiritual help is necessary to bring about real healing.

You may not be a trained counselor yourself, but the Counselor indwells you when you are filled with the Spirit. I got a crash course in consulting the Counselor through a dear friend of mine who used to call me often when she was in a crisis. I usually had no idea what to say, so I learned to lean on the Holy Spirit. I claimed the verse from Luke 12:12 which promises that when you are brought before people, you're not to worry about what you will say, for the Holy Spirit will teach you at that time what you should say. I was simple enough in my faith to believe that this promise was for me. So when she would call, I would quickly ask the Holy Spirit to help me to understand the problem, and to give me words to say. As long as I was in the Word, attached to the vine, the answers came from the truth in God's Word, not from ideas in my own empty head.

Life is very hard sometimes, and very confusing and mental health care professionals that have God's wisdom can be invaluable. God's Word is practical, it's not just for pious people who don't live in the real world. The Holy Spirit, the Counselor who has been sent to us has real answers for us, if we search for them with all of our hearts.

Today's Reading:
Proverbs 26-27; Romans 16-1Corinthians 1

September 21

THE HOLY SPIRIT: GOD

By Peggy Kalevik

Genesis 2:7 *the LORD God formed the man from the dust of the ground and breathed into his nostrils the breath of life, and the man became a living being.* 2 Corinthians 3:6 *He has made us competent as ministers of a new covenant— not of the letter but of the Spirit; for the letter kills, but the Spirit gives life.*

God gives life and He takes life. At His will or desire He causes the dead to rise. In the Old Testament God breathed into Adam the breath of life. We see God also breathed the breath of life into animals. But, man was made in the image of God and was given dominion over the animals and all things on the earth. Isaiah says it is God, the Lord, who gives breath to earth's people and life to all who walk on it. We see throughout the Bible references to the "breath of life" and the "breath of God" (Isaiah 42:5). God gives life with breath from his nostrils. This breath of God and breath of life are the essence of God's Spirit. (Who gives life?)

In the New Testament God makes it clear He wants His word to live. He makes it live in the person of Jesus Christ and His Spirit. In the Old Testament the people of God lived by the letter of the law. The law was a set of written rules, without life (Exodus 24). The New Testament on the other hand brings us into relationship with God through the shed blood of Jesus. We come to Jesus by faith and we live our lives according to the Spirit (Rom 8:4-5).

Paul writes that those who lived under the law had veiled faces and their minds were made dull, because only in Christ is the veil removed. For it is in Christ that we are afforded the opportunity to receive the Holy Spirit. Paul says, *even to this day when the old covenant is read the veil covers their face; but when anyone turns to Christ the veil is lifted. For the Lord is spirit, and where the spirit of the Lord is there is freedom. And we, who with unveiled faces all reflect the Lord's glory, are being transformed into his likeness with ever-increasing glory, which comes from the Lord, who is the Spirit* (2 Corinthians 3:18).

Prayer: Father, we who are living by Your Spirit—praise you, as I am doing today; and we will tell our children about your faithfulness.

Today's Reading:
Proverbs 28-30; 1Corinthians 2

September 22

Oh To Be Like The Lord!

By Scott Kalevik

Luke 5:16 *But Jesus often withdrew to lonely places and prayed.*

Jesus went to lonely places and prayed. He did it often. He withdrew from all of the commotion of his life and spent time praying by Himself. Don't you find that amazing? The Lord of all – the Sustainer of life – the Creator – the Beginning and the End – God the Son in human flesh spends time … no … OFTEN spends time praying in withdrawn lonely places. Why do you think Jesus did that?

Jesus taught us that He lived a life of total dependence on His Father. Jn 14:10 *Don't you believe that I am in the Father, and that the Father is in me? The words I say to you are not just my own. Rather, it is the Father, living in me, who is doing his work.* Jesus often prayed in lonely places because His whole purpose was to do and say what the Father wills. They must communicate.

Now here's a question for us … If Jesus often withdrew to pray because He chose to be totally dependent upon His Father, why don't we withdraw to pray regularly? Please excuse me if you already do … I'm asking the question of those of us who regularly allow the tyranny of the urgent to overcome our prayer lives.

I know most of us have reasons why our prayer lives receive so little attention. But consider Jesus. He leads by example. His love for the Father compelled Him to pray. His desire to faithfully accomplish the Father's will drove Him to His knees.

As you read the gospels, notice that Jesus always knew where He should go and what He should do. His ministry to others was powerful, effective and loving. He had peace that passes all understanding. Remember that anyone who abides in the Vine is promised these same things.

Look at your schedule today. Is there time to pray? What can you change about your routine to spend time with God? Perhaps it's as simple as turning off the television. I believe God has given everyone of us the time to pray. The question becomes, "Is prayer a priority in my life?" It was in Jesus' life.

Point: Jesus prayed often in lonely places because He depended completely on His Father.

Prayer: Lord, give me strength to make prayer a regular, daily practice in my life.

Practice: Find a lonely place. Withdraw from the commotion of your life and pray.

Today's Reading:
Proverbs 31-Ecclesiastes 1; 1Corinthians 3-4

September 23

THE FRUIT OF THE SPIRIT
By Beth Nelson

Ephesians 5:8-9 *Live as children of light, for the fruit of the light consists in all goodness, righteousness and truth; and find out what pleases the Lord.*

A vine can only produce fruit if there is an unobstructed flow from the plant. In the same way, it is only as the life-giving power of the Holy Spirit lives fully in us that genuine fruit will appear in our lives. Christians may have just a few of the gifts of the Spirit, but we are to have every one of the fruit of the Spirit. It is when Christians accentuate the gifts of the Spirit but neglect the fruit of the Spirit that they discredit the work of the Lord and the watching world discounts their witness. For example, oftentimes it is easier for a person to teach the Bible to others, or to be a gifted administrator than it is to live a holy life. Eric Fife in his book The Holy Spirit talks about a man named John Sung, a very gifted Chinese evangelist who had genuinely experienced God's grace, but who had a reputation as having an uncontrollable temper. He was known to dismiss up to three interpreters in the course of one sermon. He had great gifts but little fruit. Jesus said, By their fruit you will know them. Mt 7:16 A pastor may get discouraged over the small number of people in his congregation, but the fruit that he displays in his life pleases God far more than being successful in the eyes of others.

This is why the apostle Paul places such emphasis on the importance of love, a fruit of the Spirit, placing the wonderful passage on love, 1Cor 13, right in the middle of his teaching on the gifts. Jesus said, I chose you and appointed you to go and bear fruit – fruit that will last. Jn 15:6 His intention is that the Spirit in us will be allowed to blossom forth fruit in our lives. This is a life-long process, of recognizing our lack of fruit, our utter hopelessness to produce it ourselves, and of giving ourselves over to the Holy Spirit to produce in us qualities pleasing to the Lord.

In keeping with the passage that exhorts us to think about whatever is true, noble, right, pure, lovely and admirable (Phil 4:8) I find it helpful to memorize and to meditate on each of the fruit of the Spirit from Gal 5:22-23: But the fruit of the Spirit is love, joy, peace, patience, kindness, goodness, faithfulness, gentleness and self-control. Against such things there is no law.

Today's Reading:
Ecclesiastes 2-4; 1Corinthians 5

September 24

How Does The Comforter Comfort?

By Scott Kalevik

Acts 20:23 *I only know that in every city the Holy Spirit warns me that prison and hardships are facing me.*

The Spirit of God kept delivering a message to the apostle Paul. "Hardships are coming." "Prison is coming." The Holy Spirit let Paul know that trouble was on the way.

When we submit our lives to Jesus Christ and obey His commands, the Holy Spirit of God indwells us (1Cor. 6:19). Paul's experience teaches us that when the Holy Spirit of God lives inside of us, He not only communicates with us, He also brings comfort to us. Sometimes that comfort comes by knowing what's coming.

Today's verse is extremely comforting to me. Why? Because Paul never had to question whether or not God was with him when the hard things came his way. The Holy Spirit had already warned him repeatedly and prepared him to walk through the valley. When the guards slapped the chains around his ankles and wrists, Paul could rejoice in the fact that God had already told him this would happen.

Paul surrendered his life so totally to the Lord, it didn't matter to him if he had to suffer or not. Whatever the Lord planned for him was fine. As he said in Philippians 3:8 *What is more, I consider everything a loss compared to the surpassing greatness of knowing Christ Jesus my Lord, for whose sake I have lost all things. I consider them rubbish, that I may gain Christ.*

In His mercy, the Holy Spirit comforted Paul by allowing him to anticipate his coming suffering. Paul could rest assured that the plan of the Lord was being worked out in his life even though he found himself behind bars. God was glorifying His name and accomplishing His purpose through Paul! What more could any of us desire?

If you've surrendered your life to Jesus Christ, this same Comforter lives in your heart today. Listen closely for the comfort He's providing.

Today's Reading:
Ecclesiastes 5-6; 1Corinthians 6-7

September 25

THE HOLY SPIRIT: A PERSON
By Peggy Kalevik

John 14:17 *The Spirit of truth, the world cannot accept him, because it neither sees him nor knows him. But you know him, for he lives with you and will be in you.*

The Bible tells us the Holy Spirit is a person. If we believe the Bible is the inerrant word of God, there is no need or desire to question. However, as students of the Bible and church goers living in the "world", we know there are those who doubt. There are many scholars of the Bible who question the validity of the Holy Spirit as a person. The truth of today's scripture says clearly that the third member of the Trinity is a true, living being.

In this section of John, Jesus is preparing His disciples for His departure from the earth to return to the Father. He tells them He will not leave them alone, but he will send a counselor. The counselor is the Holy Spirit. The purpose of this counselor is to represent God, just as Jesus did during His stay on the earth. The Holy Spirit would be their comfort and guide. The disciples were to function in ministry in the "Spirit" or as the "Spirit" lead them; as scripture says of a number of people they will be, "filled with the Holy Spirit" (Luke 1 & 2). Jesus would indwell them with the Holy Spirit before He returned to the Father (John 20:22).

The use of the pronoun "Him" as Jesus speaks about the Holy Spirit tells us Jesus knew the spirit to be a living being, or person. The Holy Spirit exhibits the attributes of a person: joy, love and grief (Luke 10:21; Rom 8:26; 14:17; 15:30; Eph 4:30). The Holy Spirit teaches, testifies, guides, enlightens, intercedes and comforts (John 14:26; 15:26; 16:7 & 13; Rom 8:4 & 26). All these are attributes of a person not a thing. The Holy Spirit is indeed with us and He is a person. Praise God for His Spirit, we would be lost in this world without all that the Holy Spirit provides. God loves us so much He sent His Spirit to live in us. As Paul writes; the Spirit helps us in our weakness, we do not know what to pray, but the Spirit intercedes for us. What great love! He lived and died for us and never leaves us alone!

Today's Reading:
Ecclesiastes 7-9; 1Corinthians 8

September 26

LED BY THE SPIRIT

By Beth Nelson

Isaiah 30:21 *Whether you turn to the right or to the left, your ears will hear a voice behind you, saying, "This is the way; walk in it.*

If we pay attention, the Holy Spirit may lead us in ways we would never imagine. Acts 8 relates the story of Philip being directed by the Spirit to go to a very specific road. When he arrived, the Spirit of God gave him detailed instructions to go up to a chariot that was on the road and to stay near it. As he got close to the chariot he overheard someone reading from the Old Testament. Someone who didn't know what he was reading. Someone who was seeking. Someone who needed help. That day, because of Philip's obedience to the Spirit, this Ethiopian man became the very first person from Africa to become a Christian.

In this politically correct world, we wouldn't dream of knocking on a stranger's door, even if God told us to. Or would we? The other day, a good friend of mine told me an amazing story. Some friends of hers have a daughter who suffered with anorexia. As the years passed this poor young woman became so gripped by the disease, that in spite of the best efforts of numerous doctors, psychiatrists and therapists, in and out of treatment centers, she continued her downward spiral. Finally, at less than 70 lbs, she was sent home from the hospital to die. Her poor parents took her home and waited for the inevitable. One day, there was a knock on the door. A woman whom they had never met was standing there with a small vial of oil. She asked, "Is there someone in this house who needs prayer for healing?" They invited her in and she prayed over this poor dying young lady, anointing her with oil. God the Holy Spirit planted healing and hope in her life that day. It was the beginning of her journey back to life. She eventually married a wonderful Christian man and they have adopted two precious children.

As His people, bought and paid for by the precious blood of Jesus, we belong to God. Let us allow His Spirit to expand our vision to see the miraculous things that He wants to do. Let us throw off the stifling cloak of the fear of what others might think and allow God the Holy Spirit to take us by the hand and move us out as lights in a dark world.

Today's Reading:
Ecclesiastes 10-11; 1Corinthians 9-10

September 27

THE FULLNESS OF GOD

By Peggy Kalevik

Ephesians 3:19 *and to know this love that surpasses knowledge—that you may be filled to the measure of all the fullness of God.*

God in His infinite wisdom shares with us the mystery that was once hidden from view but is now made known. Paul was chosen by God to bring this message to all of us who are not of Israel. And what is this mystery? God wanted to extend the right to be part of His kingdom to the gentiles; to all who would receive Him, the message of the Gospel 'the unsearchable riches of Christ'. He intended to include the gentiles in his plan of salvation. For centuries the Jews were proud of the fact they were God's chosen people. Now God introduces a new way of thinking and uses one of them to bring the message.

Paul penned this message to the church at Ephesus to give the church a better understanding of God's purpose and grace hoping they would grow in their respect and appreciation for the priorities and goals God has for His church. Paul's ultimate point to the people of the church was that God is going to use the church to express to the entire world and the heavenly realm's; His 'manifold wisdom". *"His intent was that now, through the church, the manifold wisdom of God should be made known to the rulers and authorities in the heavenly realms, 11 according to his eternal purpose which he accomplished in Christ Jesus our Lord.* (Eph 3:10-11)

God offers us an opportunity to know Him in all his fullness. Paul prays that the Ephesians will come "to understand the love of Christ" something he considers to be immeasurable. He asks God to allow the Ephesians to be rooted and established in love, so they *"...may have power, together with all the saints, to grasp how wide and long and high and deep is the love of Christ,"* (v18). Paul wants the Ephesians to achieve what God requires of us as believers; to mature to the full understanding of faith, to reach unity in the faith and in knowledge of the Son of God, and attain to the fullness of Christ. The Holy Spirit makes the scriptures become real to us by showing us applications of the Word in our lives. This is how we come to the full understanding of the character of God. When the Holy Spirit applies scripture to our life experiences we gain greater spiritual understanding.

Point: God requires of us maturity in the faith, our unity of understanding our faith and to strive to attain the character of Christ.

Prayer: God give me a faith that is maturing every day; lead me down the path of maturity in You.

Practice: Read Ephesians for understanding and spiritual growth.

Today's Reading:
Ecclesiastes 12-Song of Songs 1-2; 1Corinthians11

September 28

WHERE YOU LEAD ME WILL I FOLLOW?
By Scott Kalevik

Matthew 4:1 Then Jesus was led by the Spirit into the desert to be tempted by the devil.

Look closely at today's verse. The Holy Spirit of God leads Jesus into one of the most difficult experiences of His life. In obedience to the Spirit's leading, Jesus went to the harsh, life-threatening environment of the desert. Jesus went without food for forty days. Jesus was alone. But on top of all this suffering lies the reality that the Spirit of God leads Jesus directly into a confrontation with the Devil.

What a crucial moment in the life of our Savior. If Jesus falls to the temptations of the Devil, He proves He is not the true Messiah. If Jesus triumphs over the Devil, He accomplishes what no man has ever accomplished. He remains sinless. He passes the test. He does what only the Messiah can do. Scripture records that Jesus, even in His weakened condition, never yields to the temptation of the Devil. Jesus never sins! Praise God!

Notice, however, that the glory of God is revealed in Jesus' life through the trial. Jesus can't pass the test if there is no test given. The Holy Spirit wants Jesus to pass the test and, therefore, He leads Jesus into the desert to be tempted by the Devil.

As the Holy Spirit leads us He knows His purpose for our lives. Perhaps the Lord has led you into a very difficult situation. Have you considered that His purpose may be to glorify Himself as you rely on Him and pass the test? Ask Him for strength to follow. Ask Him for strength to pass the test. Ask Him to glorify His name in your life no matter what the cost!

The Holy Spirit of God does not always lead us to places of comfort and peace. Sometimes we are called to the test. But in the midst of the storm, He holds onto to us and glorifies His name as we follow!

Today's Reading:
Song of Songs 3-4; 1Corinthians 12-13

271

September 29

Temple of the Holy Spirit
By Beth Nelson

1Cor 6:19 *Do you not know that your body is a temple of the Holy Spirit, who is in you, whom you have received from God? You are not your own; you were bought at a price. Therefore honor God with your body.*

Temptation is nothing new. The first temptation ever recorded involves forbidden fruit in the garden of Eden that was "pleasing to the eye." Overcome with desire, Adam and Eve justified their disobedience to God. Just as God's one rule for Adam and Eve was given for their protection, so God's rules for holy living are not for the purpose of thwarting our enjoyment of life; they are there to protect us from harm.

Temptation to immorality is as old as the history of man and is just as destructive today. It destroys bodies, lives, spirits, and families. Paul warned the Corinthian church against such behavior. Therefore, he says, flee immorality. Get as far removed from it as you can, for it gives the enemy a foothold in our lives, and the end is our destruction.

The Bible teaches that, for the believer, our bodies are temples of the Holy Spirit of God. 2Cor 6:16,7:1 says For we are the temple of the living God...let us purify ourselves from everything that contaminates body and spirit, perfecting holiness out of reverence for God. Our bodies are given to us to enjoy all the good that God intends for us; they are dwelling places of the Spirit, entrusted to us to guard and care for. Don't you know that you yourselves are God's temple and that God's Spirit lives in you?..God's temple is sacred, and you are that temple. 1Cor 3:16 As such, our bodies don't belong to us. You are not your own; you were bought at a price. Therefore honor God with your body. 1Cor 6:20

Resisting temptation isn't always easy but the Spirit will always enable us, if we purpose to resist it. God has given us a sacred trust, to care for our bodies as the temple of the Holy Spirit. He has bought us at a great and precious price. Let us care for our bodies and use them to glorify God.

Today's Reading:
Song of Songs 5-7; 1Corinthians 14

September 30

Lord, What Direction Should I Go?

By Scott Kalevik

1 Corinthians 16:8 *But I will stay on at Ephesus until Pentecost, 9 because a great door for effective work has opened to me, and there are many who oppose me.*

Decisions are a part of life. We make decisions about what to do everyday of our lives. But now that you are following Christ, how do you know if your decisions line up with what God is asking of you? Let's look at a couple of decisions made in the New Testament and see if we can ascertain some principles of godly decision making from those that have gone before us.

In 1Corinthians 16:8, Paul makes a decision. He's going to stay in Ephesus until Pentecost. His decision is justified by the fact that a great door for effective work has opened to him. He also mentions that many people oppose him. Take note of that. Opposition is no reason to quit.

Here's another example of decision making: 2Co 2:12 *Now when I went to Troas to preach the gospel of Christ and found that the Lord had opened a door for me, I still had no peace of mind, because I did not find my brother Titus there. So I said good-by to them and went on to Macedonia.*

Notice that the Lord had opened a door for ministry in Troas too. But Paul decides not to stay. Why? He misses Titus. He has no peace of mind. Both examples contain an open door for ministry but each ends differently. Paul stays in Ephesus despite opposition. He leaves Troas because he has no peace of mind.

So how do we make godly decisions? First, as you make decisions regarding the direction of your life, ask yourself if God has opened this door. Paul knew in his heart that God had opened the door in both examples. If you're not sure if God has opened the door, keep praying. He will show you.

Second, don't let the difficulty of God's calling turn you away from the task. Remember Paul stayed in Ephesus even though many opposed him. The Lord will never leave you and He is strong enough to handle any opposition.

Third, ask yourself whether or not you have a peace about your decision. Notice, the question isn't, "Am I having fun?" The question is one of peace. If you don't have that settled feeling in your heart as you pray confirming for you that you're where God wants you, it's time to reevaluate.

Today's Reading:
Song of Songs 8-Isaiah 1; 1Corinthians 15-16

273

October 1

In the hands of an Angry God

By Peggy Kalevik

Jeremiah 19:11 *and say to them, 'this is what the LORD Almighty says: I will smash this nation and this city just as this potter's jar is smashed and cannot be repaired. They will bury the dead in Topheth until there is no more room.*

The Bible tells us God is patient and longsuffering, compassionate and forgiving. But what happens when we are disobedient to the point of making Him angry? In Jeremiah 19 God is angry and He sends Jeremiah on a mission to deliver a devastating message to His people. In the previous chapter, Jeremiah tells God that the people are making plans against him; to attack him with their tongues and pay no attention to anything he says. And now, as always, he goes like a child doing exactly as his Father has told him; and when he delivers his message the Priest has him beaten and put in "stocks" over night. But God is still angry about the terrible, no, horrendous things that have occurred at Topheth in the Valley of Ben Hinnom. Verses 4-5 tell us: *"For they have forsaken me and made this a place of foreign gods; they have burned sacrifices in it to gods that neither they nor their fathers nor the kings of Judah ever knew, and they have filled this place with the blood of the innocent. They have built the high places of Baal to burn their sons in the fire as offerings to Baal—something I did not command or mention, nor did it enter my mind".* (2 Chr 33:6). It was a place of evil, wickedness and great idolatry. It is said the drums were played to cover the sound of dying children being sacrificed on the altars. God had forbidden the sacrifice of innocent children in Leviticus 18:21, yet in Jeremiah 7:31 God says they: *"...burn their sons and daughters in the fire...*

The word "Topheth" when translated into the Greek is "Gehenna", from this word which we got the original concept of hell. By Jesus' day, Topheth was still constantly burning and known as the place where the wicked were cast into the flame.

God allowed His people to be taken into exile, many of them died. He was just as angry with His children then as I'm sure He is angry with the nations today. Is this the fate we face for our disobedience? We have turned from God to do our own thing. We do not reverence Him; we do not "give Him all the praise and glory that is due His name". No, we take credit for every good thing in our lives; some of us are quick to credit/blame Him for all the bad things even though we create a lot of our own trouble.

Point: Hebrews 10:31 —"It is a dreadful thing to fall into the hands of the living God", it's even worse if He's angry with you!

Today's Reading:
Isaiah 2-4; 2Corinthians 1

October 2

SECRET SINS

By Kathy Bryant

Joshua 6:18 *But keep away from the devoted things, so that you will not bring about your own destruction by taking any of them. Otherwise you will make the camp of Israel liable to destruction and bring trouble on it.*

It's simply not possible to keep a secret from God. Especially if it involves something sinful. We probably think "if no one I know sees me in the act, then no one's the wiser". We forget that God is all knowing and all seeing.

In Joshua 6, the Israelites had a miraculous victory over Jericho, the walls fell with very little effort on Israel's part. God specifically told the people not to take the "devoted things" for themselves, because they and the silverware were to be taken to the treasury. Achan chose to ignore this admonition and stole some items and hid them in his tent.

In Joshua 7, the bible outlines Achan's actions, the losses Israel suffered in a battle they should have won, and God's anger and chastisement of Israel. The whole story has a tragic ending. Innocent lives were lost through one person's disobedience. This story seems to force us to realize that the actions of one person in most cases affect others. The consequences of a secret sin can eventually affect those around us; our families, friends, and even our congregations. Our reputation and effectiveness as a servant of the Lord could be destroyed. We are called to live our lives by faith, trust in the Lord, and live in obedience.

Like the Israelites in Joshua 7, we might experience many losses and setbacks because we do not recognize and repent of the little "secret sins" that God hates and that go against His commands.

Point: Examine your heart and mind, and acknowledge any secret sins.
Prayer: Ask the Lord for wisdom and strength to repent and turn away.

Today's Reading:
Isaiah 5-6; 2Corinthians 2-3

October 3

Jealousy Kills!

By Scott Kalevik

Genesis 4:5 *but on Cain and his offering he did not look with favor. So Cain was very angry, and his face was downcast.*

Anger and jealousy left unchecked can overpower a life. Ask Cain. He murdered his little brother. It wasn't self-defense. It wasn't fear. Cain murdered out of anger and jealousy. He couldn't admit he was wrong. He couldn't stand that his little brother's offering was acceptable to God and his wasn't.

Cain worked the soil. Abel worked the livestock. At some point in their lives, they both presented offerings to the Lord. Naturally, Cain offered the Lord fruits from the soil. Abel offered animals from the herds. That fits doesn't it? Cain brings something from his expertise – plants or fruit, and Abel brings something from his expertise – animals.

The Lord told Cain that Abel's offering was acceptable. Cain's offering of fruits and vegetables wasn't acceptable. Why not? The Lord wanted the worship He received to teach us that innocent blood must be shed to forgive sin. Animal sacrifice points to His plan of salvation. Jesus would one day die as the sinless sacrifice taking the punishment for sin upon Himself. Before the death of Jesus, however, God required His worshipers to sacrifice innocent animals to remind us that the wages of sin is death.

So, the Lord tells Cain that his offering is unacceptable. He also tells Cain to simply do what is right. In other words, the Lord wants Cain to offer that which will please the Lord – an animal sacrifice – like his brother Abel offered. The Lord promises Cain that he will be accepted if he obeys.

What's so hard about that? The only way we can truly come to God is on His terms. But Cain rejects God's instruction. Despite God's direct warning, Cain lets his anger and jealousy overpower his life. Cain murders his baby brother Abel. Rather than please God through his obedience, Cain chooses to sin against God and against his brother by ignoring God's desire and doing things his own way.

Cain had a choice. Instead of doing what God said, Cain did what he felt like doing. You and I have the same choice today. We can either behave the way God instructs us to behave and find peace, or we can let our emotions guide us and allow sin to destroy not only us, but perhaps the ones we love as well.

Today's Reading:
Isaiah 7-9; 2Corinthians 4

October 4

Philemon

By Peggy Kalevik

Philemon 8-9a Therefore, although in Christ I could be bold and order you to do what you ought to do, 9 yet I appeal to you on the basis of love.

In this letter to Philemon, Paul is asking Philemon to love and forgive. These are traits that are inherent in Christ. It is easy to say the words "I accept", "I love", or "I forgive". It's an altogether different thing to actually live a life reflecting these behaviors. Paul asks Philemon to live his life in a way which reflects his love for Christ and the Church.

If you've listened to Pastor Scott's sermons on 1 Corinthians, one thing he keeps bringing home is unity in Christ (Christ's work on the cross unifies all who believe and accept this gracious gift of salvation). Paul is doing this same thing with Philemon. Onesimus is a runaway slave who belonged to Philemon, a wealthy Asian gentile. We know Paul met Onesimus while in prison. We don't know the details of their relationship, but we can gather from reading Colossians and Philemon that Onesimus had accepted Christ and was in some way assisting Paul in his ministry (v10-13). We also know Paul has a spiritual connection to Philemon, (a slightly more mature new Christian (v6)), maybe through Epaphras. Paul uses his considerable influence as an Apostle, as an "old man", and as a servant of Christ in chains, to persuade Philemon to do what is right in the sight of God. Paul never bluntly states that Philemon should grant Onesimus complete freedom, but it is inferred. To advocate for the release of a slave in Paul's day was to attack the social institution of slavery, the Roman culture and authorities might frown on that. Paul was not trying to cause political or cultural discord. He simply wanted Philemon to do what was right "on the basis of love".

Imagine the impact of this one man's forgiveness to a slave in this fledgling Christian community. This would be "all the buzz" over coffee and tea. It would cause many to think about their own commitment and some would undoubtedly grow spiritually. It would give slaves new found status with their owners, and among themselves. Paul makes it clear in Galatians 3:26 *"You are all sons of God through faith in Christ Jesus".*

Point: As Christians we are obligated to love and forgive one another.
Prayer: Father, please teach me to love and forgive as You have loved an forgiven me.

Today's Reading:
Isaiah 10-11; 2Corinthians 5-6

October 5

WHAT HAVE YOU DONE FOR ME LATELY?

By Scott Kalevik

Exodus 17:6 *I will stand there before you by the rock at Horeb. Strike the rock, and water will come out of it for the people to drink." So Moses did this in the sight of the elders of Israel.*

These were the people that the Lord freed from the bondage of slavery to Pharaoh despite Pharaoh's great power. As the Lord instructed them, they obediently put the blood of the lamb on their doorposts. God's angel of death passed over their firstborn sons while killing the firstborn of Egypt. What an incredible miracle of God. They witnessed it first hand.

These were the people that had walked on dry ground as God parted the sea and delivered them from the Egyptian army. Can you imagine what it must have felt like to see a wall of water halted in mid-air while you walked through the middle of a sea? And then to stand on the opposite shoreline and witness that same wall of water collapse upon the pursuing Egyptian army, what impact that must have had on their faith! What an incredible miracle of God. They witnessed it first hand.

Now God was leading them through the desert to the promised land. He gave them Moses to instruct them. God provided a pillar of cloud by day and a pillar of fire by night so that His people could not possibly miss His presence or His direction. Miraculously manna appeared to supply their need for food. These people had every conceivable reason to believe in the God they followed. They were eyewitnesses to miracle after miracle.

So how do they exercise their faith? They start yelling at Moses because they're thirsty. They can't rest in God's protection and provision. They complain because they thirst.

Moses prays. God tells him to strike the rock at Horeb with his staff. Another miracle occurs. Water gushes out of the rock. But imagine how God must have felt. All of His guidance, provision, and care was met with, "Give me more."

I catch myself doing the same sort of thing from time to time. God has led and provided so abundantly yet I'm complaining or asking for more. Not today! Thank you God for all you've done! I don't need anything more except more of You! How about you?

Today's Reading:
Isaiah 12-14; 2Corinthians 7

October 6

THE GOD OF SECOND CHANCES

By Kathy Bryant

Joshua 6:25 *But Joshua spared Rehab the prostitute, with her family and all who belonged to her, because she hid the men Joshua had sent as spies to Jericho - and she lives among the Israelites to this day.*

The bible does not tell us the circumstance that caused Rehab to become a prostitute in Jericho. We know that women in the Old Testament era were vulnerable to destitution if they did not have the protection of a husband and family. We can assume that Rehab was successful in her occupation, since she had a house that was large enough to hid the two spies from the town officials who came looking for them. Rehab risked her life to protect the spies.

Joshua and the Israelites destroyed Jericho through a miracle. The Israelites took special care to get Rehab and her household outside of the city before it was burned to the ground. Imagine how Rehab might of felt. In an instant she lost her livelihood, home, and friends. Would her faith in the God of the Israelite spies be enough to provide a future for herself and her family? The last line of verse 25 tells us that "she lives among the Israelites to this day". God opened the door for a second chance for Rehab. The word lives instead of lived suggest a continuous existence. Rehab became the great-great-grandmother to King David, whose lineage, through God's covenant, would continue forever. It was the family line of our Lord Jesus. (Matt 1:5) Rehab was also included in the faith hall of fame, (Heb 11:31).

Have you ever wished you had a second chance or a do-over? Your present or past circumstances have left you with ashes. You might have been like Rehab who lost her occupation, home, family, and everything. We can take heart that through faith in God we can receive a second chance. God has a plan for us (Jer 29:11), if we have the strength to trust Him. Who knows what opportunity for greatness might be right around the corner.

Today's Reading:
Isaiah 15-16; 2Corinthians 8-9

October 7

Eyes to See God

By Peggy Kalevik

Numbers 22:31 *Then the LORD opened Balaam's eyes, and he saw the angel of the LORD standing in the road with his sword drawn. So he bowed low and fell facedown.*

If you read the "Living Hope Today" devotional regularly, you know by now there are certain stories in the Bible, particularly in the Old Testament, that I absolutely love. This story in Numbers 22-24 is one of them. It amazes me how God uses this donkey to get the attention of someone who, like Frank Sinatra, was only interested in doing it "his way". God's use of the donkey left the prophet with no doubt that God is in control.

What would you do if your dog or cat started to speak to you in English? You'd be mortified, uuh? The prophet seemed to take it in stride, and he even repents of his behavior with his donkey. But Balaam did not have the understanding he needed to grasp the power of the moment. It wasn't until His third oracle (23:27-24:9) that we can see he understands the sure greatness of the power of God. In his third oracle you can almost feel his reverence for God. Something has changed for him. The commentaries tell us Balaam never really truly accepted or adopted the ways of God, or became a true believer. But we know, that he now understands, this God is the Almighty God. That He is not like the other Gods of his day; this God has the power to control nature and everything in our world.

Try to remember the day when you knew it was God who controlled your life, not you. You didn't react with anger or dread or fear, no, it was a place and a time to really appreciate the love, protection and mercy of God. And Balaam, finally understanding that God is pleased to bless Israel, "gives in" to the power of God, and does not resort to sorcery as he had done in the past. He proceeds to speak out the blessings as God had instructed in his heart. God opened his eyes so he could see the true wonders and blessings of God to His people. Prior to this incident, Balaam didn't have the eyes to truly see God. His donkey had better vision. As the song goes "I once was lost but now am found; was blind, but now I see".

Point: Allow God to open your eyes to His plan for your life. Even in the decision you're trying to make today! God has the power to move mountains and speak through even a donkey.

Prayer: Open my eyes Lord that I may see clearly the direction in which You're leading, that I may work where You're working.

Today's Reading:
Isaiah 17-19; 2Corinthians 10

October 8

PAIN AND FAITH
By Scott Kalevik

Genesis 23:17-18 *So Ephron's field in Machpelah near Mamre—both the field and the cave in it, and all the trees within the borders of the field—was deeded to Abraham as his property in the presence of all the Hittites who had come to the gate of the city.*

It happened. Sarah died. Abraham was alone for the first time in many years. Alone with his thoughts, alone with his memories, it was time for Abraham to decide what to do.

Have you ever experienced the loss of a soul mate? Pain pierces the heart. Grief ebbs and flows like the ocean tides. Focus disappears when looking through tear filled eyes. A lot of us ponder retreat when we're really hurt. Wouldn't it have been easy for Abraham to pack up his stuff and head back home to Ur? After all, it had been many years since God commanded him to leave Ur and move to the promised land. And so far, all Abraham really had was God's promised son, Isaac. There was no land he could call his own.

But Abraham never shut down. Despite his broken heart, he continued to believe that God keeps His promises. Abraham believed so strongly in what God would do in the future that he bought a piece of property in the promised land. He knew their descendants would one day occupy this place because the Lord had promised.

Faith endured the pain of loss. Faith held on to the hope that God's character is true. Faith looked through tear-filled circumstances to envision how the world would be after God's promise came to pass.

Your pain is only temporary if you've surrendered your life to Jesus. He still keeps every promise. If your eyes are filled with tears today, remember the faith of Abraham. Continue to walk in truth by faith and wait for God. He does everything He says He will do.

Today's Reading:
Isaiah 20-21; 2Corinthians 11-12

October 9

RESCUED BY THE POWER OF GOD

By Peggy Kalevik

Daniel 6:16b *The king said to Daniel, "May your God,
whom you serve continually, rescue you!"*

Jealousy and envy seem to be the problems of the men who falsely accuse Daniel in this most beloved story of the Bible. God is able to save even from the mouths of lions. King Darius states the three things we need to learn from this story: Our God is a living God; His kingdom and His reign are forever eternal, it will never end; and He performs miraculously on behalf of His people in heaven and on the earth. Our God is an awesome God!

In this story we see men of great power stoop to treachery and deceit. The saying "absolute power corrupts absolutely" works here. The problem is these men didn't feel they had absolute power, they thought Daniel had greater influence with the King and they were jealous. Daniel was a Jew, and these men felt he was inferior to them. They didn't like the idea that Daniel had risen to this level of power. Daniel was invaluable to the smooth transition and continued running of the governmental structure. These men didn't have understanding of the Babylonian government that Daniel held from his many years in the service of the Kings of Babylon. King Darius counted on Daniel's expertise, the Persians needed Daniel.

Daniel's integrity gave these men no way to discredit him. They knew Daniel would be faithful to His God, so they devised a plan to make Daniel choose between His God and the King. Daniel understood the cost of being faithful to God, but he prayed anyway. He asked God for help, he trusted His God. His fellow administrators of course, found him in prayer and reported him to the King, who at odds with his own heart sentenced Daniel to death by loins. When the order was issued to throw him into the lion's den, Daniel did not argue, fight or make excuses; he simply trusted God and went to his fate. And the King bound by his own decree puts Daniel in the hands of God: *"May your God, whom you serve continually, rescue you!"* What a powerful farewell to the man on death row. And God did indeed rescue Daniel. God rescues and delivers, all we have to do is trust.

Point: God is alive, his power is unfathomable; He will rescue His people.
Prayer: God give me the strength, the faith/trust to lay it all in Your hands.

Today's Reading:
Isaiah 22-24; 2Corinthians 13

October 10

Seeing the Face of God
By Peggy Kalevik

Exodus 33:20 *But," he said, "you cannot see my face, for no one may see me and live."*

Over the centuries man has tried to imagine what God looks like. We have wondered, and some have even drawn pictures of how they thought he might look. But no one really knows because he has chosen to never let us see his face. Of any man we know about, Moses got the best opportunity to see Him. But God makes a point of telling him "no one may see me and live". One of our church members phoned to say she'd been pondering this issue. She was fascinated at how people try to draw pictures of God, but no one can draw a good picture because no one has ever seen him. It occurred to her that we should keep in mind, while "we can't draw God, we can draw near to God".

Moses asked God to show him His glory. He needed God's protection, power and presence; and to distinguish him and God's people from the other people of the land. But God instead said he'd allow Moses to see all of His goodness and He would proclaim His name as He passed before Moses. By allowing Moses to see His goodness and by proclaiming His name God gave Moses understanding of His whole character and nature. His name (a more clear explanation of His nature, His character, His person, His laws and or doctrine, and His ways), also encompasses His mercy and compassion. The point seems to be: "God wants us to understand His character and His nature, not to focus on what He looks like." I think it might be too overwhelming to look upon His face anyway. We couldn't handle it. Given enough time, we'd get over the awe, and then we'd be caught up in: he's black or white or, Asian or Spanish or Greek, or whatever we think makes Him more like us. The Bible records Moses' reaction to this awesome sight: *"Moses bowed to the ground at once and worshiped* (Ex 34:8)". Hopefully, we'd react the same way.

We can still draw near to God even though we haven't physically seen His face. We draw near to Him by: obeying His commands, studying His word, talking with Him, living by His standards, emulating His character, and worshiping Him. And yet in many ways we do see Him. We see Him in the works of His hands, the miracles that occur in our lives, the wonders of the Heavens and the birth of a new baby. We see Him and His love on the Cross and in the resurrection. We see Him in the enduring Word of the Bible and the life of His Church. While we haven't had the experience of seeing Him with our physical eyes, we know He is in our hearts for we see Him through the eyes of our heart.

Today's Reading:
Isaiah 25-26; Galatians 1-2

October 11

It's Only A Matter Of Time!

By Scott Kalevik

Genesis 19:24 *Then the LORD rained down burning sulfur on Sodom and Gomorrah—from the LORD out of the heavens.*

God has His limits. Yes, the mercies of God last forever in the sense that all those who have put their faith in Jesus will enjoy His mercy for eternity, but God has His limits. Push Him far enough, and He will act to stop sin.

Take Genesis 19 for example. The people of Sodom and Gomorrah had pushed God to His limit. The stench of their wickedness stirred God to action. He decided to completely destroy both Sodom and Gomorrah.

But in His love, God sent two angels disguised as men on a mission of mercy to warn Lot and his family to flee before the destruction came. Fueled by depravity and lust, the men of Sodom gathered at Lot's door. They commanded Lot to surrender his two visitors to them so they could have sex with them. At his own peril, Lot refused the mob.

The angels save Lot first by pulling him back inside the house. They strike those outside with blindness. They save Lot again by telling him to flee. Lot takes their warning. The angels follow God's order and destroy both Sodom and Gomorrah.

Most read this story and assume homosexuality was the reason God destroyed these cities. But, according to Ezekiel, God had other reasons too. Eze 16:49 *"Now this was the sin of your sister Sodom: She and her daughters were arrogant, overfed and unconcerned; they did not help the poor and needy.*

The Lord gives us the story of Sodom and Gomorrah to warn us that judgment against sin is coming. It is only a matter of time before God permanently eliminates sin from the human race. The day will come when evil will be no more.

We do well to always remember how God will ultimately deal with sin. He will destroy it. You and I must avoid sin at all costs while we flee to the Savior to escape His wrath. It's only a matter of time.

Today's Reading:
Isaiah 27-29; Galatians 3

October 12

The Hand of the Potter
By Peggy Kalevik

Jeremiah 18:6 *O house of Israel, can I not do with you as this potter does?" declares the LORD. "Like clay in the hand of the potter, so are you in my hand, O house of Israel.*

In this Chapter of Jeremiah we see clearly why people question whether or not God changes His mind. My answer is still: No, God does not change His mind! God gives us options, and he announces His intention regarding our choices. If you do what I say I will bless you. If you do not do what I say I will not bless you, and I may bring judgment upon you. It's simple and straight forward. His anger and frustration with us doesn't last forever. If we turn to Him, He will turn to us; after all He created us and maintains complete control over every facet of our lives.

At the potter's house Jeremiah learns a valuable lesson on the sovereignty of God. God wants Jeremiah to understand that just as the potter has complete control over the clay, He has complete control over the house/nation of Israel. Whenever the potter finds an imperfection in the clay he balls it up and remolds it. God does the same with the nation of Israel. When He sees their sin, weaknesses and stubbornness He remolds them, and He will continue to do this until they conform to His plan. God applies this same principle to each one of us and each nation. He fashions and molds each of us to turn us into the faith focused servant He wants us to be. When we falter or succumb to temptation He remolds us just as the potter remolds the clay; He puts us back on the path to His purpose.

Sometimes we feel we just can't go on because we're involved in some situation which seems impossible. Or, we don't have the ability or talent to complete a task; we just can't do it. Stop and think: there is nothing too hard for our creator. He can get you through any situation or enable you to perform any kind of task. There is nothing too hard for our God! He created you, and is continually molding you; He loves you enough to die for you. Trust Him! He can do it! You are in the hands of the greatest potter. If you feel you are at a place of complete brokenness, know "the Potter" wants to remold you, eliminate all your flaws and put you back together again. His love endures forever!

Point: You are in the hands of the Potter; let Him mold you to His liking.

Prayer: God, You arm me with strength and make my way perfect (Ps 18:32), let me be a blessing unto You.

Today's Reading:
Isaiah 30-31; Galatians 4-5

October 13

SUDDEN DESTRUCTION
By Kathy Bryant

Jeremiah 7:23-24 "...obey me, and I will be your God and you will be my people. Walk in all the ways I command you, that it may go well with you. (24) But they did not listen or pay attention; instead, they followed the stubborn inclinations of their evil hearts. They went backward and not forward.

It's hard to imagine that some of our loved ones and friends who have not accepted God's free gift of salvation will be lost forever. We tried to tell them about God's goodness and Jesus' sacrifice for our sins. We beg them to repent and yet, they refuse. Sometimes we see the Holy Spirit drawing them by revealing their sinfulness, but they pull away saying "they're not ready" or "they need to clean up their act". They are stubborn and want to live life on their own terms.

On September 12, 2008 in Galveston, Texas, the governor and officials from the Federal Emergency Management Agency (FEMA) warned people of the impending danger of Hurricane Ike. They told people if they refused to evacuate they could die. Several thousands of those who were warned chose to remain behind. At the height of the storm, one of those people called emergency personnel when the water level was rising in their home. That person was told it was too dangerous for anyone to go out and help them. They were also told to write their name on a piece of paper and tie it around their ankle to later identify their body if they didn't survive! People lost their lives in that storm because they refused to leave for safety!

The Lord said when he returns for his people; He will come like a thief in the night "while people are saying "Peace and Safety", destruction will come on them suddenly..." (1 Thes 5: 2-3). No one knows how long we will remain on this earth. Each day the Lord graciously allows unrepentant people another chance to repent and turn to Him. Many of the people in Galveston thought their homes would be safe in the storm. The Bible tell us that the person who listens to God's words *"... and puts them into practice is like a wise man who built his house on the rock. (25) The rain came down, the stream rose, and the winds blew and beat against that house, yet it did not fall, because it had its foundation on the rock"* (Matt 7:24-25).

Point: No disaster, whether great or small, can completely destroy a child of God who has placed their trust and faith in Jesus Christ.

Today's Reading:
Isaiah 32-34; Galatians 6

October 14

THE MEANING OF MERCY

By Scott Kalevik

2 Kings 13:4 *Then Jehoahaz sought the LORD's favor, and the LORD listened to him, for he saw how severely the king of Aram was oppressing Israel.*

You'll find the stories of many Kings in the Old Testament. You'll also find a pattern repeated over and over. When a new king is introduced, the text will either tell us that this king did what was pleasing in the eyes of the Lord, or this king did evil in the eyes of the Lord. King Jehoahaz is a king described as one who did evil in the eyes of the Lord.

What did he do that was so evil? He took no action to stop the evil practices of idolatry that were taking place when he became king. He hadn't led the people into idolatry, but he didn't stop their worship of false gods. He tolerated evil when it was within his power to stop it.

The Lord responds to Israel's idolatry with judgment. God allows the king of Aram to oppress the Israelites because of their idolatry. The Lord doesn't seem to have any problem allowing difficulties into our lives so that He can demonstrate to us that we've lost our way. Most real change comes through pain doesn't it? Most of us won't forsake our own directions and turn to God until our trouble becomes so unbearable that we are forced to recognize we don't control our lives. Praise God for trouble! It's usually how the Lord gets our attention.

King Jehoahaz was no different. The pain of oppression by the king of Aram was so intense that Jehoahaz decided to seek the Lord's favor. Did you notice what the Lord did when Jehoahaz finally turned to Him for help? The text says, *"... the Lord listened to him."* It would have been so easy for the Lord to justifiably tell Jehoahaz that He wasn't going to listen to his request because of his blatant disobedience. But the Lord shows mercy to Jehoahaz. The Lord did not give Jehoahaz the punishment he deserved. Instead the Lord provided deliverance for him and removed the oppression of the king of Aram.

Mercy means we are not given what we deserve. God is merciful. Take a good look at the trouble in your life. Perhaps God is using it to help you turn to Him. If you surrender to Him, He will listen to you. He will forgive you. His mercy is great!

Today's Reading:
Isaiah 35-36; Ephesians 1-2

October 15

DECISIONS, DECISIONS
By Beth Nelson

Joshua 24:15 *Choose for yourselves this day whom you will serve.*

On a recent trip to Minnesota I was driving around the old neighborhood where I lived over thirty-five years ago during my high school and college days. I recalled the decisions that I made at that time in my life and how they affected the course of my life: where to go to school, decisions to seek after God, deciding whom to marry. Decisions come in all shapes and sizes. Some seem inconsequential, but some of them truly test the strength of our character, like the decision of an ordinary woman named Rahab. (Joshua 2)

Rahab, the prostitute, lived in Jericho, a pagan city. Word got out that Israelite spies were staying with her and someone reported it to the king. The king ordered her in no uncertain terms to hand the men over, so Rahab made a decision. She would risk her own life to hide and protect these men. Why? Though everyone else in the city of Jericho saw the miraculous things that God was doing through the Israelites, she was the only one who admitted the truth openly: Jos 2:9-11 *"I know the Lord has given this land to you…the Lord your God is God in heaven above and on the earth below."* She knew that she would be killed for defying the king but she was willing to take that risk to be on the side of God. All she asked for in return was protection for her family when the Israelites invaded Jericho. Talk about a courageous decision! In the end, what she got was not just safety in the day of trouble, but marriage to an Israelite, then a son named Boaz who married Ruth, and years later, a great-great grandson named David, who became the beloved King David of Israel. But the story doesn't end there. Centuries later Jesus Christ, the Savior of the world, was born into this family.

We don't often think of our decisions as being that important in the grand scheme of things. But when you realize that the course of world history is directed by the large and small decisions of men and women, our own decisions take on more significance. Our little pebbles, cast into the water, cause ripples that touch others around us. When we have the courage to make the right decision, we know that God Himself is with us. And He blesses us far beyond what we can even imagine!

Today's Reading:
Isaiah 37-39; Ephesians 3

288

October 16

I Lift Up My Hands

By Peggy Kalevik

Exodus 17:16a *He said, "For hands were lifted up to the throne of the LORD. ..."*

When we lift up our hands in worship, we don't think about going into battle. However, in a way we are doing just that. We lift up our hands towards God to welcome His presence, to glorify Him, and to feel or experience His power. We want Him to be present with us as we worship Him. We want Him to enjoy our worship, we want to bless Him. But the devil is always fighting against us. He wants to hinder or block our praise and worship of God because he wants our worship. He told Jesus in the desert, *"All this I will give you,"* he said, *"if you will bow down and worship me."* (Mt. 4:9) He thinks he is worthy of our praise. In this world we are indeed at war! So, don't be afraid to lift up your hands and worship God!

Moses lifted up his hands on the top of a hill in Rephidim to bring victory over the Amalekites. As long as he held up his hands the battle went in Joshua's favor, but as soon as his hands came down the Amalekites would forge ahead toward victory. The battle was long and Moses' arms grew tired, so Aaron and Hur held up his arms, eventually sitting him on a big stone. Between the three of them they made it through the battle and Joshua and the Israelite army were victorious. Moses held up his hands to God for strength and power for his people. The Israelites won the battle because as Moses said: "For hands were lifted up to the throne of the LORD". God spoke to Moses after the battle saying Joshua would remember it forever and he would be encouraged.

Many of the Psalms speak about lifting up hands to God, but none really express the great power in lifting up our hands to God as does this verse from Exodus. Moses' purpose was not to worship, but to appeal to God for His strength, power and deliverance. We worship God to thank Him for His strength, power and deliverance, protection and provision, and mercy; need I say more? In this world we will have troubles, trials, battles, and tribulations; but He has overcome the world, and for that alone we should lift up our hands and worship.

Today's Reading:
Isaiah 40-41; Ephesians 4-5

October 17

Extreme Opposites Extreme Love

By Herb Hubbard

Romans 8:35-39 *Who shall separate us from the love of Christ? Shall trouble or hardship or persecution or famine or nakedness or danger or sword? 36 As it is written: "For your sake we face death all day long; we are considered as sheep to be slaughtered."*

Today's text is one that we are probably familiar with and yet as I look at this text, I find it interesting. Paul uses extreme opposites to demonstrate just how all encompassing God's love is for us. Pauls deals with people first in verse 35: not our parents, children, spouse, employer, no one can separate us from the love of Christ. Then Paul deals with the issues of death and life, angels and demons, the present and the future. No powers(small or great), neither height nor depth; (and then, just to make sure we get it) he finishes with nothing else in all of creation can separate us from the love of God. God demonstrated his extreme love for us when he exchange his righteousness for our opposite unrighteousness. Paul makes this clear in chapter 5:8 *But God demonstrates his own love for us in this: While we were still sinners, Christ died for us.*

So even sin cannot separate us from the love of God but it can keep us from a right relationship with him. His will for us is to enter into that relationship with him. Are you in opposition with him today? Do you feel separated from him? God has already made the provision for you in Christ Jesus to live in his perfect love, the rest is up to you.

Point: Nothing can stop God's love from reaching you.
Prayer: Lord Jesus, thank you for your love and help me to live my life as someone worthy of God's love.
Practice: Surrender any areas of your life that you may feel have separated you from God's love.

Today's Reading:
Isaiah 42-44; Ephesians 6

October 18

SAID FAITH VS. REAL FAITH

By Kathy Bryant

Act 8: 20 "...may your money perish with you, because you thought you could buy the gifts of God with money!"

Simon was a magician in ancient Samaria. He was able to do impressive magic tricks leading people to believe he had great powers. The church in Samaria was growing exceedingly. Simon befriended some of the Christians, and he began to fellowship with them. He was even baptized into the fellowship. The bible said Simon believed, but it is this belief that is in question. In Romans 10:10 the bible says *"For it is with the heart that you believe and are justified, and it is with your mouth that you confess and are saved"*. Simon may have believed he could become a member in the body of Christ through baptism, but he failed to believe in his heart. We can see in Acts 8:19 that Simon thought he could add to his "powers" by tapping into the Holy Spirit. He even wanted to buy the Holy Spirit!

Many people today may be a member of the church, but they can not tell you if they've made a profession of faith in Christ. They enjoy the fellowship with believers and, like Simon, may even be baptized. They want the things they can get out of the church, but they want to be lord of their own lives. In Jn 10:27 Jesus says *"My sheep listen to my voice; I know them, and they follow me"*. Christians have a relationship with the Lord Jesus that dwells in their heart. Simon's attempts to buy the Holy Spirit resulted in a rebuke by Peter and a judgement from God (Act 8: 20-21). No one can tell if someone has a "said faith" like Simon's or a "real faith" through the Lord Jesus as a child of God. Each person knows in their heart who's the Lord of their lives. It's urgent that everyone knows where he or she stands with the Lord. No one knows the length of time we have on earth. Let's make sure we will spend eternity with the Lord, or we might hear Him say, *"...I never knew you. Away from me, you evildoers"* (Matt 7:23).

Today's Reading:
Isaiah 45-46; Philippians 1-2

October 19

WHAT'S YOUR EXCUSE?
By Beth Nelson

Exodus 4:11 *The Lord said to him, "Who gave man his mouth? Who makes him deaf or mute? Who gives him sight or makes him blind? Is it not I, the Lord? Now go; I will help you speak and will teach you what to say."*

The people of Israel had been slaves in Egypt for hundreds of years and they were crying out in misery and agony. God could have spoken a word and had them walk effortlessly out of Egypt. So why didn't He? God doesn't override man and nature to accomplish His tasks. He uses them. And God wanted to use Moses.

However, when God told Moses that He had picked him for the job, He, the Maker of the Universe, ran into major resistance. First of all, Moses was astounded that God had picked him for this task. "Who am I, that I should go to Pharaoh?" Then Moses' mind raced through every worst-case scenario that he could think of, "What if they don't believe me or listen to me and say, 'The Lord did not appear to you?'" Then, realizing his inadequacies he said, "O Lord, I have never been eloquent...ever!" And finally, he dug his heels in and said, "O Lord, please send someone else." Moses finally agreed to the task, as long as he can lean on Aaron, his brother, for support. In the challenging days ahead, God never abandoned Moses, and with signs and wonders He delivered His people out of slavery in Egypt.

Has the Lord spoken to you – about someone that needs the Lord, or a task that needs to be accomplished or changes that need to be made – in your neighborhood, in your church, in your country? We, like Moses, can make every excuse why we shouldn't be the ones to do something. "I'm not trained… What if?.. Ask someone else… I just don't want to do it." *Jesus said, "Anyone who has faith in me will do what I have been doing. He will do even greater things than these, because I am going to the Father."* Jn 14:12 Could it be we dream too small? The God that is in us is great and mighty. We are never adequate for the job but if God calls us, He qualifies us. What could possibly be our excuse?

Today's Reading:
Isaiah 47-49; Philippians 3

October 20

OH! WHAT A BOOK!

By Scott Kalevik

2 Timothy 3:16 *All Scripture is God-breathed and is useful for teaching, rebuking, correcting and training in righteousness, 17 so that the man of God may be thoroughly equipped for every good work.*

Many of us have heard, "You should read your Bible" from grandparents, parents, preachers and friends. Some of us have heard it all of our lives. Have you ever asked yourself, "Why should I read my Bible?" Paul laid it out for Timothy in our passage today.

First, Scripture is "God Breathed." The Bible comes right from God Himself. Peter said it this way in his second letter: 2Pe 1:20 *Above all, you must understand that no prophecy of Scripture came about by the prophet's own interpretation. 21 For prophecy never had its origin in the will of man, but men spoke from God as they were carried along by the Holy Spirit.*

Second, Scripture is useful for teaching. Some of us think we know it all and that we don't need advice about how we should live. Others of us understand that God knows more than we do. God has given us His word to instruct us in every area of life … if we'll listen.

Third, Scripture is useful for rebuking. The Lord is willing to let us know when we're going the wrong way or thinking the wrong things! In Matthew 16 we listen to Jesus rebuke Peter for thinking that his way was better than Jesus' way! God uses His word to tell us things like STOP THAT or YOU'RE WRONG!

Fourth, Scripture is useful for correcting us. When Jesus told the Sadducees they were badly mistaken for not believing in the resurrection of the dead, He said it was because they did not know the Scriptures or the power of God (Mt. 22:29). Scripture corrects our misconceptions about who God is and what He wants.

Fifth, Scripture trains us in righteousness. Want to know how to live a godly life? The Bible lays it out verse by verse. Why should we read our Bibles? Paul summarizes by telling us that Scripture thoroughly equips us for every good work. Want to be effective as a Christ follower? Read His word and obey.

Point: God has given us His word for many tremendous reasons.
Prayer: Lord, help me read Your word.
Practice: Discipline yourself to read His word each day! You'll reap the benefits!

Today's Reading:
Isaiah 50-51; Philippians 4

October 21

I AM

By Scott Kalevik

John 8:58 "I tell you the truth," Jesus answered, "before Abraham was born, I am!" 59 At this, they picked up stones to stone him, but Jesus hid himself, slipping away from the temple grounds.

Blasphemy is a terrible sin. Webster says that blasphemy is: the act of insulting or showing contempt or lack of reverence for God - the act of claiming the attributes of deity. Now the Jews of Jesus' day were particularly sensitive to anyone who dared to claim equal status with God. If they thought you were equating yourself to God as an equal, they would kill you by stoning you to death.

God told Moses that His name is I AM (Ex. 3:14). Imagine the uproar in Jerusalem centuries later when a Jewish carpenter from Nazareth sat in the temple courts and said, *"before Abraham was born, I am."* Every listener realized that Jesus used the exact same title for Himself that God used for Himself in Exodus 3:14. In other words, Jesus unmistakably, undeniably, equates Himself with God.

The fact that everyone understood what Jesus said is clear from verse 59. The people responded by trying to stone him to death. In their view, Jesus had committed blasphemy. In their minds He called Himself God and He deserved to be executed. But in reality, Jesus merely spoke the truth. He declared Himself God because He is God.

There are many lessons for us here. First, Jesus is God. Not just, as many say, a good teacher or an enlightened leader, but God in the flesh! He deserves worship from us!

Second, notice that Jesus doesn't back off the truth even though He understands that they will want to kill Him for telling them the truth. Even in the face of certain persecution, Jesus tells the truth. Are we so bold?

Third, Jesus loves even His enemies enough to make sure they hear the truth. He gives them a chance to surrender to Him as Lord knowing that their desire will most likely be to kill Him. Do we love our enemies or, friends for that matter, enough to tell them that Jesus is I AM – God in the flesh?

Today's Reading:
Isaiah 52-54; Colossians 1

October 22

The Inheritance

By Beth Nelson

Luke 12:15 *A man's life does not consist in the abundance of his possessions.*

A man died, leaving an inheritance to two sons. One son arrived first and seized the money, telling his brother, "I got here first so this is mine." His brother, stewing over this injustice yet helpless to do anything about it, left the house and got caught up in a large crowd. Literally thousands of people were gathering to see Jesus, jostling and trampling on one another. Jesus gazed over this huge crowd and began to speak about the preciousness of every human being, that even the very hairs of our heads are numbered. And don't be afraid of powerful people. Be in awe of God and honor Him with your lips and with your life and the Holy Spirit will be with you.

Suddenly Jesus was interrupted with someone shouting out from the crowd, "Teacher, tell my brother to divide the inheritance with me." Excuse me? Wasn't that a bit rude?

What would you do if you were interrupted right in the middle of a powerful sermon? Ignore the man? Perhaps ask him to come and talk to you about his problem afterwards? Well, instead of putting him off, Jesus recognized that this man was having trouble focusing on spiritual truths. His mind was so consumed with his brother's sin against him that he couldn't think about anything else. So Jesus switched gears and began to speak to the primary heart-need of this man, and of all of mankind: put God first in your life. Don't be greedy for material things. Your life is so much greater than the accumulation of wealth. Let your first focus of the day and your last focus at night, be toward God. God knows what you need; let Him order your life.

Have you ever been in that situation? I certainly have; so bothered by something going on in my life that I have trouble clearing my mind and quieting my spirit to listen to the Lord. Just like the worthless junk mail takes over my mailbox, there are many things that crowd out what's really important in my life. I need to regularly toss out anything that begins to take first place so that I can once again hear the voice of the Savior.

Today's Reading:
Isaiah 55-56; Colossians 2-3

October 23

A Time to Speak and a Time to be Silent

By Peggy Kalevik

Genesis 37:5 *Joseph had a dream, and when he told it
to his brothers, they hated him all the more.*

Joseph was a special person, God used him to save His people from famine and certain death. God spoke to, and through, Joseph a number of times. Joseph seemed innocent in all he did, but on occasion he spoke up when maybe silence would have served him better. He didn't understand that some things are best left unsaid. Sure, God was giving him insight into his future, but I don't recall reading anywhere that God told him to tell his family. It might have been better for Joseph to be silent, but what would have happened to God's people if he had?

Joseph's brothers hated him because they knew their father loved Joseph above them all. I imagine their hearts were hurt. Jacob loved Joseph more because his birth came when Jacob was old, and he was born through Rachel. Jacob had a special robe made for the boy. So, his brothers hated him.

God was preparing Joseph for his future. God showed him he would be a powerful man; his brothers would all bow down to him. Most of us would've kept this information to ourselves, but Joseph was young and immature. This was a time to be silent. Joseph thought his brothers would find this as exciting as he did; but they didn't. They took action on the hatred they felt for him when opportunity came. One of the brothers decided they should kill him and throw him in the cistern and all his dreams would be lost with him. But praise God for Rueben and Judah, they saved their little brother's life! They spoke up at just the right time. Think about it. If the two of them had said nothing the rest of this story would never have happened; and God would have used some other way to save his people. But someone did say the words, and God's plan was set in motion. For some reason we may never understand, God used these circumstances in Joseph's life to put Him where He needed him to be. It's a perfect example of how God can turn a bad situation around for His good.

Point: When God speaks to you do you automatically think you need to tell someone? Or, do you ask God: "is this just for me or should I share it with others?" Think about it before you speak, there could be consequences.

Today's Reading:
Isaiah 57-59; Colossians 4

October 24

THE COVER-UP

By Kathy Bryant

Genesis 3:7 *"Then the eyes of both of them [Adam and Eve]
were opened, and they realized they were naked, so they sewed
fig leaves together and made coverings for themselves".*

The story of Adam and Eve eating the fruit from the tree of knowledge is familiar to most people. It is at this point most Christians believe humanity fell from grace, and sin and death entered into the world. While reading the above passage, I noticed a deeper meaning to the actions following the eating of the fruit. I wondered when Adam and Eve ate from the tree of knowledge why they didn't acquire brilliant minds. The Bible says the first thing they realize is they are naked; a physical response.

We have experienced the same feelings when we find ourselves in sin i.e., lying, dishonesty, committing malicious acts, etc. We give little thought of the immediate consequences. As we try to cope with our actions, the next feeling we may experience is the realization that someone may find out what we've done. We could be exposed (naked) before our family, friends, or community. We might begin to "cover-up" our actions by blaming someone else; our environment, our mood, etc.; just like Adam and Eve tried to cover their nakedness (sin) with fig leaves, even trying to hide from God. We too try to hide our sin from God by not telling Him where we were spiritually or emotionally when we committed the sin.

If the Lord chooses to discipline us, we might be quick to shift the blame; much like Adam and Eve blamed each other for their fall into temptation. Before the fall, Adam and Eve were naked. In a sense there was no barrier between them and the Lord. I believe the Lord wants us to be naked before Him. He will not accept our attempts to cover-up our sins.

Point: Lord, help us to be honest before you. You know everything about us, and you know whatever we do. Lord, help us to keep in our mind not to cover-up our mistakes before you.

Today's Reading:
Isaiah 60-61; 1Thessalonians 1-2

297

October 25

Memorial Stones
By Beth Nelson

Joshua 4:7 *These stones are to be a memorial to the people of Israel forever.*

When I first heard the song, *"Generations"* by Sarah Grove with the lyrics "generations will reap what we sow," it stopped me in my tracks. A picture formed in my mind of not just my husband or my children, but great-great-great grandchildren being affected by how I decide to live my life today - a pretty sobering thought. Then my mind turned and I thought about all of the prayers that God has answered and how those touchstones in my life will be lost to future generations unless I think of some way to pass them on. We Americans talk about leaving this world a better place than we found it, and what could be more important than passing on faith in the one true God?

But how do we go about doing this? Well, this must be important to God, too, because the Bible records that God is big into memorials of all shapes and sizes. He commanded the people of Israel to put some of the manna in a jar "and keep it for generations to come, so they can see the bread I gave you to eat in the desert when I brought you out of Egypt." Ex 16:32 After the Lord stopped the flow of the Jordan River and the Israelites crossed over on dry ground, they were to set up twelve stones taken from the middle of the dry river bed so that "In the future when your descendants ask their fathers, 'What do these stones mean?' tell them, 'the Lord your God did to the Jordan just what he had done to the Red Sea..so that all the peoples of the earth might know that the hand of the Lord is powerful and so that you might always fear the Lord your God.'" Josh 4 Based on the command of Jesus to remember Him, believers to this day commemorate the New Covenant by the taking of communion. The common thread through the centuries is, "remember to tell future generations what I have done for you."

I need to build my own pile of stones, so to speak, so that I will never forget, and perhaps more importantly, future generations will know without a doubt.

Today's Reading:
Isaiah 62-64; 1 Thessalonians 3

October 26

THREE STRIKES! YOU'RE OUT!

By Kathy Bryant

1 Samuel 2:25 *"If one man sins against another man, God mediates for him; but if a man sins against the Lord, who will intercede for him? His sons, however, did not listen to their father's rebuke ..."*

Eli, a priest in Shiloh, spoke words of correction to his two sons Hophni and Phinehas. His sons however did not listen. Although, the bible does not tell us how Eli sons were raised, their behavior as adults suggest they were spoiled and allowed to do whatever they wanted. They were corrupt and even as priests they did not know the Lord (1 Sam 2: 12).

Hophni and Phinehas made three grave errors as they served in the Temple. The three strikes they commit draw God's anger against them. (1) They forced the people to give them the best part of the sacrificial meat for their own use, before it was presented to the Lord. (The correct manner in which the priest should treat the sacrificial offering was outlined in Numbers 18.) The people grew to dislike making sacrifices because of Hophni and Phinehas's tactics; (2) They openly slept with prostitutes, instead of maintaining purity as priests; (3) They ignored Eli's (their father) attempts to warn them of their sins. The Lord sent a man to prophesy to Eli saying that he and his sons had been judged and would die.

The Bible tells us in several places that a wise child should honor their parents and listen to their instruction (Prov 3:1). Parents are told to train their children in the way they should go (Prov 22:6). The entire chapter of Deuteronomy 4 is devoted to how parents should interact with their children. Sometimes parents do everything the Lord instructs and still their children go their own way. Job understood that children have the ability to sin against God, so he offered sacrifices to God on a regular basis to ask for forgiveness of any sins his children might have committed (Job 1:5). It seems that both parent and children have a responsibility to God. Children should honor and listen to the wisdom of their parents, and parents should instruct and pray for their children before the Lord.

Today's Reading:
Isaiah 65-66; 1Thessalonians 4-5

October 27

Esau's Rejection
By Peggy Kalevik

Genesis 25:31-32 Jacob replied, "First sell me your birthright." 32 "Look, I am about to die," Esau said. "What good is the birthright to me?"

In the beginning of her pregnancy, God tells Rebekah: *"Two nations are in your womb, and two peoples from within you will be separated; one people will be stronger than the other, and the older will serve the younger."* God is always true to His word. As Moses might say, "As it is written, so it shall be done". Even in the womb the feud began, Jacob and Esau wrestling for position. Before their father died, Esau who is terribly hungry after a day of hunting forfeits his birthright for a bowl of soup! It was a hastily made decision which haunted his people forever. In addition, the Bible says Esau despised his birthright (Gen 25:34).

Esau, like many of us, was sure of his "rights". He thought it was a sure thing; he was after all the firstborn! But God didn't see it that way. He wanted Esau to value this honor and to take it on with the reverence and responsibility that came with it. Jacob on the other hand wanted the birthright bad enough to take it through bribery and deceit. As a result, Jacob received the blessing which should have been given to Esau. Esau was bitter and angry and makes a vow to kill Jacob after their father dies.

This story has always bothered me; I thought it was so unfair. I couldn't understand why God allowed Jacob to succeed through deception and lies. How many times have you made a quick snappy statement you didn't really mean and later wished you could take it back? Isn't that all Esau did? Praise God, He understood Esau's heart, soul and mind. God knew Isaac loved Esau, but Esau wasn't the one to carry out the plan He had for His people. And, Esau didn't care about the great honor that was to be bestowed upon him. He despised it; he found it to be contemptuous and rejected it; all the while thinking, "I'm the firstborn, my father must bless me". Again, like a lot of people today, he was wrong. Some of the things we think are our "right" are really privileges. And this was a privilege God didn't see fit to give to someone who didn't understand the value or responsibility of it.

Point: Be careful to honor God and the blessings He bestows, knowing that all "rights" are at His discretion.

Today's Reading:
Jeremiah 1-3; 2Thessalonians 1

October 28

OBEDIENCE

By Beth Nelson

1 Samuel 15:22 *Does God delight in burnt offerings and sacrifices as much as in obeying the voice of the Lord? To obey is better than sacrifice.*

I had been feeling spiritually flat for a few months when I heard a preacher speak about prayer. He made the point that if you're feeling spiritually stagnant and your prayers feel like they're hitting the ceiling and bouncing back, go back to the last thing that God told you to do and begin to do it. I hadn't thought of that before. I remembered the last thing that God had told me to do, and I also knew that lately, I had been lax in doing it. Refocusing on my obedience was a key in being spiritually revitalized.

Obedience to God is a theme that starts with the beginning of creation and runs all the way to the modern-day church. The first recorded act of disobedience was not when the world was infested with evil, but when life was literally perfect. Yet Satan knew just how to entice Adam and Eve to doubt God enough to disobey Him. Years later, God gave his people commandments and decrees in order to protect them from harm. He said, *"Hear, O Israel, and be careful to obey so that it may go well with you and that you may increase greatly in a land flowing with milk and honey."* Deut 6:3 God knows that living in this world brings enough trouble without our carelessly bringing more on ourselves. It is His gracious intent to protect us from ourselves and from the evil one.

Jesus said, *"If anyone loves me, he will obey my teaching. My Father will love him, and we will come to him and make our home with him."* John 14:23 Jesus was crystal clear in teaching us what to obey. And that's where we start whenever we wonder what God's will is for us. The Holy Spirit is God's gift to us, to enable us to obey when we simply cannot do it in our own strength. And the more our hearts desire to obey God, the more God makes His home in our lives. Spiritual valleys do come at times, but they won't last forever if we choose to obey.

Today's Reading:
Jeremiah 4-5; 2 Thessalonians 2-3

October 29

WHO WILL STAND IN THE GAP?

By Mike Scheimann

Ezekiel 22:30 *I looked for a man among them who would build up the wall and stand before me in the gap on behalf of the land so I would not destroy it, but I found none.*

This passage from Ezekiel is a sad testimony to the spiritual decline of the Israelites, and the magnitude to which they, as a country, had fallen away from God. He could not find one person to stand in the Gap on Israel's behalf. How do you think we as both American believers, and as individual Christians would come out if God were searching for somebody to stand in the gap? Either on behalf of this country and it's people, or as individuals standing in the gap on behalf of our loved ones, and our church body.

God's call to "stand in the gap", is a serious calling. He expects someone to step up. Someone who is courageous enough to follow His plan and obey His will and commands, even if they are unpopular with those around them. He is calling for somebody to stand and pray earnestly, humbly, and consistently for our country, our family members, our church body, and our friends.

A dear friend in our church is a prime example of one who has stood in the gap for her children, her grandchildren, and now her great grandchild. She has done this quietly, but earnestly for many many years, and has never given up. She is an example that we can all follow. Are you willing to stand with us?

Point: If God were writing this same verse about America, would you be one that He could find to stand in the gap for our country and your loved ones?

Prayer: Mighty God, please help us to have the courage, strength, and desire to be willing to stand for you in that gap, in prayer and obedience.

Practice: Make a written list of people who need intercession with God, on their behalf. Include family members, children, church members, friends, our country, and our troops overseas. Write the name and what the special need is, and then pray earnestly

Today's Reading:
Jeremiah 6-8; 1Timothy 1

October 30

He Prayed
By Peggy Kalevik

Luke 6:12 *One of those days Jesus went out to a mountainside to pray, and spent the night praying to God.*

Jesus understood and spoke the truth of God. He was obedient and faithful to God and He always prayed. Take a look through the Gospels and see how many times He was in prayer. If we want to be like Him, one of the most important things we can do is to be people of prayer. It was His first source of strength, comfort, wisdom and peace. He spoke with His Father continuously. How much time do we spend with God?

Over the years I've heard lots and lots of people say, "I want to be like Jesus". We sing songs saying it, but do we really mean it? We can find time to watch around 145 hours of TV every month (2003 Census report) and to play computer games, but we don't have time to pray and sit with God. Do we really understand what it means to be like Jesus? I've heard the "reasons", "well He's Jesus; you can't expect me to know as much scripture as He does, or pray as much as He does". These are just excuses; we do what we want to do! If we gave up half our TV time and devoted that time to studying the Bible and prayer, our lives would change dramatically!

Luke 5:16 shows us that Jesus' notoriety for His healing power was starting to preclude Him from having privacy, and hinder His ministry. After healing a man of leprosy he withdraws to a lonely place to pray. Instead of enjoying the prominence of His new reputation, He seeks His Father. His goal is always to do the will of the Father. And how do we know the will of the Father? We study His word and we pray. In Luke 6 Jesus went out to a mountainside to pray when He was on the verge of making a big decision. He prayed all night, and the next morning He chose His disciples. He needed to hear the voice of His Father in heaven. He prayed and then He made the decision. Prayer is the key to staying in line with the will of God. We study and we pray; there is no other way. He prayed. He is God. How much more do we, mere mortals, need to pray?

Prayer: Father, teach me to pray three times a day, and be willing to pray more if you call me to it.

Practice: Jesus Prayed: Matt 6:9-13; 11:25; Mark 1:35; 8:6; Luke 3:21; 5:16; 6:12-13; 10:21; 11:1-4; 22:31-32 & John 11:4-42; 12:27; 17:1-26

Today's Reading:
Jeremiah 9-10; 1Timothy 2-3

October 31

THE SKIES ARE TALKING!
By Beth Nelson

Psalm 19:1 *The heavens declare the glory of God; the skies proclaim the work of his hands. Day after day they pour forth speech; night after night they display knowledge.*

After the memorial service for my parents held in Minnesota we stepped outside and saw an awesome sight - the sky was filled with a dazzling display of colorful aurora borealis. We stood there speechless for it was such a fitting tribute to this couple who spent most of their lives serving the people of Alaska. God seemed to be communicating a message to us in that night sky.

God has been known to use the heavens as His tablet – writing messages to mankind. And He can do this, for as the prophet Isaiah wrote in 760 BC , *"Lift your eyes and look to the heavens; Who created all these? He who brings out the starry host one by one, and calls them each by name."* Is 40:26 The oldest book in the Bible, Job (1520 BC), records a conversation where God says to Job, *"I created Pleiades and Orion and the Bear, I brought forth the constellations in their seasons and set up dominion over the earth. I laid the earth's cornerstone – while the morning stars sang together and all the angels shouted for joy."* Job 38

Recently, professor Rick Larson did extensive research, trying to locate the star of Bethlehem. He pored over clues in the Bible and other historical documents, combining them with the latest planetary tracking software. In the year 4 BC he located the star that the Magi would have seen moving across the dark middle eastern sky (www.bethlehemstar.net). The morning stars singing together were none other than Jupiter and Venus, so unusually close that they seemed to be one huge star. And this bright star moved in the sky and then stood still over the town of Bethlehem. The sight moved him to tears, for it was exactly as the scriptures had recorded.

Think of this - when the Creator placed the stars and planets in the sky, measuring their orbits with mathematical precision. He planned that centuries later, at a precise time in history, these signs would come together and herald the coming of the Savior of the world! The heavens do indeed declare the glory of God! The skies do indeed proclaim the work of His hands! For centuries they have been pouring forth speech and displaying knowledge. That God is awesome is too small a word. Let us bow down in worship. Let us kneel before the Lord, our Maker!

Today's Reading:
Jeremiah 11-13; 1Timothy 4

November 1

WHAT WILL YOU SAY?

By Herb Hubbard

Acts 3:4-6 Peter looked straight at him, as did John. Then Peter said, "Look at us!" 5 So the man gave them his attention, expecting to get something from them. 6 Then Peter said, "Silver or gold I do not have, but what I have I give you. In the name of Jesus Christ of Nazareth, walk."

Have you ever been confronted by someone in a shopping center or grocery store parking lot? Just as you are getting out of your car or maybe as you approach the store someone hits you up for your spare change. They give you their story hoping to recieve from you whatever you are willing to give. We probably all have the same action or reaction. If we notice them we will duck and go the other way or if they catch us off guard we will keep moving using the "just say no" approach. Peter is headed into the temple at the time of prayer. He is accompanied by John and as they approach the gate a man asks them for money.

It appears that this man must be accustomed to the "just say no" approach because Peter has to tell him to look at them. Then Peter tells him, *"Silver and gold I do not have but what I have I give you. In the name of Jesus Christ of Nazareth walk."* Wow! This surely exceeded what the man must of thought he was going to get. Remember this is the same Peter that had denied Christ. What do you already have that God has given to you? Maybe it would be worth a bit of spare change just to see what God can do through you. We already have the testimony of what God has done for us through Christ and we have the gospel to share and the promise that he will never leave us. If we are willing to follow as God provides the opportunity we can help those crippled by sin to "walk" in the new life only Christ can provide. What will you say next time someone asks you for something? Will you just keep moving or will you give them what you already have?

Point: Be prepared and willing to share what you already have from God

Prayer: God give me the boldness to share the Gospel of Jesus Christ whenever you give me the opportunity.

Practice: As you start each day ask God for the opportunity to share him with at least one person and see what God does with what you already have.

Today's Reading:
Jeremiah 14-15; 1Timothy 5-6

November 2

DUTIES OF THE SHEEP: PART 1. FOLLOW
By Peggy Kalevik

John 10:27-28 *My sheep listen to my voice; I know them, and they follow me. I give them eternal life, and they shall never perish; no one can snatch them out of my hand.*

Jesus calls us His sheep. We are His sheep if we recognize His voice, and follow Him. He tells us in John 14:15 that *"if you love me, you will obey what I command."* Jesus knows His sheep and they love Him; they are loyal and obedient. To those who follow in love, loyalty and obedience He gives eternal life. To those who refuse to believe all that He has said and done, He says, *"…you do not believe because you are not my sheep".*

What does it mean to follow Jesus? At least 20 times in the Gospels Jesus said "follow me". It is an invitation to live in the manner in which He lived. He came at the will of the Father and everything He did was as the Father commanded. He was obedient and humble. To be good followers we first need to accept Him as our Lord and Savior and repent of our sins (Matt 4:17; Luke 13:3; 15:7). In Mark 8 Jesus says: *"If anyone would come after me, he must deny himself and take up his cross and follow me".* To deny oneself in this context is not to deny us of some "thing", but rather to let go of what or who we think we are, or what you want. He wants us to renounce self. 2 Corinthians 5:15 says: *"And he died for all, that those who live should no longer live for themselves but for him who died for them…"* So, we need to deny self and follow His example. He has left us with plenty of examples to follow, in fact He tells us in John 13:15, *"I have set you an example that you should do as I have done for you."* In addition, we need to do as he has commanded, and that is to love the Lord our God with all our heart and with all our soul and with all our mind, the greatest commandment (Matt 22:37-38). Then we need to make disciples of all nations "teaching them" everything He has commanded, the great commission (Matt 28:18-20). I've had a few people tell me evangelism is not their gift. Well it's not about gifting, it's about obedience. God has given you all you need to speak to someone about Him. Blessed are all who fear the LORD, who walk in his ways. (Psalm 128:1)

Point: You must study and understand His word to know His ways in order to follow well.

Today's Reading:
Jeremiah 16-18; 2Timothy 1

November 3

DUTIES OF THE SHEEP: 2. LISTEN TO HIS VOICE
By Peggy Kalevik

Isaiah 28:23 *"Listen and hear my voice; pay attention and hear what I say".*
Matthew 17:5b *"This is my Son, whom I love; with
him I am well pleased. Listen to him!"*

As God speaks to His people about their behavior and what will happen as a result of that behavior. He tells them to "listen, pay attention". Verses 16-19, considered to be messianic, God is calling His people to faith in Him; He would be their sanctuary, their refuge. After much cajoling, God tells them to listen and hear His voice, and pay attention. He is calling us to do the same. We are no more morally strong in our society than the people of Jerusalem in 701 B.C., if anything we're worse. In Matthew 17:5 God tells us to listen again; this time not just to Him but to His Son. Do we have any doubt we need to listen, or any doubt about who we are to listen to?

So, how do we recognize His voice? As in following, the best way to hear His voice is to understand His Word. While God can choose whatever method He wants, His Word is His primary way of speaking to us. He also uses other people, our conscience and the circumstances of our lives. But, all these should be evaluated against and/or filtered through what He has told us in His Word.

Understanding His Word helps us to understand/discern between what He is telling us and what the world is telling us. If we don't study His word we will become easily confused and good decision making may become impossible. God has given us the Holy Spirit to guide us. The Holy Spirit pricks our conscience when we find ourselves in uncomfortable circumstances. It tells us when or if we're going the wrong direction. This is God's voice in our ear, our heart and spirit. Listen to that little voice, it's telling you the right way to go. God's voice is rooted in His holy scripture; everything He tells us will be reflected there in some way. We must study His word for understanding and to sharpen our ability to hear His voice. The more time we spend with Him the more understanding we will gain enabling us to hear His voice with more clarity.

Point: A good sheep listens to his/her shepherd. Whether you turn to the right or to the left, your ears will hear a voice behind you, saying, "This is the way; walk in it." (Isa 30:21)

Today's Reading:
Jeremiah 19-20; 2Timothy 2-3

November 4

GOING HOME
By Scott Kalevik

John 14:2 *In my Father's house are many rooms; if it were not so, I would have told you. I am going there to prepare a place for you. 3 And if I go and prepare a place for you, I will come back and take you to be with me that you also may be where I am.*

My father's life has changed a lot in the last few months. One year ago he was living at home with the occasional help of an assistant. Today he lives in a nursing home. As I sat in his room this week speaking with him, I couldn't help but think of all the things he's lost as he's aged. He lost his wife in 2001. His best friend died a few years ago. I was sitting next to him when the doctor told him he couldn't drive anymore.

He can't really stand anymore. He's unable to keep his balance very well. Most days he feels like he's on the high seas. Talking is difficult and slow. Buttons refuse to be buttoned. Writing is a memory. Feeding himself has become a real challenge. Practically every possession he's ever owned has either been sold, given away, or is sitting in my garage. The medical experts unintentionally confront his dignity day after day with their pokes and procedures. As dear Lois VanSciver once told me, "Getting old isn't for sissys!"

Perhaps you've helped a loved one through this stage of life. Perhaps you're going through this stage yourself. In either case, Jesus' words today are like healing balm to the soul. He goes to prepare a place for all of the people who have surrendered their lives to Him. Jesus is coming back to take His followers to be with Him. And did you notice the last part? Why is Jesus taking His followers? So that we can be where He is! God wants to be with us!

Yes, most days are difficult for my father. I'm not enjoying this much either. But both my father and I – and you too – can find joy in Jesus' words. Jesus taught us that this world is not our home. Though we lose everything this world has to offer, we are still bubbling over with the hope of His promise. One day Jesus will take us to the home He has prepared for us to be with Him forever.

Today's Reading:
Jeremiah 21-23; 2Timothy 4

November 5

To Seek and to Save

By Peggy Kalevik

Luke 19:10 *For the Son of Man came to seek and to save what was lost.*"

This passage of scripture comes at the end of a number of valuable lessons from the Master. Jesus shows us He is no respecter of persons; He's not concerned with our position in society or the balance in our bank accounts. The Pharisees were right about one thing, *"This man welcomes sinners and eats with them."* Jesus tells us in Luke 5: 31-32…, *"It is not the healthy who need a doctor, but the sick. I have not come to call the righteous, but sinners to repentance."*

God sent His Son to restore us to relationship with Him. Jesus crossed every social, cultural, religious, racial, ethical, gender and economic barrier to complete His mission. In this little section of Luke 19:1-10 we see in the story about Zacchaeus that the Gospel is universal. From the reaction of the crowd it seems that the chief tax collector, was a person of poor character, disliked and distrusted. At least the people thought him to be a "sinner". But Jesus knew him, knew his heart, and said I "must" stay at your house. Jesus implies an urgent divine necessity, He knows this man's name and He sees an urgent need to spend time with Him. Zacchaeus is on the divine agenda of the Master. The fact that the world doesn't see the worth of this man doesn't mean he isn't valuable or loved by God. We have a tendency to judge the world according to our standards. But it's God's standard that matters.

In His effort to share the Gospel with Zacchaeus (who does receive the message), Jesus gave no thought to what the people around Him thought about His actions. He was true to His mission. Similarly in Luke 5 Jesus eats with tax collectors. In His mission to bring these people to the truth of the Gospel, Jesus commits a fairly serious social blunder. He has dinner at the home of Levi the tax collector. Sharing a meal with someone was a significant social statement. It meant there was fellowship between them. Short of committing a flagrant sin with sinners, nothing would break the wall of separation between the religious holy people and the despised sinners more decisively than having dinner with them. Well, He seeks each of us with the same tenacity; all we need to do is respond like Zacchaeus.

Point: He came to seek and to save that which was lost; we are all valuable to Him. Be found by Him today!

Today's Reading:
Jeremiah 24-25; Titus 1-2

November 6

Belonging

By Scott Kalevik

Romans 1:6 *And you also are among those who are called to belong to Jesus Christ.*

Need a place to belong? While touting our independence, most of us crave a place to belong. Like the theme song from the old sitcom Cheers, people want a place where everybody knows your name and they're always glad you came.

Community is hard to come by in modern America. Although most of us are surrounded by people, few of us feel connected to very many. We sit in our traffic jams with our windows up. We wave at our neighbors while closing the garage door. We work in our cubicles. Our yards are fenced. Our ears are plugged with ipods while we pass each other on the street. Even at home, our televisions command our attention and keep us from talking to one another. Although we have the need to experience community, many of us live in relative isolation. Although we go to our bar-b-ques or bowling leagues or bar stools trying to belong, our isolation leaves us in a position where very few people really know us.

I'm so glad the Lord has called us to belong to Him! To belong to Jesus allows you and me to experience what it is like to really be known by someone. His Holy Spirit lives in us. He created us and knows everything about us. And He loves us anyway!

To belong to Jesus is the greatest privilege of life. To think that the Lord of all has called us to belong to Him ... who are we that He is mindful of us? What a loving and gracious God we serve. Thank God for the cross of Jesus! His death and resurrection open the door to our belonging.

Because we've surrendered our lives to Jesus and now belong to Him, we also belong to each other. His church is that community of people who belong to Jesus. If you've surrendered to the Lord, you belong.

Today's Reading:
Jeremiah 26-28; Titus 3

November 7

WALKING BY FAITH IN SPITE OF THE RAIN
By Peggy Kalevik

Genesis 2:5b ... *for the LORD God had not sent rain on the
earth and there was no man to work the ground,*
Genesis 7:4 *Seven days from now I will send rain on the earth for forty days and forty
nights, and I will wipe from the face of the earth every living creature I have made.*

If I read the Bible correctly, God had not sent rain on the earth until He tells Noah that He's sending forty days and nights of rain. Think about the level of faith it takes to do something God is telling you to do when you don't understand at all. Noah had great faith; it took great faith to be obedient under these circumstances. Yet Noah was obedient and because of his obedience he was blessed, and the rest of creation with him.

I imagine that Noah was thoroughly confused when God told him it was going to rain forty days and forty nights. What is rain? What is an ark? Think about your own life: what happens when you find yourself in a situation that seems like fun but you know it's a bad environment, do you listen to that soft voice that's saying "you need to leave" or do you stay because you don't want to look foolish to your friends. What about that nagging feeling that God is prodding you to tell a friend about Jesus, yet you just can't muster up the courage. These are simple situation when compared to Noah's dilemma. Yet we sometimes don't have the faith to respond in obedience to the voice of God. Noah in total ignorance to what was about to happen obeyed God. Noah had great faith and great respect for the all powerful God.

Are you walking by faith today? Is God speaking to you in terms that you can't accept and can't understand? God knows everything! Note that He didn't even bother to explain to Noah what rain is, He simply gave Him instructions about what to do. If God is speaking to you today and you don't understand just follow the instructions. When the rain comes you'll be prepared, and you'll be blessed!

Prayer: God give me the grace and peace to be obedient to your voice in all situations.

Today's Reading:
Jeremiah 29-31; Philemon

311

November 8

CLARITY
By Beth Nelson

Jeremiah 29:11 *"for I know the plans I have for you," declares the Lord, "plans to prosper you and not to harm you, plans to give you hope and a future."*

I just had my eyes checked and found out that my eyesight had deteriorated. The doctor gave me a prescription for trifocals. To go from reading glasses to trifocals was a big change! Nevertheless, I'm out shopping for new glasses.

Who of us, if we cannot see clearly, will not seek help from a professional? We must, if we want to be able to navigate in the world around us. Yet when it comes to how to live our lives, we prefer to stumble along by ourselves in a fuzzy world.

Daniel, as a young man, knew and honored the Word of God and he bravely resisted the enticing ways of Babylon. "Daniel resolved not to defile himself with the royal food and wine." What happened? "God caused the official to show favor to Daniel and to his friends. To these four young men God gave knowledge and understanding of all kinds of literature and learning. And Daniel could understand visions and dreams of all kinds." At the end of a trial period, the king himself questioned them and found them to be "ten times better" in every matter of wisdom and understanding than anyone in his entire kingdom. "So they entered into the king's service." Dan 1:1-21 Daniel stood firm and obeyed what he already knew, and God blessed him with more.

The psalmist says in Ps 119 *"Your word is a lamp to my feet and a light for my path. Oh, how I love your law! I meditate on it all day long. Your commands make me wiser than my enemies, I have more insight than all my teachers."* Do you and I want that kind of blessing in our lives? It's there for us as well! We have the same choices today: whether to stumble aimlessly through life, or to obey the clear Word of God.

Today's Reading:
Jeremiah 32-33; Hebrews 1-2

November 9

UNCONVENTIONAL TRUTH!

By Scott Kalevik

Luke 22:51 *But Jesus answered, "No more of this!" And he touched the man's ear and healed him.*

Eleven disciples were sound asleep in the Garden. Jesus had asked them to pray with Him, but they were too tired. Jesus was in such anguish that He sweat drops of blood as He prayed. It was the night of His betrayal and arrest.

A crowd of armed men approached. Judas walked up and kissed Jesus on the cheek. And then it happened. Malchus, the servant of the High Priest, began to scream in pain as the flash of sharpened steel grazed the side of his head. Peter, doing his groggy best to defend Jesus, had sliced off Malchus' ear with a sword.

Now conventional wisdom suggests that Jesus should be proud of Peter for his bravado. After all, this crowd of armed men wants to hurt Jesus. Peter should get a pat on the back from His Lord for his brave defense – right? Conventional wisdom might also applaud the cutting off of Malchus' ear. You're supposed to defeat your enemies, right?

Jesus is unconventional. His love extends even to His enemies. He rebukes Peter for his misplaced display of aggression. Then Jesus reaches out and performs the last miraculous healing of His earthly ministry. Jesus heals Malchus' ear. Jesus heals one of the very men that came to lead Him to His death! The Lord loved Malchus enough to put him back together even though Malchus was there to tear Jesus' life apart.

Those of us who claim to follow Jesus are well advised to evaluate our attitudes towards those who mean us harm. Generally, our first instinct is to defend ourselves or retaliate against those that hurt us. Jesus' first instinct was to follow His Father and fulfill His purpose even if it meant suffering.

Mt 5:44 *But I tell you: Love your enemies and pray for those who persecute you,* Ro 12:19 *Do not take revenge, my friends, but leave room for God's wrath, for it is written: "It is mine to avenge; I will repay," says the Lord. 20 On the contrary: "If your enemy is hungry, feed him; if he is thirsty, give him something to drink. In doing this, you will heap burning coals on his head."* Our God is unconventional!

Today's Reading:
Jeremiah 34-36; Hebrews 3

November 10

Because He is Worthy
By Beth Nelson

Hebrews 13:15 *Let us continually offer to God a sacrifice
of praise – the fruit of lips that confess his name.*

Oklahoma U's women's basketball team was undefeated in their regular season this year and were expected to go all the way to play for the title. But a big upset in the Final Four quashed those hopes. After their unexpected loss, OU's basketball star, senior Courtney Paris pulled her teammates into a huddle for the last time. A reporter, interviewing Courtney afterwards, asked her what she was doing. Visibly shaken after the loss she said, "I pulled the girls together so that we could pray. We always pray after games."

The writer of Hebrews says, "Let us continually offer to God a sacrifice of praise." Why? Because it redirects our thoughts and hearts off of our ever-changing circumstances, and onto our loving and almighty and changeless God. King David learned to praise God whether life was smooth or rocky. In fact, David often found himself in dire straits. Yet in Ps 103 he writes, *"Praise the Lord, O my soul, and forget not all his benefits..who redeems your life from the pit and crowns you with love and compassion."* David knew from experience that though life may be full of "pits" God has the infinite capacity to redeem the creatures he has made. For that and much more, He is worthy to be praised.

I don't think I've ever felt like thanking God when difficulties arise but I also don't think that He expects me to. However, like young Courtney, I can and I should praise and acknowledge Him in all of my life, even if it seems like a sacrifice. Let me not forget all that He's done for me. He is worthy of all of my praise!

Today's Reading:
Jeremiah 37-38; Hebrews 4-5

November 11

ACCOUNTABLE
By Scott Kalevik

*Ezekiel 33:7 "Son of man, I have made you a watchman for the house of Israel;
so hear the word I speak and give them warning from me. 8 When I say to the
wicked, 'O wicked man, you will surely die,' and you do not speak out to dissuade
him from his ways, that wicked man will die for his sin, and I will hold you
accountable for his blood. 9 But if you do warn the wicked man to turn from his
ways and he does not do so, he will die for his sin, but you will have saved yourself.*

The Lord told Ezekiel he was accountable. Ezekiel wasn't accountable to save the Israelites – as if he could. He wasn't accountable to get them to change their ways. Again, we don't control the behavior of others. But Ezekiel was accountable to tell the people that they were in danger of God's judgment because they were not following Him.

Ezekiel was commanded to warn the Israelites about the dangers of living in disobedience to God. Notice in verse nine that once Ezekiel speaks the Lord's word, then the people become accountable for their own sin. They are no longer able to disobey God with the excuse of not knowing any better. Once told, they know. Once they know the truth, each of them is held accountable for living out the truth. But Ezekiel must speak.

In the New Testament, the Lord Jesus calls His followers 'salt' and 'light'. We who love Him are called to arrest the moral decay in society like salt arrests the rotting of meat. We are to be like light – shining the love and truth of the Lord in every setting.

The Lord has told us to speak the truth in love. We are accountable.

Today's Reading:
Jeremiah 39-41; Hebrews 6

November 12

The Grass is Always Greener...

By Kathy Bryant

Psalm 73:2-3 *"But as for me, my feet had almost slipped; I had nearly lost my foothold. For I envied the arrogant when I saw the prosperity of the wicked"*

In our current economic times, many families are feeling the effects of unemployment, no medical insurance, and an uncertain future. On the other hand, some people seem to be doing really well in this environment. They're buying up real estate and stocks, and they seem to be prospering on the misery of others. The super rich live in mansions, drive high performance cars, they have a staff of people to tend to their needs, and they are the beautiful people. In Psalms 73, Asaph wrote about similar people. He said *"they have no struggles; their bodies are healthy and strong. They are free from the burdens common to man; they are not plagued by human ills"* (vs 4-5) Asaph goes on to describe in detail the behavior of the "privileged" people who were condescending to "ordinary" people. They were insecure in their attempts to protect their wealth, and their hearts were harden to the point of questioning the existance of God. This passage in Psalm 73: 4-12 could have been ripped from our local newspaper, People magazine, or Newsweek.

It's the other half of the psalm that many of us can relate to. Many of us try to live life by following the commands of the Lord, but instead of the good things coming our way, it seems we are plagued and feel punished every morning. (Ps 73:14) Like Asaph, our hearts could become grieved and our spirit embittered when we look at other people with envy in our hearts.

Can we be saved from ourselves? Absolutely! Our salvation is in God. The Lord is holding us during times of trouble, and he will guide us with sound counsel. (Ps 73:23-24) The wicked may enjoy themselves for now, but unless they repent and turn to God, they will perish. So it does not pay to envy unbelievers who seem to be doing better than us, because their future might not be a bright as they planned.

Today's Reading:
Jeremiah 42-43; Hebrews 7-8

November 13

Overcoming the Devil's Attacks
By Mike Scheimann

1 John 4:4 You, dear children, are from God and have overcome them, because the one who is in you is greater than the one who is in the world.

When I was a young lad, a girl told me that when it comes to chocolate, resistance is futile. It turned out that she was wise beyond her years. I am unable to resist a piece of chocolate if I see one there waiting to be devoured. It is one thing to try and resist chocolate, but to try and resist and defend the temptations and attacks of the Devil, is a serious matter. To give in to the Devil's temptations could have eternal ramifications. To be defeated by his attacks and be led into sin, could be more than we could handle. The Devil is always on the prowl, waiting to devour us, and prove how sinful and weak we really are. Some might say, I am not strong enough to defeat Satan. He is the ruler of this world, and the ruler of darkness. He knows every trick in the book. I am just a mere mortal.

However, if you think that, you are wrong! Once you accept God into your life, you now get His power and His strength to fight off the devil. Don't be fooled. The Devil and God are not two equal adversaries, fighting for the upperhand. God created the Devil, and has defeated him. And God will ultimately destroy him when the time has come. God will chain him and cast him into the lake of fire for all eternity.

Point: When God is with you, who can be against you? You are greater than the devil or anything he can bring against you, as long as you are a child and servant of God.

Prayer: Christ, our strength, our fortress, our rock. You created Lucifer, and then cast him out of heaven when he sinned. You also defeated him by defeating death and sin, by dying on the cross so that we might live thru you. We have faith that you will deliver us.

Practice: Take a long hard look at the weaknesses you see in your life. The chinks in your armor that the devil is attacking. Ask God to help you overcome those weaknesses and turn them into strengths.

Today's Reading:
Jeremiah 44-46; Hebrews 9

November 14

BE READY
By Beth Nelson

1 Peter 3:15 *In your hearts set apart Christ as Lord.*

In April of this year the NCAA women's basketball championship games were broadcast on national television. Before the games each player was asked to tell something about themselves. When it came time for Angel McCoughtry, the star player for the Louisville team to speak, she said simply, "I'm a Christian."

How would you and I answer the question: Who are you? The apostle Peter wrote to the dispersed Christians scattered among the nations, *"Who is going to harm you if you are eager to do good? But even if you should suffer for what is right, you are blessed. Do not fear what they fear; do not be frightened. But in your hearts set apart Christ as Lord. Always be prepared to give an answer to everyone who asks you to give the reason for the hope that you have. But do this with gentleness and respect."* 1Pet 3:13-15

Peter uses the words, *"In your hearts set apart Christ as Lord."* If I prepare my heart before the Lord, then I will hear His voice and I'll be ready to give an answer for the hope that is in me. Jesus also talked about being ready, about preparing ahead of time for whatever would follow. In Luke 12:35 Jesus said, *"Be dressed ready for service and keep your lamps burning."* Did He mean literally stay dressed all the time? No, He was talking about keeping my heart right before Him, making Him Lord of my life daily, always being ready to answer or to serve when called. We never know, we can't anticipate what will happen this day. But if we're always ready, we won't miss the opportunity.

Angel McCoughtry had a minute to speak on national television. Her heart was prepared and she didn't hesitate to honor her Lord with her answer. She may not have won the championship game, but she had already won a prize far greater, one which can never be taken away from her.

Today's Reading:
Jeremiah 47-48; Hebrews 10-11

November 15

Transcendent God (1)

By Peggy Kalevik

Exodus 33:20 *"But he said, "you cannot see my face, for no one may see me and live."*

God spoke to Moses often, but still He tells Moses no one may see Him and live. God goes on to provide elaborate measures to let Moses see His back. God is so far out of our realm of understanding we can't even comprehend the reason for this mystery. Essentially God showed Moses the aftereffects of His glory because God is Spirit and has no form to which we can relate. We are continually saying God is sovereign, but He is also transcendent and immanent. Adam and Eve are perhaps the only humans to experience both the transcendent and immanent God. However, they damaged/changed that relationship for themselves and for us. Moses and Abraham both enjoyed outstanding relationship with God, but they experienced an "immanent God". The transcendent God is one of such greatness and power that we can't fully grasp an understanding of Him.

The Merriam-Webster Dictionary gives us these "words" to define transcendent: exceeding usual limits: surpassing; extending or lying beyond the limits of ordinary experience; being beyond the limits of all possible experience and knowledge; being beyond comprehension. I like the last one best, "beyond comprehension" because it really fits the God we serve. We try to understand Him. We want to understand Him, but, the more we learn the more we understand we don't understand! He is a Mighty, Awesome God!!

When we think of our transcendent God we should think in a way that relates to His sovereignty. As Christians we believe in the sovereignty of God; that is we know all things are under God's rule and control, and nothing happens without His direction or permission. When we say we believe or understand He is transcendent, we are saying God is above all, and He is distinguished or distinct from all he has made; he transcends it all. The Bible gives us many scriptures to support this view, Old and New Testament passages. *"For you, O LORD, are the Most High over all the earth; you are exalted far above all gods."* (Psalms 97:9); *"One God and Father of all, who is over all and through all and in all."* (Eph 4:6) All things are done according to His will. He has forgotten nothing and He is never surprised by anything that happens. God is sovereign in all things. He is the most powerful of all powers. He is the only God; there is no other!

Today's Reading:
Jeremiah 49-51; Hebrews 12

November 16

Transcendent God (2)

By Peggy Kalevik

Isaiah 55:8-9 *"For my thoughts are not your thoughts, neither are your ways my ways," declares the LORD.*

What drives our thoughts, what motivates our actions? Sometimes we are motivated by purely selfish reasons, needs or desires. We are often conflicted in our decision making and we lose our perspective. God's ways are always righteous and holy. In fact, in this scripture from Isaiah He gives us a key to understanding Him. His thoughts are not our thoughts, and His ways are not our ways. His ways and thoughts are higher than ours, because His ways and thoughts are ordered and directed by righteousness. His ways and thoughts are without error and indecisiveness. He is always right and just.

We continually strive to understand God. But the truth is God is outside of our little world; He "transcends" time, space and our reality. Picture Him holding the universe in His hand. How can we understand the one who holds the universe in His hand? We don't even understand the universe! He knew we wouldn't be able to understand, so He made provisions for that. He gave us the Old Testament and in it He told us He was coming. Then He came and lived among us; that gave us more scripture, the New Testament. How would we ever understand anything about Him if He hadn't given us His Word? He came to us, we couldn't get to Him.

In the words of R.C. Sproul, our God is holy, separate, and different from man in everyway; and, He is "awesomely unique" (from *"The Holiness of God"*). This is our transcendent God; the God that Adam and Eve knew and walked with. His greatness is so great that He spoke the world into existence (Gen 1:3-29). As the prophet Elijah prayed, fire came down and consumed the offering and water (1Kings 18:38). So powerful is He that He can make the sun stand still in the sky until His people defeat their enemies (Josh 10:13). So awesome is He that He decided to come to us, as one of us, and live on the earth among us. Then He went to the cross to die for us, and rose from the dead and returned to Himself on high in the Heavenly realms (the Gospels); Wow!

Point: Our God is an awesome, holy, transcendent God!

Prayer: Father, Lord of all, help me to understand You better and appreciate how awesomeYou really are.

Today's Reading:
Jeremiah 52-Lamentations 1-2; Hebrews 13

November 17

Immanent God: Immanuel

By Peggy Kalevik

Matthew 1:23 *"The virgin will be with child and will give birth to a son, and they will call him Immanuel"—which means, "God with us."*

"But will God really dwell on earth? The heavens, even the highest heaven, cannot contain you. How much less this temple I have built!" (1 King 8:27) The wisest man who ever lived, Solomon understood that God could not be contained in a building, but he built the temple anyway. He desired a place where the name of God would reside, would rest. Here Solomon shows us a heart that understands and loves God. The heavens, even the highest heaven, cannot contain You. God is bigger than our Church building yet He is there, resting and residing. In His prayer Solomon makes known his heart and begs God to hear the prayers that are offered in the temple and be present. He understands that God's dwelling is in heaven far above and outside our understanding, but he knows that God is here with us as well.

In the Gospels we meet our God close-up in the person of Jesus Christ. He is near; He came to save us; to indwell us. This is God in His immanent being. He lives with us and in us; yet He remains distinct/distinguished from us and all His creation. Colossians 1:16-17 tells us that He is immanent and transcendent: *"For by him all things were created: things in heaven and on earth, visible and invisible, whether thrones or powers or rulers or authorities; all things were created by him and for him. He is before all things, and in him all things hold together."* This scripture is referring to Jesus Christ; but isn't He God? God came to us; Immanuel! The God who is above us, whose power and holiness we can not comprehend. Yet He is with us. *"In Christ all things hold together";* the earth, the planets, the universe, all its inhabitants; human, animal, plants, the solar system, all things are under His control. And still the Bible tells us that He is with us; He is near; He is immanent! God lives in and among, and watches over all that He has created. He is an awesome God!

Point: God's great power, holiness, majesty and deity did not stop Him from coming to us and making a way to have personal relationship with us. God is with us, He is near. His Spirit indwells us.

Today's Reading:
Lamentations 3-5; James 1

November 18

Immanent God

By Peggy Kalevik

Jeremiah 23:24 *Can anyone hide in secret places so that I cannot see him?" declares the LORD. "Do not I fill heaven and earth?" declares the LORD.*

God is inescapable! We cannot escape His presence, or His reach. Yet He is transcendent and distinct from man and all of His creation. He is both transcendent and immanent at the same time. God is able to be with us, within us and yet be distinct from us. We've done a number of devotionals on the omnipresence of God, but not many, if any, on the immanence of God. The two are closely related. Our understanding of omnipresence is that God is always with us, every where all the time. Immanent means "to be within or near; existing within or inherent in something; existing in all parts of the universe. The two words give us a full meaning of God's presence in our lives. God is always present within His creation, though distinct from it. God is the source of our existence and He sustains all of His creation.

"Am I only a God nearby, declares the LORD, and not a God far away?" (Jer 23:23) God denounces the false prophets. The prophets act as though they can avoid God's watchful gaze, that He doesn't know their every move. God, through Jeremiah, makes it plain He sees and hears all. They will not escape His gaze or His judgment. He is a God who is nearby and far away, He knows their hearts.

What is it that makes us think that we have greater wisdom than God? Is it that ego or that need to be in control? As fallible humans we run the risk of making a horrible mistake when we think we know better than the all powerful, all knowing, all seeing God. He is not "only a God nearby". 1 Corinthians 4:5b tells us: *"He will bring to light what is hidden in darkness and will expose the motives of men's hearts."* This is speaking of the return of Christ when all Christians will have their works examined. But how could He do that if He didn't understand what we are doing right now. If our heart is not motivated by His purpose and His word He is aware and He will act accordingly. We make a mistake when we think we can out smart Him. He is in you and me, He knows you and me. He is here with us right now.

Point: God is nearby, He is loving, comforting, ready, and always on time.

Today's Reading:
Ezekiel 1-3; James 2

November 19

COME HOLY SPIRIT

By Kathy Bryant

John 16:7-8 *"But I tell you the truth: It is for your good that I am going away. Unless, I go away the Counselor will not come to you; but if I go, I will send him to you. When he comes, he will convict the world of guilt, in regard to sin and righteousness and judgment.*

The Holy Spirit has a unique place in the Godhead. As born-again Christians we believe the Godhead consists of God the Father, God the Son, and God the Holy Spirit. Yet in Acts 2 the Holy Spirit takes a prominent role in the young church. The Holy Spirit has always been around. In Genesis 1:1 His presence was often referred to as the "Spirit of God"; but in Acts his role becomes more defined. The Holy Spirit convicts a person of sin. It is the Father who draws an unbeliever to faith in Jesus, by working in their mind and heart to confess their sins. (John 6:44) The Holy Spirit begins to guide the new believer on how to live in the righteousness of Jesus, by revealing God's truths in the bible, by prayer, and through a teacher. The apostle Paul defines the role of the Holy Spirit as the teacher in 1 Cor 2: 9-16. Paul gave a detailed explanation about how man cannot comprehend the ways of God using his own reasoning, unless the Holy Spirit teaches him spiritual things *"We have not received the spirit of the world but the Spirit who is from God that we may understand what God has freely given us. This is what we speak, not in words taught us by human wisdom but in words taught by the Spirit, expressing spiritual truths in spiritual words."*

Lastly, the Holy Spirit convicts us of the coming judgement. In Act 17: 29-31 the bible says God overlooked some of man's idolatry due to ignorance. But since the coming of Jesus, His death and resurrection all men will be commanded to repent or face the judgement of eternal death. God's judgment was seen before through his treatment of the rebellious angels and the world before the flood. (2 Peter 2:4-5) The Holy Spirit will continue to remind the believer, and the unbeliever, that the day of judgement is a real point in time.

Point: Let us appreciate the presence of the Holy Spirit in our lives.

Today's Reading:
Ezekiel 4-6; James 3

November 20

FOLLOW ME

By Scott Kalevik

John 13:36 *Simon Peter asked him, "Lord, where are you going?" Jesus replied, "Where I am going, you cannot follow now, but you will follow later."*

Peter listened when Jesus said, "Follow Me" to him some three years before. Peter obeyed, left everything, got up and followed Jesus. At first, following Jesus was really pretty simple for Peter. Peter got up every morning and found Jesus. Then, wherever Jesus went that day, Peter went with Him. Peter had literally been following Jesus day after day for three years.

But just before Jesus went to the cross, He told Peter that He was going somewhere that Peter couldn't follow Him – at least not immediately. Jesus tells Peter that he will follow later, but not now. What a shock it must have been to Peter to understand that his ability to literally follow Jesus was about to be disrupted! Peter objects to Jesus' statement and tells Him that he'd be willing to die for Him. Jesus predicts Peter's failure through denial and abandonment.

Peter was about to learn a new way of following Jesus. Following wouldn't be like it had been for the last few years. Instead of operating by literally finding Jesus each day and following Him, Peter would have to learn how to follow Jesus in the power of the promised Holy Spirit.

Peter, using his own strength and ability to follow Jesus, failed miserably. Peter denied the Lord three times at His trial and abandoned Him to face crucifixion by Himself. But Peter following Jesus after being filled with the Holy Spirit was unstoppable. Even though Jesus wasn't literally physically walking in front of him each day as before, Peter learned how to respond to the leading of the Holy Spirit. Many came to faith in the Lord. Miracles were accomplished. Healings abounded.

Like Peter, we must learn to depend on the Holy Spirit's power and direction if we are to follow Jesus today. We must abandon our dependence on our strength and allow the Holy Spirit to minister through us. The Lord produces heavenly fruit through a the soul totally yielded to Him.

Today's Reading:
Ezekiel 7-9; James 4

324

November 21

It's the Law

By Kathy Bryant

Acts 15: 5, 10 *"Then some of the believers who belonged to the party of the Pharisees stood up and said, "the Gentiles must be circumcised and required to obey the Law of Moses"... Now then why do you try to test God by putting on the necks of the disciples a yoke that neither we nor our fathers have been able to bear?*

The Rule of Law was developed to preserve order in a society. It was used to establish government, the judiciary, and law enforcement. Order was established in society by outlining privileges and punishment. Without the Rule of Law society would fall into anarchy and rebellion. People left on their own may eventually default to their basic lawlessness or whatever they see fit. (Judge 21:24-25)

When the early church was being established, Pharisees, who had become believers, thought the gentiles should be forced to obey the law which included the Ten Commandments and the additional 500 plus man-made laws. The Apostles understood the danger of imposing these oppressive laws on the new believers; thus they strongly opposed the attempts by the Jerusalem council to establish this law. The law was established by God to show people that we can never fulfill or measure up to the law. We need Jesus, and the grace of God, to walk by faith instead of a set of rules. Jesus said "Take my yoke upon you and learn from me, for I am gentle and humble in heart, and you will find rest for your souls. For my yoke is easy and my burden is light". Most people, like those in Galatians 3, feel comfortable living within defined parameters and rules. Paul said "So the law was put in charge to lead us to Christ that we might be justified by faith. Now that faith has come we are no longer under the supervision of the law" Gal 3: 24-25. No one obeying the law can ever achieve salvation. We need the grace of God through faith in Jesus Christ, to obtain salvation.

Today's Reading:
Ezekiel 10-12; James 5

November 22

OUR FATHER
By Peggy Kalevik

John 20:17 *Jesus said…'I am returning to my Father and your Father, to my God and your God.'"*

Our earthly fathers have many roles to fill. They must provide for the family; love, mentor and care for their children. They are expected to teach their children and disciple them. At the same time they need to be a great husband and friend to their wife. To do all these things a father needs to live a Godly life; to be faithful, obedient servants of God. This is essential to being a great father. If you have or had a father like this, you are blessed. Some of us never had the experience of having an earthly father at all. Jesus says God is our Father, which is a great blessing to those who have an earthly father and to those who do not. God watches over, cares for, loves, mentors, teaches, disciplines, befriends, and shelters us everyday. And He is faithful to us, *"God, who has called you into fellowship with his Son Jesus Christ our Lord, is faithful"* (1Cor 1:9).

The Bible tells us "to all who received Him, to those who believed in His name, He gave the right to become children of God". If you've received and believed in Him (Jesus), God is your father. Rejoice in that fact; there is no father on this planet that can compare. If you have godly parents, you have heard how good God has been to them throughout their lives; the many blessings He has bestowed upon them. How He provided when they couldn't make their pay checks stretch far enough. Or, how when they or their parents were ill and the doctors couldn't help, God brought healing. But you never fully understand until you experience His power in your own life. When God shows up and brings comfort, provision or healing to you; or holds you in His arms when you need to cry, you start to understand the love God has for you. You know He is your Father. Know, receive, feel, and enjoy the love that your Father has for you.

Point: No matter who you are, or where you're from, if you have received and believed Him, God is your father.

Prayer: Father, I love you, thank you for the many blessings, and the great love You show to me!

Today's Reading:
Ezekiel 13-15; 1Peter 1

November 23

CREDENTIALS AND COMPASSION!

By Scott Kalevik

Luke 7:16 *They were all filled with awe and praised God. "A great prophet has appeared among us," they said. "God has come to help his people."*

Two large crowds converged on the outskirts of a tiny village called Nain. One crowd was following Jesus into town. The other was following a casket to the cemetery.

A poor widow lady had not only suffered the loss of her husband, but now she suffered the loss of her son as well. We're not told how her son died. But to be without a husband or a son in those days meant severe hardship. Very little work was available to widows. Very little support was given from society. It's why God keeps telling his people to care for the widows and orphans throughout scripture (i.e. James 1.27).

As Jesus watched the funeral procession pass, His heart was filled with compassion for the grief stricken mother. Lk 7:13 *When the Lord saw her, his heart went out to her and he said, "Don't cry."*

But Jesus did much more than simply speak those words: Lk 7:14 *Then he went up and touched the coffin, and those carrying it stood still. He said, "Young man, I say to you, get up!" 15 The dead man sat up and began to talk, and Jesus gave him back to his mother.*

To the weeping widow Jesus says, "Don't cry." To the dead son Jesus says, "Get up!" And with a word from Jesus, the son begins to speak. He's alive again.

Jesus proves His credentials. The dead come to life at His word. Just like the creation account in Genesis when God spoke creation into existence, Jesus speaks life into this woman's son. Only God can do that. Jesus clearly proves His credential as the Messiah and Lord of life.

Jesus also proves that God cares. He cares particularly for those who have no other hope. This woman's grief is turned to joy unspeakable. Her future now holds the hope of having family and life without the burden of poverty because her son is there to take care of her.

Jesus is God and He cares for you too! How will you serve Him today?

Today's Reading:
Ezekiel 16-18; 1Peter 2

November 24

THANK YOU LORD

By Peggy Kalevik

Psalm 100:4 *Enter his gates with thanksgiving and his courts with praise; give thanks to him and praise his name.*

We give thanks to you, O God, we give thanks, for your Name is near; men tell of your wonderful deeds. (Ps 75:1) We do tell of His wonderful deeds. In Psalm 101 David says, I will sing of your love and justice; to you, O LORD, I will sing praise. And we do sing His praise because He is worthy of all our praise. We do give thanks because it is the appropriate response to all that He has done for us.

The Bible clearly tells us that God wants our submission, obedience and praise. If we believe His word and worship Him, then we are acknowledging that He is our Lord and our God. We come before Him in humble submission and worship. Our lives should reflect the love that He has shown us.

We should thank God as soon as we rise in the morning, for every answered prayer and all the marvelous works of His hand throughout our day. Stop for a second right now and think: "Have I thanked God today?" If you haven't now is a good time. Thank Him for waking you this morning, for health and strength and life. Thank Him for the air you are breathing right now, and the water you used to shower. These things we take for granted everyday are not guaranteed, they are all a result of His love and His mercy for us.

We enter His gates when we come into the sanctuary to worship, or when we kneel in our prayer closet to pray. As we enter, let go of every thought other than your love, gratitude and worship of Him. Come before Him with praise, lifting up your voice to sing His praise. Shower Him with love for His great deeds on your behalf. Spend a moment today thanking Him for the many blessings, the years of protection over your life and the love He shows your family.

Who is like the LORD our God, the One who sits enthroned on high, who stoops down to look on the heavens and the earth? (Psalms 113:5-6). No one is like you, O LORD; you are great, and your name is mighty in power. Who should not revere you, O King of the nations? This is your due. Among all the wise men of the nations and in all their kingdoms, there is no one like you (Jer. 10:6-7). "…Then Jesus looked up and said, "Father, I thank you that you have heard me" (John 11:41).

Today's Reading:
Ezekiel 19-21; 1Peter 3

November 25

We Will Serve the LORD
By Peggy Kalevik

Joshua 24:15 *But if serving the LORD seems undesirable to you, then choose for yourselves this day whom you will serve... But as for me and my household, we will serve the LORD."*

At the end of his life Joshua sat God's people down to have a little talk. He knew these people; he understood their stubbornness, their weaknesses, and their fears. Joshua is giving his farewell address to the leaders and all the people of Israel. He recounted all the things that God had done for them up to this time. He was going to bring them to a choice point, and he wanted to be sure no one would feel that they didn't have all the information they needed to make a good decision. He's really saying, I'm old (110) and I have tried to do everything for you that God commanded me to do; now you must choose, for yourselves which path you will take (Joshua 23 & 24). After all they'd been through you'd think they would be true faithful believers and followers of God, but apparently some people were still worshiping other gods. Joshua tells them to fear the LORD and serve Him with faithfulness; throw away the gods their forefathers worshiped beyond the river and in Egypt and serve the LORD. The people have seen the power of God displayed on their behalf, they have been provided for, protected, delivered, and loved by Almighty God. Joshua's call is to be loyal, faithful, and true to God if they want to continue to live in His favor. But he is not deciding for them, he allows them the privilege of making their on decision. He tells them in today's verse: *"But if serving the LORD seems undesirable to you, then choose for yourselves this day whom you will serve, whether the gods your forefathers served beyond the River, or the gods of the Amorites, in whose land you are living. But as for me and my household, we will serve the LORD."* Note that God does not change; He has always given us choice. We are not forced to worship Him, never have been never will be. But the day we stand before Him on the throne, there will only be one choice.

I challenge you to read Exodus, Numbers, Deuteronomy and Joshua and view a life lived in total surrender to the will of God. Joshua was an exceptional person, he always stood for God, and he was certain of his God, his faith was unmovable. When we think of him we most often think of the phrase that Moses spoke to him in the assembly of all the people as he charges Joshua with the leadership of the people. I give you Moses words today hold them in your heart. "Be strong and courageous"... the Lord himself goes before you and will be with you; he will never leave you nor forsake you. Do not be afraid; do not be discouraged (Deut 31:7-8).

Today's Reading:
Ezekiel 22-24; 1Peter 4

329

November 26

TIME FOR GOD

By Mike Scheimann

Hosea 10:12 *Sow for yourselves righteousness, reap the fruit of unfailing love, and break up your unplowed ground; for it is time to seek the Lord until He comes and showers righteousness on you.*

A wise person once said "God loves you because of who God is, not because of anything you did or didn't do." God has loved us for all time. Before we were even born. Before He even created the world, God knew who you were and He loved you. In fact, He loved you, and still loves you, knowing all the sins that you were going to commit. He knows all our sinful deeds, lies, and even our thoughts. He knew the sin we would have in us, before there was even time, but yet He still loved each and every one of us, and still does. With all His heart. God made time for us. Literally! He created the days and the seasons. Are we making time for God? Are we taking time in our busy lives to show the God who has loved us for all time, and will continue to love everyone for all eternity, that we love Him back? Do we take the time to tell Him we love him every day? Do we show our love for Him, by loving others? Do we talk, pray, worship, and adore Him every day in every spare moment? Are you taking the time to seek the Lord? Don't wait until it is too late. Seek and follow Him so that you may be showered with righteousness. Not wrath!

Point: God doesn't expect much from us in our relationship with Him. He doesn't expect flowers or candy, or gifts. All He wants is our sincere love, and obedience to Him and to be number one in our lives.

Prayer: Almighty Father, our Maker and Creator. You who formed us in the womb, and gave us our very lives. Please forgive us when we don't take the time and effort to show you how much we love you. Thank you for your unconditional love, and your infinite patience.

Practice: Make a list of the priorities in your life. Is God at the top of your list? He should be above family, spouse, money, job, and even your own life.

Today's Reading:
Ezekiel 25-27; 1Peter 5

November 27

Who Am I Following?
By Beth Nelson

Proverbs 3:5-6 *Trust in the Lord with all your heart and lean not on your own understanding; in all your ways acknowledge him, and he will make your paths straight.*

In 1913 a renowned explorer named Stefansson set sail on a ship, the Karluk, along with twenty-four scientists and crew, to look for land that he felt certain was hidden beneath the polar ice. Six weeks later, the Karluk became stuck fast in a pack of ice north of Alaska, and Stefansson left the ship, under the pretense of going hunting. Just then, the wind and currents began propelling the ice pack, and for months the passengers were virtual prisoners on the ship as it drifted steadily northwest for hundreds of miles into the vast Arctic Ocean. A year later, the Karluk had sunk to the bottom of the ocean and most of the passengers had perished.

The image is a tragic one, of intelligent, well-intentioned people joining an expedition and then sailing helplessly off to their deaths. They put their trust in one man, a man who had his facts wrong.

The Bible says, *"Be self-controlled and alert. Your enemy the devil prowls around like a roaring lion looking for someone to devour."* 1Pe 5:8 In speaking of Satan, Jesus said, *"..there is no truth in him...he is a liar and the father of lies."* Jn 8:44 He regularly leads people down what looks like a rosy path – straight to their deaths. Praise God that we are not without hope in this world, for Jesus came to lead us back to safety, back to the arms of God. He is "the way and the truth and the life" Jn 14:6

There is an old hymn, *Jesus, Savior, Pilot Me*, which says, Jesus, Savior, pilot me over life's tempestuous sea; unknown waves before me roll, hiding rock and treacherous shoal. Chart and compass come from thee; Jesus, Savior, pilot me. We are not left to drift helplessly, but we have a Savior who stays with us through all of life, and who will guide us safely home.

Today's Reading:
Ezekiel 28-30; 2Peter 1

331

November 28

Consider It Pure Joy
By Herb Hubbard

James 1:2-4 Consider it pure joy, my brothers, whenever you face trials of many kinds, 3 because you know that the testing of your faith develops perseverance. 4 Perseverance must finish its work so that you may be mature and complete, not lacking anything.

Consider it pure joy, you have got to be kidding! Who in their right mind would consider it pure joy when you face trials of many kinds? I know I have felt that way many times in the middle of the trial.

It is hard to consider it pure joy. Even just facing one trial at a time can be overwhelming depending on the situation. The part that makes it unbearable is when nothing is gained or at least when it seems that nothing has been gained. I like the wording in verse 3 "the testing of your faith develops perseverance". I like to think of it as if I were developing a roll of film. The way things were done before instant everything was to take your pictures, send them in, wait for a week and get the developed pictures back. It is always so much fun to look back and remember. What is especially fun is to get a roll developed that maybe you took months or even years ago. To look back and compare to the present helps you to see the changes of those in the pictures. It doesn't matter if the people in the pictures are young or old. You will be able to see how much they have changed.

If we could go back and develop an old picture of when we first became a christian we would see just how much we have grown and matured in the Lord. Then we would be able to say amen to these verses in James and truly be able to count it as pure joy knowing that the testing of our faith has and is developing us into the image of Christ.

Point: The testing of your faith is not in vain but is constantly developing you into the image of Christ.

Prayer: Lord help me to consider it pure joy knowing that the testing of my faith does develop perseverance.

Practice: Take time to reflect on what God has done in your life maybe it will give you a clearer picture of what he is doing now.

Today's Reading:
Ezekiel 31-33; 2Peter 2

November 29

THE PURPOSE OF THE CHURCH
By Peggy Kalevik

Romans 15:5-6 *May the God who gives endurance and encouragement give you a spirit of unity among yourselves as you follow Christ Jesus, so that with one heart and mouth you may glorify the God and Father of our Lord Jesus Christ.*

What was or is God's purpose for the Church? I think there are four major things that God wants us to do as His Church body. The first and most important is to glorify the Head of the Church that is Jesus. The second thing is to evangelize those who have not heard, and third to educate and edify the body. Lastly, I believe that in educating the body, we are also expected to minister to the community around us. Not just believers but all people in the community.

Matthew 28:1-18-20 tells us what Jesus expects believers to do. We don't need a theologian to explain it to us, its perfectly clear. We are to go and make disciples of all nations, baptizing them in the name of the Father the Son and the Holy Spirit. We are to teach them everything He commanded. How hard is that to understand? Yet we squirm around in our seat when someone asks us about evangelizing. It doesn't make any exceptions; it doesn't say you need a special gift. Just "go", and make disciples of all nations. Matthew 22:37-40 gives us the first and greatest command, the charge to love the Lord your God with all your heart, with all your soul and with all your mind. And also the second greatest command, to love our neighbor as our selves. Note that it doesn't qualify "neighbor". This is the reason I believe we should serve our community as a whole, not just believers. These two scripture references give us the foundation of what the Church is all about.

Romans 15 rounds out the purpose of God's Church: *"For everything that was written in the past was written to teach us, so that through endurance and the encouragement of the Scriptures we might have hope. May the God who gives endurance and encouragement give you a spirit of unity among yourselves as you follow Christ Jesus, so that with one heart and mouth you may glorify the God and Father of our Lord Jesus Christ"* (Rom 15:4-6).

Point: The Church is to love and glorify God, love one another, serve (the body and the community), teach and evangelize.

Today's Reading:
Ezekiel 34-36; 2Peter 3

November 30

THE CHURCH
By Peggy Kalevik

Matthew 16:18 *and I tell you that you are Peter, and on this rock I will build my church, and the gates of Hades will not overcome it.*

In a moment of instruction Jesus tells Peter that He will build His Church on the rock. There is much debate about the use here of the Greek word for rock (petros) because Peter in Greek carries the same meaning as "rock". But, the point of this passage is Jesus' acknowledgement that He is the Messiah and He will build His Church.

Most often in the New Testament the word "church" (*ekklesia* – to call out) refers to a Christian body of believers or Jesus followers. Acts 7:38 speaks of Moses being with the assembly (NIV) church (KJV), a reference to Ex 19:17. Moses' assembly in Ex 19 was composed of God's people, the Israelites; the first "called out". Now God has sent Jesus with the gift of salvation for all those who believe; those who follow Him are His Church.

I believe most Christians point to this place as the beginning of the Christian Church. Some however, believe the Christian Church started with the Council at Nicea in A.D. 325. During the reign of Emperor Constantine I, Christianity became the official religion of the Roman Empire in A.D. 326. Constantine called the Council of Nicea to bring unity to the doctrine of the Christian Church (Catholicism). This is how we arrived at the once a week meeting, usually on Sunday, that we still observe today. The Church grew, but for all the wrong reasons; the people came because of its prosperity, its lavish buildings and powerful bishops. (There's much more to this part of the story. If you're interested, may I suggest a little research, http://www.britannica.com Constantine-I).

While we're glad Constantine stopped the persecution of Christians, we can't applaud everything that came out of his accomplishments on behalf of the Church. Still, it is part of Church history. I lean towards the way of the early Church; its pure focus on the message of Christ, and its power and compassion. It also had miraculous blessings, love, caring, understanding of the scriptures and rejoicing in the testimonies of the Saints. In all the things I read about Constantine these things are never mentioned. I believe we are "called out" to live our lives in harmony with the Word of God and the message of the cross.

Point: Father, please reach down and redeem Your Church, save us from ourselves.

Today's Reading:
Ezekiel 37-39; 1John 1

December 1

What if there was no hope?

By Mike Scheimann

Isaiah 40:31 ...*but those who hope in the Lord will renew their strength. They will soar on wings like eagles; they will run and not grow weary, they will walk and not faint.*

Have you ever found yourself in a hopeless situation? How many times have you looked at films or pictures of orphans, homeless people, or battered and abused wives and children; the look of hopelessness in their eyes and on their face? No hope for food, for shelter, or a warm bed to sleep in, and no hope of a mother's embrace for comfort. There are many millions of people in this world, in fact many right here in our own country, that go through life with no hope. What little glimmers of hope they do find in their lives are usually temporary, or quickly dashed. They see no future here on earth and certainly no future beyond their inevitable death. It is truly heartbreaking to see the sadness in their eyes. Just imagine the saddness of a whole world living without hope. What if none of us had a hope for our souls, or our future after death? Can you imagine what this world would be like if no one on earth was concerned about the consequences of their actions, or the penalty of their sins? If people just did whatever they felt like, whenever they felt like it? When people have no hope for a future, they live for the present. We must thank God that He has through His grace and mercy, and the death of His Son, given us hope when there was none. He has given us not only the hope for a future, but the promise of a future.

Point: God knows how hopeless, how weak, and how lonely we are without His presence in our lives and in our world. That is why He has promised to renew our strength, and to help us to soar like eagles.

Prayer: Dear Loving Father, Help us to share Your love and hope with the lost souls around us.

Today's Reading:
Ezekiel 40-42; 1John 2

December 2

God's Plan Will Prevail

By Mike Nelson

Ecclesiastes 3:14 *I know that everything God does will endure forever; nothing can be added to it and nothing taken from it so that men will revere him.*

Herod, called the Great, was a man who by political intrigue and cunning negotiation had been given the position of King of the Jews by the Roman government. He did not qualify for this position for he was only half Jewish and had not won a military victory. He was called Great because he built the new Temple in Jerusalem that rivaled the magnificence of King Solomon's original. He further established his position as King by executing the prior ruler, then killing one of his own wives and two of his sons due to his concern over their desire for shared power. Whenever he was confronted with a challenge to his position as King, he would react with decisive acts of violence to rectify this challenge.

God's plan will not be changed by the evil intents of earthly kings. God knew before the beginning of time of the Wise Men's desire to follow His celestial confirmation of the Messiah's coming and of their desire to worship Him. He knew what Herod's response would be. God warned Joseph of Herod's intent to kill Jesus and also provided the financial means (gold, frankincense and myrrh) to pay for the trip to Egypt and for the extended stay that would be mandated until it was safe to return. God sent His Son in the fullness of time to be born of a virgin, to live under Roman rule, and to be born into financial poverty; to literally change the hopes and dreams of true seekers of God of His plan for mankind's spiritual and physical salvation. Herod has a scant mention in history and his Temple was totally destroyed by the Romans in 70 AD but God's plan for mankind continues on to this day and wise men and women still seek His Messiah and worship Him with great joy when they find Him.

Today's Reading:
Ezekiel 43-45; 1John 3

December 3

LOVING AND DISCIPLINING
By Gwen Taylor

John 6:66 *From this time many of his disciples turned back and no longer followed him.*

When I reflect on loving God with all my heart, soul, mind and strength, I realize that God will not settle for second best. He wants us to involve him in every thought, decision, action and service. Even the first two commandments talk about God being the first and only God. He wants us to have HIS purpose as our motivator and we are to be directed by the Holy Spirit. As He states in Luke 14:26-27, we must be willing to give up everything to put him first. Even the thing we love most. It is the cost of discipleship. Many people realize the cost of putting God first and they do as many disciples did in John 6:66, *"From this time many of his disciples turned back and no longer followed him."* People cannot let go of their most prized items such as family, work, money, etc. and, therefore, do not serve God any longer. The cost is too great. This is often what happens to newer Christians, Mark 4:18-19 (parable of the weeds). When I think about my own life, I realize that I sometimes allow other things to take all my energy and time and when God ask me to do something for him or someone else I feel exhausted. God wants the first 10% from us and not what is left over. Too often we allow other things to crowd God out such as work, entertainment and family activities; then we are too tired to devote any energy, passion or love to the things of God, i.e. studying God's word and serving others. The fact is, if we are to follow him and be his disciple we must give him our best.

If we truly understand the Bible from the front to the end we should know the only reason for sending Jesus was so God could have relationship with his creation. His purpose is to seek and save the lost. Matthew 28:18-20 simply states that we, his disciples must be about our father's business of reaching the lost and making disciples. Christians have failed badly here. We have not shared the love of God through Christ to non-believers as often as we should, or spent time with the people who accept Christ, growing them as disciples. We must get better at this mission because we all know the end of time is upon us and we should be as God, not willing that any should perish.

Today's Reading:
Ezekiel 46-48; 1John 4

337

December 4

BEHIND THE SCENES!

By Scott Kalevik

John 1:14 *The Word became flesh and made his dwelling among us. We have seen his glory, the glory of the One and Only, who came from the Father, full of grace and truth.*

To the casual observer it appeared so routine there was no reason to notice. A lady was pregnant. It was time to deliver. She had a baby boy. But behind the scenes, God was changing the world forever.

At the time of His birth, very few people were in on what God was doing. Mary spoke with an angel. Joseph had a dream. Some shepherds heard the host of heaven declare the King's birth. Three guys from a foreign land had followed a star to find Him. Zechariah, Elizabeth, Simeon and Anna were in on it to varying degrees. But, by and large, God's entrance into life as a human was unrecognized for decades. Instead of a regal grand entrance worthy of a King, Jesus enters the human drama with barely a blip on the radar screen of life.

God enters time and space as a flesh and blood human named Jesus. And once on the planet, Jesus waits in almost total silence for thirty years before beginning His public ministry.

It is good for us to understand that many times God chooses to accomplish His plan without fanfare. Oh sure, Jesus' public ministry would eventually bring Him the recognition of the world. Some hated Him. A few loved Him. But for years and years only a handful of people had any inkling that God was up to something over at Joseph and Mary's house. That helpless little baby boy was happy to spend years growing and developing until the time was right for Him to fulfill the Father's purpose for His life. To most it appeared that nothing was happening. But the majority was ignorant. God's salvation plan was right on time.

Don't think God's moving fast enough for you? Can't see what He's up to? Don't understand why He's taking so long to 'fix it'? Remember how He came. God has heard your honest prayer. He'll work it out in His time even if most fail to recognize what He's doing. Pay attention and keep following Jesus.

Today's Reading:
Daniel 1-3; 1John 5

338

December 5

THE STAR OF BETHLEHEM

By Peggy Kalevik

Matthew 2:10 *When they saw the star, they were overjoyed*

Many scholars and theologians have researched and studied the star of which the Magi or Wise Men spoke in the scriptures. Some believe it is the planet Venus, still others believe it is Jupiter. The Magi followed the star to Bethlehem and made inquiries as to the location of the one who was born King of the Jews. We have read this story many times, but have you ever stopped to think why the Magi had to ask the residences of the land "where is this one born King of the Jews". If they're following the star, why didn't they keep going until they came to the place where its beam pointed? The speculation is that the star is really an Angel. It is apparent that once the Magi reach Bethlehem they can't see the "star" anymore. Otherwise they wouldn't have to ask. When King Herod heard that there were Wise Men asking questions about this new born king, he summoned them in secret. After their discussion with the king, scripture says in Matt 2:9-10 *"After they had heard the king, they went on their way, and the star they had seen in the east went ahead of them until it stopped over the place where the child was. 10 When they saw the star, they were overjoyed."* While we may be able to see why this raises questions in the minds of the researchers, it only increases the believer's awe of God.

Through our faith and knowledge about the all powerful God we serve, we know that He is sovereign, omnipotent, omnipresent, and omniscient, so we know that nothing is too hard for Him. Wouldn't it be just like God to make the star invisible until after the Magi had completed their visit with the evil hearted King Herod. As soon as the meeting is finished, there's the star (once again) and they are able to go right to the location of the child. Read verse 12 to think even more about the depth of God's word. Does it imply that the Magi spent the night with Mary, Joseph and the child? What do you think?

Point: God made the heavens and the earth, He controls their every moment. With men this is impossible; but with God all things are possible. (Matt 9:26)

Prayer: Father, give me faith that I may understand Your power and know that You can do the impossible.

Practice: Read more about it: http://www.scripturescholar.com/ VenusStarofBethlehem.htm

Today's Reading:
Daniel 4-6; 2John

December 6

Pick Me! Pick Me!

By Beth Nelson

Isaiah 57:15 *For this is what the high and lofty One says – he who lives forever, whose name is holy: I live in a high and holy place, but also with him who is contrite and lowly in spirit, to revive the spirit of the lowly and to revive the heart of the contrite.*

Poor Zechariah and Elizabeth, they're such a nice couple, it's too bad they don't have any children. They would have been such good parents! Every time I see them, I feel pity for them. Maybe it's something they did. Now they're getting too old to have children anyway.

Matthew records that this childless older couple, Zechariah and Elizabeth, felt themselves disgraced among the people. Yet they were both upright in the sight of God, and followed all of the Lord's commandments and regulations blamelessly. And their hearts remained humble and true before their Maker. Zechariah did not falter in his assigned religious duties and beyond that, he did not give up praying for a child. His heart was still soft and open to the Lord – accepting whatever the Lord's will was for him but remaining diligent in praying for the desires of his heart. The Bible doesn't say why this couple was picked by God to parent John the Baptist. We can surmise that there were other couples that God could have chosen for this all important forerunner to the Christ. What we do know is that God always looks on the heart, not on outward appearances as we might. And God loves to do the impossible, to bring glory to Himself – to show that He alone is able to accomplish what we in our own power, cannot.

I am humbled when I think of this couple with contrite hearts, faithfully serving God year after year, asking God for this child whom they thought they might never have. Scripture says that God lives with those who are lowly in spirit He bends His ear to hear their cries, and He revives their hearts.

Zechariah and Elizabeth were not perfect, yet their constant faith in God and their vulnerability as a childless couple somehow pleased God. Perhaps because of this, God blessed them with such a miracle that Luke says neighbors were filled with awe and people everywhere were talking about them. Their names are recorded in the Holy Scriptures, to be remembered and honored forever.

Today's Reading:
Daniel 7-9; 3John

December 7

HE'S MORE THAN A BABY!

By Scott Kalevik

1Corinthians 10:3 *They all ate the same spiritual food 4 and drank the same spiritual drink; for they drank from the spiritual rock that accompanied them, and that rock was Christ.*

Christmas is the time of year we celebrate the birth of Jesus. The majority of sermons in Christian congregations will correctly declare that God infiltrated time and space as He came to earth as the baby Jesus! Although it's true, Jesus was born as a baby in Bethlehem, Bethlehem's manger was not the place Jesus came into existence.

The fact is, Jesus never came into existence. Scripture tells us clearly that Jesus is what the theologians call "preexistent." In other words, there never has been a time, including all of eternity past, when Jesus did not exist. Jesus is eternally alive, past, present and future.

Note that today's verse from the New Testament is speaking of Jesus' work in the Old Testament. It describes Jesus supplying His people as they walked in the desert with Moses. Here are a few other verses that attest to Jesus' deity and His preexistence. Ponder them carefully:

Col 1:17 *He is before all things, and in him all things hold together.*

Jn 1:1 *In the beginning was the Word, and the Word was with God, and the Word was God. 2 He was with God in the beginning.*

Jn 8:58 *"I tell you the truth," Jesus answered, "before Abraham was born, I am!"*

Jn 17:5 *And now, Father, glorify me in your presence with the glory I had with you before the world began.*

Jesus' birth in Bethlehem declares God's willingness to empty Himself of His heavenly splendor in order to live in the confines of human flesh. But the Lord we serve didn't begin there. He has always been. His power is incomparable. He created this world. He sustains this world. He will destroy this world by fire at the end of time. And, this same Lord of all, Jesus, loves you to death.

Today's Reading:
Daniel 10-12; Jude

December 8

Judah's Judgment

By Peggy Kalevik

Ezekiel 21:27 A ruin! A ruin! I will make it a ruin! It will not be restored until he comes to whom it rightfully belongs; to him I will give it.'

God is an awesome Father. He disciplines His children; He purges them until they are cleansed. Ezekiel is given the task of relaying to God's people the sorrowful message of destruction and captivity for the sins they have committed. God used Babylon's King Nebuchadnezzar to be His sword of judgment against His people. Zedekiah, the descendant of Judah currently on the throne, was to lay down his crown. The high priest of Judah was to lay down his turban. The crown and the turban would not be worn again until the one "comes to whom it rightfully belongs."

The life of Ezekiel was a strategy board for God. He used the prophet to demonstrate His plan, His power, and His Lordship over His people. Ezekiel would bear the burden of delivering God's message to a hard, obstinate, disobedient people. Imagine going in to tell an ancient day King to take off his crown. Not an easy task! If you recall, Zedekiah was put on the throne by Nebuchadnezzar after his nephew Jehoiachin (only having served three months) was taken into captivity. Today's passage points out to us the reason God had to bring Christ. Man, no matter how wise or royal, is capable of living a spotless life. These kings were simply human. They did wrong in the eyes of God. They could do no less. God's anger was so fierce Ezekiel repeats ruin three times to stress the intensity of God's wrath. Since the time Adam and Eve were in the garden, man has committed sin. God knew then he would bring a Savior. The spotless Lamb of God would take away the sin of the world. Zedekiah, his father and His father's father would never be able to wash away their own sin, much less the sins of the world. They were the cause of God's anger. They had done unspeakable things. They proved that we need a Savior. Zedekiah was the last King of Judah. The crown awaited the one to whom it rightly belonged.

Point: We need a Savior. Christ is the one to whom the crown belongs.

Prayer: Lord, help me to worship the Savior in this season with true understanding of who He is and why you sent Him.

Today's Reading:
Hosea 1-3; Revelation 1

December 9

THE BEST OF TIMES

By Beth Nelson

John 8:12 *he said, "I am the light of the world. Whoever follows me will never walk in darkness, but will have the light of life."*

"It was the best of times, it was the worst of times," wrote Charles Dickens in the opening line of A Tale of Two Cities. I can think of several "worst of times" in my life with family struggles where there seemed to be no way out, losses that brought deep pain. In the midst of those times, you wonder if they will ever end, if you will ever feel joy again.

Into this very dark and hopeless world was born a holy baby in Bethlehem, a bright light, the only hope for all mankind. "Arise, shine, for your light has come!" Is 60:1 There is no darkness that is greater than God's light. As the star shone brightly in the dark sky, just so radiantly does God transform the darkest night into His glorious light.

Isaiah 51:11-16 says, *"gladness and joy will overtake them, and sorrow and sighing will flee away. I, even I, am He who comforts you. I, the Lord your God have covered you with the shadow of my hand."* God our Father covers us with His protective hand. Jesus our brother is with us in our darkest of nights. The Spirit has been sent to bring comfort to our sorrowing souls. The everlasting God is our refuge and strength, a very present help in time of trouble. There is no tragedy, no sin, no difficulty that God is not greater yet.

Let the babe in the manger symbolize new life for you and for me, for all who are tired and worn and sad. Let us come humbly, gratefully, burdens in hand, and place them reverently there. For surely He has borne our griefs and carried our sorrows and just as surely there is healing in His wings. Is 53:4,Mal 4:2

The worst of times will not last forever, for God sent His best to us. Together we cry, "Come, Lord Jesus!" Rev 22:20 We welcome Your light into our darkness today.

Today's Reading:
Hosea 4-6; Revelation 2

December 10

PLACED IN THE CRADLE BUT BORN FOR THE CROSS

By Peggy Kalevik

Luke 2:7 ... She wrapped him in cloths and placed him in a manger...
Matthew 26:39 Going a little farther, he fell with his face to the
ground and prayed, "My Father, if it is possible, may this cup
be taken from me. Yet not as I will, but as you will."

This child born and placed in the manger was born for the Cross; because we need a Savior! We can't atone for our own sin. Our omniscient Father sent His Son to die for the sins of the world. The beauty of the Cross is its saving sacrifice. The Cross and its shame brought us salvation and gave us life. Though we deserve death, the one on the cross was neither you nor I. It was the babe from the manger.

Jesus willingly gave His all for us. I've been asked; did He dread going to the cross? We all dread the tough things life throws our way. We find excuses not to complete a task which seems unbearable; we dread hearing bad news whatever it may be. In human form Christ prayed in the garden: "My Father, if it is possible, may this cup be taken from me." I've never thought of His prayer as dread, but of knowledge. It lets us know that He was human, and yet all the while He is God. His prayer simply stated is: Father, if you can achieve your goal some other way please do it. Jesus' prayer came from a heart in great anguish; His sorrow was deep enough to kill. He was not only concerned with His suffering and/or death on the cross, but also about the wrath of God. So He prays in agony. With all our sufferings in this world, we cannot imagine what He went through. When He was with us as a man, He was the epitome of what God wants us to be. He knew His purpose and He knew the will of the Father who sent Him. Do we know our purpose and the will of our Father? In His human state even in great agony, His greatest desire is to do the will of the Father that He loves. So, He also prays: "Yet not as I will, but as you will." This is an appropriate state of mind and heart; it's not confusion or double mindedness. We always strive to pray in the will of God, but sometimes in certain situations we may not understand His will. So it's the humble obedient heart that prays "let Your will be done" even when it hurts.

Point: At birth He was placed in the cradle but His purpose was fulfilled on the Cross. His will, His desire and His heart - to do the will of the Father.

Today's Reading:
Hosea 7-9; Revelation 3

December 11

The Good Shepherd
By Kathy Bryant

John 10:27 *"My sheep listen to my voice; I know them, and they follow me"*

Animal behaviorists have studied sheep for years and have discovered some interesting traits. Sheep are able to recognize and retain in their memory other sheep and human features for up to two years. Sheep are known for their flocking (herding) and following instincts. As recently as 2006, there was a report of 400 sheep in eastern Turkey plunging to their death when one sheep tried to cross a 15-meter ravine. In biblical times, shepherds would lead their sheep to large pastures occupied by other sheep. The sheep were comfortable around other sheep, and the shepherd would share the watch responsibility with the other shepherds. When it was time to go the shepherd would make a sound which only his particular sheep would respond to and follow their shepherd out of the pasture (John 10: 3-5) The Lord Jesus understood this relationship between the shepherd and the sheep. Sheep are helpless against attacks from predators. Jesus says of himself: *"I am the good shepherd. The good shepherd lays down his life for the sheep. The hired hand is not the shepherd who owns the sheep. So when he sees the wolf coming, he abandons the sheep and runs away. Then the wolf attacks the flock and scatters it."* (John 10: 11-12) We are like sheep. Most of us feel comfortable in a group rather than alone. Safety in numbers! We are helpless against the attacks of the evil one, unless we are under the protection of Jesus our Lord. Those of us who claim Jesus as our shepherd hear his voice through the study of His words in the bible and through prayer. We better learn the sound of his voice the more time we spend in his presence. We can only hope to achieve total trust like sheep who, at a signal from the Lord, will stop what we are doing and follow him; because we know wherever He leads there will be safety and security even when we don't know the way.

Today's Reading:
Hosea 10-12; Revelation 4

December 12

The Babe in the Manger

By Peggy Kalevik

Luke 2:12 *This will be a sign to you: You will find a baby wrapped in cloths and lying in a manger."*

The baby in the manger was more than a beautiful child; He was a gift on a mission. He came to seek and to save that which was lost. He came not for power, He already had that, but for love. He came to give us the greatest gift ever given; the gift of God, eternal life in Him, Christ Jesus our Lord. He was an extraordinary child, the child of promise.

The manger, while an unlikely throne for the King, was the perfect setting for one so humble and meek. The message the angel gave the shepherds provided enough specific information that they would know they'd found the right child when they saw Him. It was common for newborns to be wrapped in strips of cloth, but none were likely to be found lying in a manger. The shepherds were able to find the baby just as the angel told them. But did they really understand the power of this seemingly helpless child, or the awesome presence before them?

Mahalia Jackson wrote a song for Christmas back in the 50's entitled *"Sweet Little Jesus Boy"*. It expresses deep sorrow and remorse over the cruel treatment of our Lord when he came in human flesh. It's a song like no other Christmas song. When you hear it you can't help but feel the sorrow over what we did to Him. She sings, "They made you be born in a manger, and we didn't know who you was". Do we know Him today? Do we live according to His commands to us? He told us: "Love the Lord your God with all your heart and with all your soul and with all your mind" the first and greatest commandment. Secondly He says to "love our neighbor as ourselves". All the law and the prophets hang on these two commands. Yet we couldn't even receive Him in love; we didn't know who He was. Maybe the shepherds understood, but there are a lot of days when I think we still don't have a clue.

Point: He came to us in a manger but His purpose and His destiny on earth was the cross. He came for the cross to give us life.

Today's Reading:
Hosea 13-14; Revelation 5

December 13

LOVING GOD, WISEMEN STYLE

By Beth Nelson

Matthew 2:10-11 *When they saw the star, they were overjoyed. On coming to the house, they saw the child with his mother Mary, and they bowed down and worshiped Him. Then they opened their treasures and presented him with gifts.*

We sing a song which goes, Come let us worship and bow down. Let us kneel before the Lord our God, our Maker. Matthew writes that when the journey of the Wisemen was over, when they reached their final goal, what did they do? With hearts full of awe they bowed to the ground and worshiped the child. This is a fitting and right response to being in the presence of the King of Kings and the Lord of Lords.

Who were these Wisemen, these strangers from Persia, who were watching the clues in the sky, who sacrificed their time and their wealth to travel more than 700 miles on the backs of camels? They came in order to see for themselves the one prophesied in Micah 5:2 *"Out of you will come one who will be ruler over Israel."* Perhaps they were descendents of Daniel, that young Israelite who was brought to Babylon some 600 years earlier and taught by the best scholars of the land. Daniel remained true to the one true God. In any case, it's possible they had some Jewish roots, for what we do know is that finding the child was all-important to them. They didn't hesitate and miss the opportunity. They knew the scriptures, they were watching, and they were ready. They journeyed many days – for what? To bow down before this babe, to worship Him, to give Him gifts, symbols of their love, their allegiance, their reverence.

I am reminded again this Christmas that God asks for the love of His people. He has given us everything we need for life and what He asks of us in return is to *"love the Lord your God with all your heart and with all your soul and with all your mind."* Mt 22:37 Do we love God? Have we given Him our hearts?

Let us ask God to rekindle that love in our hearts once again this Christmas, to place Him first in our hearts and in our lives. The Wisemen were so moved by being in the presence of Jesus that they bowed down and worshiped Him. Let us draw near to our King and worship and love Him with all that we are, for He alone is worthy. Oh come, let us adore Him, Christ the Lord!

Today's Reading:
Joel 1-3; Revelation 6

December 14

GIVING GIFTS
By Scott Kalevik

John 1:14 The Word became flesh and made his dwelling among us. We have seen his glory, the glory of the One and Only, who came from the Father, full of grace and truth.

The word 'incarnation' has 'carne' or 'flesh' at its root. 'Incarnation' means 'to be in flesh.' The Christmas season is a time when our thoughts are once again focused on the incomprehensible fact that God Himself took on flesh or was incarnated in the Person of Jesus.

God spoke in times past through prophets, through the revelation of His word, through His creation, and through mighty deeds. But in Jesus we see God Himself coming to personally walk among us. Every word Jesus spoke was the word of God. Every miracle Jesus did was God working His will among men. Every command Jesus issued was then and is now the command of God.

It's hard to fathom the fact that the little baby in the manger created the universe before He entered His own creation in flesh and blood. But that's the wonder of the birth of Christ. The Lord of all gave up His majesty in exchange for a manger. Ultimately, He laid down His crown to be nailed to a cross.

Praise, worship and obedience are all we really have to give such a King. Today, as we contemplate how He emptied Himself to be born of Mary, let's do two things. First, let's worship Jesus. He is worthy of all praise! Second, ask Him for power and strength to forsake sin and follow Him. Our gift, meager as it may be, is a gift Jesus laid down His life to give us the opportunity to offer. We offer Him all we have.

Today's Reading:
Amos 1-3; Revelation 7

December 15

Rewarding The Faithful!
By Scott Kalevik

Luke 2:25-26 Now there was a man in Jerusalem called Simeon, who was righteous and devout. He was waiting for the consolation of Israel, and the Holy Spirit was upon him. 26 It had been revealed to him by the Holy Spirit that he would not die before he had seen the Lord's Christ.

Scripture tells us that God rewards those who earnestly seek Him (Heb. 11:6). Simeon was a man who followed with all of his heart. Our text tells us Simeon was righteous and devout. The Holy Spirit was upon him. He loved the Lord and proved it each day by earnestly following Him!

Simeon apparently studied and learned that God was going to send His Messiah. The long awaited Deliverer would come. Sin would be forgiven through the work of the Messiah. Simeon believed it with all of his heart because the Old Testament Scripture describes it so clearly. But one day something very interesting happened to Simeon.

We don't know if it happened while he was praying. Maybe he was reading God's word. Maybe he was just sitting at his kitchen table. But one day the Holy Spirit tapped Simeon on the shoulder and told him about something that was going to happen. The Holy Spirit told Simeon that he would not die until he had seen the Lord's Christ!

Imagine the joy of that message. Not only would all those prophecies about the coming of Messiah be fulfilled in Simeon's day, but Simeon would have the privilege of seeing the Messiah for himself before he died.

And one day, true to His word, the Spirit led Simeon to the Temple just when Joseph and Mary brought Jesus. Simeon held the baby Jesus. Simeon got his shout on! He praised God! He blessed Joseph and Mary! God had rewarded him with great privilege.

We serve a God who blesses His people generously! Don't let yourself be discouraged. Follow earnestly! Read, pray, listen, serve! Remember the blessing God gave Simeon. This same Lord watches over you today!

Today's Reading:
Amos 4-6; Revelation 8

December 16

Follow That Star: Balaam's Fourth Oracle
By Peggy Kalevik

Numbers 24:17 *I see him, but not now; I behold him, but not near. A star will come out of Jacob; a scepter will rise out of Israel. He will crush the foreheads of Moab, the skulls of the sons of Seth.*

In this, his fourth oracle, Balaam fast-forwards to the return of Christ. He also touches on His first arrival. His overall focus, however, is a picture of Christ's royal power over all the enemies of God and His people. Balaam singles out the Edomites and the Moabites because of their bold hatred toward God's chosen people.

Balaam starts this verse with information giving us insight into its longevity. He sees Him "not now" and "not near". And indeed His arrival was some 1,400 years away. His return would be another 2,000 or more years away. Ever wonder why God would give us so much time to ponder these things. Why not wait until the time is only two years away?

But our focus today is "the star". The use of the terms "star" and "scepter" denote monarchy or deity. The people of Balaam's day recognized these symbols as such. Many times the monarchs were considered gods or the sons of God, and in this case, Jesus is the Son of God. Another significant thing is this is the first mention of the coming "star"; and is the real point of today's reading. In Matthew 2:2 we read the interesting question of the "Magi" and ponder in awe the length of time mankind has been striving to understand this star of prophesy. The question: "Where is the one who has been born king of the Jews?" has been answered. But how many understood His coming prior to the date of His birth, death and resurrection? Balaam may not have understood. But he knew God was using him for a purpose that day; long before the arrival of the star of which he spoke and whose arrival he would not see in his lifetime. "We saw His star in the east and have come to worship Him."

Point: God's word is always pointing us to His purpose.

Prayer: Father, I praise You for Your Word, it gives light to all who hear and receive it. May all people read and understand it and know that You are the LORD of lords.

Today's Reading:
Amos 7-9; Revelation 9

December 17

THE GIFT

By Kathy Bryant

John 3:16 *"For God so loved the wold that he gave his one and only Son, that whoever believes in him shall not perish but have eternal life"*

One of the expressions of love and caring during the Christmas season is giving gifts. The act of gift giving takes many forms. Some people give their time to volunteer service rather than exchanging material presents. Some people seek out the unprivileged in the community and buy things to meet their physical and financial needs. Still others embrace the commercial aspect of Christmas and participate in the month long shopping spree from Thanksgiving to Christmas. The primary recipients of these purchases are children, family and friends. The euphoria of the season tends to wane in January when the bills start to roll in if credit was used to pay for the gifts. In fact, we might even question our spirit of generosity, because we spent more than we earned during the season. In addition, some of these gifts we searched for at great lengths are sometimes forgotten hours after they are opened or days later are broken in pieces.

On the other hand, God's gift to the world was the most perfect gift that was ever given. Jesus Christ was born in Bethlehem, to redeem the human race back to God. Jesus was the sinless sacrifice who would shed his blood and die on a cross for our sins. (Ish 9:6-7) The wise men, or Magi, came from the East and they brought gifts to present to Jesus. The actual date that they arrived has been estimated from the time Jesus was a newborn or a toddler. (Matt2: 16) The wise men brought Frankincense, Gold, and Myrrh. Each item symbolized Jesus' identity and mission on Earth. The Frankincense was used in Jewish worship and it showed that people would worship Jesus. Gold was associated with Kings. Jesus was the King of Kings. Finally, Myrrh was a perfume and was used to prepare a body for burial. It showed that Jesus would suffer and die. On Christmas day when we celebrate the birth of Jesus, let us be mindful that every person was offered the most perfect gift in the form of Jesus Christ. Will you receive or reject God's gift to the whole world?

Today's Reading:
Obadiah - Jonah; Revelation 10

December 18

The Bright Morning Star
By Peggy Kalevik

Revelation 22:16 *"I, Jesus, have sent my angel to give you this testimony for the churches. I am the Root and the Offspring of David, and the bright Morning Star."*

Astrologers have dubbed the morning star to be the planet Venus. On May 18, 2004 the New York Times reported that the morning star would appear again on June 8th for the first time since 1882. The article stated that Venus would return for its shining hour. The occurrence of the planet, the transit of Venus as it is called, only happens twice each century. So, what is the Bible telling us in today's scripture? (http://www.dawnbible.com/2004/0408-hl.htm)

In Revelation 2:25-28, to the Church at Thyatira, Jesus says, *"Only hold on to what you have until I come. To him who overcomes and does my will to the end, I will give authority over the nations— 'He will rule them with an iron scepter; he will dash them to pieces like pottery' — just as I have received authority from my Father. I will also give him the morning star."* God is telling us that He will give us, the Church at Thyatira, "the light". As Venus light is so bright that it can be seen even in the light of day, so this light will be for us. Peter says it best in 2 Peter 1:19: *"And we have the word of the prophets made more certain, and you will do well to pay attention to it, as to a light shining in a dark place, until the day dawns and the morning star rises in your hearts."* The day dawning is the second coming of Christ and the morning star is a reference to the Messiah. This verse tells us that the light of the Messiah will illuminate and transform the hearts of believers. It's not hard to believe that a planet could be described using these same characteristics, after all who made the planets? The dark place that Peter refers to here is the world in which we live; we have turned from God's light to the darkness of sin.

Today's scripture tells us that Christ is the Messiah that Israel is waiting for, that He is the "Root and the Offspring of David", and He is the promised Morning Star of Revelation 2:28.

Point: Jesus is the Bright Morning Star, the light of the world.
Prayer: Come, Lord Jesus Come, we who read Your word and hear Your voice, say come.

Today's Reading:
Micah 1-3; Revelation 11

December 19

MARY AND OUR OBEDIENCE

By Beth Nelson

John 14:23 *"If anyone loves me, he will obey my teaching. My Father will love him, and we will come to him and make our home with him."*

This time of year we rightly celebrate the birth of our Lord. After all, it was the most significant event in the history of our planet, when God Himself came to earth to be born, to live, to die and to be raised to life to save us from our sins. With hearts full of gratitude for all that this means to us, we sing, "Hark the herald angels sing, glory to the newborn king! Peace on earth and mercy mild, God and sinners reconciled." And God accepts our praise and our prayers of adoration. We decorate our homes with lights, signifying Jesus, the light of the world. We place manger scenes with Mary, Joseph and the baby Jesus on our mantels and outside on the snow for all to see. It is the time we've set aside to celebrate our Savior's birth.

But lest we only go this far and no farther, consider this piece of history. One day Jesus was teaching a group of people when one of the women shouted out, "Blessed is the mother who gave you birth and nursed you." In His reply, Jesus immediately brought their attention back to what he considers "blessed" in God's kingdom. He said, "Blessed rather are those who hear the word of God and obey it." He seized this teachable moment to emphasize a divine truth: we are not to get stuck reverencing the people whom God uses. Not even Mary with her heart of submission and faith.

God, the unchanging yet ever-living and dynamic God urges us to fix our hearts and minds on knowing the word of God and obeying it. Mary was not unimportant. But our obedience to God is just as important. Do we know the word? Most importantly, do we obey it? If you do, you are indeed blessed in the eyes of God.

Point: Let us be willing to see our celebration of Christmas with fresh new eyes. Maybe even to break with tradition and the way we always do it to follow a more personally obedient path. Study the Word and ask God what He would have you to do, for then

Today's Reading:
Micah 4-7; Revelation 12

December 20

FOLLOW THAT STAR: THE MAGI
By Peggy Kalevik

Matthew 2:2 *"Where is the one who has been born king of the Jews? We saw his star in the east and have come to worship him."*

Who are these men the King James Bible calls "wise men", the Magi? The Jews have possessed formal knowledge of the Scriptures for centuries, yet they are not looking for the Messiah, and have not prepared for his arrival. These men have come from "the east", following a star they say is "His star". Why is it these men, whom the Jews would consider "pagan", are aware of "His star"? They are aware He is "born" King of the Jews, not that he would become King of the Jews.

No doubt you have read this passage countless numbers of times, but have you noticed the title the Magi use for Jesus is the same as the inscription that is over his head on the cross - "King of the Jews" ? (Matt 27:37) God loves to repeat himself. In doing so, he speaks to us; he knows we don't really get it the first time.

While scholars cannot agree precisely on the identity of the Magi, there is some consensus that at the time the New Testament was written the word "magi" covered a varied group of men who studied dreams, astrology, magic, and books concerning the mysteries of the future. It is generally agreed this particular group of men studied ancient Jewish books and made astrological calculations based on the information they discovered in the books. They believed what they read and followed through on their belief. Apparently, a star appeared in the east just as the information they'd gathered told them. That star led them to Bethlehem. Their desire was to worship this King. God spoke to these non-Jewish men, and told them of the arrival of this "one who has been born king of the Jews". After they had given him the appropriate gifts and worshiped Him, God protected them and His son by sending the Magi home by a different route. Are we searching the scriptures for revelation of God?

Point: We must study and search the scriptures just as these men did. God wants to reveal Himself to us just as He did with these men. A wise man knows God.

Prayer: Show me your ways, O LORD, teach me your paths; guide me in your truth and teach me.

Practice: Research where Balaam came from. What does he have in common with the Magi?

Today's Reading:
Nahum; Revelation 13

December 21

CHRISTMAS IS NO ACCIDENT!

By Scott Kalevik

Matthew 1:22-23 *All this took place to fulfill what the Lord had said through the prophet: 23 "The virgin will be with child and will give birth to a son, and they will call him Immanuel"—which means, "God with us."*

To many of us, Christmas is about family, football, food, finances and fun. But to God, Christmas is about fulfillment. The Lord takes special care to make sure we understand that the birth of Jesus is the fulfillment of His plan. In fact, Matthew's gospel mentions fulfillment five times while describing the entrance of our Savior into this world.

Hundreds of years before the birth of Jesus, God inspired His prophet Isaiah to write about a virgin giving birth to a son (Is. 7:14). When Matthew describes the angel telling Joseph not to divorce Mary because of her pregnancy, he emphasizes that Jesus' birth by the virgin was fulfilling this specific prophecy of the Old Testament.

In other words, God wants us to recognize that the birth of His Son was no accident. Orchestrated and planned since before time began, the Lord even shows us how the details of Jesus' birth were foretold.

What is God telling us? First, He is telling us that He loves us. He was not surprised by our disobedience. He did not abandon us to hell. The Lord planned to provide a way for us to be forgiven for our sin while maintaining His justice and holiness. He came Himself to die for us! All we are asked to do is to believe and repent and follow Him.

Second, the Lord tells us Jesus is the fulfillment of prophecy because He wants us to know that Jesus really is His Son. There is no other Savior. History points to no other person whose life was predicted and fulfilled so specifically.

As we focus on Christmas this year, let's thank God for His provision. He not only came to earth, He told us He was coming. He is always true to His word. Praise God!

Today's Reading:
Habakkuk; Revelation 14

December 22

MESSIAH: THE SON OF DAVID

By Peggy Kalevik

Isaiah 53:12 Therefore I will give him a portion among the great...because
he poured out his life unto death, and was numbered with the transgressors.
For he bore the sin of many, and made intercession for the transgressors.
Luke 1:32 He will be great and will be called the Son of the Most High.
The Lord God will give him the throne of his father David,

In Acts, chapter 3, Peter reacts to the amazement of the crowd as they watch the healing of a man who was lame from birth: "why does this surprise you?" The men he's speaking to have been taught from their childhood about the one who would come. God told them (and us) about the coming messiah through Moses (Dt 18:17-18), David (Ps 8), Isaiah (9, 42, & 53) Jeremiah (23:5-6; 31:5, 31; 33:15-16) and many others. Yet they were surprised to see this miracle occurring among them! Isaiah gives us a picture of the suffering messiah, one who will give His all for mankind. He starts chapter 53 with a very telling question which was appropriate in the setting Peter found himself at the colonnade. "Who has believed our message?" Isaiah ends chapter 52 with an equally ominous statement: "For what they were not told, they will see, and what they have not heard, they will understand". The people Peter addressed had been told; and they had heard. Now they could see His great power at work in the miraculous healing of this man. Isaiah's suffering messiah has been revealed to us just as God told us. He lived as a man (Ps 110:1; Isaiah 11:10; Dan 7:13-14), but He is the risen King (Isaiah 9:6-7; Dan 7:27; 9:24-26). He came, He lived and taught, He suffered, He died, and He rose again! (The Gospels)

Luke 1 recalls a title most commonly used when speaking of God in the Old Testament, "the Most High". He reminds us of the revelations about the Messiah coming from David's lineage. The angel Gabriel gives us affirmation of that promise by saying the Lord God will give Him the throne of His Father David (2 Sam 7:13; 16; Ps 2:6-7; 89:25-27; Isa 9:6-7).

When we see scenes of the babe in the manger this year, let us remember how "God" came to us as a child for the specific purpose of saving a dying world. He came to give us life, love, peace, and the certainty of eternal life. God told Solomon of His promise to David, saying he will always have a man on the throne. God keeps his promises! (1 Kings 9:5)

Point: David still has a man on the throne, His Son the Messiah.

Today's Reading:
Zephaniah 1-3; Revelation 15

December 23

Mary's Song

By Peggy Kalevik

Luke 1:46-47 *"My soul glorifies the Lord and my spirit rejoices in God my Savior,"*

Mary sings a song of praise, a song that has become known as the "Magnificat". This is a song of deep piety and knowledge of the scriptures. It is a song that puts into words gratitude and love for a God who lifts up the lowly and downcast, feeds the hungry and blesses the waiting heart. Imagine a child expressing such adoration and understanding of God. And God knows her heart, He chose her above all the women of the world.

Hannah exhibits a similar kind of love and knowledge in her prayer in 1Samuel 2. Hannah is one of the downcast and she is overjoyed at what the Lord has done for her. Hannah speaks of the poor who have been raised to sit with nobles. Mary sees the nobles overthrown from their position of power. Though Hannah sings a song of great faith and praise unto God, Mary's song supersedes hers with its messianic voice and shows that Mary understands the importance of her role in God's plan.

In today's scripture Mary acknowledges her dependence on God, her Savior. By recognizing God as her Savior, she acknowledges herself as a sinner in need of salvation. In our celebration of Christmas we rarely think of our lives from the perspective of being a sinner. Mary is rejoicing but in the midst of her rejoicing, she makes known to God that she understands her position in relationship to Him. And that while she is blessed by the fact that He chose to use her, she understands that it is not about what she has done. She receives and rejoices over the blessing, understanding that the savior of the world will be born in her. She acknowledges God's sovereignty. And her cousin Elizabeth rejoices with her. We can rejoice in the fact that the savior will be born in us too if we let Him. This Christmas, let go of the gift giving and receive the gift of God. If you don't know the savior, let Him be born in you today.

Point: If you don't know the LORD, let this song lead you to receive Christ as your savior.

Prayer: Dear Lord Jesus, I know that I am a sinner, and I need your forgiveness. I believe that you died for my sins. I want to turn from my sins. I now invite you to come into my heart and life. I want to trust You as Savior and follow You as Lord.

Today's Reading:
Haggai; Revelation 16

December 24

WHEN WAS JESUS REALLY BORN?

By Scott Kalevik

Luke 2:12 *This will be a sign to you: You will find a baby wrapped in cloths and lying in a manger."*

There is no evidence to support the idea that Jesus' birthday is December 25th. No Biblical account offers the exact date of Jesus birth and, therefore, we don't know the exact date of Jesus' birth. Most scholarship agrees that His birth was likely around 6 B.C. to 4 B.C., but due to lack of evidence, precision has been replaced with probability.

Why didn't God tell us the exact date? I believe He didn't tell us because He didn't want us to miss the point. The point God is making through the birth of Jesus is that God came to earth. God came to pay the price of death, even death on a cross, for our sin. Jesus arose from the dead. Jesus is alive today! The date on which Jesus was born is a distant second to these awesome truths about Him!

So how did we end up celebrating Jesus' birth on December 25th? Many ancient cultures held festivals in late December. The most common reason for the festivals was that the long nights of Winter would soon be replaced by the long sun of Summer. Seeing that paganism celebrated their false gods during this season, church leaders, perhaps as early as 273 A.D., decided to commandeer the date to celebrate the birth of Christ. Western Christians first celebrated Christmas on December 25 in 336, after Emperor Constantine declared Christianity as the empire's religion.

Don't miss the point of Jesus' birth this season. Christmas is not about celebrations of solstice, food, family, football or gifts. Christmas is the celebration of God's loving us enough to come into this world to rescue us! Jesus loves us enough to empty Himself of heaven's grandeur. He willfully chose swaddling clothes and a manger and, eventually, a cross, to tell every one of us that He wants relationship with us. He paid the price for our sin. Why not give Him the gift He wants most from you this year: The gift of your surrendered life!

Today's Reading:
Zechariah 1-3; Revelation 17

December 25

REJOICE!

By Peggy Kalevik

Isaiah 44:23 *Sing for joy, O heavens, for the LORD has done this; shout aloud, O earth beneath. Burst into song, you mountains, you forests and all your trees, for the LORD has redeemed Jacob, he displays his glory in Israel.*

This is the day that we celebrate the birth of our Savior, understanding that He was not born on December 25th, we have chosen this day to remember His birth and the miraculous way in which He came to us. It was a virgin birth, the one and only, born of the Holy Spirit, not by the will of man. He willingly came as a child in accordance with God's word and plan, that we might be set free "…and a little child will lead them" (Isaiah 11:6).

Isaiah writes of God's Chosen: *"… O Israel. I have made you, you are my servant; O Israel, I will not forget you. I have swept away your offenses like a cloud, your sins like the morning mist. Return to me, for I have redeemed you"* (Isaiah 44:21-22). Luke writes of God's redemption in the Song of Zechariah. Zechariah was told by the angel that his son would "go before the Lord", that he would make ready a people prepared for the Lord. But at the birth of his son Zechariah sang of the one who God sent to redeem His people, a horn of salvation for the house of David, and we know this is not John the Baptist. Both Isaiah and Zechariah are speaking of our Savior, Jesus. John did prepare the way, for the Savior who came to redeem us. Although many including some of His own have rejected that redemption, He gave us an open door to salvation. This child that came through the virgin has saved us from our sin and the wrath of an all mighty, all powerful God.

Through Isaiah God told His people to remember that He has made them, He is determined to forgive their offenses and sins, they only need to return to Him and He will redeem them. In the New Testament God comes again in the person of Jesus to redeem His people. Throughout history God shows His love for His people. The coming of our Lord was the ultimate display of God's love for us. He loved us so much that He gave His only son. Its amazing that God calls on nature to rejoice; we should be rejoicing so loud that nature's rejoicing is drowned out. Rejoice over the goodness of God. Rejoice heavens and earth, and the people of God, for Emmanuel has come!

Today's Reading:
Zechariah 4-6; Revelation 18

December 26

THE ORDINARY BECOMES EXTRAORDINARY!
By Scott Kalevik

Luke 2:8 *And there were shepherds living out in the fields nearby, keeping watch over their flocks at night.*

It probably started out just like any other night. Stars twinkling above while sheep munched the grass as the little campfire swirled about in the breeze. The shepherds no doubt kept their eyes peeled on the rolling hills for any sight or sound of predators. There was no way to know God was about to make an announcement. Without warning, the darkness fled, as the gleaming angel of God appeared. Scripture says the glory of the Lord shone around them. This was not an ordinary night of watching the sheep! They were terrified!

I've never seen an angel that I know of. Have you? It would be enough just to view such an awesome heavenly being. But God had more in mind. The text tells us that a 'great company of the heavenly host' also appeared with the angel. Even though the angel told the shepherds not to fear, I can only imagine that they were quaking in their sandals when the whole group appeared.

And why did this great throng from heaven appear? To give praises to God! Lk 2:14 *"Glory to God in the highest, and on earth peace to men on whom his favor rests."* The angel and the great company of heavenly host can't hardly contain themselves as they celebrate the coming of God to earth – the birth of Jesus!

Three things: 1) Heaven rejoiced when Jesus came to earth! Why? Because God wants relationship with us! He wants it so much that He celebrated sending His Son to earth to die! Heaven was happy because God's plan of salvation was coming to fulfillment in Jesus!

2) The Lord reveals His heavenly host to unassuming shepherds out in the hills. The religious elite that were supposed to know so much about God have no clue. It's the humble shepherds that see the glory of the Lord shining around the heavenly host as they praise God!

3) The shepherds praise God after seeing Jesus for themselves!

Praise God for His salvation today! Humble yourself before Him! This ordinary life becomes extraordinary when we see what God is doing!

Today's Reading:
Zechariah 7-9; Revelation 19

December 27

MARVEL AT GOD'S CREATION
By Mike Scheimann

Psalm 111:2 *Great are the works of the Lord; they are pondered by all who delight in them.*

I once read that "Life isn't neccessarily tied with a bow, but it is still a gift". We live in one of the most beautiful areas of this country. We can look out our windows and see the majestic mountain range, capped in freshly fallen snow. We can stare up into the sky and see just a glimpse of this vast universe and galaxies that God has created. We know that God hung each star in it's place and named each of them. Since there are billions of stars out there, that is even more awe inspiring. God created everything from the smallest most delicate flower, to the mighty Ponderosa Pine, towering over a 100 feet in the air. He made the smallest molecules of DNA come together to form a human body so intricate, and complex, that to this day modern science still has no clue how it all works. Everything that God has made has its order in this world, and was made perfectly. How often do we take those mountains for granted? How often does God give us a beautiful orange and red sunset, and we ignore it and watch TV? Do we still take time to smell the flowers, or are we too caught up in the rat race? One of my good friends told me that he likes to sit and look out the windows at the farm house and watch the foxes, and racoons. He truly marvels at God's Creation. Do you?

Point: God has given us beauty and majesty in this world that even the greatest artist could not begin to capture on a canvas, yet how often do we overlook it all?

Prayer: Father, forgive us for not taking the time to stop and delight in all that you have done. Forgive us for taking it for granted sometimes.

Practice: Next time you are looking out your window, or driving, or doing your devotions, take some time to ponder the great works of the Lord. Once you realize just how awesome and amazing they really are, you will surely delight in them.

Today's Reading:
Zechariah 10-12; Revelation 20

December 28

A Servant's Love

By Peggy Kalevik

John 13:5 after that, he poured water into a basin and began to wash his disciples' feet, drying them with the towel that was wrapped around him.

On the day before His crucifixion Jesus finds Himself washing the feet of His disciples. If our need for the approval of others is the bases for our Christian service this is the story to help us get over it. Jesus shows us a selfless act of "agape" love as only He can. In John 15 He tells us: My command is this: Love each other as I have loved you. As He carries out this lesson in humility He shows them how much He loves them. He instructs them that they should follow His example; they should do for each other as He has done for them (Jn 13:14). The custom of washing a person's feet was more than just good etiquette, it served a purpose. Back then people walked everywhere wearing sandals. There was no pavement, so everyone's feet got really dirty. When they entered a home the household servant washed their feet. It was a serious violation of etiquette or hospitality not to wash the feet of guest arriving at someone's home. At this meeting of Jesus and the disciples, there was no servant to perform this task and none of the disciples took the initiative (I wonder why?). Jesus, understanding the customs and the hearts and minds of the disciples, took the opportunity to perform this common task in order to show his love for them. In John 17, Jesus prays for His disciples saying while He was with them He protected and kept them safe. God gave the disciples to Jesus and He accepted responsibility for them, by protecting, teaching, instructing and praying for them (John 17:6-12). Now, in an act of total humility, He's washing their feet to show them this great love. Paul says: *"He made himself nothing, took on the very nature of a servant... he humbled himself and became obedient to death— even death on a cross!"* (Phil 2:7-8)

This entire episode is pointing to several facts: 1) Jesus wanted these men to understand the love He had for them and for all who follow Him. 2) He wanted them to follow His example; 3) He wanted them to be servants; 4) He wanted them to see that a disciple must be humble; and last but not least of all these 5) He wanted them to love one another.

Point: "...the Son of Man did not come to be served, but to serve," (Mt 20:28) We must follow His example!

Today's Reading:
Zechariah 13-14; Revelation 21

362

December 29

THE POWER OF LIFE AND DEATH

By Kathy Bryant

John 2:19 *Jesus answered them, "Destroy this temple, and I will raise it again in three days."*

In AD 70 the Temple of Jerusalem was burned to the ground. Jewish historian Josephus wrote about the siege by the Roman armies under the Roman general Titus. The Romans assaulted the city on great platforms, killed the priests, and looted the temple treasury. The temple was set on fire and burned to the ground. The fire was so hot the gold forming the mortar between the stones melted and was taken by the soldiers; so there was "not one stone left on top of another" (Matt 24:2). The temple was never rebuilt and many of the Jews and Christians living in Jerusalem scattered. Jesus had prophesied the devastation less than forty years previously. In the verse above, Jesus spoke of His death and resurrection, but the Jews thought he meant the building. When Jesus was brought before the Sanhedrin to be tried by the High Priest, two men accused Jesus of saying he would destroy the temple. They misquoted and misunderstood Jesus' reference to the temple of His body. Jesus proved he was God when he said "… I will raise it again in three days". Jesus, the Incarnate, had authority over life and death in other peoples lives, like with Lazarus (John 11:38-44). And with Himself, in John 10:17-18 Jesus said; *"The reason my Father loves me is that I lay down my life—only to take it up again. No one takes it from me, but I lay it down of my own accord. I have authority to lay it down and authority to take up again."* Only God Himself has the power to lay down His life and to take it up again. In John 10:30 Jesus said; "I and the Father were one". As born-again Christians we can trust the Lord and be at peace with the fact of death, because just like Lazarus, Jesus can raise us up from the dead to be with him.

Today's Reading:
Malachi 1-4; Revelation 22

December 30

WHEN BAD THINGS HAPPEN

By Beth Nelson

Romans 8:28 *And we know that in all things God
works for the good of those who love him.*

Axel Karlson, a missionary for the Swedish Covenant Church, traveled to
Caucasia in southern Russia in the 1880's. A devout Christian who loved the Lord,
he was arrested by Russian authorities and put in prison in Siberia. During those
three horrific years in prison he became fluent in the Russian language. Eventually,
the government of Sweden was able to secure his release. His church changed course
and sent him to Alaska instead, where one of the first people that he met was a
Russian-born man named Sergei Ivanoff. Sergei directed him to settle in the village
of Unalakleet, where the village chief was also fluent in Russian. Axel Karlson grew to
love the Eskimos in this region, and established the first Christian church in that part
of western Alaska. God used Axel and his willingness to be obedient to God's call
on his life, in spite of extreme difficulties and discouragement along the way. When
he wrote about his life he said, "That was how I came to Unalakleet, and even today
I have the assurance within me that God's invisible hand led me there." The gospel
spread to surrounding villages and today, there are thriving Covenant churches
throughout most of western Alaska, with hundreds of second, third and fourth
generation Christians who are humbly and simply living lives saved by grace.

Axel Karlson lived in Unalakleet for twenty-three years and is buried in
the cemetery there, with a monument that states, "When he came there were no
Christians; when he left there were no heathen." I'm sure that years later, he could
look back and see how God used all of these detours and difficulties, to accomplish
exactly what He intended.

We are not always blessed to see the fruit of our labor during our lifetime, as
Reverend Karlson was. But what we do know is that nothing in all creation will be
able to separate us from the love of God. And as the scriptures say with such certainty,
"We know that in all things God works all things for the good of those who love
him, who have been called according to his purpose."

Today's Reading:
Exodus 23-25; Luke 1

December 31

Pulling Back The Curtain!

By Scott Kalevik

Matthew 17:2 *There he was transfigured before them. His face shone like the sun, and his clothes became as white as the light.*

There is a scene in The Wizard Of Oz when Dorothy and friends believe they are in the presence of "The great and terrible Oz." Oz spits fire and thunders his questions as they tremble in his presence. That is until Dorothy's little dog Toto runs over and pulls back the curtain revealing a mere man moving the levers that control the not so great and terrible Oz. Suddenly, fear evaporates. Oz is a fraud. He's not real. Oz has absolutely no power. He is not God.

Popular thinking says that we all get to choose whatever we want to believe for ourselves. We're told that everybody's belief system is valid. We should honor all faiths. You get to decide what truth is true for you. All spiritual roads eventually lead to the same place they say. No one has a right to say that any belief system is not true. To do so would be "intolerant."

The Bible speaks forcefully against the popular thinking of our day. All spiritual roads do NOT lead to the same place. In fact, the Bible goes so far as to declare without apology that knowing Jesus is the ONLY way possible to know God. Jn 14:6 *Jesus answered, "I am the way and the truth and the life. No one comes to the Father except through me.*

All other belief systems practiced in this world will experience the fate of Oz. The curtain will be pulled back at the end of time. The belief system will be exposed as a lie. No amount of popular sentiment will change the truth. Jesus will remain the Way, the Truth, and the Life on that day just as He is today.

When walking this earth, Jesus allowed Peter, James and John to witness His transfiguration. Heaven pulled back its curtain as Jesus was changed before their eyes. His face shone like the sun and His clothes became as white as light. Instead of a fake god with no reality, the disciples saw the Truth.

The Holy Spirit compels us to tell others about Jesus. Knowing the Truth and knowing that the curtain of reality will be drawn back to expose all other beliefs as insufficient must motivate us to follow the Spirit's leading and speak the truth in love with whom ever God leads.

Today's Reading:
Exodus 26-27; Luke 2-3

The Message of The Cross

God loves you! No matter what you've done, no matter how many mistakes you've made in your life, God wants to forgive you and make you whole! God wants relationship with YOU! The Bible assures us that *"There is no condemnation for those who are in Christ"* (Romans 8:1). The question is, "How can I be in Christ Jesus?"

Do you believe you are a good person?

Most of us do. Yet, if we examine our lives, we can see that we have repeatedly done what God forbids. We've lied. We've stolen. We've used God's name as a curse word (blasphemy). Truthful examination of our lives forces us to acknowledge we've done a lot of other things that directly disobey what God has commanded. You can never be right with God until you recognize that you've disobeyed Him. If you think you're basically a good person, Heaven's doors are not open to you. But ...**If you know you've disobeyed God's law then**
You Can Be Made Right With God Through Jesus Christ!
 * We all disobey God. Every one of us has broken God's law. Our disobedience has severed the relationship God intended to have with us: *There is no one righteous, not even one; there is no one who understands, no one who seeks God. All have turned away, they have together become worthless; there is no one who does good, not even one.* (Romans 3:11-12)
 * The Bible calls our disobedience 'sin.' God's penalty for sin is death. Since we've sinned against God, we deserve to be condemned: *Therefore, just as sin entered the world through one man, and death through sin, and in this way death came to all men, because all sinned*—Romans 5:12. *For the wages of sin is death, but the gift of God is eternal life in Christ Jesus our Lord.*— Romans 6:23
 * The good news is that God provides a way for us to be transformed from His enemy, deserving His punishment, to His child inheriting eternal life with Him. God sent His one and only Son, Jesus, to die on the cross. Jesus was punished for our sins. Jesus took my place and your place on the cross. Even though Jesus never disobeyed His Father, He died to pay our penalty on the cross! *For Christ died for sins once for all, the righteous for the unrighteous, to bring you to God. He was put to death in the body but made alive by the Spirit,* (1 Peter 3:18)
 * Jesus loves you enough to die for you! He has the power to forgive your sin, and make you right with God: *If we confess our sins, he is faithful and just and will forgive us our sins and purify us from all unrighteousness.*(1 John 1:9) *Therefore, there is now no condemnation for those who are in Christ Jesus* (Romans 8:1)
 * Want to avoid God's punishment? Want to be His child instead of His enemy? If you're sorry for your disobedience to God, ask Jesus to forgive you and make you right with God. Then repent or turn away from sin and obey God's word. *Yet to all who received him, to those who believed in his name, he gave the right to become children of God* (John 1:12)
 Pray something like this: "Lord Jesus, I know I deserve to die for disobeying

You. Please forgive me for my sin. Thank You for being punished in my place on the cross! Lord, please come into my life. I don't want to sin anymore. Help me obey Your word. I want to live like You want me to live. I surrender my life to You. Please fill me with Your Holy Spirit and guide me from this day forward. Thank you Jesus, for loving me, forgiving me, and for changing my life today! Amen.

* If you prayed that prayer, you've begun a new life in Christ - forever. Read your Bible. Obey. *Therefore, if anyone is in Christ, he is a new creation; the old has gone, the new has come*! (2Corinthians 5:17)
Take a minute and email Pastor Scott to tell him
about what God has done for you today!
Gdluvsu@hotmail.com

9 781462 004690